# WORLD DIRECTORY OF ENERGY INFORMATION

# VOLUME 1: Western Europe

# WORLD DIRECTORY OF ENERGY INFORMATION

## VOLUME 1: Western Europe

Compiled by Cambridge Information and
Research Services Limited

## Facts On File, Inc.

119 West 57th Street,
New York, N.Y. 10019

WORLD DIRECTORY
OF ENERGY
INFORMATION
Volume 1: Western Europe

Published in the United Kingdom in 1981 by Gower Publishing Company Limited, Westmead, Farnborough, Hants, England.

Published in the United States of America in 1981 by Facts On File, Inc., 119 West 57th Street, New York, N.Y. 10019

Compiled by Cambridge Information and Research Services Limited, Sussex House, Hobson Street, Cambridge CB1 1NJ

Edited by Christopher Swain BA and Andrew Buckley BA

**Library of Congress Cataloging in Publication Data**
Main entry under title:
World Directory of Energy Information.
  Includes indexes
  Contents: v. 1. Western Europe

  1. Power resources—Information
Services—Directories.  I. Cambridge
Information and Research Services Ltd.
TJ163.17.W67    333.79    81-754
ISBN 0-87196-563-1    AACR2

Printed in Great Britain

# Contents

# Illustrations

Each country review in Part Two contains illustrations of production and/or consumption in the following energy sectors:

- Oil
- Coal
- Gas
- Electricity

Tables are also included showing the patterns of primary fuel supply and final energy consumption and net import/export movements of coal, crude oil, oil products, natural gas and electricity. Imports of crude oil are analysed by country of origin.

# Introduction

Few people are today ignorant of the importance of energy to everyday life and well-being. In Western Europe, which is heavily dependent on the international flow of energy, issues of energy supply and conservation are given intensive consideration. The issues are complex, as is the energy economy of Europe. A wealth of information and ideas is being generated continuously from all sources—governmental, industrial, scientific and academic.

Despite the importance of the subject however, the essential basic information concerning energy in Western Europe remains dispersed and often difficult to obtain. It is to help overcome this problem that this first volume of the World Directory of Energy Information has been compiled, following contact with many of the organisations involved and extensive fieldwork and analysis. It is believed to be the only book of its kind and includes statistical and other information specially prepared for the purpose. It also contains reference sections, which indicate a multitude of sources, both organisational and bibliographical, to which reference can be made for further information.

The World Directory of Energy Information is divided into four parts, Parts One and Two deal with the main elements of the energy economy of Western Europe as a whole and of individual countries. Parts Three and Four are reference sections on energy organisations and publications.

Part One, entitled Europe's Energy Framework, gives an overall view of the main features of energy in Western Europe in a series of ten maps and tables. These illustrate the scale of energy consumption, the pattern of international movements of energy and the variation in circumstances of individual countries. They also summarise in graphic form the state of indigenous energy resources and plans to reduce import-dependence.

Part Two, Country Reviews, looks in greater detail at the 17 individual countries. These country profiles follow a standard format. Key energy indicators identify total energy consumption, per capita energy consumption and the extent of dependence on imports of energy in total, and oil in particular. These are followed by sections dealing with: recent trends in the general development of the economy and energy consumption; the pattern of energy supply and consumption; the oil, coal, gas and electricity industries; foreign trade in each energy form; and a review of the state of official policies on energy supply and energy conservation.

Entries in Parts Three and Four are grouped along broad geographical lines. This recognises the transnational nature of many energy organisations and of most energy issues. An international section is followed by sections on Great Britain and Ireland (United Kingdom and Republic of Ireland); Scandinavia (Denmark, Finland, Norway and Sweden); and Continental Europe (Austria, Belgium, France, Greece, Italy, Luxembourg, Netherlands, Portugal, Spain, Switzerland and West Germany).

Part Three contains information on the activities of more than 400 organisations in the energy sector. It includes government departments, official agencies, state undertakings, private companies, professional institutions and trade associations. In the case of most of the energy supply companies figures taken from the latest available financial accounts provide an indication of the scale of operations.

Part Four consists of a wide-ranging bibliography of over 900 publications relevant to the supply and consumption of energy in Western Europe. The details appear within the same geographical groupings as adopted in Part Three. The bibliography is completed by a set of indexes. Index One is an alphabetical listing of all publications. Index Two contains a detailed classification by subject matter, sub-divided by country. Index Three contains reference information on the publishers.

*ACKNOWLEDGEMENTS*

The editors wish to record and acknowledge the cooperation and assistance received from many sources throughout Europe in compiling this book. Their contributions have made possible the piecing together of the complex picture of the European energy scene. Particular acknowledgement for help in this undertaking is due to British Petroleum Company, the Electricity Council, the Institute of Petroleum, the Institution of Gas Engineers and the National Coal Board.

The statistical content of Parts One and Two is based mainly on published information of the Organisation for Economic Cooperation and Development, the Statistical Office of the European Communities and the United Nations, supplemented by a variety of local sources for individual countries.

# Part One:
# Europe's Energy Framework

# Europe's Energy Framework

Western Europe constitutes one of the world's main areas of energy consumption. With a generally high level of industrialisation and a total population of some 350 million people, annual consumption of energy is equivalent to nearly 1,240 million tonnes of oil, well over 4,000 litres of oil per person. Although the inventory of indigenous energy resources is not without significance, the area as a whole is dependent on imported energy to the extent of 55 per cent of total requirements.

The dependence on imports is particularly crucial in the case of oil, of which more than 85 per cent is imported. In common with all other western countries oil has been the mainstay of economic growth during the last three decades and all West European countries are wrestling with the problem of maintaining economic growth while containing the demand for oil. To this end plans and programmes exist for the expansion of nuclear power and the greater exploitation of indigenous resources. These efforts to increase the supply of energy are now being increasingly complemented by a wide range of policies for energy conservation. An important factor in restraining demand is the rising real cost of energy, which all governments have come to acknowledge.

The availability of adequate supplies of energy is fundamental to the future prosperity of all West European economies. Each country faces a unique situation, but the main energy issues are international, with the supply problem common to all. Recognition of this has brought a growing tendency towards coordination of both policy development and supply operations, reinforcing the existing inter-dependence.

## Energy Consumption

Figure 1 illustrates the scale of energy consumption in individual West European countries. The four most populous countries, France, Italy, the United Kingdom and West Germany, account for nearly 70 per cent of energy consumption. There is however quite a spread between them in terms of consumption per head, with West Germany ranked sixth and Italy fourteenth on this basis. This reflects essential differences in industrial development and climate. Generally, it is the Scandinavian countries which emerge with the highest average levels of energy consumption and the industrialising Mediterranean countries with the lowest. The notable exception is Luxembourg, which has a somewhat unusual economic structure and pattern of energy consumption.

## Energy Imports

The sources of imported energy are shown in Figure 2. The Middle East is of predominant importance, supplying approximately one-third of all Western Europe's energy needs and a high percentage of oil imports. But Africa and Eastern Europe are also important. European imports of oil from Africa have started to decline in the face of growing North Sea production. But this has been offset by rising imports of coal and natural gas. At the same time, Western Europe continues to obtain sizeable quantities of oil and gas from (or through) the Soviet Union and of coal from Poland.

## Import-Dependence

Within Western Europe countries vary greatly in the degree of dependence on imported energy (Figure 3). Most countries have resources which make a useful contribution to the energy balance. Norway now occupies the enviable position of producing more than twice as much energy as it consumes. The Netherlands and the United Kingdom import only a minor percentage of their energy requirements. At the other extreme are several countries—Belgium, Denmark, Italy and Luxembourg—which have minimal resources in relation to their requirements. Between these groups lie the majority of West European countries, which maintain significant energy production of one form or another, but which nevertheless remain highly dependent on imports for some fuels.

## Oil Import Targets

The crucial dependence on external sources for oil has led to attempts to coordinate policies for limiting oil consumption. Under the auspices of the International Energy Agency, which includes almost all West European countries, maxima for oil imports over the next few years have been adopted. Figure 4 shows how the target levels for 1985 relate to those for 1980. Denmark, Norway and the United Kingdom anticipate a significant reduction of oil imports as a result of increased exploitation of indigenous resources and conversion to the use of coal. But a number of countries are still allowing for a rise in imports so as not to impede chances of economic growth. The general target for Western Europe in total is to keep the increase in oil imports to two per cent between 1980 and 1985. But, given the deteriorating situation in the world economy, imports are unlikely to be much higher than the current level anyway.

## Energy Prices

One factor behind the poor state of the international economy, and a significant restraint on energy consumption, is the rising real cost of energy, and of oil in particular. Table 5 gives indicative figures for oil prices in 1973 and 1980. In absolute terms the greatest increase is in motor gasoline and the least in heavy fuel oil. But because of the high unit price of the former and low unit price of the latter the position is reversed in terms of percentage increase. Whichever way the increases are looked at, they are very large for such a relatively short period of time. In the case of motor gasoline the increase would have been greater if taxes and duties had been raised in line with the rate of inflation.

Part B of the table relates consumer prices for oil products to prices of other energy forms. The most obvious feature of the table is that the rise in price of primary fuels has been compounded in the case of electricity. This is to a large extent an expression of the technology of electricity generation, which converts only one-third of primary fuel input into the electrical equivalent of its calorific value. It is noticeable that coal prices rose least on average, but moves have been made to price natural gas more in line with its value in premium uses rather than as a boiler fuel.

## Indigenous Resources

Figure 6 highlights the significant level of indigenous resources enjoyed by the majority of West European countries. Each symbol on the map indicates production equivalent to at least ten per cent of total energy requirements. A number of countries have substantial contributions from more than one energy form. Primary electricity is perhaps the least obtrusive of these, but plays a major role. Production of hydro-electricity is widespread, but unutilised potential is now limited. To complement this several countries are in the process of building up nuclear generating capacity.

## Nuclear Power Programmes

By the beginning of 1980 total nuclear generating capacity in Western Europe was over 43,000MW (Figure 7). Countries with the largest capacities were France (10,500MW) and West Germany (9,800MW). The United Kingdom's construction programme has progressed only slowly in recent years, so that the country now ranks third in the European league. Italy, the other major consumer of energy, has so far made little use of nuclear power, despite its dependence on imported energy. Of greater significance has been the scale of construction programmes in Sweden and, for their size, those in Finland and Switzerland.

Energy policies envisage the construction of some 65,000MW during the 1980s. The French programme involves tripling existing capacity to nearly 34,000MW. Major programmes are also anticipated in Spain and Italy, adding 10,000MW and 8,000MW respectively, although there is some doubt as to how much of this capacity can be on stream by 1990. Several countries have no nuclear power station and no commitments to build any during the 1980s, although in the case of Greece one may be built by 1990. Following the referendum rejecting nuclear power, the outlook in Sweden is uncertain. No new plant will be built during the 1980s, but those already in operation or nearing completion will remain in service.

# FIGURE 1 ENERGY CONSUMPTION

Total Energy Consumption in
Million Tonnes of Oil Equivalent

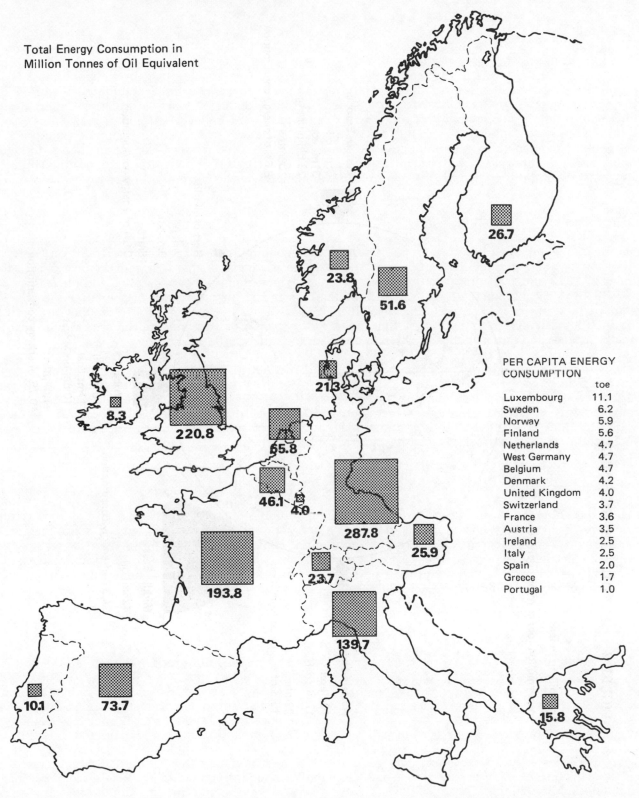

PER CAPITA ENERGY
CONSUMPTION

| | toe |
|---|---|
| Luxembourg | 11.1 |
| Sweden | 6.2 |
| Norway | 5.9 |
| Finland | 5.6 |
| Netherlands | 4.7 |
| West Germany | 4.7 |
| Belgium | 4.7 |
| Denmark | 4.2 |
| United Kingdom | 4.0 |
| Switzerland | 3.7 |
| France | 3.6 |
| Austria | 3.5 |
| Ireland | 2.5 |
| Italy | 2.5 |
| Spain | 2.0 |
| Greece | 1.7 |
| Portugal | 1.0 |

# FIGURE 2    EUROPE'S ENERGY IMPORTS

mt=million tonnes

mtoe=million tonnes of oil equivalent

M³=cubic metre

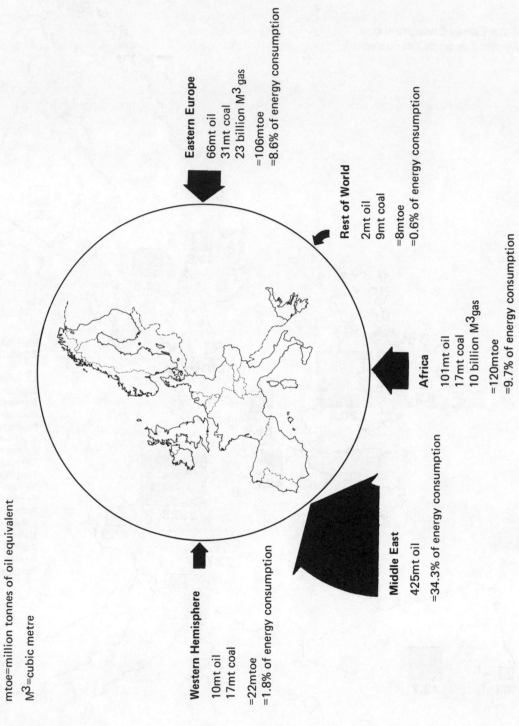

**Western Hemisphere**

10mt oil
17mt coal

=22mtoe
=1.8% of energy consumption

**Eastern Europe**

66mt oil
31mt coal
23 billion M³gas

=106mtoe
=8.6% of energy consumption

**Rest of World**

2mt oil
9mt coal

=8mtoe
=0.6% of energy consumption

**Africa**

101mt oil
17mt coal
10 billion M³gas

=120mtoe
=9.7% of energy consumption

**Middle East**

425mt oil

=34.3% of energy consumption

**Energy Transmission**

The increasing real cost of supplying energy to the West European economies has caused greater attention to be paid to diversification of energy sources and the efficiency of energy supply. Commercial and technological considerations have led to a high level of integration in the transmission of energy within Western Europe, as is shown in Figures 8-10. To these considerations are now added those of strategic security and optimal overall use of economic resources.

Oil pipelines are already well developed (Figure 8). Continental Europe is moving perceptibly towards the completion of a pipeline network for transporting natural gas in great volumes, based on indigenous resources, the sub-Mediterranean pipeline and terminals for importing liquefied natural gas at strategic locations around Europe (Figure 9). The map in Figure 10 illustrates the network of principal high-voltage electricity transmission lines throughout Western Europe, including international connections of over 200kv. These links are being reinforced, and provide an important means of assuring electricity supply in the most efficient manner.

# FIGURE 3   IMPORT-DEPENDENCE

Imported Energy as Percentage
of Total Energy Consumption

☐ Less than 20%

▦ 40-65%

▨ 66-80%

▩ 81% or more

*NB  Norway is a net
exporter of energy

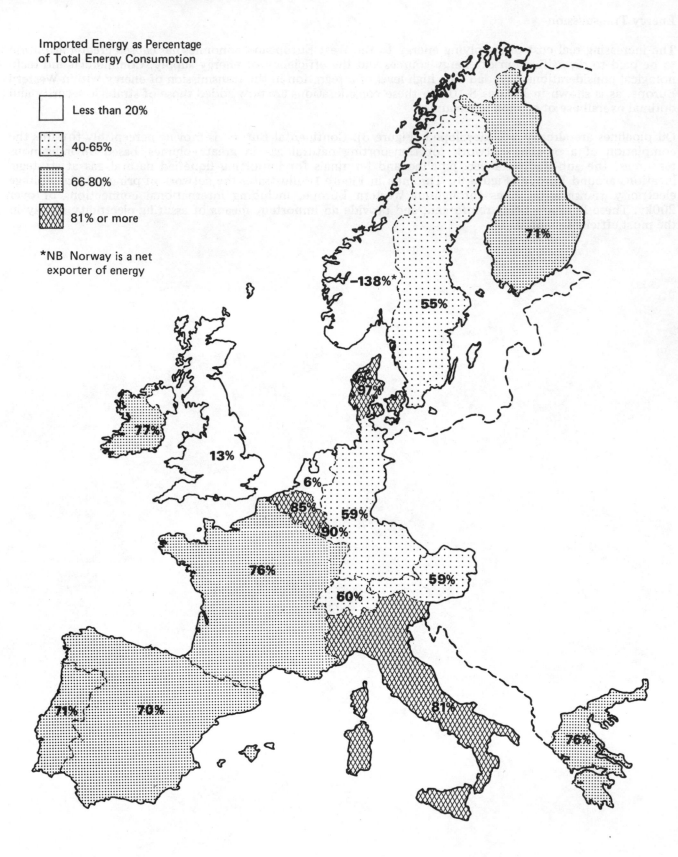

# FIGURE 4 — 1985 OIL IMPORT TARGETS

Maximum Planned Import Levels
in 1985 compared with 1980

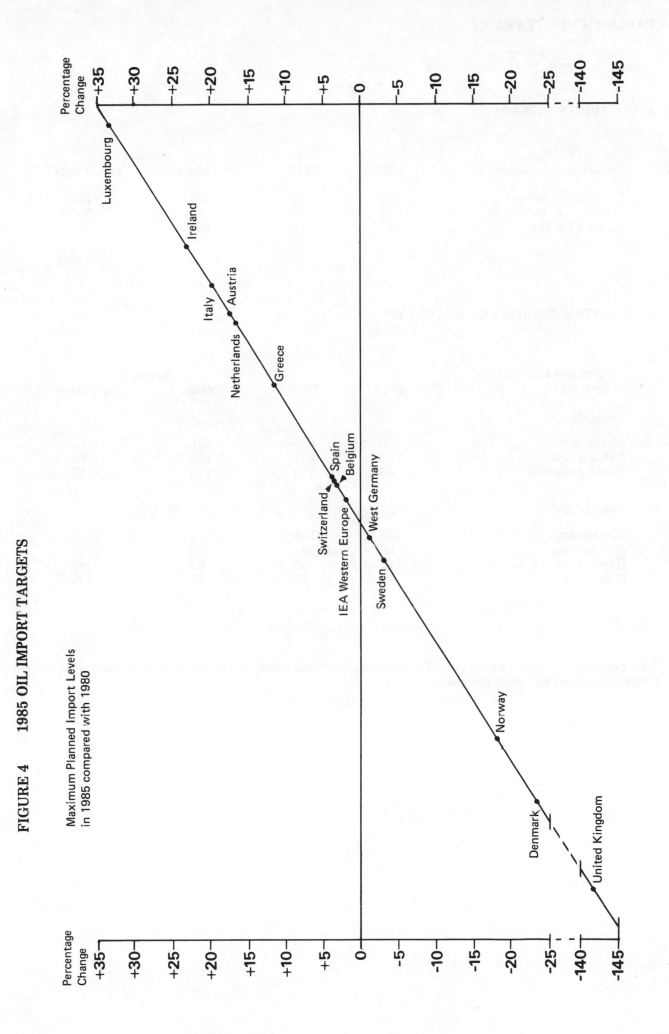

# TABLE 5 ENERGY PRICES

## A OIL PRICES 1973-80*

| (dollars per cubic metre) | 1973 | 1980 | Increase dollars | Increase percentage |
|---|---|---|---|---|
| Premium Gasoline | 250 | 735 | 485 | +194 |
| Heating Gas Oil | 55 | 345 | 290 | +527 |
| Heavy Fuel Oil | 25 | 175 | 150 | +600 |

## B RELATIVE ENERGY PRICES 1973-78*

| (dollars per tonne of oil equivalent) | 1973 | 1978 | Increase dollars | Increase percentage |
|---|---|---|---|---|
| **Domestic** | | | | |
| Electricity | 450 | 888 | 438 | + 97 |
| Natural Gas | 163 | 301 | 138 | + 85 |
| Heating Gas Oil | 63 | 177 | 114 | +181 |
| **Industrial** | | | | |
| Electricity | 252 | 553 | 301 | +119 |
| Natural Gas | 56 | 131 | 75 | +134 |
| Heavy Fuel Oil | 28 | 97 | 69 | +246 |
| Coal | 43 | 90 | 47 | +109 |

*Average prices to main categories of consumers, including taxes, for Belgium, France, Italy, Netherlands, United Kingdom and West Germany.

# FIGURE 6    INDIGENOUS ENERGY SOURCES

Symbols Indicate Production Equivalent to at least
10% of National Energy Consumption

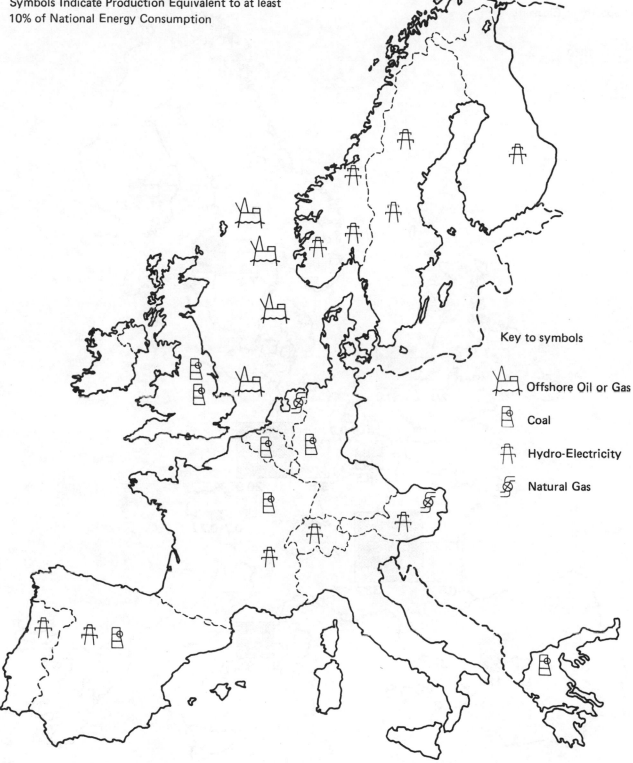

Key to symbols

Offshore Oil or Gas

Coal

Hydro-Electricity

Natural Gas

# FIGURE 7   NUCLEAR POWER CAPACITY 1980 and 1990

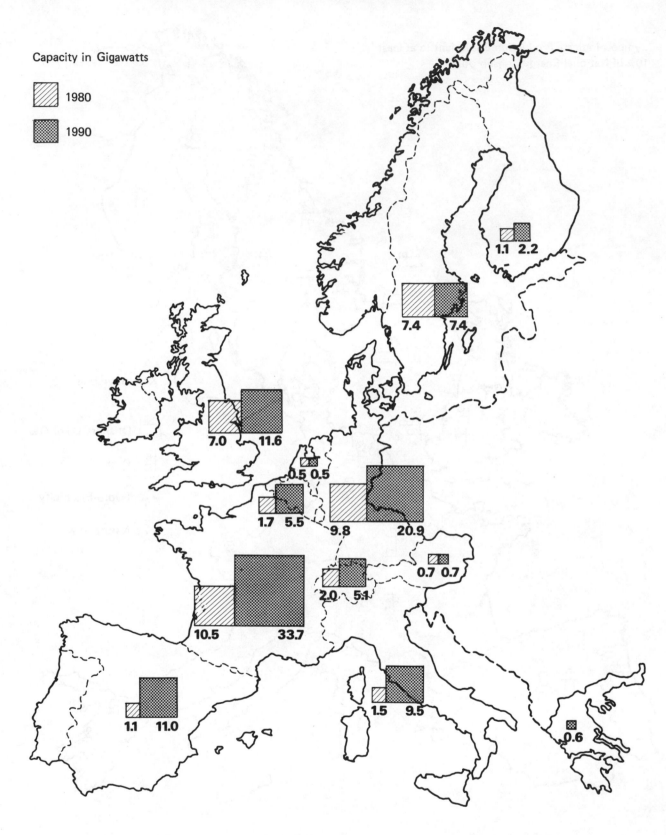

Capacity in Gigawatts

1980

1990

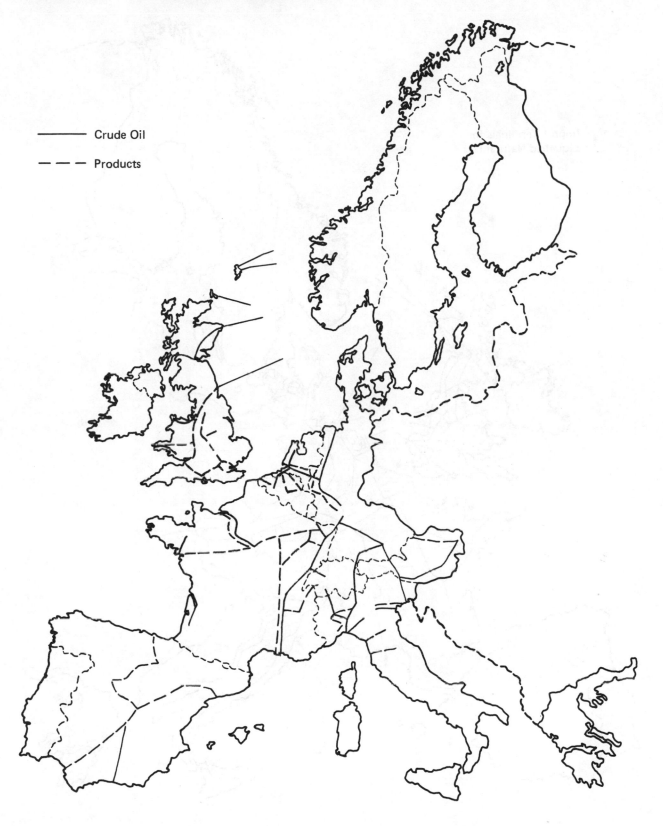

**FIGURE 8    PRINCIPAL OIL PIPELINES**

Crude Oil

Products

# FIGURE 9 NATURAL GAS TRUNK PIPELINES

 Import Terminals for
Liquefied Natural Gas

# FIGURE 10   THE HIGH-VOLTAGE ELECTRICITY NETWORK

Principal High-Voltage Transmission Lines
and Underwater DC Cables

# Part Two:
# Country Reviews

# Austria

## KEY ENERGY INDICATORS

Energy Consumption
    —million tonnes oil equivalent                25.9
Consumption Per Head
    —tonnes oil equivalent                     3.5
    —percentage of West European average    97%
Net Energy Imports                        59%
Oil Import-Dependence                   90%

*Austria has an average level of energy consumption per head and has a significant base of indigenous energy production, notably in primary electricity. It is nevertheless heavily dependent on imported energy, especially oil. Existing production areas of oil and natural gas provide some promise of finding further reserves to exploit and there are possibilities of uranium deposits. A referendum on the use of nuclear power has blocked development of this energy form for the foreseeable future, so that import-dependence is not likely to fall. For Austria the issue is the balance between dependence on international energy markets and increasing links with Comecon.*

## ENERGY MARKET TRENDS

*Trend of Energy Consumption*

Energy Consumption
    +1.6% p.a.

Gross Domestic Product
    +3.1% p.a.

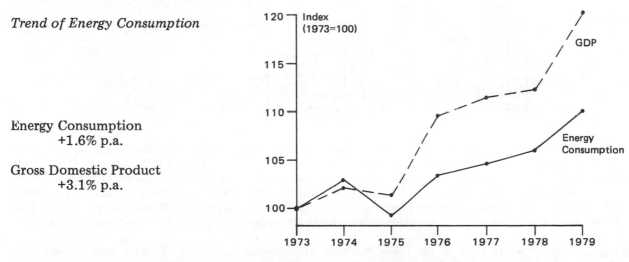

The Austrian economy recovered well from the oil supply crisis of 1973. Gross Domestic Product fell back slightly in 1975, but since then has risen steadily. The average rate of growth of GDP since 1973 has been over three per cent per annum. Economic growth in this period has been achieved at the cost of only a moderate rate of growth in total energy consumption, averaging half that of GDP. Energy consumption was rising at a greater rate than this, but following a sharp drop in 1975 the upward trend has been contained. Two reasons behind the good performance of the economy have been the increased availability of primary electricity and the existing agreements for the supply of natural gas from the Soviet Union.

*Pattern of Energy Supply and Consumption*

| Primary Fuel Supply (percentage) | | Final Consumption (percentage) | |
|---|---|---|---|
| Oil | 50 | Industry | 37 |
| Solid Fuel | 7 | Residential | 32 |
| Natural Gas | 19 | Transport | 21 |
| Primary Electricity | 24 | Other | 10 |
| TOTAL | 100 | TOTAL | 100 |

Oil meets half of Austria's total primary energy requirement. This is less than is the case on average in Western Europe and reflects the presence of considerable hydro-electric potential as well as indigenous reserves of natural gas, coal, and oil. Primary electricity provides two-thirds of the electricity consumed, with the balance made up principally by coal-fired plant.

Although there are some major industrial centres in Austria, including energy-intensive industries such as steel-making, the proportion of final energy taken by this sector is more than two per cent below the European average. This is offset by the high proportion used in the residential sector, 32 per cent compared with 28 per cent on average.

## ENERGY SUPPLY INDUSTRIES

Energy supply is dominated by two major state undertakings. ÖMV, formerly the Österreichische Mineralölverwaltung, is responsible for the importation of crude oil and natural gas, the refining of crude oil and exploration for uranium. Österreichische Elektrizitätswirtschafts AG-Verbundgesellschaft oversees the operations and planning of electricity supply. Other local public authorities are involved in the sale of gas and electricity. Private companies play an important role in the distribution of oil products.

### Oil

*Oil Production and Consumption*

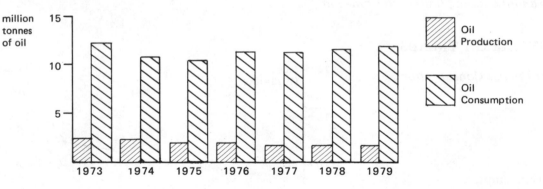

There has been indigenous production of crude oil for many years, but today it accounts for only a minor part of total crude oil used and production is on a downward trend. In 1970 production of 2.8 million tonnes was achieved, but since that time the level of production has fallen by more than a third. Exploration work is continuing, by ÖMV and by the Shell/Mobil partnership company Rohöl-Aufsuchungs Gesellschaft (RAG) in the main existing producing areas of Lower Austria and Burgenland and in Upper Austria. Secondary recovery techniques are widely used in order to maximise indigenous production.

Refining capacity is concentrated in the ÖMV refinery at Schwechat, outside Vienna, and close to the main producing areas. But the refinery, which has a capacity of 14 million tonnes per annum relies for the larger part of its feedstock on crude oil imported through the pipeline spur from the Trans Alpine Pipeline, which runs from Trieste across western Austria into southern Germany. The spur line, the Adria-Wien Pipeline (AWP), is owned by ÖMV, with a 51 per cent holding, and the international oil companies involved in marketing in Austria. These are primarily Shell and Mobil, with smaller shares held by British Petroleum, Exxon, Compagnie Française des Pétroles and AGIP. These companies have their crude oil processed by ÖMV at Schwechat. Total throughput in the refinery is over ten million tonnes per annum. The Danube provides an important artery for transporting oil products but a products pipeline has also been built from Schwechat to the Linz area, thus avoiding disruptions to supply in winter or when there is low water on the Danube.

# Coal

*Coal Production and Consumption*

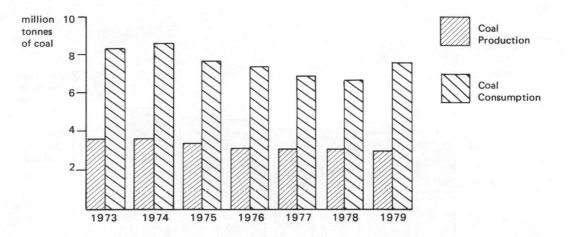

Coal production in Austria now amounts to around three million tonnes per annum. Output has been on a downward trend, but will receive a boost with development of a new mine in Styria with a capacity of one million tonnes per annum. Production in Austria is entirely of lignite and, as is the case with the new mine, largely used in power stations. The country is reliant on imports for requirements of hard coal and coke.

The principal coal producing company is the Graz-Köflacher Eisenbahn- und Bergbaugesellschaft (GKEB), which is a subsidiary of the state holding company ÖIAG. GKEB operates mines in the Graz area of Styria including the new lignite mine being brought into production at Oberdorf. In total, this company will then account for around three-quarters of Austrian indigenous production.

# Gas

*Gas Production and Consumption*

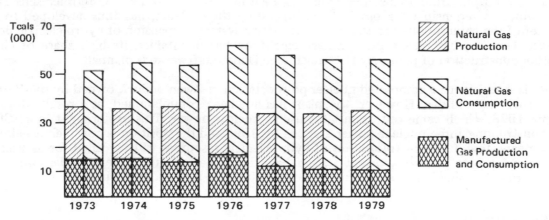

Austria's own production amounts to somewhat under half of the country's consumption of natural gas. Production from gas fields has in fact been rising, although output of associated gas has fallen as production of crude oil has declined. The pipeline system connects main consuming centres in Upper and Lower Austria, Burgenland and Styria. Manufactured gas, which is mainly used by industry, has provided the equivalent of half the amount of indigenous natural gas.

The main supplementary supply of natural gas is being imported by ÖMV from the Soviet Union. ÖMV supplies gas to industrial companies and local undertakings and handles nearly 90 per cent of all supplies. Soviet gas is imported at Baumgarten, on the Czechoslovakian border, for transport via the Trans-Austria Gasleitung (TAG) to the south, and via the West Austria Gasleitung (WAG) to the west. These lines are basically transit lines for moving Soviet gas to Italy and to France and West Germany, but considerable quantities are to be drawn off by ÖMV for Austrian consumption.

ÖMV has negotiated a long-term contract with the Soviet Union for the importation of gas up to the year 2000. With the construction of the second trunkline (WAG) and the increasing demand for natural gas, ÖMV is engaged in negotiating for supplementary quantities of Soviet natural gas.

## Electricity

*Electricity Production*

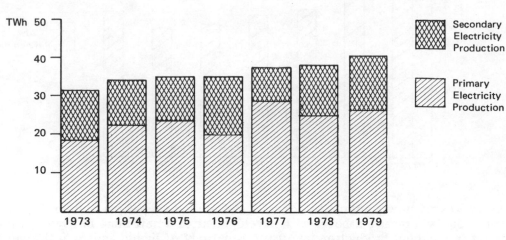

Approximately two-thirds of electricity is generated from hydro-electric resources. In the public supply system, which represents 90 per cent of the total, this primary energy form accounts for 70 per cent of electricity production. The balance of electricity is supplied by thermal power stations. The public supply system is co-ordinated by Österreichische Elektrizitätswirtschaft AG-Verbundgesellschaft, which distributes electricity to regional or municipal undertakings. The bulk of electricity fed into the public system is provided by a small number of major power companies.

Austria's hydro-electric power derives from two principal sources: firstly, the normal exploitation of individually minor rivers in the mountain areas; secondly, from the steady movement of the large mass of water in the Danube. Additional plants on the Danube have been built since the mid 1960s, raising the electricity output from this source from 1.3 TWh in 1963 to 8.0 TWh. Österreichische Donaukraftwerke AG, which is reponsible for building and operating these plants, has thus developed to meet about one quarter of the total supplied to the public electricity system. Expansion of hydro-electric power, principally on the Danube, has meant that primary electricity has maintained its high share of electricity supply. Further construction of plants by Österreichische Donaukraftwerke is planned.

There is in existence a completed nuclear power station at Zwentendorf, owned by the Verbundgesellschaft and provincial utilities. However, the plant has not been commissioned, as a result of a referendum held in late 1978, which came out against the use of nuclear power. This has brought to a halt the programme for constructing three nuclear power stations by 1990 and the position is not likely to alter for some time. This means that further exploitation of hydro-electric resources will be called for as well as construction of thermal power plants. A power station based on a new lignite mine is under construction in Styria. Other projects, using Polish and Hungarian coal as fuel, are also under discussion.

## ENERGY TRADE

*Net Imports/(Exports) 1973-79*

|                                   | 1973  | 1974  | 1975  | 1976  | 1977  | 1978  | 1979  |
|-----------------------------------|-------|-------|-------|-------|-------|-------|-------|
| Coal (million tonnes)             | 4.8   | 5.0   | 4.3   | 4.2   | 3.7   | 3.7   | 4.5   |
| Crude Oil (million tonnes)        | 6.6   | 6.4   | 6.1   | 7.4   | 7.0   | 7.9   | 8.8   |
| Oil Products (million tonnes)     | 2.9   | 2.3   | 2.2   | 2.5   | 2.3   | 2.2   | 2.1   |
| Natural Gas (000 million M$^3$)   | 1.5   | 2.0   | 1.8   | 2.7   | 2.3   | 2.8   | 2.9   |
| Electricity (TWh)                 | (1.5) | (3.0) | (4.5) | (2.2) | (3.9) | (2.8) | (3.8) |

Austria has a significant level of trade in all main energy forms. Over four million tonnes of coal per annum is imported, including substantial quantities of hard coal and processed coke. Most of the country's oil requirement is imported, mainly in the form of crude oil, though there is quite a lot of cross-border movement between Austria and Switzerland and West Germany, giving a net product import of over two million tonnes per annum. Increasing consumption of natural gas is met by imports from the Soviet Union. Only in the case of electricity does Austria have a net export position, owing to the existence of its substantial hydro-electricity production, which provides cheap base-load power for neighbouring countries. Net exports of up to 4.5 TWh per annum have taken place, representing well over ten per cent of production, but this position is likely to be eroded if additional power demand is met from conventional thermal plant.

*Sources of Imported Crude Oil*

| | | |
|---|---|---|
| (percentage) | | |
| Middle East | | 58.0 |
| Iraq | 41.8 | |
| Saudi Arabia | 12.7 | |
| Other | 3.5 | |
| | | |
| Africa | | 21.7 |
| Libya | 11.2 | |
| Algeria | 6.1 | |
| Nigeria | 4.4 | |
| | | |
| Eastern Europe | | 20.3 |
| | | |
| TOTAL | | 100.0 |

Austria's import requirement for oil is met largely by crude oil. Iraq is by far the dominant source of crude oil, reflecting the proximity of the export terminal in the eastern Mediterranean to the TAL pipeline terminal at Trieste. Saudi Arabia, the largest Middle East exporter of crude oil, occupies a relatively minor role in total supply. The Soviet Union, which has its main export terminal on the Black Sea, is the second largest supplier of crude oil. Eastern European sources also account for over a quarter of imports of finished products, but, as may be expected, the neighbouring countries with extensive refining capacity, namely Italy and West Germany, furnish the bulk of product imports.

## ENERGY POLICIES

The development of energy policy in Austria has been conditioned by the result of the 1978 referendum on the use of nuclear power. Prior acceptance of the outcome of the referendum by Parliament has meant that at least for some time nuclear power cannot be considered, despite the presence of the completed but unoperated Zwentendorf power station. From a purely technical point of view a two-thirds majority of Parliament is required even to accept a new referendum. Austria must therefore look to other lines of policy to restrain demand and increase supply, even though this may ironically involve the importation of nuclear generated electricity from Eastern Europe.

### Energy Supply

On the supply side of the energy question Austria is looking to natural gas and coal to provide greater shares in energy supply. Through the agency of ÖMV and general trading agreements with Eastern Europe, it is hoped to raise natural gas imports to 4,000 million cubic metres per annum and utilise Polish and Hungarian coal. It is conceivable that more complex arrangements could be made whereby electricity generating plant might be constructed in eastern Europe and electricity exported to Austria. However, this would further increase Austria's dependence on Comecon countries since it would not be able to resort to world markets for coal supplies.

### Energy Conservation

Several measures have been adopted to economise on the use of energy, mainly taking the form of fiscal incentives. Tax allowances and accelerated depreciation are allowed for investments in energy-saving processes and equipment, including the installation of combined heat and power plant and equipment to use wastes. Loans may also be made. In addition, information and advisory services are provided.

# Belgium

## KEY ENERGY INDICATORS

Energy Consumption
—million tonnes oil equivalent     46.1
Consumption Per Head
—tonnes oil equivalent     4.7
—percentage of West European average     132%
Net Energy Imports     85%
Oil Import-Dependence     100%

*Belgium is a highly industrialised country with several energy-intensive industries. Energy consumption per head is well above the average for West European countries. Most of the energy resources for the economy have to be imported, including all of its oil requirement. The only indigenous form of energy is coal, but this is an industry in decline. Investment is being made in nuclear power capacity, but this will have only a limited impact. With a view to meeting an increasing amount of energy demand from natural gas and diversifying geographically its sources of supply, a terminal for liquefied natural gas is being built at Zeebrugge.*

## ENERGY MARKET TRENDS

*Trend of Energy Consumption*

Energy Consumption
−0.2% p.a.

Gross Domestic Product
+2.4% p.a.

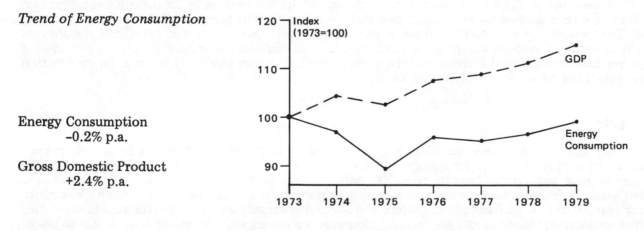

In the two years following the 1973 oil supply crisis energy consumption in Belgium fell by more than ten per cent, reflecting the impact on the country's energy-intensive industries. The economy as a whole seems to have survived that period well, maintaining growth of over four per cent in Gross Domestic Product in 1974 and sustaining only a small decline in 1975. Since that time economic growth has been relatively good and accompanied by only a small increase in energy consumption. In fact, total energy consumption has only just returned to the level of 1973, whereas Gross Domestic Product has grown by 2.4 per cent per annum on average.

*Pattern of Energy Supply and Consumption*

| Primary Fuel Supply (percentage) | | Final Consumption (percentage) | |
|---|---|---|---|
| Oil | 54 | Industry | 44 |
| Solid Fuel | 23 | Residential | 27 |
| Natural Gas | 18 | Transport | 16 |
| Primary Electricity | 5 | Other | 13 |
| TOTAL | 100 | TOTAL | 100 |

Oil accounts for over half of primary energy supply, although this figure is below the average for Western Europe. Both coal and natural gas are major contributors to the energy balance, with both being used to some extent for generation of electricity, which helps to contain the amount of fuel oil needed in that sector. Belgium has been an obvious market for the export availability of natural gas from the Slochteren field in the Netherlands. Primary electricity is almost entirely nuclear, and contributes around a quarter of total electricity.

Belgium is an industrialised country, with several energy-intensive consuming industries such as steel making and petrochemicals manufacture as well as oil refining for export purposes. As a result the share of final energy consumption attributable to industry is well above the European average, at 44 per cent, compared with 39 per cent. Consumption in each of the other sectors is somewhat below average, but appreciably so only in the case of the transport sector. Only 16 per cent of final energy is consumed in transportation, compared with over 20 per cent on average, and reflects the size of the country, the importance of seaborne trade and the use of inland waterways for freight movements.

## ENERGY SUPPLY INDUSTRIES

Although private companies are involved in the supply of all energy forms in Belgium, the State and local authorities maintain a close control through legislation and institutional arrangements. However, the position and power of local and regional public bodies is strong enough to offset central government decisions in some of the key issues of supply. In the supply and distribution of oil and coal there is much less official involvement.

## Oil

*Oil Consumption*

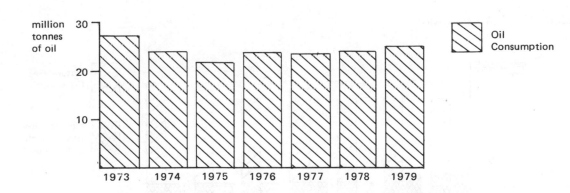

Belgium is dependent on overseas supplies of oil, and the port of Antwerp has developed as one of the key centres of refining and trading in northern Europe. This position is reinforced by its potential for supplying the demand for oil in the hinterland of the Rhineland and southern Germany. In order to overcome limitations on the capacity of Antwerp to accommodate the very large crude oil tankers, a pipeline has been built from Rotterdam to Antwerp, with an extension to Feluy. The main refiners in Antwerp are Exxon, Petrofina and British Petroleum. The Feluy refinery is operated by Standard Oil of California. The country's other major refinery is at Ghent, which is fed by pipeline from Zeebrugge.

The major international oil companies, including Shell, which is based in the Netherlands and has a large amount of refining capacity at Rotterdam, are responsible for the supply of most of the crude oil and products in Belgium. But the Belgian company, Petrofina, is also a leading supplier and marketer, and owns, jointly with BP, one of the main refineries at Antwerp. Independent companies also play a role in importing and distribution, both for the Belgian and for the West German and other inland markets.

## Coal

*Coal Production and Consumption*

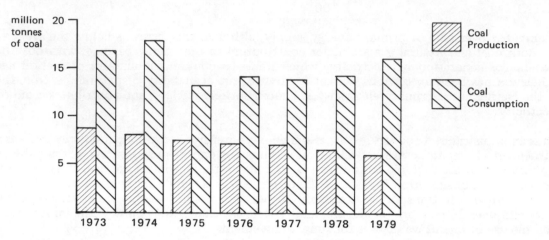

The mining industry in Belgium has been in decline for many years, with production from areas which are being worked out or costly to operate. Production of hard coal now amounts to only six million tonnes per annum and has fallen by 30 per cent since 1973, despite the change in the general situation for coal demand since the oil supply crisis of that year. The total requirement for hard coal has in fact remained at about 15-16 million tonnes per annum, but an increasing proportion has to be met by imports. Additional quantities of coke, for industrial use, are also imported.

Electricity generating plant consumes about one-third of hard coal availability. Industry is a more significant market and has a large requirement for coke. There are several energy-intensive industries in Belgium and these utilise both coke and the resultant gas.

## Gas

*Gas Production and Consumption*

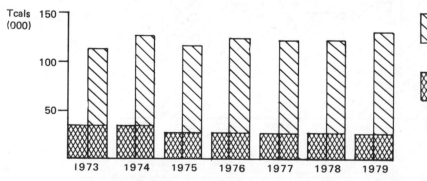

There is very little production of natural gas in Belgium itself, but it is well placed to link into the Dutch export system. Over 15,000 million cubic meters per annum is imported through a trunkline which crosses the Dutch border to the north of Antwerp and passes close to Brussels. The line then extends south-west to the French border. Other trunklines supply all the main centres of industry and population. One line serves the south and extends into Luxembourg. A significant amount of gas is derived from various industrial processes, but this is used within the steel industry and other energy-intensive industries.

The transport system for natural gas is operated by Distrigaz, which sells gas either directly to bulk industrial consumers or to local undertakings for general public supply. Well over half is sold directly by Distrigaz. The rest is sold by numerous undertakings under the control of local towns or communes. For the most part these undertakings represent a grouping of local authorities in combination with private companies.

The overall gas sector is supervised by the Comité de Contrôle de l'Electricité et du Gaz, on which industry and trade unions are represented. However, the government has the leading role on this committee, which is particularly concerned with questions of investment planning and tariffs. In order to supplement supplies of Dutch natural gas a terminal is being built at Zeebrugge for the importation of liquefied natural gas. Initially this is to come from Algeria, although other sources of supply have now become practicable.

**Electricity**

*Electricity Production*

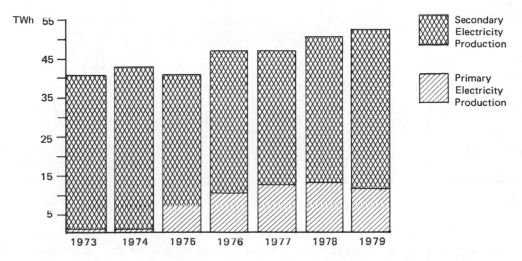

Electricity for the public supply system is almost entirely produced by private industrial companies. A small quantity is produced by plant run by local towns or communes. A more significant quantity, around ten per cent, is produced by industry for its own consumption. Arrangements for public distribution and sale of electricity are the responsibility of local authorities. Nearly 80 per cent of the public supply is sold by undertakings in which a number of communes and private sector companies are involved.

Both production and distribution are, however, closely controlled by the State. The Comité de Contrôle de l'Electricité et du Gaz, on which industry and trade unions are represented, is empowered to co-ordinate operating procedures, long-term planning and the setting of tariffs.

With limited indigenous energy resources, the decision has been taken to develop nuclear power capacity. At present there is a 870 megawatt station in operation at Tihange. This is the second largest power station in Belgium, and larger units are being built, both at Tihange and Doel, north of Antwerp, and at Chooz, which is across the French border. France participates in the Tihange capacity and in return Belgian companies are involved at Chooz. Already, nuclear power and associated pumped storage plant account for more than 20 per cent of electricity produced. The government's objective is that nuclear power should be used for supplying half of the country's electricity demands in the mid 1980s.

**ENERGY TRADE**

*Net Import/(Exports) 1973-79*

|  | 1973 | 1974 | 1975 | 1976 | 1977 | 1978 | 1979 |
|---|---|---|---|---|---|---|---|
| Coal (million tonnes) | 8.0 | 10.0 | 6.6 | 7.5 | 6.6 | 7.4 | 10.2 |
| Crude Oil (million tonnes) | 37.3 | 30.5 | 29.0 | 29.2 | 36.6 | 33.1 | 33.8 |
| Oil Products (million tonnes) | (6.5) | (0.5) | (5.0) | (4.7) | (10.3) | (6.5) | (5.5) |
| Natural Gas (000 million M$^3$) | 9.4 | 11.0 | 10.8 | 11.5 | 11.3 | 11.2 | 12.5 |
| Electricity (TWh) | (0.8) | (0.3) | (0.9) | (3.4) | (1.4) | (2.8) | (1.2) |

Belgium has very limited indigenous energy resources, confined to production of around six million tonnes per annum of hard coal. In addition to this well over 10 million tonnes of coal and coke is imported to meet inland demand. Other Community countries, principally West Germany, supply more than half of the imports, but significant quantities are obtained from other main exporters, namely, the United States, Poland, South Africa, the Soviet Union and Australia.

Belgium has to import all of its oil requirements and has a significant level of natural gas imports too, mostly from the Netherlands. In the electricity sector a large base load of nuclear power plant has been constructed, which has put Belgium into the position of being a net exporter of electricity. Because of the country's strategic position in relation to West Germany, which is a major importer of finished products, refining capacity is utilised for export processing and supply to independent bulk markets.

*Sources of Imported Crude Oil*

| (percentage) | | |
|---|---|---|
| Middle East | | 82.9 |
| Saudi Arabia | 45.5 | |
| Iran | 12.9 | |
| Iraq | 7.0 | |
| United Arab Emirates | 7.0 | |
| Qatar | 5.7 | |
| Kuwait | 4.8 | |
| | | |
| Africa | | 10.5 |
| Nigeria | 8.8 | |
| Other | 1.7 | |
| | | |
| United Kingdom | | 2.6 |
| Other | | 4.0 |
| | | |
| TOTAL | | 100.0 |

The Middle East is by far the most important source of crude oil for Belgian refineries and Saudi Arabia, the world's largest individual exporter of crude oil, accounts for almost half of all crude oil imports. A significant amount of Nigerian crude oil is run, but very little from North African sources. Despite the country's location and refinery activity, only limited quantities of North Sea oil have been imported so far.

## ENERGY POLICIES

The principal areas in which government policies have influenced the energy industries continue to be of an operational nature, although decisions have been taken which affect the future pattern of energy supply.

### Energy Supply

The government has a continuing presence in the operation of all the energy industries. Through the Comité de Contrôle de l'Electricité et du Gaz it is directly concerned with the setting of tariffs. Through a related committee the day-to-day operation of both gas and electricity systems is controlled. Prices of petroleum products are also controlled and there is a joint government/industry committee which discusses pricing. The short-term health of mining is subject to decisions by the government concerning subsidies for consumers or producers and other forms of financial or social assistance.

The government wishes to press ahead with construction of nuclear generating capacity, sometimes in the face of opposition from local authorities. Steps have been taken, with the construction of the terminal at Zeebrugge for importing liquefied natural gas, to diversify the sources of supply of this important form of energy. Belgium is unlikely to be able to increase imports from the Netherlands, and indeed may have to consider some reduction, although additional supplies may be available from the North Sea via the Dutch trunklines. It remains the intention to cut down on the use of natural gas by industry.

### Energy Conservation

Official activity in energy conservation has hitherto concentrated on the provision of information and advice to both industry and the general public. Schemes of financial assistance were in force for a time, involving interest subsidies or special tax allowances, but these have now been discontinued. One area in which a scheme is being considered is in combined heat and power systems, which should be of particular relevance, given the existence of numerous energy-intensive industrial consumers.

# Denmark

## KEY ENERGY INDICATORS

Energy Consumption
    —million tonnes oil equivalent         21.3
Consumption Per Head
    —tonnes oil equivalent             4.2
    —percentage of West European average   117%
Net Energy Imports                97%
Oil Import-Dependence            97%

*Denmark has above-average consumption of energy per head, reflecting the generally high standard of living in the country. But it is highly dependent on imported energy. This import-dependence will be reduced through the development of offshore oil and gas resources. These promise to make a significant contribution to energy supply by the late 1980s and involve establishing a natural gas supply system. Development of these resources, combined with a major substitution of coal for oil in electricity production has enabled a decision on construction of a nuclear power station to be left in abeyance.*

## ENERGY MARKET TRENDS

*Trend of Energy Consumption*

Energy Consumption
    +1.3% p.a.

Gross Domestic Product
    +1.9% p.a.

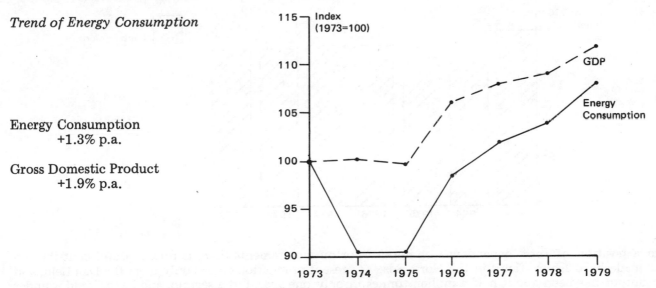

Following the oil supply crisis of 1973 and the related general economic recession energy consumption in Denmark fell dramatically. The impact on economic growth was much less marked, although Gross Domestic Product stagnated during 1974 and 1975. Since then GDP has risen at a reasonable rate to raise the overall average to nearly two per cent per annum. The rate of increase in energy consumption has been greater than that of GDP since 1975, and is tending to offset the advantage gained in 1974 and 1975.

*Pattern of Energy Supply and Consumption*

| Primary Fuel Supply (percentage) | | Final Consumption (percentage) | |
|---|---|---|---|
| Oil | 79 | Industry | 20 |
| Solid Fuel | 19 | Residential | 40 |
| Natural Gas | — | Transport | 23 |
| Primary Electricity | 2 | Other | 17 |
| TOTAL | 100 | TOTAL | 100 |

The main change in the pattern of fuel supply has been a shift from the use of oil to greater use of coal, mainly in electricity generating stations. But reliance on oil is still very high. This is in part a reflection of the high proportion of final consumption in the residential sector, where gas has occupied only a small share. At 40 per cent of final consumption the residential sector is well above the West European average of 28 per cent. Use of energy in transport and agriculture is also above-average.

The scope for a further major shift from the use of oil to coal is limited by the fact that industry accounts for only 20 per cent of final energy consumption, compared with the West European average of 39 per cent. The main factor leading to a reduction in use of oil products will be the development of a natural gas system using indigenous North Sea resources, which will have a significant impact on the residential and commercial sectors.

## ENERGY SUPPLY INDUSTRIES

The organisation of electricity production and distribution has been subject to overall government supervision, and the industry associations which coordinate operations now have increased formal governmental support and supervision. The state is playing a key part in the development of a natural gas supply system and has set up a state agency to deal with supply and bulk distribution. Private companies have an essentially free hand in supplying oil products, although they are subject to close scrutiny on questions of pricing and competition.

## Oil

*Oil Consumption*

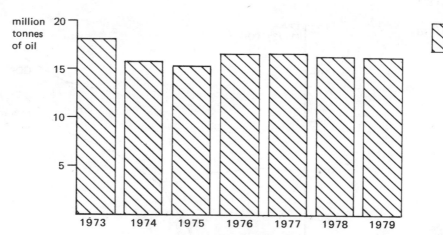

 Oil Consumption

From a position of total dependence on imports for oil requirements there is now a useful contribution being made by offshore fields in the North Sea. At present production comes only from the Dan field, and peak output has been about half a million tonnes in only one year. But a second, and larger, field is under development. Named Gorm, this field is expected to produce at a maximum rate of two million tonnes per annum in the late 1980s. Yet another field, Skjold, has been discovered and a decision concerning development has yet to be made. This would be capable of production at a rate similar to the existing Dan field.

All exploration and development in the North Sea is carried out by the Dansk Undergrund Consortium, which has exclusive rights. DUC comprises the Danish firm of AP Moeller, which has oil and shipping interests, and Danish affiliates of the international oil majors Chevron, Shell and Texaco. Shell is a leading marketer in Denmark with a refinery at Fredericia and Texaco is one of the main marketers in West Germany with a refinery at Heide close to the Danish border.

Other principal oil marketers in Denmark are Esso and Gulf, which have refineries at Kalundborg and Stigsnaes respectively. Between them the affiliates of the international companies account for a large part of sales, but there are also a number of independent fuel importers and distributors and a network of co-operatives. Individual major industrial users can also arrange direct imports of fuel.

## Coal

*Coal Consumption*

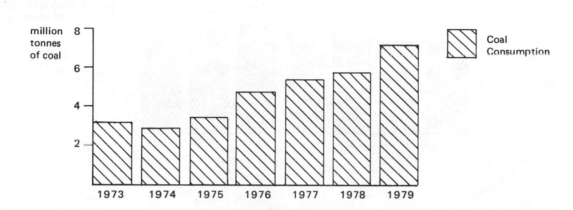

There is no indigenous production of coal in Denmark but a substantial import trade has been built up by independent fuel importers and in particular by electricity producers and other major industrial companies who can import bulk shipments direct to their installations. During the last two years installations at power stations at Aabenraa and Stigsnaes have been upgraded so as to be able to import coal in large carriers of 100-150,000 deadweight tons.

## Gas

*Gas Production*

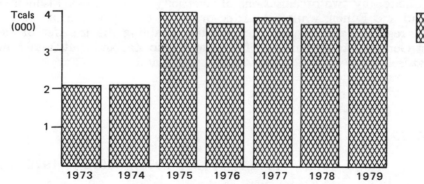

Exploration activity in the Danish sector of the North Sea has revealed a significant amount of natural gas. Although requiring major investment in relation to potential output, particularly when compared with projects for exploiting some of the much larger gas reserves found in the United Kingdom and Norwegian sectors, the government has decided that this gas should be exploited and landed in Denmark. Development work is to be undertaken by the Dansk Undergrund Consortium, which has contracted with the state-owned Dansk Olie og Naturgas for the supply of 55,000 million cubic metres over a 25-year period commencing in the mid 1980s.

At present there is a substantial production of manufactured gas in the overall energy supply picture. Total production has reached up to 4,000 teracalories per annum, equivalent in heating value to 400,000 tonnes of oil. This type of gas is likely to be largely supplanted in the domestic supply system as offshore gas is brought in, although requiring virtually a new supply network. It is envisaged that around half a million households will be supplied ultimately with natural gas.

## Electricity

*Electricity Production*

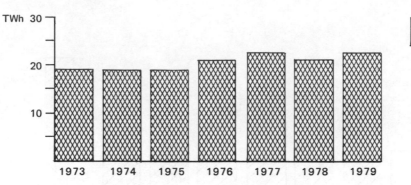

Electricity is produced almost entirely from conventional thermal power stations using either coal or heavy fuel oil. There is only a negligible amount of electricity produced by hydro-electric plant and as yet there is no nuclear power station in Denmark. Since the mid 1970s there has been a major shift from the use of fuel oil to the use of coal as key power plants have been converted to dual firing. By 1978 nearly 60 per cent of electricity was being produced in coal-fired plant and since that time the proportion has been rising towards 80 per cent.

There are some 120 electricity undertakings in Denmark of which 108 are either municipally owned or co-operatives. Many are of limited local significance and the bulk of electricity in the public supply system is generated by only 11 undertakings, operating 18 main power stations. Most of these major installations also provide district heating. The amount of heat supplied in this way totals 6,000 teracalories, equivalent to 7,000 GWh. But this is only about one-third of the total amount of district heating produced, as there are many smaller scale local schemes.

Electricity supply is co-ordinated by two organisations of electricity undertakings. Elsam is responsible for electricity supply in Jutland and Funen, while Elkraft co-ordinates the operation of utilities on Zealand, Lolland and Falster. Both regions have external power cables enabling the transfer of electricity from Norway, Sweden and West Germany to Jutland and from Sweden to Zealand, but there is no high-voltage connection across the Great Belt between Funen and Zealand or Lolland.

## ENERGY TRADE

*Net Imports/(Exports)1973-79*

|                              | 1973  | 1974  | 1975 | 1976 | 1977 | 1978 | 1979 |
|------------------------------|-------|-------|------|------|------|------|------|
| Coal (million tonnes)        | 3.1   | 3.6   | 4.1  | 4.2  | 5.6  | 6.2  | 7.8  |
| Crude Oil (million tonnes)   | 9.8   | 9.4   | 7.9  | 7.6  | 7.3  | 7.7  | 8.3  |
| Oil Products (million tonnes)| 8.7   | 7.8   | 8.5  | 8.5  | 9.6  | 8.7  | 7.5  |
| Electricity (TWh)            | (0.2) | (0.1) | 0.9  | 0.8  | 1.6  | 3.7  | 3.7  |

Denmark is heavily dependent on imported energy, with no indigenous sources of coal and negligible capacity for hydro-electric production. The development of offshore natural gas is still in the early stages. Imported oil, approximately half as crude oil for the domestic refineries and half as finished products imported from other major export refining centres, forms the basis of energy supply. Until recently oil was the predominant fuel used in power stations. This has been changing rapidly as plant has been converted to use coal, although retaining the capability to burn heavy fuel oil if desired. Over the five years 1973 to 1978 imports of coal doubled and rose again substantially in 1979. This is despite the fact that Denmark has been increasing its importation of electricity via the power cables linking the north of the country with Norway and Sweden.

*Sources of Imported Crude Oil*

| (percentage) | | |
|---|---|---|
| Middle East | | 35.1 |
| Saudi Arabia | 15.2 | |
| Iran | 8.4 | |
| Kuwait | 5.2 | |
| United Arab Emirates | 4.3 | |
| Other | 2.0 | |
| | | |
| United Kingdom | | 34.0 |
| Eastern Europe | | 21.4 |
| Western Hemisphere | | 3.8 |
| Nigeria | | 3.5 |
| Other | | 2.2 |
| | | |
| TOTAL | | 100.0 |

The United Kingdom has become the most important source of crude oil for Danish refineries, reflecting their proximity to North Sea resources and also the fact that these refineries are unable to accommodate the largest tankers engaged in long-haul crude oil movements. Nevertheless, Middle East countries, in particular Saudi Arabia, remain important sources of crude oil. There is also an appreciable supply from Eastern Europe. Denmark imports only a limited quantity of crude oil from African countries, as North Sea crude oil avoids the need for additional supplies of light low sulphur crude oil.

*Sources of Imported Coal*

| (percentage) | |
|---|---|
| Poland | 50.3 |
| South Africa | 14.3 |
| USSR | 8.3 |
| EEC countries | 17.4 |
| Other | 9.7 |
| | |
| | 100.0 |

In its drive to diversify its sources of energy supply and pattern of fuels there has been a substantial growth in imports of coal from the nearest source, Poland. While this country remains the leading source of imports, other principal exporting countries are now beginning to supply increasing amounts. South Africa has become an important supplier and supplies from Australia are increasing. In addition Denmark is well located to benefit from supplies from West Germany, which is the European Community's main exporter of coal.

## ENERGY POLICIES

The oil supply crisis in 1973-74 highlighted the precarious nature of the Danish energy situation, with its reliance on imported oil for a large part of its requirements. The continuing awareness of actual and potential energy supply difficulties since that time has brought about a number of changes in policies in the energy sector. The need to re-examine the country's use of energy has also been underlined by the economic problems arising from much higher prices in international energy markets, which have helped to undermine the country's basic financial stability.

### Energy Supply

From a position of reliance on one form of energy Denmark has been moving quite rapidly towards a more diverse basis for energy supply. The government has been keen to see exploited the discoveries of oil and gas found offshore by the Dansk Undergrund Consortium and the decision has been taken that natural gas should be landed in Denmark and be used as the basis for a new gas system, rather than be piped to West

Germany. West Germany already has the capacity to absorb large quantities of natural gas and is landfall for the associated gas produced in the Ekofisk field. Although landing Danish gas for the West German market may well have been more economic overall, from the Danish point of view the use of the gas is seen as an important increase in security of supply. It would also enable the country to contemplate the use of liquefied natural gas at some later stage.

A second major move towards diversification of supply has been the shift of a substantial amount of electricity production to the use of coal as boiler feed. This shift has been encouraged by the price level in the international coal trade and by the nearby availability of coal from Poland. Having attained a high level of coal use in power generation the aim now is to diversify the sources of coal drawn upon by utilities.

Electricity supply has been co-ordinated by the two industry groupings Elsam and Elkraft. These two organisations were originally voluntary co-operative groups responsible for operational activities and co-ordination of long-term planning, particularly in relation to the import of electricity from Norway and Sweden. The role of these groupings has been reinforced by statute since 1978, under the general supervision of the Danish Association of Electricity Supply Undertakings.

The development of offshore oil and gas, combined with the new extensive ability to use coal for electricity production has meant that the question of developing nuclear power plant has fallen into abeyance. Until late 1979 the objective of Danish energy policy was to diversify into a four-fuel economy. However there is strong opposition to the development of nuclear power and the subject was to have been put to a national (advisory) referendum during 1980. The present government has felt that progress in the utilisation of other energy sources, combined with firm energy conservation measures, has made a decision about nuclear power less urgent.

### Energy Conservation

Denmark has been one of the countries most active in energy conservation. This has taken the form of letting consumer prices rise to international market levels in order to restrain demand, and attaching specific energy taxes to all forms of energy. A number of specific measures to reduce consumption have also been taken, including speed limits, imposition of a car-free day on vehicle owners and restrictions on heating and lighting. In order to encourage investment in energy-saving developments in industry and commerce financial assistance is made available by the government.

An important area in which Denmark already has a leading role is in the use of combined heat and power systems. There are many such plants throughout the country and new ones are to be encouraged. The government has embarked on a long-term programme for extending the use of district heating systems and increasing the use of combined heat and power plants.

# Finland

## KEY ENERGY INDICATORS

| | |
|---|---|
| Energy Consumption | |
| —million tonnes oil equivalent | 6.7 |
| Consumption Per Head | |
| —tonnes oil equivalent | 5.6 |
| —percentage of West European average | 157% |
| Net Energy Imports | 71% |
| Oil Import-Dependence | 100% |

*Finland has a high average level of energy consumption, reflecting the general standard of living and the demands of the northerly climate. The country has important hydro-electric production, but is dependent on foreign sources for oil, coal and nuclear fuel, although it may be able to exploit indigenous resources of uranium. Two nuclear power stations are now in operation and a limited natural gas supply system has been established based on imports by pipeline from the Soviet Union.*

## ENERGY MARKET TRENDS

*Trend of Energy Consumption*

Energy Consumption
+2.8% p.a.

Gross Domestic Product
+2.3% p.a.

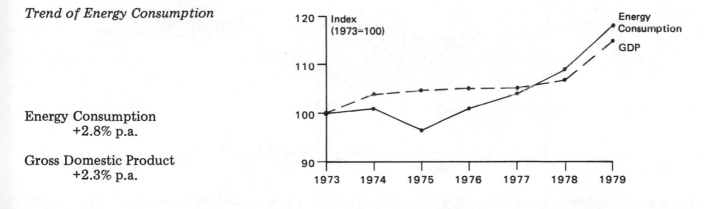

Despite its high dependence on imported energy and on international trade Finland suffered no decline in Gross Domestic Product subsequent to the 1973 oil supply crisis, although the economy stagnated for several years. Only recently has there been significant economic growth, and associated with this has been an increased rate of growth in energy consumption. Consumption of energy fell back in 1975, but has risen strongly since that time as nuclear plant has become available and supplies of natural gas have built up. Since 1973 energy consumption has risen faster than GDP on average.

*Pattern of Energy Supply and Consumption*

| Primary Fuel Supply (percentage) | | Final Consumption (percentage) | |
|---|---|---|---|
| Oil | 52 | Industry | 43 |
| Solid Fuel | 31 | Residential | 33 |
| Natural Gas | 4 | Transport | 15 |
| Primary Electricity | 13 | Other | 9 |
| TOTAL | 100 | TOTAL | 100 |

Oil accounts for over 50 per cent of primary fuel supply and consumption has increased rapidly to meet the energy requirements of an expanding economy, since the country's significant hydro-electric resources are virtually fully exploited. During the 1980s however the contribution from natural gas and nuclear power will increase and substitution of coal for fuel oil will be greater, especially in the production of electricity. Peat and wood still constitute a significant proportion of the total of solid fuel availability.

The proportion of energy consumed in the residential sector is about 20 per cent greater than the West European average, but the greater use of natural gas and increased use of combined heat and power plant will permit a further shift away from the use of oil products. The transport sector, which is most dependent on oil products, is smaller than in most countries, as a result of the general concentration of economic activity in the south and south-western parts of the country. The industrial sector contains several industries which are energy-intensive. Some of the major plants in these industries may be able to convert to the use of coal instead of oil.

## ENERGY SUPPLY INDUSTRIES

The State is closely involved in the energy supply industries, either directly through ownership of Neste Oy, in the oil sector, and Imatran Voima, the electricity undertaking, or indirectly because of the State monopoly in oil importing and trade agreements with the Soviet Union. Other gas and electricity companies are run by various municipalities. The distribution and marketing of oil and coal products is largely carried out by private companies.

### Oil

*Oil Consumption*

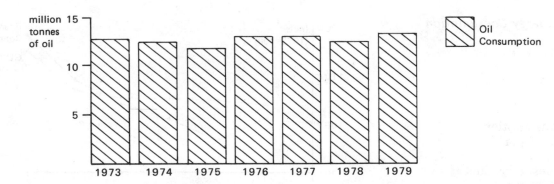

There is no indigenous production of oil. The importation of crude oil and petroleum products is closely controlled and in practice operated through the state oil company Neste Oy. Neste operates two refineries, at Porvoo on the south coast and Naantali on the west coast. These enable most product requirements to be met, but some additional quantities have to be imported.

Neste plays a leading role in the distribution and marketing of oil products and is a major participant in two of the main marketing companies, E-Öljyt and Kesoil. Several of the international oil companies are also represented, notably Shell, Esso and British Petroleum. There are a number of smaller Finnish firms, some of which have been set up primarily to handle products imported from the Soviet Union.

## Coal

*Coal Consumption*

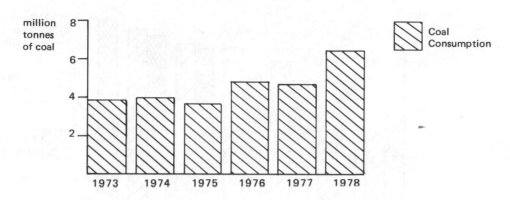

There is no coal mining activity in Finland. But there is a substantial market using coal, amounting to some five million tonnes per annum. Coal is used in electricity generation, including the largest power station, the 1,000 MW plant of Imatran Voima at Inkoo. Special solid fuels are also needed for a number of industries. Peat and wood are the only forms of solid fuel produced in Finland. These make a useful contribution to the overall energy balance. In the north of the country some small power units generate electricity from peat.

## Gas

*Gas Production and Consumption*

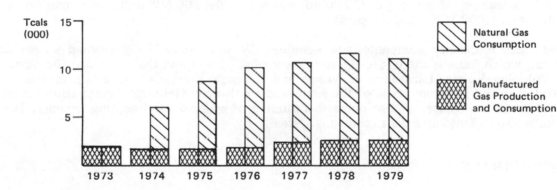

There are no resources of natural gas in Finland and it is only in recent years that an extension has been constructed to the Soviet Union's pipeline system enabling Soviet natural gas to be moved into Finland. Neste Oy, the state-owned oil company, is operator of the pipeline system based on this imported gas, which is so far restricted to a small part of south-eastern Finland.

The natural gas is being used for a variety of markets, including electricity generation. This is partly a reflection of the lack of any national supply grid at this stage, so that consumption is limited to the area closest to the import pipeline. Meanwhile gas is manufactured from oil at a number of municipal plants, the Helsinki Energy Board (Helsingin Energialaitos) producing 25 million cubic meters per annum for local supply in the densest network.

## Electricity

*Electricity Production and Consumption*

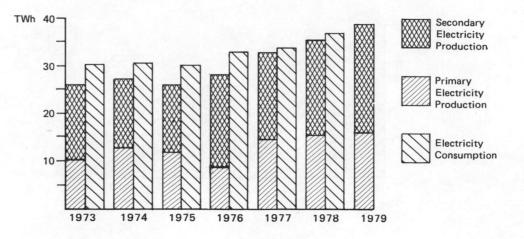

Electricity supply is closely controlled by the state through several different channels. It owns the largest individual producer of electricity, Imatran Voima Oy, which also controls and operates the national transmission system. Imatran Voima plays the leading role in the Power Producers' Co-ordinating Council, Sähköntuottajien Yhteistyövaltuuskunta (STYV), which deals with overall matters of investment, transmission and operations. STYV includes other public sector producers and the organisation of industrial electricity producers, several of which are ultimately state-owned companies.

Imatran Voima developed as the company responsible for exploiting hydro-electric resources in the lakeland area of south-eastern Finland. It is the main shareholder in other companies producing hydro-electric power in the north, but is also heavily involved in building up thermal generating capacity. Imatran Voima has a nuclear power station at Loviisa, which has a capacity of 840 MW, and is a participant in the second nuclear power station, at Olkiluoto, where the first 660 MW unit is in operation. At Inkoo Imatran Voima has a 1,000 MW coal-fired plant.

Other main electricity companies are Kemijoki Oy and Oulujoki Oy (owned 90 per cent by Imatran Voima), which harness the hydro-electric power of the Kemi and Oulu rivers in the north of the country, and Pohjolan Voima, Länsi-suomen Voima and Helsingin Energialaitos, the operations of which are concentrated in the populous areas of the south and south-west. Helsingin Energialaitos supplies both gas and electricity in the capital. It also operates a number of major district heating schemes. The second city of Turku is also to build up a district heating system.

## ENERGY TRADE

*Net Imports/(Exports) 1973-79*

|                                   | 1973 | 1974 | 1975 | 1976 | 1977 | 1978 | 1979 |
|-----------------------------------|------|------|------|------|------|------|------|
| Coal (million tonnes)             | 3.8  | 4.9  | 4.8  | 3.7  | 5.1  | 5.7  | 6.1  |
| Crude Oil (million tonnes)        | 9.5  | 9.5  | 9.6  | 11.1 | 11.6 | 10.5 | 12.7 |
| Oil Products (million tonnes)     | 4.1  | 4.1  | 3.1  | 2.3  | 1.7  | 1.3  | 2.2  |
| Natural Gas (000 million M$^3$)   | -    | 0.4  | 0.7  | 0.8  | 0.8  | 1.0  | 0.9  |
| Electricity (TWh)                 | 4.3  | 3.1  | 4.0  | 4.0  | 0.9  | 1.3  | 0.7  |

Finland has limited indigenous energy resources and therefore imports coal, crude oil, finished products, and in more recent years, natural gas. Natural gas is imported through a pipeline from the northern part of the Soviet Union, and the Soviet Union is also the principal supply source for crude oil and oil products. The supply of energy products takes place under the general long-term trade agreement which exists between the two countries, although volumes are negotiated more frequently and prices are related to general international price levels. The construction of nuclear plant and the natural gas pipeline also form part of bilateral trade and construction contracts.

*Sources of Imported Crude Oil*

| (percentage) | | |
|---|---|---|
| Eastern Europe | | 57.8 |
| Middle East | | 36.7 |
|    Saudi Arabia | 16.4 | |
|    Iran | 11.0 | |
|    Iraq | 9.3 | |
| United Kingdom | | 3.6 |
| Other | | 1.9 |
| TOTAL | | 100.0 |

The Soviet Union accounts for upwards of 60 per cent of crude oil imports. The balance derives mostly from Middle East sources. In the case of oil products imports come almost entirely from the Soviet Union.

Imports of coal have risen to over six million tonnes per annum. For the most part this is hard coal imported from Poland, which is the most easily accessible source.

## ENERGY POLICIES

As a country highly dependent upon imported energy, Finland has become increasingly conscious of the need for developing an energy policy to cover all aspects of supply and conservation. The state is already involved in both main aspects of energy policy.

### Energy Supply

During 1978 and 1979 an intensive study of the country's energy situation was carried out. The overall objective on the supply side is to reduce the extent of import-dependence, especially dependence on oil. There are limits to what can be done to increase domestic supply, but it is expected that the use of peat, of which there are large reserves, can continue to be increased, with the possibility of this source meeting between five and ten per cent of energy needs by 1990.

Secondly, more intensive investigation of possible uranium resources is to be carried out. At present the country's nuclear power stations use imported fuel. When fully operational the Loviisa and Olkiluoto Stations should supply 30 per cent of all electricity, and a decision has been taken to build a third nuclear power station.

### Conservation

As a northerly country Finland sets fairly high standards in design and construction of buildings to reduce waste of energy. There is also an increasing amount of combined heat and power generation in the many district heating schemes.

Still higher standards in design and construction are to be required, including better insulation, such as triple glazing. A range of financial incentives are to be made available to encourage investment in energy-saving measures, both by companies and private individuals.

Prices of energy products, in common with other basic commodities, are subject to official control. Taxes on products, especially oil products, have been used to promote the objectives of conservation policy. Duty on motor fuels has been increased considerably in the recent past, in order to restrain consumption. Part of the revenue from this source is being used to subsidise bus operations and encourage the use of this form of transport.

# France

## KEY ENERGY INDICATORS

Energy Consumption
    —million tonnes oil equivalent      193.8
Consumption Per Head
    —tonnes oil equivalent      3.6
    —percentage of West European average      102%
Net Energy Imports      76%
Oil Import-Dependence      99%

*France is the third largest consumer of energy in Western Europe, but has only modest indigenous resources in the form of coal, natural gas and hydro-electric power. Dependence on imported energy is high and in the case of oil almost total. Despite the presence of energy-intensive industries such as petrochemicals and steel-making, consumption of energy per head is close to the average level for Western Europe, reflecting the potential for further industrialisation in some parts of the country. In order to sustain continued economic growth, but at the same time reduce its dependence on imported energy, particularly oil, the French government has made significant headway with its programme of nuclear power plant construction.*

## ENERGY MARKET TRENDS

*Trend of Energy Consumption*

Energy Consumption
    +0.9% p.a.

Gross Domestic Product
    +2.9% p.a.

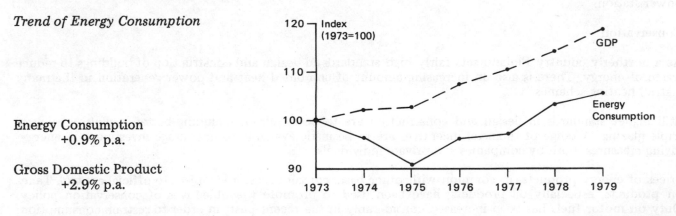

The French government has been more active than many others in constraining energy consumption, especially in the residential and commercial sectors. Through prices and taxes as well as direct controls, in the form of rationing of heating oil, energy consumption has been limited without a serious impact on economic growth. Energy consumption fell in both 1974 and 1975, although even in the latter year the country avoided a real decline in Gross Domestic Product. Since 1975 energy consumption has been increasing at a greater rate than Gross Domestic Product, but some of the benefit gained in terms of energy conservation appears to have been maintained.

*Pattern of Energy Supply and Consumption*

| Primary Fuel Supply (percentage) | | Final Consumption (percentage) | |
| --- | --- | --- | --- |
| Oil | 59 | Industry | 38 |
| Solid Fuel | 16 | Residential | 29 |
| Natural Gas | 12 | Transport | 22 |
| Primary Electricity | 13 | Other | 11 |
| TOTAL | 100 | TOTAL | 100 |

The pattern of primary fuel supply to the French economy is changing quite rapidly. Consumption of coal and natural gas has been increasing and France is well into a major programme to construct nuclear power stations. As a result the proportion of primary energy derived from oil is falling. Nevertheless, it still accounts for nearly 60 per cent of total primary energy input.

The pattern of final energy consumption shows that the share taken by industry is slightly below average, despite the existence of certain major energy-consuming industries, and perhaps reflects the fact that France is not so intensively industrialised as some other West European countries, such as Belgium or West Germany. The transport sector on the other hand absorbs slightly more than the average owing to the long distances between some of the key cities and industrial centres. The proportion consumed in the residential sector is also above average despite attempts to encourage energy conservation.

## ENERGY SUPPLY INDUSTRIES

The state is directly involved in all of the energy industries. Most coal is produced in the nationalised mines and production of electricity and gas is carried out by state undertakings. In the oil sector the distribution and marketing of products is regulated and the state oil and gas enterprise ERAP has been given support and resources both to ensure a leading presence in the domestic sector and to assure the country of more secure energy resources abroad.

### Oil

*Oil Consumption*

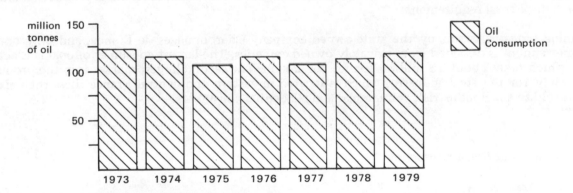

Despite continuing exploration efforts, both onshore and offshore, significant quantities of oil have not so far been revealed. About one million tonnes per annum is produced from fields in Aquitaine and the Paris Basin. Almost as significant are the natural gas liquids produced in association with gas in the Lacq area.

The importation of crude oil and products is subject to a licensing system, which has been used to assure the country of adequate refining capacity and a significant role for French companies, approximately 50 per cent of product sales. As an adjunct to this system prices are subject to official maximum levels.

Leading positions in refining and marketing are held by Compagnie Française des Pétroles, in which the state holds approximately 40 per cent and by the specially created state company Entreprise de Recherches et d'Activités Pétrolières (ERAP), which has expanded through the absorption of the oil interests of ANTAR. Several of the international major oil companies are represented in France, namely, British Petroleum, Mobil, Shell and Exxon.

Independent distributors have maintained a role, particularly in the supply of heating oil and industrial fuel oil, but they have not been able to capitalise to any great degree on the availability from time to time of lower cost imports, on account of the import control system.

The size of the country has led to a considerable use of pipeline transport. Although major refineries are to be found at several points around the coast, such as the Marseilles area, Bordeaux, Le Havre and Dunkirk, many refineries have been built inland, closer to centres of consumption. Several refineries along the Seine Valley and the Paris Basin, as well as the refinery at Valenciennes, are supplied from Le Havre, where the largest crude carriers can be accommodated. Refineries at Feyzin, near Lyon, and in Alsace and Lorraine are supplied by the South European Pipeline from Fos, near Marseilles.

## Coal

*Coal Production and Consumption*

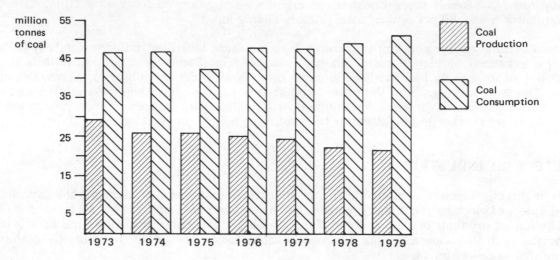

There is an important coal-mining industry in France, although production has been on a downward trend and this is likely to continue. Production of hard coal amounts to less than 19 million tonnes per annum, which is 30 per cent lower than in 1973. About half of this output is obtained from mines in Lorraine. The rest is mined mostly in the Nord—Pas de Calais area and the south central part of the country. In addition about three million tonnes per annum of lignite is obtained. But in total, indigenous production amounts to less than half of total requirements.

The mining industry is run by the state-owned company Charbonnages de France, and only one million tonnes per annum is obtained from privately owned collieries. The largest consumer of coal is Electricité de France, which takes about 18 million tonnes per annum. The second largest market is in the production of coke, mainly for the steel industry, which is located in eastern and central France. Less than six million tonnes is sold to small industrial, commercial and residential consumers.

## Gas

*Gas Production and Consumption*

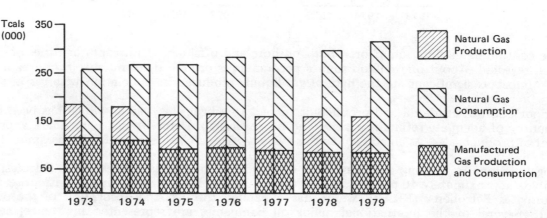

Natural gas production approaches 8,000 million cubic metres per annum, or some 30 per cent of requirements. The balance is imported by pipeline or in liquefied form. Pipeline gas from the Netherlands is used in the north-eastern part of the country. Liquefied natural gas is imported via terminals at Fos, on the Mediterranean, at Le Havre, on the north coast, and at St Nazaire on the Atlantic. These terminals are strategically located in relation to consumption and the existing natural gas resources at Lacq in the south-west. From the beginning of 1980 supplies of Soviet natural gas are being imported across the West German border. Gaz de France has an agreement for up to 4,000 million cubic metres per annum from this source.

The supply and distribution of gas is undertaken by the state enterprise Gaz de France. Industry is by far the largest sector of consumption for gas, taking close to half of the availability of natural gas. In addition energy-intensive industries, such as steel-making, consume most of the gas derived from coking operations. Electricité de France uses about ten per cent of the natural gas for electricity production.

## Electricity

*Electricity Production*

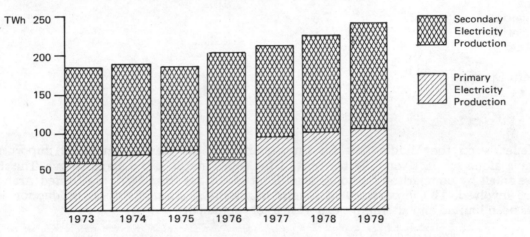

The production of electricity for public supply is undertaken principally by Electricité de France. A separate state undertaking, the Compagnie Nationale du Rhône is responsible for hydro-electric production from the river Rhône, where it has a number of installations. The steel industry and some other large industrial companies produce electricity for their own consumption and Charbonnages de France, the state coal-mining company, operates more than 20 power stations, which contribute seven per cent of total supplies.

Less than 50 per cent of electricity is produced from conventional coal- or oil-fired thermal plant. The most significant single source is hydro-electric power, derived from the potential of the Alps and Pyrenees. To this is added an increasing share attributable to nuclear power plant. The proportion of nuclear electricity now approaches 20 per cent and there is a major construction programme underway designed to add 27,000 MW of capacity by 1984. Output from nuclear stations has risen more than five-fold during the last ten years. Natural gas is used to generate about six per cent of total supply.

## ENERGY TRADE

*Net Imports/(Exports) 1973-79*

|  | 1973 | 1974 | 1975 | 1976 | 1977 | 1978 | 1979 |
|---|---|---|---|---|---|---|---|
| Coal (million tonnes) | 14.5 | 19.5 | 19.1 | 20.1 | 22.4 | 24.3 | 27.5 |
| Crude Oil (million tonnes) | 134.9 | 130.7 | 106.1 | 121.1 | 117.4 | 115.1 | 126.7 |
| Oil Products (million tonnes) | (6.7) | (3.7) | (2.6) | (1.5) | (5.6) | (3.6) | (4.2) |
| Natural Gas (000 million M$^3$) | 9.1 | 10.9 | 11.3 | 14.1 | 15.0 | 16.5 | 18.1 |
| Electricity (TWh) | (3.0) | (0.2) | 2.5 | 2.1 | 5.0 | 4.3 | 5.8 |

With virtually total dependence on imported oil, France is the second largest importer in Europe. In 1979 total imports of crude oil rose to 127 million tonnes, against which is to be set only a relatively small net export trade in finished products. France also imports a large amount of coal. The quantity involved increased significantly in 1974 and since 1976 has continued to rise rapidly. Since 1973 the level of net imports has more than doubled. A similar trend has taken place with natural gas. Between 1973 and 1979 imports rose from 9 to 18 thousand million cubic metres. Since 1973 a net export position in electricity has turned into a deficit.

*Sources of Imported Crude Oil*

| (percentage) | | |
|---|---|---|
| Middle East | | 75.3 |
| Saudi Arabia | 36.1 | |
| Iraq | 19.8 | |
| United Arab Emirates | 7.0 | |
| Iran | 5.4 | |
| Kuwait | 3.9 | |
| Other | 3.1 | |
| | | |
| Africa | | 16.1 |
| Nigeria | 7.8 | |
| Algeria | 4.1 | |
| Other | 4.2 | |
| | | |
| Eastern Europe | | 4.2 |
| Other | | 4.4 |
| | | |
| TOTAL | | 100.0 |

France depends on the Middle East for three-quarters of its massive crude oil import requirements. Saudi Arabia alone supplies some 37 per cent of the total. Iraq is also a major source. The shares of other sources are small by comparison, although significant quantities from Iran, the United Arab Emirates and Nigeria are involved. The importance of Algeria has declined considerably as production in the former colony has been limited and alternative export markets obtained.

## ENERGY POLICIES

The French government has been very aware of its dependence on imported energy, especially oil, for many years. This was intensified by the oil supply crisis of 1973. It has much of the legislation and instruments necessary to influence developments in the energy sector, as well as direct control over the state undertakings. It has adopted bold lines of policy in seeking to reduce its import-dependence and limit the growth of energy consumption.

### Energy Supply

The key element in French policy towards reducing dependence on oil, which must be imported, has been the decision to press ahead with a major programme of nuclear power station construction. The use of solid fuel and fuel oil is expected to decline. Only a limited additional contribution is expected to be obtained from hydro-electric resources during the current plan.

The existing and long-standing system of licensing the importation of crude oil and oil products provides a means whereby the government can keep the overall balance of payments cost of oil to a minimum, although more is to be expected from energy conservation in this respect. Exploration in French offshore areas is considered to be of some importance. This is carried out by the state oil company ERAP, and other companies operating in the French oil market are encouraged to search for oil and gas. On the other hand there is less of a commitment to maximise the use of indigenous coal resources.

### Energy Conservation

Since 1973 the French government has taken a keen interest in energy conservation and the potential of unconventional forms of energy, such as tidal and solar power. Through the Agence pour Economies d'Energie over 100 million francs per annum has been used to provide financial support for investment by industry in energy-saving equipment. Loans of up to 25 per cent are available. The Agence is responsible for encouraging public awareness of energy conservation, but the government has also felt the need to enforce direct controls on oil consumption, particularly in the use of oil for central heating systems.

# Greece

## KEY ENERGY INDICATORS

Energy Consumption
    —million tonnes oil equivalent          15.8
Consumption Per Head
    —tonnes oil equivalent              1.7
    —percentage of West European average     47%
Net Energy Imports                   76%
Oil Import-Dependence             100%

*Greece is still in the process of industrialisation, and although it has some energy-intensive industries has a level of energy consumption per head only half that of the West European average. There are indigenous resources of lignite and hydro-electric power, which are being further exploited in order to limit energy imports without restricting economic growth unduly. Greece is currently entirely dependent on foreign sources for oil, which means that overall import-dependence is high. A commercial oil field is being developed offshore, but further exploration activity in the Aegean Sea is impeded by the state of relations between Greece and Turkey.*

## ENERGY MARKET TRENDS

*Trend of Energy Consumption*

Energy Consumption
+4.4% p.a.

Gross Domestic Product
+3.7% p.a.

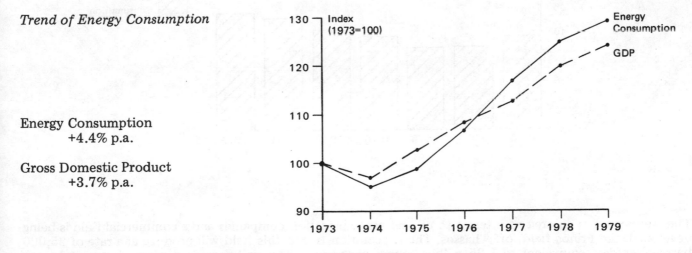

Greece is one of the least industrialised countries in Europe and is still in the development stage. It has had a high average rate of economic growth. Unfortunately, high growth and rapid industrialisation have inevitably been accompanied by even more rapid growth in energy consumption. Thus, while Gross Domestic Product has been rising at 3.7 per cent per annum, consumption of energy has been increasing by nearly four and a half per cent.

*Pattern of Energy Supply and Consumption*

| Primary Fuel Supply (percentage) | | Final Consumption (percentage) | |
| --- | --- | --- | --- |
| Oil | 72 | Industry | 39 |
| Solid Fuel | 23 | Residential | 15 |
| Natural Gas | – | Transport | 34 |
| Primary Electricity | 5 | Other | 12 |
| TOTAL | 100 | TOTAL | 100 |

Greece can make a significant contribution to its energy requirements from indigenous resources. There are extensive deposits of lignite in both the north and south of mainland Greece. These are being increasingly utilised. In addition there is hydro-electric potential in the mountain areas and this resource is particularly useful in helping to minimise the need to import oil for electricity generation. A firm decision has not yet been taken concerning the project to build the country's first nuclear power station. But for the major part, 70 per cent, of its requirements of primary energy Greece is reliant on imported oil.

Rather as a matter of coincidence, considering the stage of development which Greece has reached, the proportion of final energy consumed by industry is the same as for Western Europe as a whole. Yet the transport sector is well developed and takes a disproportionate share of final consumption. The low level of energy consumption per head is, however, shown by the small proportion consumed in the residential sector.

## ENERGY SUPPLY INDUSTRIES

State agencies are closely involved in energy supply. Electricity production and distribution is the sole responsibility of a nationalised undertaking, the Public Power Corporation, which also operates the major coal mines to serve its power stations. The oil sector is subject to controls on refining and importing and the state itself has refining interests.

### Oil

*Oil Consumption*

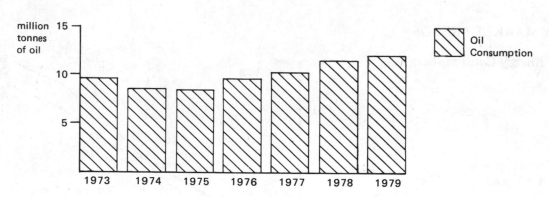

The Aegean sea is an area of interest to oil and gas exploration companies and a commercial field is being developed, the Prinos field, off Thassos. The expectation is that this field will produce at a rate of 25,000 barrels per day, equivalent to 1.25 million tonnes per annum. This will provide a minor, but useful, contribution to help contain the country's balance of payments problems arising from the increasing cost of imported oil.

There are four oil refineries in Greece, of which one, at Aspropyrgos, near Athens, is owned by the state. This refinery supplies about half of the products consumed in Greece. The other refinery primarily concerned with supplying the Greek market is at Thessaloniki, in the north of the country. This refinery is owned by the Exxon group. Two other refineries have been built, each by a Greek shipping group, geared to processing crude for export markets, although also supplying some oil products to the home market. One of these is at Corinth, owned by the Vardinoyannis group; the other at Elevsis, to the north of Athens, and owned by Latsis.

Although Exxon is the only foreign company involved in refining, a number of other major international oil companies have marketing operations, purchasing their product requirements from Greek refinery companies.

Prices of oil products are controlled by the state. Increasing state involvement has been reflected in the setting up of the Public Petroleum Corporation, which is responsible for encouraging offshore exploration and will participate in future development work.

## Coal

*Coal Production*

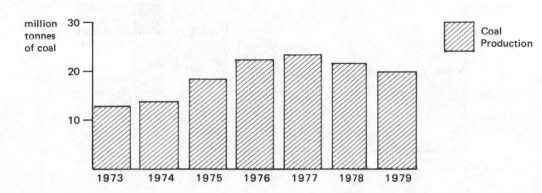

Greece has considerable reserves of lignite which are currently supporting production at the rate of 22-23 million tonnes per annum. Output from these lignite mines is dedicated to power stations of the Public Power Corporation, and are operated by the Corporation. The largest mine is at Ptolemais, which produces over 18 million tonnes per annum. Most of the balance of production is obtained from the Megalopolis mine. A small amount is being produced at Aliveri.

The remainder of Greek requirements for coal is met by importing hard coal or manufactured coke. These quantities are relatively small, amounting to under half a million tonnes per annum, and are for industrial use. There is little consumption of coal in the residential or commercial sectors.

## Gas

*Gas Production*

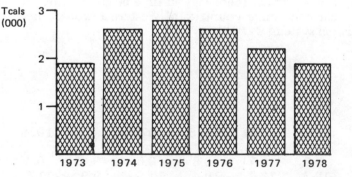

There is no production of natural gas in Greece and no system for distribution of imported gas has as yet been developed. The country is remote from international trunklines supplying major centres of energy consumption and the scale of potential use in Greece itself has not justified the development of facilities for importing liquefied natural gas. However, long-term energy plans involve consideration of a link to either the Italian trunkline carrying Algerian gas, crossing the Adriatic to Corfu, or to the Soviet based system which extends to Bulgaria.

Gas is manufactured, mainly in the course of industrial operations, including oil refining. For the most part this gas is consumed by the industries themselves and only a small, and declining, proportion is sold for public supply.

**Electricity**

*Electricity Production*

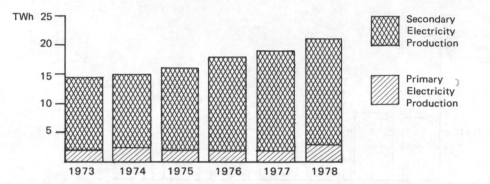

The production and public supply of electricity is the responsibility of the state undertaking, the Public Power Corporation. About 65 per cent of its electricity is produced from indigenous resources. Power Stations at Ptolemais, near the Yugoslav border, and at Megalopolis, towards the southern end of the mainland on the Peloponnese, have been built to utilise large lignite deposits. The Ptolemais mine also supplies a recently built station at Kardia. These are three of the largest stations in Greece, having a total capacity of nearly 1,800 MW. In all, lignite provides 54 per cent of the Power Corporation's supply. The mountainous terrain also provides the scope for hydro-electric power. Some of these plants are quite large with a capacity of 320-440 MW. Hydro-electric stations supply over ten per cent of electricity.

The balance of the Power Corporation's electricity is derived from oil-fired stations. This includes the remaining large plants in the Athens area, which use fuel oil, and the many small local turbine generators on individual islands in the Aegean Sea. Corfu is linked to the mainland and there are cable links from the Peloponnese at Corinth and Patras. Euboea also has two cable links to the mainland.

The Public Power Corporation sells around 30 per cent of its output to bulk industrial consumers, and purchases surplus electricity from private energy producers which have generating plant. The Greek system has links to Albania and Yugoslavia, through which there may in time be greater integration and scope for optimisation with the grids of the main consuming countries of Western Europe. There is also a project to link up with the Bulgarian transmission system.

**ENERGY TRADE**

*Net Imports/(Exports) 1973-79*

|                                | 1973 | 1974  | 1975  | 1976  | 1977 | 1978 | 1979  |
|--------------------------------|------|-------|-------|-------|------|------|-------|
| Coal (million tonnes)          | 0.7  | 0.7   | 0.8   | 0.6   | 0.6  | 0.4  | 0.3   |
| Crude Oil (million tonnes)     | 12.7 | 13.7  | 10.4  | 11.9  | 9.9  | 11.6 | 15.7  |
| Oil Products (million tonnes)  | 1.7  | (0.8) | (3.4) | (0.2) | 0.5  | 0.3  | (2.7) |

Imported energy is almost entirely in the form of crude oil. The overall level of oil imports, including net trade in oil products, has been relatively stable since 1973, as rising energy demand has been met from indigenous resources. In consequence, imports of coal have declined. There are marginal deficits or surpluses from year to year in electricity exchanges between Greece, Albania and Yugoslavia.

*Sources of Imported Crude Oil*

| | | (percentage) |
|---|---|---|
| Middle East | | 87.1 |
| Saudi Arabia | 60.1 | |
| Iraq | 22.5 | |
| Other | 4.5 | |
| | | |
| Eastern Europe | | 6.5 |
| | | |
| Africa | | 6.4 |
| Libya | 5.9 | |
| Other | 0.5 | |
| | | |
| TOTAL | | 100.0 |

Middle East sources account for an overwhelming proportion of Greek crude oil imports. Saudi Arabia alone supplies over 60 per cent. Iraq, which is the nearest oil exporting country of significance, is also a major supplier. Efforts are being made to diversify sources of crude oil and the state agency has contracted for half a million tonnes per annum of Nigerian crude oil. The Soviet Union, which has an export terminal on the Black Sea, is the third largest individual source of oil.

## ENERGY POLICIES

The state has been partially involved in the energy industries for some years, namely in coal production and electricity supply. It has however only recently established the Public Petroleum Corporation. This factor taken together with the limited exploration and development activity so far means that there will continue to be reliance on outside expertise and finance in this sector.

### Energy Supply

The government has adopted a programme for the period 1978 to 1987, which envisages a major development of indigenous resources in order to meet increasing demands for electricity as well as reducing the amount of fuel oil required. This programme is well advanced, although one element, the construction of the country's first nuclear power station, has been postponed until at least 1987. However, progress is being made on expansion of lignite-fired plant and the construction of new hydro-electric schemes. Capacity to draw energy from these two sources is expected to be increased by 2,400 MW and 1,600 MW respectively in the period to 1987.

### Energy Conservation

The government is also paying attention to the way in which energy is used. Half of the consumption of energy by industry is by energy-intensive industries. For these a system has been instituted, setting targets for reductions in energy consumption. To assist with the introduction of processes using less energy, interest-free loans of up to 50 per cent of the cost of investment are being proposed. Tax allowances are to be available to private consumers as well as industry to encourage the introduction of solar heating plant. Private consumption of motor gasoline is being progressively penalised through higher prices and taxes and more direct constraints, such as restrictions on the use of private cars are being contemplated.

# Ireland

## KEY ENERGY INDICATORS

| | |
|---|---|
| Energy Consumption | |
| —million tonnes oil equivalent | 8.3 |
| Consumption Per Head | |
| —tonnes oil equivalent | 2.5 |
| —percentage of West European average | 70% |
| Net Energy Imports | 77% |
| Oil Import-Dependence | 100% |

*Ireland is still only partially industrialised by comparison with other north European countries. Its energy consumption per head is accordingly well below the average, at 70 per cent. Growth is continuing at a relatively high rate leading to increased demand for energy. Although there are some indigenous resources, in the form of natural gas, dependence on imported energy is likely to increase. In view of this the main theme of energy policy must be to seek a high level of security of supply for imported oil and diversification to use a greater proportion of coal.*

## ENERGY MARKET TRENDS

*Trend of Energy Consumption*

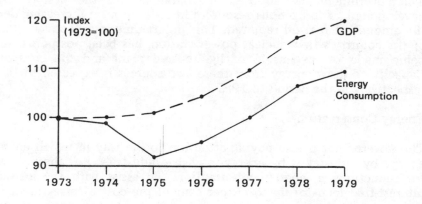

Energy Consumption
+1.6% p.a.

Gross Domestic Product
+3.1% p.a.

Irish energy consumption fell back in 1974 and 1975 following the oil supply crisis. The decline was nearly seven per cent in the latter year. Despite this the economy still recorded positive real growth in Gross Domestic Product. Since 1976 this growth has accelerated, bringing with it increasing consumption of energy. However, through a combination of enforced constraints on consumption and the operation of conservation policies aimed at curbing energy-intensive industrial development, the rate of growth of energy consumption has been kept well below the growth rate of the economy. This represents a valuable gain to the economy and is in contrast to the pattern of growth and energy consumption in the developing countries of southern Europe.

*Pattern of Energy Supply and Consumption*

| Primary Fuel Supply (percentage) | | Final Consumption (percentage) | |
|---|---|---|---|
| Oil | 75 | Industry | 30 |
| Solid Fuel | 16 | Residential | 32 |
| Natural Gas | 6 | Transport | 27 |
| Primary Electricity | 3 | Other | 11 |
| TOTAL | 100 | TOTAL | 100 |

Oil is the mainstay of the Irish economy accounting for three-quarters of primary energy input. This has to be entirely imported. Indigenous resources consist primarily of hydro-electric power generated from some of the larger rivers in the west of the country and reserves of peat which are being exploited as fuel for a number of power stations. There is some production of coal but this amounts to only 5—10 per cent of the supply of this form of energy. A new indigenous resource, offshore natural gas, is beginning to be tapped for supply to a power station and some bulk industrial users in the Cork area.

The pattern of final energy demand reflects the state of development of the Irish economy, which has been one of the fastest growing in Europe. New industrial projects continue to be established, but consumption by this sector is still relatively low. On the other hand transport systems are more fully modernised with a high level of private transport. Consumption in this sector is well above average, 27 per cent compared with 21 per cent. Consumption is also above average in the residential sector, partly in reflection of the situation in industry, as there are many parts of the country in which household consumption, particularly of electricity, is low.

## ENERGY SUPPLY INDUSTRIES

Up to the present time the supply of oil, the country's main form of primary energy, has been largely left to the international oil companies. Electricity production and distribution is under state control. The development of natural gas offshore has led to the creation of a state undertaking with sole responsibility for supply and distribution. Increasing concern about the international oil supply situation and the need to encourage greater exploration effort in Irish waters means that an increasing role may be played by the recently established state petroleum corporation.

**Oil**

*Oil Consumption*

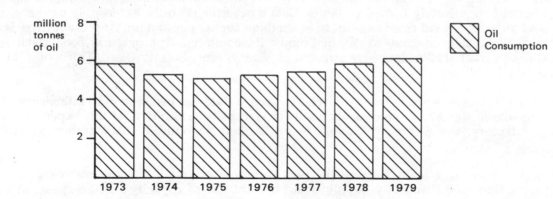

At present Ireland is reliant on imports for its key form of primary energy. Offshore exploration activity has shown some promise, but the only field of significance found so far is over 100 miles off the west coast in deep water, and where conditions for exploitation would be even more arduous than in the North Sea. This find was made by Phillips in the Porcupine Trough area, but is not considered to be commercially viable under current circumstances.

The focus of the supply of products for the Irish market is the refinery at Whitegate, near Cork, which has a capacity of less than three million tonnes per annum. The main oil marketers, Esso, Shell, Texaco and British Petroleum, participate in the refinery, which is operated by Esso. But increasing quantities of oil products are being imported, particularly into the Dublin area, where one-third of the population is concentrated. Gulf operates a large trans-shipment terminal for crude oil at Bantry Bay on the west coast, but this has not led to construction of refining capacity.

The state has not hitherto been directly involved in the oil products market. Government influence has been felt mainly through the operation of controls on prices, which has been a factor causing additional disruption to supplies in the face of high and volatile prices in the international oil market. The Electricity Supply Board has also been involved in direct importation of fuel oil from Eastern Europe. Encouragement has been given to the privately owned company Aran Energy Limited, which was set up to participate in offshore exploration and development. Aran is involved in consortia led by BP and Amoco, which are undertaking exploration activity.

The promise of worthwhile discoveries of oil was a major factor behind the decision to set up the Irish National Petroleum Corporation in 1979, although increasing concern about the country's reliance on foreign sources and companies for this vital form of energy also played a part. One of its first main tasks is to seek to diversify the sources of oil and in particular to negotiate with producer-country governments.

## Coal

### Coal Consumption

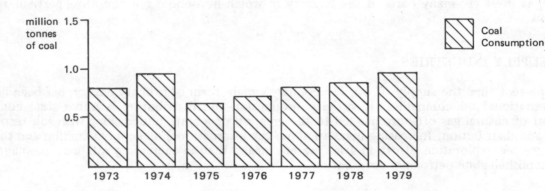

There is only a very limited amount of indigenous coal production, amounting to 30-60,000 tonnes in any one year, produced by privately owned collieries. Coal is nevertheless quite extensively used in the residential sector, and imports of hard coal range up to one million tonnes per annum. At present there is only one small power station using coal, at Arigna in County Roscommon. Approval has been given for a new 600MW coal-fired power station to be constructed at Moneypoint, County Clare. This would be supplied with imported coal.

Research and development work is being undertaken using a fluidised bed system to establish whether low-grade coal deposits in the Arigna area can be used for electricity generation. If this experimental work is considered satisfactory, the Electricity Supply Board is likely to build a 40MW station to exploit these resources.

Of greater significance as a solid fuel are the peat resources of Ireland. These are being exploited for electricity production. The Electricity Supply Board has 450MW of capacity based on peat, which implies a capacity to use well over 2,000 tonnes of peat per hour. Peat extraction, which is controlled by the state agency, the Irish Peat Development Authority, takes place mainly in central Ireland, although there are also peat-fired generating plants in the western counties.

## Gas

### Gas Production

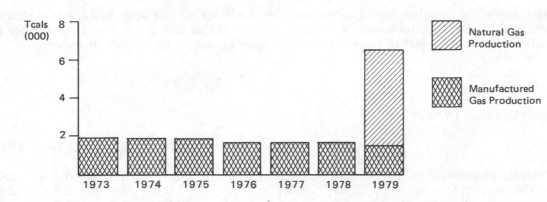

In late 1978 Ireland became a producer of natural gas, with the bringing on stream of the offshore field discovered by Marathon off Kinsale Head to the west of Cork. This field is expected to provide around 1,300 million cubic metres per annum of gas over a twenty-year period. The advent of this important new indigenous resource led to the establishment in 1976 of the Irish Gas Board, with the general responsibility to develop a natural gas supply system. Hitherto gas supply was entirely a matter of producing towns gas for local supply in Dublin, Cork and some others of the larger towns. This is carried out by a variety of private, co-operative and municipal companies.

Initial arrangements for the use of the Kinsale Head gas have inevitably meant its supply to a small number of bulk consumers. The two principal consumers are the Electricity Supply Board and Nitrigin Eireann Teoranta. The ESB will use some in its existing plant at Cork, but is building a new 270MW station at Cork to be fired by natural gas. This is due for completion by 1981, when the field will be reaching its maximum production rate. Nitrigin Eireann Teoranta will use the gas as a feedstock for fertiliser production. The balance of natural gas output will be used by bulk industrial consumers in the Cork area. However, the Irish Gas Board is examining alternative end-uses which would make better use of the gas.

## Electricity

### Electricity Production

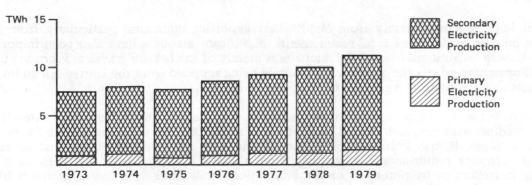

The production and distribution of electricity is the sole responsibility of the Electricity Supply Board, which is a nationalised undertaking. The ESB has built up a significant proportion of capacity based on indigenous fuels but remains reliant on oil imports for the bulk of its production. Out of a total capacity of 2,900MW, 65 per cent is based on oil. The Cork station, of 200MW, now uses natural gas and to this will be added the new plant, of 270MW, at Cork in 1981. At that stage all three indigenous fuels, peat, natural gas and hydro-electric power, will each have an output capacity of 450-500MW.

Thereafter, it is hoped that coal-fired plant will make a greater contribution to electricity supply and directly supplant fuel oil, even though it too must be imported. In 1979 permission was given for the construction of the country's first major coal-fired station, to be located at Moneypoint, County Clare, on the north side of the mouth of the Shannon. This plant will have a capacity of 600MW and may be in operation by 1986.

Preliminary planning of a nuclear power station has been undertaken. The proposed site is at Carnsore Point, County Wexford. There has, however, been much opposition to this project and no further progress is expected until the whole subject of nuclear power has been examined by a public tribunal.

## ENERGY TRADE

*Net Imports/(Exports) 1973-79*

|                             | 1973 | 1974 | 1975 | 1976 | 1977 | 1978 | 1979 |
|-----------------------------|------|------|------|------|------|------|------|
| Coal (million tonnes)       | 0.7  | 0.8  | 0.6  | 0.5  | 0.8  | 0.8  | 1.0  |
| Crude Oil (million tonnes)  | 2.7  | 2.7  | 2.6  | 1.9  | 2.3  | 2.3  | 2.4  |
| Oil Products (million tonnes)| 3.0 | 2.7  | 2.6  | 3.3  | 3.5  | 3.7  | 4.0  |

Ireland imports the larger part of its energy requirements in the form of oil. This is either imported as crude oil to be processed in the oil refinery at Whitegate or as finished products. After a decline from a combined total of 5.7 million tonnes in 1973 to 5.2 million tonnes in 1975, imports have risen steadily to exceed six and a half million tonnes per annum. However, there has been a noticeable change in the pattern of supply. Throughput at the refinery was at a maximum in 1973 and 1974, but has fallen back somewhat since then. At the same time imports of products have increased, such that they now account for nearly two-thirds of oil imports compared with one half in 1974.

*Sources of Imported Crude Oil*

| (percentage) | | |
|---|---|---|
| Middle East | | 86.8 |
| Saudi Arabia | 49.1 | |
| Iraq | 13.8 | |
| Iran | 13.4 | |
| Kuwait | 10.5 | |
| | | |
| Eastern Europe | | 6.5 |
| United Kingdom | | 4.2 |
| Other | | 2.5 |
| | | |
| TOTAL | | 100.0 |

Crude oil imports come mainly from Middle East exporting countries, particularly from Saudi Arabia, which supplies around half of total requirements. Significant amounts have also been imported from Iraq, Iran and Kuwait. Crude oil from these countries is mainly of the heavier grades as is crude oil from Eastern Europe. For lighter crudes the Whitegate refinery is being supplied from the United Kingdom, where all the participants in the refinery have access to offshore production.

Approximately two-thirds of imports of finished products are brought in from the United Kingdom. Both Esso, the leading marketer, and Texaco have refineries at Milford Haven, in south-west Wales. There are also refineries of Shell, British Petroleum and Esso on the west and south coasts of England and Wales. The balance of product requirements is supplied from various European refineries belonging to companies marketing in Ireland or by purchases on the international bulk market, including products from the Soviet Union. Eastern European sources are also prominent in the supply of coal. Poland is the main supplier.

## ENERGY POLICIES

The Irish government is becoming increasingly involved in energy matters. This is a reflection of uncertainties in the international oil supply system, actual and prospective developments of offshore oil and gas resources, and the highly controversial proposal for a nuclear power station. In the last few years state agencies for natural gas and oil have been set up, and these are likely to become more active.

## Energy Supply

Two issues underlie the government's concern with oil supply. Firstly, the country is highly dependent on this form of energy, which at present must be entirely imported, and secondly the government is unwilling to leave oil supply completely in the hands of international major companies, which have preferred to import products rather than increase refining capacity and which have limited supplies in the face of price controls in the market place. As a result the Irish National Petroleum Corporation has been set-up and is likely to seek some security and diversification through government-to-government supply arrangements.

It is, however, equally a plank of the government's policy to diversify away from dependence of oil, at least in the absence of a major discovery of indigenous resources. Further exploitation of peat and hydro-electric power is to be expected and examination of the project to build a nuclear power station is being progressed. But in the near term diversification of fuels almost certainly means increasing the use of coal. To this end permission has been given to construct a 600MW plant on the Shannon.

## Energy Conservation

It is of equal concern that economic growth should not lead to excessive growth in energy consumption. Conservation aspects therefore are prominent in government policy. A key role in this respect is played by the Industrial Development Authority, which is responsible for encouraging new industrial development in Ireland. Energy conservation is to be an important criterion in assessing the types of industry which will best benefit the country. All grants and incentives provided by public agencies are to be co-ordinated with energy conservation in mind.

Grants of up to 35 per cent may be made available towards investment in energy-saving equipment. A similar proportion of the cost of energy surveys can also be covered. There are energy audit systems in operation for certain key industries and a range of information and advisory services. Grants are made towards studies of waste heat utilisation schemes and the cost of providing equipment. Additional measures aimed at energy conservation include speed limits on vehicles, the extension of thermal insulation standards for buildings and grants for conversion of domestic heating systems to the use of solid fuel.

# Italy

## KEY ENERGY INDICATORS

Energy Consumption
—million tonnes oil equivalent — 139.7

Consumption Per Head
—tonnes oil equivalent — 2.5
—percentage of West European average — 70%

Net Energy Imports — 81%

Oil Import-Dependence — 98%

*Italy has the second largest population in Western Europe, 57 million people. Energy consumption per head is however well below the average. Although the northern part of the country has reached an advanced state of economic and industrial development, there remain large areas in the southern half of the country in only a semi-developed state, with low levels of energy consumption in all sectors. Italy is poor in indigenous fuels and its growth has been based on imported energy, notably oil. This dependence is continuing to increase in the absence of a nuclear power programme and effective energy conservation. Even diversification to increase the use of coal is making only slow progress.*

## ENERGY MARKET TRENDS

*Trend of Energy Consumption*

Energy Consumption
+0.9% p.a.

Gross Domestic Product
+2.4% p.a.

In 1974, the year following the oil supply crisis, consumption of energy continued to rise, reflecting a continuation of previous trends which overrode supply difficulties in the oil sector. Consumption of energy did fall appreciably in 1975, but resumed its upward path thereafter. Despite the financial burden on the balance of payments of dependence on imported oil, the country has so far managed to sustain the required levels of imports without a severe financial crisis. In the period since 1973 the rate of increase in energy consumption has been small in relation to growth of the economy. However, this seems to be more likely to be a result of short-term changes in the pattern of economic activity than from effective energy conservation achievements.

*Pattern of Energy Supply and Consumption*

| Primary Fuel Supply (percentage) | | Final Consumption (percentage) | |
|---|---|---|---|
| Oil | 67 | Industry | 46 |
| Solid Fuel | 7 | Residential | 27 |
| Natural Gas | 17 | Transport | 20 |
| Primary Electricity | 9 | Other | 7 |
| TOTAL | 100 | TOTAL | 100 |

Oil is by far the most important form of primary energy in the Italian economy, accounting for two-thirds of total input. There is little indigenous coal available and a ready supply of imported oil has until recent years led to a key role for oil in electricity generation. The amount of indigenous natural gas is limited, but has been such as to provide an established system for distribution of natural gas and imports, as gas or in liquefied form, have been built up. There is a useful contribution from hydro-electric sources, although there is little untapped potential remaining, unless associated with nuclear/pumped storage plant.

Industry consumes 46 per cent of final energy, a proportion well above the West European average of 39 per cent. This is mainly a reflection of the development of a number of energy-intensive industries, such as petrochemicals, export-based oil refining and heavy engineering. But a further factor is the relatively low levels of energy consumption per head in the residential and service sectors.

## ENERGY SUPPLY INDUSTRIES

State undertakings play a key part in the supply and distribution of oil, gas and electricity. Ente Nazionale Idrocarburi (ENI) is involved in all phases of the oil industry, Ente Nazionale per l'Energia Elettrica (ENEL) produces 80 per cent of electricity and has overall responsibility for supply and distribution. SNAM, a subsidiary of ENI, is responsible for supply operations connected with natural gas. Private companies, and particularly Italian concerns, are prominent in oil refining and marketing.

## Oil

*Oil Consumption*

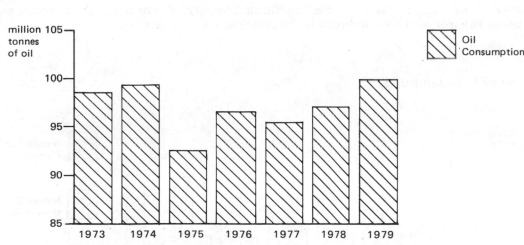

Indigenous production of oil is very small, and even with the development of a new field at Malossa in 1978 production remains less than two million tonnes per annum. Exploration continues, both onshore and offshore, mainly carried out by ENI.

Despite the lack of its own oil resources, Italy has built up a very large refining sector, based on its geographical position between the main export sources of crude oil in the Middle East and the consumer markets of Europe. In the years before the oil supply crisis of 1973 extensive refinery capacity was built in southern Italy and the islands of Sicily and Sardinia. These developments were particularly encouraged by the state because of the lack of industrial activity and employment in these areas. Out of a total of 180 million tonnes per annum of capacity 70 million tonnes is to be found in Sicily and a further 23 million tonnes in Sardinia, whereas the main centres of consumption lie in the north of the country. As a result, this capacity is severely under-utilised.

ENI is the leading marketer of oil products in Italy. Its position has been increasingly reinforced as the international oil companies have either withdrawn from the Italian market, as in the case of Shell, or limited their operations in the face of prices controlled at low levels. ENI itself operates several refineries, with a total capacity approaching 40 million tonnes per annum. The next largest refining operation belongs to the private Italian Monti group, which includes the largest refinery at Milazzo in Sicily. However, this group has been particularly badly hit by the reduction in international oil trade and loss of export-refining contracts and at least half of its capacity may be added to ENI's holding.

## Coal

*Coal Production and Consumption*

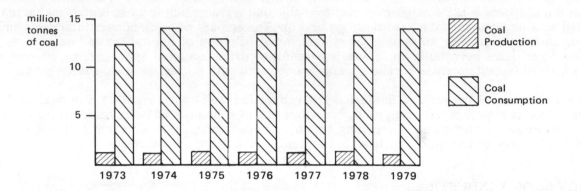

There is very little production of coal in Italy, although efforts are being made to increase activity. Lignite is mined at two locations in Valdamo and Perugia, and this is used as fuel for local power stations. Total consumption of coal by electricity producers is still at a low level, although it increased from under two million tonnes in 1978 to over three million tonnes in 1979. Increasing amounts of coal are expected to be imported for this purpose, particularly from Poland and South Africa, although ENEL is experiencing difficulty in obtaining permission to convert capacity to coal-firing.

The largest market for coal is the coke manufacturing industry, where ten million tonnes per annum of hard coal is used. The iron and steel industry is the principal user of the coke.

## Gas

*Gas Production and Consumption*

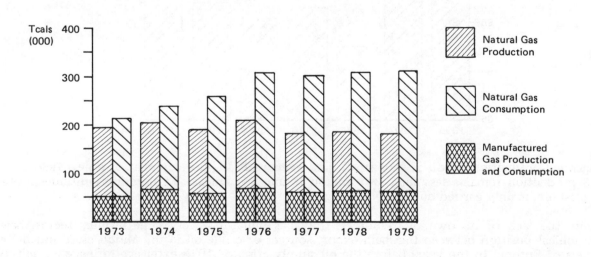

Natural gas is produced from both onshore and offshore fields. The principal producing area is in the Po Valley in northern Italy. Reserves are currently estimated at some 200,000 million cubic metres, and support a rate of production of 13,000 million cubic metres per annum. The total amount of energy supplied by gas produced in Italy is 50 per cent higher than this when account is taken of gas produced in coking, oil refining and other operations, but this is consumed by energy-intensive industrial consumers.

Production and distribution of natural gas through the public supply system is the responsibility of SNAM SpA, which is a subsidiary of the state-owned ENI. SNAM is also responsible for securing additional imported supplies. Natural gas is imported from the Netherlands and the Soviet Union into northern Italy. Existing arrangements allow for up to 7,000 million cubic metres per annum to be brought in from the Netherlands. Similar quantities could be brought in from the Soviet Union.

However, SNAM is concentrating on developing the infrastructure and contractual arrangements for importing even larger quantities of gas from Algeria. A 2,500 km trunk pipeline reaching Bologna, in northern Italy, is expected to be completed in 1981, capable of carrying over 12,000 million cubic metres per annum of gas. In the first year some 4,000 million cubic metres is to be imported.

## Electricity

*Electricity Production*

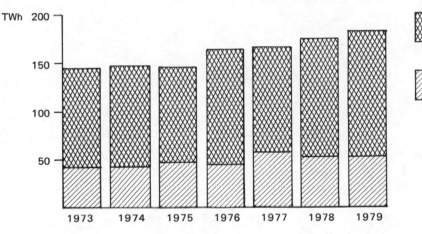

The state undertaking ENEL is responsible for the basic public supply of electricity, import/export arrangements, the development of rural electrification and furthering work on geothermal energy. ENEL supplies 95 per cent of electricity fed into the public supply system, the remainder being produced by small municipal undertakings. Distribution to public consumers is in the hands of around 160 local authorities in individual cities and towns. In addition to the public supply system over 18 per cent of total electricity production is produced by industrial companies for their own consumption.

Oil-fired power stations contribute 55-60 per cent of ENEL's electricity production and conventional thermal plant 70 per cent in total. The use of coal is limited, although growing. On the other hand a comparable amount of electricity is derived from burning natural gas and this is likely to be reduced in the future. Hydro-electric power is an important source of energy, providing 27 per cent of public supply, and is the second largest source of electricity. So far ENEL has been able to develop only a small nuclear capacity. Three small plants, with a total capacity of 600 MW were built in the 1960s and in 1978 a major plant, of 860 MW, was completed at Caorso, near Piacenza. Another of 1,000 MW is due for completion in the mid 1980s at Viterbo, to the north of Rome. A further five nuclear power stations are planned, but with no firm construction schedules, owing to continued opposition to the development of nuclear power.

## ENERGY TRADE

*Net Imports/(Exports) 1973-79*

|                                   | 1973   | 1974   | 1975  | 1976  | 1977  | 1978   | 1979   |
|-----------------------------------|--------|--------|-------|-------|-------|--------|--------|
| Coal (million tonnes)             | 11.2   | 12.5   | 13.0  | 11.8  | 12.1  | 11.3   | 11.3   |
| Crude Oil (million tonnes)        | 128.9  | 120.0  | 95.9  | 102.8 | 105.8 | 110.6  | 114.0  |
| Oil Products (million tonnes)     | (22.8) | (15.3) | (5.6) | (4.8) | (9.8) | (15.3) | (14.3) |
| Natural Gas (000 million M$^3$)   | 2.0    | 4.1    | 8.7   | 11.8  | 13.0  | 14.2   | 14.8   |
| Electricity (TWh)                 | 0.9    | 2.3    | 2.6   | 1.1   | 2.8   | 2.1    | 5.4    |

The importation of crude oil looms large in the energy trade of Italy. The level of imports has however remained fairly static since 1976, after taking into account the net export trade in oil products. To these quantities of crude oil and product movements can be added the export-refining of crude oil which remains entirely in bond in the refineries.

Growth in energy imports has been reflected primarily in the figures for natural gas. Since 1973 imports have risen from a modest 2,000 million cubic metres to nearly 15,000 million cubic metres in 1979, representing more than half of total consumption. There has been a net import of electricity, principally from Switzerland, usually between two and three terawatt hours per annum, but this increased to 5.4 terawatt hours in 1979. The level of net imports of coal shows that little progress has been made in switching away from oil to this form of primary fuel.

*Sources of Imported Crude Oil*

|                       |       |       |
|-----------------------|-------|-------|
| (percentage)          |       |       |
| Middle East           |       | 71.6  |
|   Saudi Arabia | 32.9 |       |
|   Iraq      | 22.0  |       |
|   Kuwait    | 10.8  |       |
|   Other     | 5.9   |       |
|                       |       |       |
| Africa                |       | 20.5  |
|   Libya     | 14.7  |       |
|   Other     | 5.8   |       |
|                       |       |       |
| Eastern Europe        |       | 6.4   |
| Other                 |       | 1.5   |
|                       |       |       |
| TOTAL                 |       | 100.0 |

Italy depends on Middle East sources for over 70 per cent of its crude oil imports. Saudi Arabia is the leading supplier of crude oil, but ENI in particular has established import arrangements with Iraq too, which covers one-fifth of total requirements. Kuwait is also a significant source of crude oil, reflecting the high proportion of heavy fuel oil required for electricity generation and industrial use in Italy. By contrast only a small proportion of Middle East crude oil imports are of the lighter type. For this type of crude oil Italy relies on African sources, especially Libya. Italian companies, including both ENI and smaller independent refiners, have also had long-standing arrangements with the Soviet Union for imports from the Black Sea.

## ENERGY POLICIES

With the existence of large established state undertakings in the form of ENI, for oil and gas, and ENEL, for electricity, Italy is well equipped organisationally to implement new government policy initiatives both at home and abroad. However, the adoption of clear long-term policies, just as much as the implementation of short-term operational measures, is bedevilled by a lack of consensus amongst political groups at the national level, and lack of cohesion between national and regional governments. The actual operations of the state organisations is also affected by these considerations.

### Energy Supply

In 1977 the government adopted a long-term energy policy based on greater use of coal and a major growth in the use of nuclear power. ENEL's construction programme includes five new stations, in addition to the one under construction near Rome. However, because of opposition at both national and regional levels, no progress has been made with this programme and there has effectively been a moratorium on the development of nuclear power. The aim of the plan was to raise output of nuclear power from 30 TWh in 1978 to 75.5 TWh by 1990, or over 18 per cent of projected electricity consumption.

The scale of use of coal for electricity generation is supposed to increase to an even greater extent, to provide over 26 per cent of electricity. Some units have been converted to coal-firing but ENEL is experiencing difficulties in obtaining permits from regional authorities.

In any event the use of oil is actually expected to increase in the early 1980s. Faced with problems in securing adequate supplies even now, the government is seeking to encourage greater interest in supplying the Italian market on the part of the international oil companies. Principally this is to be done by allowing marketers to recover margins competitive with other European markets. Greater activity is looked for from foreign companies in exploration too, but it seems unlikely that ENI's privileges in this respect will be withdrawn.

### Energy Conservation

Allowing the controlled selling prices of oil products to rise represents the main instrument of policy in encouraging conservation in the part of consumers as much as in assuring adequate supplies. Taxes on motor gasoline have been increased on a number of occasions. Further restrictive measures have been announced establishing limits to the number of days on which central heating systems can be used, and abolishing the preferential prices for motor gasoline for tourists.

Little progress has been made in actively encouraging energy conservation in industry. A reporting system for energy consumption is in operation, but grant and loan schemes have not been developed as in other industrial countries of Western Europe.

Activity in developing the use of additional indigenous energy resources and minimising wastage is being undertaken principally by ENEL. Research and development work on geothermal energy, combined heat and power schemes and the use of waste is being carried out, and recent legislation has empowered both ENEL and local authorities to distribute heat.

# Luxembourg

## KEY ENERGY INDICATORS

Energy Consumption
—million tonnes oil equivalent     4.0
Consumption Per Head
—tonnes oil equivalent     11.1
—percentage of West European average     311%
Net Energy Imports     90%
Oil Import-Dependence     100%

*The economy of Luxembourg and its requirements for energy are dominated by the presence of the ARBED steelworks, and other related businesses in steel-making and metal-working. This leads to a high demand for energy and, as the total population of Luxembourg is only some 360,000, consumption per head is over three times as great as the average for West European countries. What is more, virtually all of the energy to meet the needs of this industry has to be imported. The only indigenous resource of energy lies in the limited hydro-electric potential of this small country, providing approximately sufficient electricity for the non-industrial sectors. Oil, which is mainly used in the residential, transport and services sectors, has to be entirely imported.*

## ENERGY MARKET TRENDS

*Trend of Energy Consumption*

Energy Consumption
–3.0% p.a.

Gross Domestic Product
+1.2% p.a.

The circumstances of the iron and steel sector of the economy have had an overwhelming influence on the trend of energy consumption. The industrial sector of the Luxembourg economy is centred on this energy-intensive activity, which is responsible for no less than 25 per cent of Gross Domestic Product. As it has been one of the sectors most badly hit by rising energy prices and the recession in world trade since 1973, the economy has followed an uncertain path. Energy consumption is still 15-20 per cent below the 1973 level. However, other sectors of the economy have fared relatively well, particularly the services sector, and this had by 1978 offset the fall in Gross Domestic Product attributable mainly to the decline in steel and metal-working.

*Pattern of Energy Supply and Consumption*

| Primary Fuel Supply (percentage) | | Final Consumption (percentage) | |
|---|---|---|---|
| Oil | 31 | Industry | 70 |
| Solid Fuel | 40 | Residential | 16 |
| Natural Gas | 10 | Transport | 11 |
| Primary Electricity | 19 | Other | 3 |
| TOTAL | 100 | TOTAL | 100 |

The pattern of primary fuel supply in Luxembourg shows a very high proportion of coal and a much lower proportion of oil. This reversal of the usual situation is the result of the use of coal by the steel-making industry. In fact that industry accounts for virtually all coal supplies, and such is the dominance of this industry and the related metal-working industries that the whole pattern is distorted by these activities. Oil is little used by them but large quantities of natural gas and electricity are. Coal, natural gas and the larger part of electricity consumed in Luxembourg have to be imported. True primary production of electricity, from the country's hydro-electric resources, amounts to no more than eight per cent of total energy input.

The dominance of the steel industry is made clear by the pattern of final energy consumption. The proportion consumed by industry as a whole is 70 per cent, compared with the West European average of 39 per cent. Proportions for the residential and transport sectors are correspondingly low. These sectors are dependent primarily on oil and electricity for their energy supplies.

## ENERGY SUPPLY INDUSTRIES

Energy supply in Luxembourg reflects the two main aspects of the economy. On the one hand is a small population, of 360,000 people, 75 per cent of whom are concentrated in the capital city. On the other hand the country includes a major centre of the steel-making industry, which is an intensive consumer of energy. As a result large-scale production of energy is carried out within the industrial sector for its own use, and large imports of energy are made directly on its behalf. But the rest of the economy relies on small scale distribution of oil products and local distribution of electricity and gas.

## Oil

*Oil Consumption*

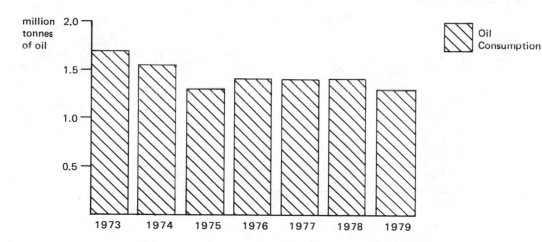

There are apparently no indigenous resources of oil and there is little evidence from neighbouring parts of West Germany, France or Belgium to hold out much promise in this respect. Furthermore the sum of the country's requirements for oil is insufficient to justify establishing a refinery within Luxembourg. The country is therefore supplied from refineries or import terminals in neighbouring countries. The supply of oil products is undertaken by affiliates of several of the international companies, including Shell and Chevron (Standard Oil of California).

There are in any event several refineries fairly close to Luxembourg. The nearest refinery is at Hauconcourt, to the north of Metz, in which the participants are Compagnie Française des Pétroles, Elf and the French affiliate of Exxon. There is also a refinery at Klarenthal, in Saarland, which is owned 50 per cent by Saarbergwerke AG. Other participants are again CFP and Elf, along with Charbonnages de France. However, as a result of the Benelux arrangements, and in particular the Belgium-Luxembourg Economic Union, there are obvious lines of communication with the main centres of product supply in Belgium and Netherlands.

## Coal

*Coal Consumption*

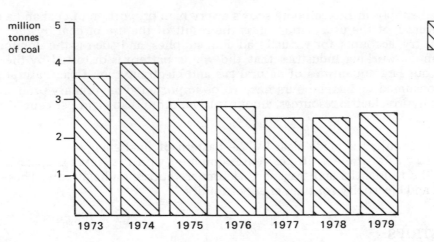

Although a large-scale steel-making industry has developed in the south of Luxembourg, based originally on supplies of iron ore from Lorraine, there is no indigenous production of coal. There is, however, production on a large scale in both Lorraine and Saarland. The steel industry gives rise to a large requirement for coal and coke in relation to the scale of energy consumption in the rest of the Luxembourg economy. Consumption is of the order of 2.5 million tonnes per annum in the form of coke, and approximately half a million tonnes per annum as hard coal. EEC countries are naturally the principal sources for this coal, but even in the case of Luxembourg it has proved worthwhile to bring in some supplies of South African coal.

## Gas

*Gas Production and Consumption*

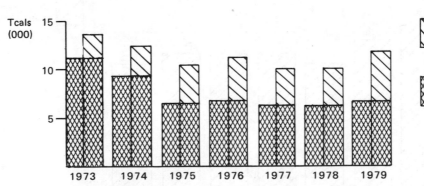

Luxembourg has no indigenous resources of natural gas, but it is able to import gas from the Netherlands indirectly via the Belgian network, one spur of which crosses the Luxembourg border at Pétange. This is close to the main industrial area in the south of Luxembourg, and the gas is consumed entirely in this area. Of the total of some 500 million cubic metres per annum imported currently, the steel industry absorbs 80 per cent. The rest is supplied to the public gas distribution authorities in the city of Luxembourg and in Esch-Sur-Alzette. Towns gas is also supplied by the public authorities in Dudelange, also in the southern industrial area and in Diekirch, the principal town in the centre of the country.

A large amount of gas is produced in the industrial sector, particularly in course of steel-making. This is used by the industries themselves to produce electricity, of which they are the country's principal consumers.

## Electricity

*Electricity Production and Consumption*

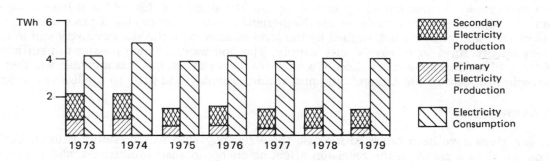

The main public supply of electricity is provided by Compagnie Grand-Ducale d'Electricité du Luxembourg (CEGEDEL) which operates under a concession from the state. CEGEDEL supplies public consumers directly and bulk high-tension supplies to industrial consumers and other communal and municipal distributors. The main source of public power supply is hydro-electric plant on the rivers Moselle and Sûre. The principal hydro-electric plant is at Vianden, operated by the Société Electrique de l'Our.

The bulk of the electricity consumed by industry is either produced by the industrial companies themselves or imported direct from the Belgian network or from Rheinisch-Westfäliches Elektrizitätswerke, the major West German utility. The industrial companies, and notably the steel producers, use blast furnace gas, coke-oven gas, and imported natural gas to generate most of their own output of electricity. The balance is based on oil-fired plant.

Consideration has been given to construction of a nuclear power station in Luxembourg, and in 1975 a contract was placed for its construction at Remerschen, on the Moselle. However, the basic energy situation of Luxembourg is such that its total electricity requirement is relatively small and construction of a major plant would be too closely tied up with the fortunes of the country's industrial activities. These are particularly uncertain at the present time and the project has been shelved.

## ENERGY TRADE

*Net Imports/(Exports) 1973-79*

|  | 1973 | 1974 | 1975 | 1976 | 1977 | 1978 | 1979 |
|---|---|---|---|---|---|---|---|
| Coal (million tonnes) | 3.6 | 3.9 | 2.9 | 2.8 | 2.3 | 2.5 | 2.5 |
| Oil Products (million tonnes) | 1.7 | 1.4 | 1.3 | 1.5 | 1.4 | 1.4 | 1.4 |
| Natural Gas (000 million M$^3$) | 0.3 | 0.4 | 0.5 | 0.5 | 0.5 | 0.6 | 0.6 |
| Electricity (TWh) | 2.0 | 2.7 | 2.4 | 2.6 | 2.5 | 2.5 | 2.7 |

Luxembourg produces only a limited amount of electricity from its indigenous hydro-electric resources and to meet the overall needs of the economy imports a high proportion of its needs, approximately 65 per cent. Oil is imported entirely as finished products, as there is no refinery in Luxembourg. For the most part these are supplied from Belgian refineries, with smaller quantities from the other neighbouring countries of France, Netherlands and West Germany. Natural gas is imported from the Netherlands via the Belgian network. Coal and coke is obtained primarily from neighbouring countries, but about 25 per cent of supplies originate in South Africa.

## ENERGY POLICIES

Despite being heavily dependent on imported energy, the Luxembourg government has not had to intervene directly in questions of energy supply. It is to some extent circumscribed in what it could do, according to the terms of the economic union with Belgium, although on many issues the interests of Luxembourg and Belgium could be similar. In fact, the strength of the less energy-intensive sectors of the economy has enabled Luxembourg to override the problems which have arisen so far.

### Energy Supply

Problems of energy supply are not critical for Luxembourg. Its consumption of oil products is modest, and to some extent may be supplanted by increasing use of natural gas, for which it has an assured long-term contract for supplies from Gasunie in the Netherlands, subject to paying a price acceptable to Gasunie. Imports of coal and coke are determined by the level of activity in the steel industry and in any case coal is the major energy form in relatively easy supply. The one way in which greater self-sufficiency might be attained would be through construction of a nuclear power station, but it is arguable whether this would be an economic proposition for Luxembourg and would probably add little to the level of security of supply.

### Energy Conservation

So far, few steps have been taken to increase the efficiency with which energy is used. Consumption has been contained as a result of the recession affecting energy-intensive industries, and the slow overall rate of growth of energy consumption is mainly attributable to the increasing role of service sector activities in the economy. Encouragement of just such a structural change, which the government is doing, may indeed prove to be the most successful means of limiting energy consumption while maintaining economic growth.

The government has adopted measures to tighten up the system for granting permits for installing heating systems and requires higher standards for insulation in new buildings. Space-heating is subject to some restrictions. Subsidies, of up to 25 per cent of investment costs, are being made available to private consumers. The government also provides information and advisory services, both to the public and to industry and commerce.

# Netherlands

## KEY ENERGY INDICATORS

Energy Consumption
    —million tonnes oil equivalent            65.8
Consumption Per Head
    —tonnes oil equivalent                 4.7
    —percentage of West European average   132%
Net Energy Imports                     6%
Oil Import-Dependence                 97%

*The Netherlands is a highly developed country with one of the highest standards of living in Western Europe. Energy consumption per head is accordingly well above the average. The economy is based on hydrocarbon energy, natural gas, of which there are very large indigenous reserves, and oil, for which the country is almost entirely dependent on imports. Nominally production and consumption of energy are close to balance, as in terms of energy potential exports of natural gas are approximately equivalent to imports of oil and coal. However, in practice, the Dutch government is now trying to confine the use of natural gas to its most appropriate uses and increase the rate of substitution by other fuels, even though these must be imported.*

## ENERGY MARKET TRENDS

*Trend of Energy Consumption*

Energy Consumption
    +1.1% p.a.

Gross Domestic Product
    +2.8% p.a.

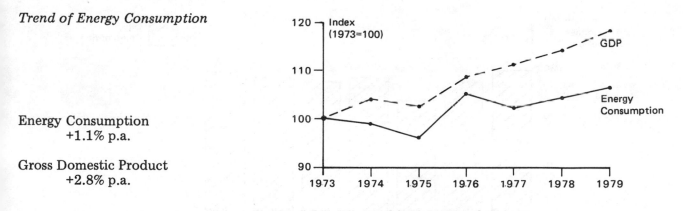

The performance of the Netherlands economy since 1973 provides a good illustration of recent developments in terms of economic growth and energy consumption. The oil supply crisis of 1973 checked the forward movement of the economy, although only after a time-lag, whereafter the economy recovered somewhat. Subsequent rates of economic growth have been lower than prior to 1973, but have been associated with a relatively low rate of increase in consumption of energy. On average, the economy has been growing at nearly three per cent per annum but consumption of energy has increased at little more than one per cent per annum. This is partly a reflection of the impact of energy conservation and partly a result of the lower level of activity in energy-intensive industries.

*Pattern of Energy Supply and Consumption*

| Primary Fuel Supply (percentage) | | Final Consumption (percentage) | |
|---|---|---|---|
| Oil | 50 | Industry | 40 |
| Solid Fuel | 4 | Residential | 28 |
| Natural Gas | 45 | Transport | 16 |
| Primary Electricity | 1 | Other | 16 |
| TOTAL | 100 | TOTAL | 100 |

The pattern of primary fuel supply reflects the existence of the extensive reserves of natural gas discovered in the Netherlands and its offshore areas. Exploitation of these resources has led to the widespread use of natural gas in all sectors of the economy. Nevertheless, oil accounts for a higher proportion of energy input, and this may well rise as efforts are made to cut down on the use of natural gas, particularly where it is being used as a boiler fuel.

Primary electricity is derived almost entirely from one commercial nuclear reactor, and there is little hydro-electric potential. The use of coal is still quite limited, although on a rising trend.

The pattern of energy consumption shows both industrial and residential sectors accounting for shares very close to the West European average. However, as may be expected in a small country, particularly one in which water-borne transport is important, consumption in the transport sector is less than average. Consumption in the commercial sector is correspondingly high.

## ENERGY SUPPLY INDUSTRIES

The state is involved as a joint partner in the exploitation, supply and export of the country's large natural gas deposits. Its role in other energy industries is much less, although the electricity industry is subject to general supervision. The Netherlands is the base for the Royal Dutch/Shell Group, one of the largest international oil companies, and Rotterdam has developed as one of the key centres of the international oil market.

## Oil

*Oil Consumption*

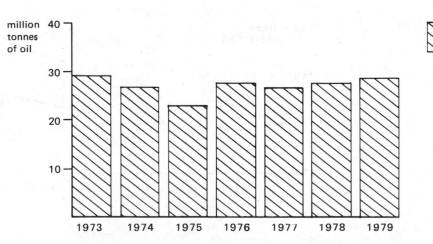

There is only a very small quantity of oil produced in the Netherlands in conjunction with the extensive exploitation of natural gas fields. Production amounts to only one and a half million tonnes per annum or about five per cent of the country's requirement. Yet the Netherlands has developed as the centre of north European oil activities as a result of its geographical location and the initiative of the port authority in developing Rotterdam's ability to handle ever larger crude oil tankers.

Total refining capacity exceeds 90 million tonnes per annum. This is somewhat less than in the mid 1970s when the total was 100 million tonnes per annum, and reflects the closure of old or high-cost units in the face of reduced demand for oil products. Even so, capacity is greatly under-utilised. The domestic economy requires less than a third of existing capacity, and product exports have fallen from 42 million tonnes in 1973 to around 30 million tonnes per annum. Most of the major international oil companies have refineries in the Netherlands, the two largest belonging to Shell and British Petroleum, having a capacity of 25 and 23 million tonnes per annum respectively, both located at Rotterdam. The Shell refinery is one of the most sophisticated and a key centre of that group's European activities. Exxon and Standard Oil of California have refineries at Rotterdam too. Other refineries belong to Mobil at Amsterdam, and Compagnie Française des Pétroles, at Vlissingen.

The companies refining crude oil all have sizeable marketing operations, especially the Dutch-based Shell company, which supplies 25-30 per cent of the market. But other independent distributors and marketers have built up sales through purchase of bulk cargoes, either sold by the refining companies, or imported from other export sources. The entrepot and storage capability of Rotterdam forms the basis of the world's largest open market for oil products.

## Coal

*Coal Consumption*

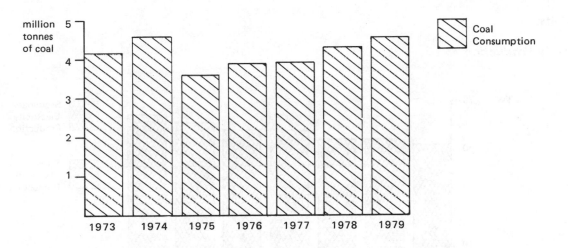

Coal is no longer produced in the Netherlands and what requirements there are have to be imported. Since 1973 imports have been on a rising trend. Imports are largely of hard coal which is used in coking plants. About one million tonnes per annum is used by utilities to generate electricity. Less than four per cent of electricity is derived from coal.

## Gas

*Gas Production and Consumption*

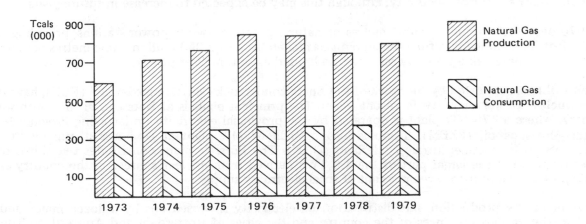

Since the early 1960s the Dutch energy economy and gas industry have been transformed by the exploitation of the large reserves of natural gas. A large part of these gas resources, including the massive

Groningen field, are exploited by Nederlandse Aardolie Maatschappij (NAM), a partnership of the Shell and Exxon groups. On the basis of these reserves natural gas has become a mainstay of the energy economy and large quantities are sold on long-term contracts to gas supply undertakings in West Germany, France, Belgium, Switzerland and Italy. The Netherlands itself absorbs over 45,000 million cubic metres per annum and export sales are at a similar level. In view of the change which has taken place in the general energy situation and relatively disappointing results from recent exploration activity, efforts are being made to reduce the consumption of natural gas at home and limit export commitments.

The transmission of natural gas, and operation of the main trunklines is the responsibility of Nederlandse Gasunie. The state holds a 50 per cent share in Gasunie, ten per cent directly and 40 per cent through Dutch State Mines, and the NAM partners own the other 50 per cent. Gasunie supplies the 150 or so public distributors, industrial bulk consumers and handles export contracts. It has also become involved in contracts to import gas from the North Sea and from Algeria, in liquefied form, in order to supplement supplies.

The public supply system, comprising mostly local and regional partnership undertakings belonging to local authorities, handles only just over half of domestic sales. The rest is consumed by electricity utilities and bulk industrial consumers, buying direct from Gasunie. These two sectors each take up approximately 25 per cent of natural gas supplies.

## Electricity

*Electricity Production*

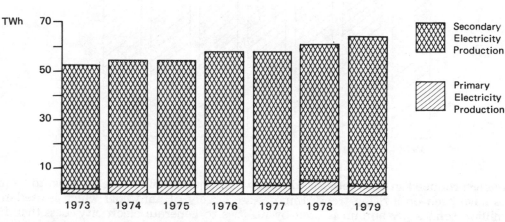

In common with most other industrialised countries a large proportion of electricity is generated by oil-fired plant. But the Netherlands is unusual in using natural gas as its main fuel input for electricity production, reflecting the importance of the country's only significant energy resource and the widespread use of gas throughout the economy. In contrast, coal has been the least important fuel source, providing less than four per cent of electricity, although this may be expected to increase in future years.

In 1975 over 11,000 million cubic metres of natural gas were used in power stations, providing two-thirds of all electricity. Since that time the amount has fallen back to 9,000 million cubic metres per annum, with an increasing share being taken by oil, and to a limited extent, nuclear power.

Dutch utilities, supported by the work of the Energieonderzoek Centrum Nederland (ECN), have developed some nuclear power capacity in recent years. The principal plant is at Borssele, in the south-west of the country, where a 470 MW plant is operated by the provincial electricity undertaking Provinciale Zeeuwse Energie-Maatschappij (PZEM). There is also a small 54 MW plant at Dodewaard, run by the Gemeenschappelijke Kernenergiecentrale Nederland (GKN). The Borssele plant contributes two-thirds of PZEM's power output and the larger part of the 4.5 TWh derived from nuclear sources in the country as a whole. This represents more than seven per cent of total electricity supply.

The bulk of the production and distribution of electricity is carried out by a dozen major undertakings based in the various provinces of the country and the cities of Rotterdam and Amsterdam. These undertakings carry out sale and purchase of electricity between each other to increase the degree of optimisation of total operations. Three utilities in the southern part of the country optimise their activities through the Zuidelijke Economische Optimalisatie (ZEO) for transactions between themselves and other provincial undertakings.

## ENERGY TRADE

*Net Imports/(Exports) 1973-79*

|  | 1973 | 1974 | 1975 | 1976 | 1977 | 1978 | 1979 |
|---|---|---|---|---|---|---|---|
| Coal (million tonnes) | 2.1 | 3.3 | 3.8 | 3.9 | 4.3 | 4.8 | 5.0 |
| Crude Oil (million tonnes) | 72.2 | 64.6 | 55.2 | 63.9 | 58.9 | 55.3 | 60.5 |
| Oil Products (million tonnes) | (32.0) | (28.8) | (23.6) | (26.2) | (23.3) | (19.8) | (21.2) |
| Natural Gas (000 million M$^3$) | (34.6) | (45.5) | (51.1) | (56.0) | (57.0) | (48.2) | (53.0) |
| Electricity (TWh) | (1.3) | (1.5) | (0.3) | (0.3) | 0.7 | 0.3 | 0.1 |

Netherlands trade in most energy forms has shown considerable change since 1973. The net import of crude oil and oil products in 1979 was only slightly less than in 1973, but total movements are much less, reflecting the decline in the international oil products trade and the efforts of several countries to refine crude rather than import finished products.

Net exports of natural gas are unlikely to return to the level reached in 1977, as the Dutch government pays increasing attention to limiting its export commitments and conserving the country's only significant indigenous resource. A steady growth in coal imports has been taking place as electricity utilities and industrial consumers change from fuel oil or natural gas.

*Sources of Imported Crude Oil*

| (percentage) | | |
|---|---|---|
| Middle East | | 63.9 |
| Saudi Arabia | 32.3 | |
| Kuwait | 14.5 | |
| Iran | 9.1 | |
| Iraq | 3.4 | |
| Other | 4.6 | |
| | | |
| Africa | | 25.0 |
| Nigeria | 22.5 | |
| Other | 2.5 | |
| | | |
| United Kingdom | | 8.1 |
| Other | | 3.0 |
| | | |
| TOTAL | | 100.0 |

The Middle East is the predominant source of crude oil used in Dutch refineries. Saudi Arabia alone supplies one-third of the country's requirements. The importance of Saudi Arabia and Kuwait has increased as the availability of crude oil from Iran has been cut back in recent times. African sources are also prominent and Nigeria is the second largest individual source of crude oil. The North Sea has become of some importance for lighter crude oils, but its role is limited by comparison with that of Nigeria.

## ENERGY POLICIES

The changed situation in world energy markets since 1973 has caused the Dutch government to take an increasing interest in the energy sector. Its direct involvement is confined to a total 50 per cent holding in Nederlandse Gasunie. There is no direct intervention in the oil sector, although concern at the impact which volatile prices in the bulk markets may have on internal price levels.

### Energy Supply

The principal concern of government policy is that indigenous natural gas reserves should be conserved and that no additional long-term contracts for export should be concluded. Indeed, the Netherlands is prepared to see increasing imports of natural gas in the interests of conserving its own reserves, which should have greater long-term value. Preparations are being made to develop a terminal for importing liquefied natural gas. This would be for other countries as well as the Netherlands. The terminal is to be at Eemshaven, in the north of the country, partly because this region lacks industrial activity, but also because of concern about the safety issue if it were located in the Rotterdam area.

While accepting existing commitments to export natural gas up to the end of the century, the government is determined to obtain current market values for its gas. To this end it has made contingency plans which would enable it to cut off export movements. At the same time as limiting export commitments, greater attention is being paid to the exploitation of smaller deposits of natural gas, both onshore and offshore. It is also clear that electricity producers and energy-intensive industrial consumers will find decreasing quantities of natural gas being made available for their purposes.

### Energy Conservation

The government has not introduced legislation to enforce conservation but has been active in a number of other ways. Regulations on standards of insulation have been tightened and subsidies are available for insulation. Grants of up to 29 per cent are available for insulating commercial buildings, grants of 25 per cent for energy-saving investment and up to 50 per cent for demonstration projects. The 25 per cent grant is also available to industrial companies and public authorities for investment in combined heat and power or waste incineration schemes. In addition a wide range of information and advisory services is provided. Gasunie is active in this way and in promoting higher levels of efficiency in gas equipment.

# Norway

## KEY ENERGY INDICATORS

Energy Consumption
    —million tonnes oil equivalent         23.8
Consumption Per Head
    —tonnes oil equivalent              5.9
    —percentage of West European average   164%
Net Energy Imports                   -138%
Oil Import-Dependence              nil

*Norway is virtually self-sufficient in energy, thanks to the existence of ideal conditions for generating hydro-electric power and the discovery during the last ten years of extensive reserves of oil and gas in the North Sea. The availability of cheap hydro-electricity has permitted the establishment of energy-intensive industries and progress towards a high standard of living, with energy consumption per head well above the West European average. The country is now in the happy position of being able to husband the exploitation of offshore resources and is not pressed to make a decision on nuclear energy.*

## ENERGY MARKET TRENDS

*Trend of Energy Consumption*

Energy Consumption
    +3.2% p.a.

Gross Domestic Product
    +4.4% p.a.

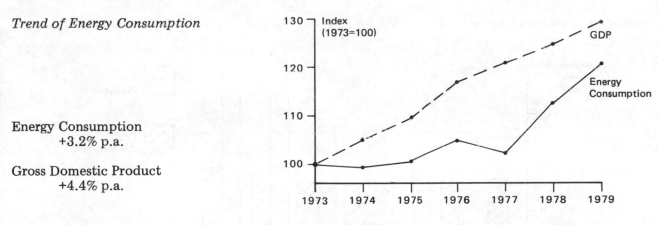

Norway suffered from the impact of the 1973 oil supply crisis only insofar as the physical supply of oil to industrial nations was affected. At that time the output from offshore fields was only just coming on stream. But the country has escaped the more persistent effects of loss of purchasing power and balance of payments deficits which have become a major feature of most other countries by virtue of its relatively large indigenous resources. Energy consumption fell only slightly in 1974 and again in 1977, Norway's consumption being affected more by markets for industrial output and by the weather than by restraints of price or conservation policies. On average the consumption of energy has risen at over three per cent per annum, supporting a relatively high rate of economic growth. Gross Domestic Product has been increasing at well over four per cent per annum, partly as a result of expansion of the energy production industries.

*Pattern of Energy Supply and Consumption*

| Primary Fuel Supply (percentage) | | Final Consumption (percentage) | |
|---|---|---|---|
| Oil | 41 | Industry | 45 |
| Solid Fuel | 3 | Residential | 24 |
| Natural Gas | 2 | Transport | 19 |
| Primary Electricity | 54 | Other | 12 |
| TOTAL | 100 | TOTAL | 100 |

Norway is blessed with great potential for hydro-electric power generation and this has been thoroughly exploited over the years, such that this energy source provides over half of total energy supply. The balance is almost entirely derived from oil, the share of which must be close to its minimum, since electricity is widely used in industry and the residential sector. There is no general use of gas and natural gas which has been discovered in the North Sea has been sold to the British Gas Corporation or major gas distributors in West Germany, Belgium and France.

Industry accounts for a relatively high proportion of final energy demand, 45 per cent, compared with the West European average of 39 per cent. This reflects the past establishment of energy-intensive industries, notably aluminium smelting based on the ready availability of hydro-electric power. Both transport and residential sectors take smaller shares in final consumption than on average. In the case of transport this is in part a reflection of the concentration of population and activity in the Oslo region and the use made of coastal shipping for many movements between the main coastal towns.

## ENERGY SUPPLY INDUSTRIES

With an economy that has been traditionally based on indigenous hydro-electric power, public authorities have been closely involved in the supply of energy. But until the last decade the growing oil market was left to private companies, and particularly to the major international companies, to supply. However, the development of large scale oil and gas operations in the North Sea, combined with the increasingly important political aspect of world energy issues, has led to the state taking a direct interest in energy operations and policies.

### Oil

*Oil Production and Consumption*

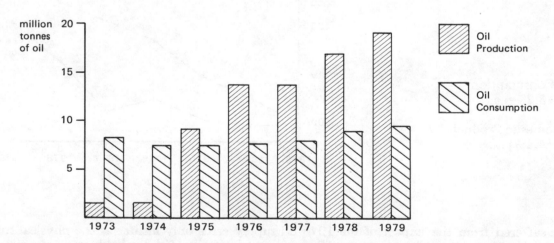

The discovery of major oil and gas resources in the North Sea has transformed the situation in the Norwegian oil industry, in terms of both supply and structure. The Ekofisk field was discovered in 1970 and was one of the first to be developed. It was also found that there were a number of other significant deposits of oil and gas in the same part of the North Sea. As a result oil and gas are collected in one total system to be piped to the north-east of England, in the case of crude oil and natural gas liquids, or to Emden, in North Germany, in the case of natural gas.

But the giant Statfjord field, which lies at 61 degrees north, and is estimated to contain recoverable reserves of about 340 million tonnes of oil, is to load crude oil into tankers at the field, so that the direct movement of some crude oil into Norwegian refineries is expected, especially to the Mongstad refinery, north of Bergen.

To date, the main international companies involved in Norwegian offshore oil production have not been those with refining and marketing interests in Norway, where Exxon and Shell are the leading marketers. Exxon operates a refinery at Tønsberg on the south-east coast, and Shell has a refinery at Stavanger. Shell has an interest in one of the fields forming part of the Ekofisk system and a small share in the Statfjord development. But the principal foreign companies involved are Phillips, the operator for the Ekofisk complex, Mobil, the operator for Statfjord, and French exploration companies.

However, with the development of indigenous resources has come a greater involvement in all phases of the industry, on the part of Norwegian companies and the Norwegian government. Norsk Hydro, which is the country's largest industrial company and a major consumer of energy has interests in the Ekofisk field and exploration operations. It is also a participant in the Mongstad refinery, which was commissioned only in 1975. The state oil company, Statoil, which was set up in 1972, is majority participant in the refinery and has built up important marketing activities. Statoil has been a 50 per cent shareholder in oil exploration concessions issued since 1974.

## Coal

*Coal Production and Consumption*

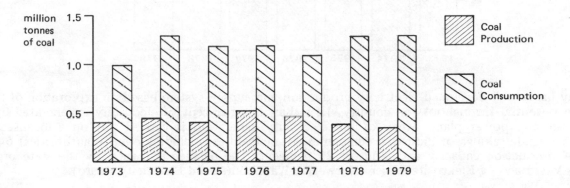

Coal production of up to half a million tonnes per annum takes place on the island of Svalbard (Spitsbergen) which is under joint Norwegian and Soviet administration. Approaching half of this output is exported. On the other hand there are imports of coal into Norway, of both hard coal and coke. The use of coal in Norway is very limited, and confined to industrial consumption where special cokes and solid fuels are required.

## Gas

*Gas Production*

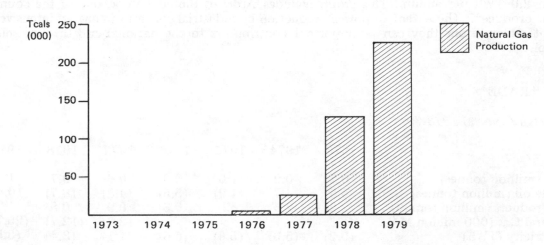

The ready availability of electricity and lack of onshore natural gas deposits have prevented the emergence of a gas supply industry in Norway. There has therefore been little economic incentive to try to land in Norway the increasingly large quantities of offshore gas being produced. Gas from the Ekofisk development and from the Frigg field has thus been contracted to gas suppliers in the major European gas markets of West Germany, Belgium, France and the United Kingdom. It is also possible that gas made available from the development of the Statfjord field will be piped to the United Kingdom as well. However, as technology develops in the fields of pipelaying or in-situ processing (e.g. through conversion into electricity at the field) Norway may seek to use future gas resources more directly for its own energy balance.

## Electricity

### Electricity Production

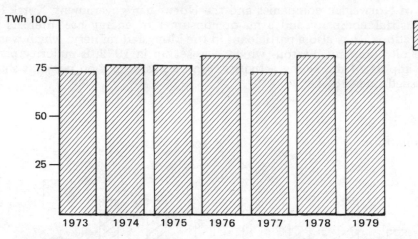

Norway has a well developed electricity production and supply system based on exploration of the hydro-electric potential throughout the country. Less than one per cent of electricity is generated by conventional thermal power plant. Much of the electricity generation is carried out on a localised basis by municipal undertakings or industrial companies. Municipalities (including county authorities) own 54 per cent of production capacity and industry 20 per cent. The balance is owned by the state organisation Norges Vassdrags- og Elektrisitetsvesen (Norwegian Watercourse and Electricity Board).

The co-ordination of supply is undertaken by the Samkjøringen av Kraftverkene i Norge, the Norwegian Power Pool. The Power Pool conducts buying and selling operations between all member undertakings in order to balance the supply and demand for electricity and optimise operational and long-term arrangements between all four Scandinavian countries. The Power Pool operates with four regions—Oslo, Bergen, Trondheim and Narvik. The main net flow of electricity is between the Bergen and Oslo regions.

Both NVE and Norsk Hydro, the country's largest industrial company, operate plant in many parts of Norway. Norsk Hydro is in fact the third largest producer of electricity after NVE and the Oslo municipal power undertaking, which itself owns a complex of plants within the Oslo Region. Oslo Lysverker generates over 5.5 TWh per annum, and Norsk Hydro over 5.0 TWh per annum. Only four other enterprises generate more than 2.0 TWh per annum. This group includes Årdal og Sunndal Verk, one of the country's main aluminium producers. The extent of power production by industrial concerns in energy-intensive industries means that on occasions they can be important contributors to the national grid through selling to the Power Pool.

## ENERGY TRADE

### Net Imports/(Exports) 1973-79

|                                  | 1973  | 1974  | 1975  | 1976  | 1977   | 1978   | 1979   |
|----------------------------------|-------|-------|-------|-------|--------|--------|--------|
| Coal (million tonnes)            | 0.7   | 0.9   | 1.0   | 0.9   | 0.6    | 0.7    | 1.2    |
| Crude oil (million tonnes)       | 5.6   | 4.7   | (1.9) | (5.5) | (4.8)  | (8.7)  | (10.4) |
| Oil Products (million tonnes)    | 2.2   | 2.5   | nil   | 0.3   | 0.9    | 0.8    | 1.7    |
| Natural Gas (000 million M$^3$)  | -     | -     | -     | -     | (2.6)  | (12.7) | (25.7) |
| Electricity (TWh)                | (5.2) | (5.5) | (5.6) | (6.6) | (1.1)  | (3.4)  | (3.5)  |

In the West European context Norway is unique in having a net export of energy, in fact net exports exceed the country's own internal consumption of energy. This is a comparatively recent phenomenon. Norway's hydro-electric potential has enabled it to export significant quantities of electricity, approaching ten per cent of production in some years. But the major contributions have come from the build-up in production of Ekofisk crude oil and gas in the mid 1970s. Total combined production of oil, gas and gas liquids from the Ekofisk system, the Frigg gas field and the Statfjord field is expected to exceed 60 million tonnes of oil equivalent throughout the 1980s.

*Sources of Imported Crude Oil*

(percentage)

| | | |
|---|---|---|
| United Kingdom | | 49.0 |
| | | |
| Middle East | | 25.0 |
| Saudi Arabia | 15.1 | |
| Iran | 8.5 | |
| Other | 1.4 | |
| | | |
| Eastern Europe | | 12.8 |
| Nigeria | | 11.1 |
| Other | | 2.1 |
| | | |
| TOTAL | | 100.0 |

The output from Ekofisk and Frigg fields is physically landed abroad, so that there is no particular advantage in using Norwegian North Sea crude oil in the three main refineries. Nevertheless, United Kingdom sources, including Teesside, where the Ekofisk terminal is located, provide the largest share of crude oil imports. However, because of the pattern of product demand and particular corporate interests in refining in Norway, crude oil is imported from a number of leading petroleum exporting countries.


## ENERGY POLICIES

The existence of offshore oil and gas resources well beyond the obvious requirements of Norwegian consumption is an all-pervading factor in the running of the economy and in other political issues. Explicit action to limit the amount of exploitation of offshore oil and gas resources has not yet been taken, although there has in effect been a moratorium until recently on exploration to the north of the sixty-second parallel. While encouraging Norwegian firms to participate as much as possible in exploration, development and onshore-related work, there is increasing concern about the indirect impact of the North Sea bonanza on the general manufacturing base of the economy.

### Energy Supply/Disposal

The state has come to play a leading role in all aspects of exploration and development for oil and gas. Through the state oil company, Statoil, it automatically obtains a 50 per cent share in new developments and has the dominant voice in questions of field development. Up to the present time political considerations have not prevailed over the clear-cut economics of landing large quantities of oil and gas outside the country, although the agreement to pipe Ekofisk oil to England was linked to an undertaking to supply natural gas liquids to the new petrochemical plant at Rafnes in southern Norway at no additional freight cost. It is increasingly likely that future developments, particularly if taking place in more northerly waters or close to the Norwegian coast, will be weighed against the potential onshore gain in terms of economic development, although overall economic policy is mindful of the problems which could arise, particularly in the northern parts of the country, for traditional industries.

The latest White Paper on energy policy envisages further exploitation of hydro-electric potential, although there are now limits to how much more can be generated in this way, and the construction of thermal power plant at some stage during the 1980s, using either coal or fuel oil as boiler feed. Primarily these thermal stations would be an insurance against low rainfall and the need to meet peak power demand.

An advisory committee set up by the government came to the conclusion that in principle nuclear plant would be acceptable on safety grounds, but there is no question of this form of energy becoming a key issue for some time.

## Conservation

As a complement to its policy of proceeding with further hydro-electric schemes, which are subject to opposition on environmental grounds, the government is devoting more resources to energy conservation and research into alternative forms of energy. In particular, more stringent standards in building construction are to be required, and taxes and subsidies are to be used more extensively to encourage the use of forms of transport which are not energy-intensive.

The White Paper also suggests that energy prices, particularly electricity prices, should move towards the long-term marginal cost of electricity supply. Since the historic cost of producing hydro-electricity has been relatively low, this would involve a fundamental change in the situation facing certain energy-intensive industries.

# Portugal

## KEY ENERGY INDICATORS

| | |
|---|---:|
| Energy Consumption | |
| —million tonnes oil equivalent | 10.1 |
| Consumption Per Head | |
| —tonnes oil equivalent | 1.0 |
| —percentage of West European average | 29% |
| Net Energy Imports | 71% |
| Oil Import-Dependence | 100% |

*Portugal is perhaps the least developed country in Western Europe and is in an early stage of industrialisation. Energy consumption per head is markedly lower than in either Spain or Greece, at less than 30 per cent of the European average. Energy consumption is, however, rising steadily. Portugal has a useful indigenous resource of hydro-electric power but growth is founded on oil, which must all be imported. No oil or natural gas of significance has been found and the scale of industry and population in Portugal is unlikely to justify imports of liquefied natural gas. There is as yet no firm project to build a nuclear power station. Despite this dependence on imported oil, no definite shift towards the use of coal has yet taken place.*

## ENERGY MARKET TRENDS

*Trend of Energy Consumption*

Energy Consumption
+4.9% p.a.

Gross Domestic Product
+2.3% p.a.

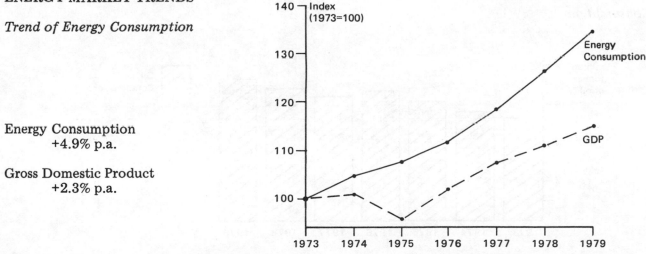

Energy consumption has continued on its upward trend despite the oil supply crisis of 1973. Rising energy demands seem to have been inevitable given the low base from which industrial growth has been taking place. Even in 1975, when Gross Domestic Product fell by 4.4 per cent, energy consumption increased by 2.5 per cent. Overall in the period since 1973 Portugal has recorded a reasonable growth in GDP, but in association with much greater rate of growth in energy consumption. In this respect its recent history has been similar to that of Spain and Greece, which are also in the process of industrialisation, although Portugal seems to have fared worse than the other two countries in terms of the GDP growth achieved at such cost to the balance of payments.

*Pattern of Energy Supply and Consumption*

| Primary Fuel Supply (percentage) | | Final Consumption (percentage) | |
|---|---|---|---|
| Oil | 69 | Industry | 40 |
| Solid Fuel | 5 | Residential | 12 |
| Natural Gas | – | Transport | 35 |
| Primary Electricity | 26 | Other | 13 |
| TOTAL | 100 | TOTAL | 100 |

The Portugese economy has a base-load of indigenous energy in the form of hydro-electric power from its mountain areas. This provides about a quarter of primary fuel supply. The balance is almost entirely made up of oil and oil-based energy, and it has been oil that has supplied the foundation of Portugal's recent rapid industrial development.

Coal accounts for a remarkably small proportion of total energy supply. This may be partly attributed to the sizeable discoveries of oil which were made in former colonial territories, such as Angola and Cabinda. But a greater role for coal in the future seems likely.

The pattern of final energy consumption is notable for the high proportion used in the transport sector. This sector may perhaps be considered the most fully developed, whereas Portugal is still relatively under-developed from an industrial point of view, and the amount of energy used in the residential sector is a reflection of the low general level of living standards, although the mild climate is also a contributory factor. As development progresses it is to be expected that industry will take up a larger share, even if Portugal seeks to limit the extent of growth by energy-intensive industries.

## ENERGY SUPPLY INDUSTRIES

Since the transition to a democratic regime in Portugal, control of basic industries, including the energy sector, has been put more explicitly under state control with new undertakings established in the oil and electricity industries. Private companies continue to play a part in the distribution of oil products and the international oil companies may become more involved in the search for indigenous hydrocarbon resources.

### Oil

*Oil Consumption*

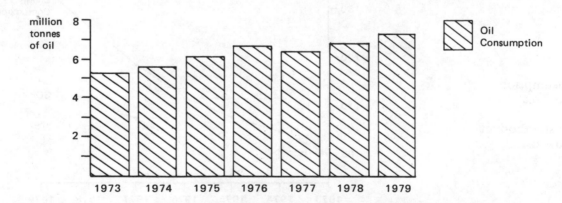

Portugal has no indigenous production of oil, which is a basic element in the process of growth in the national economy. Total imports of oil amount to around 7.5 million tonnes per annum.

A central role in the oil industry is played by the state oil company Petroleos de Portugal (Petrogal), which is responsible for import and export arrangements, has the monopoly in oil refining and controls marketing arrangements. There are three refineries with a total capacity of 19.5 million tonnes per annum. The main refinery is at Sines, to the south of Lisbon, a modern refinery of ten million tonnes per annum capacity linked to a petrochemical plant. The refinery was initially built with the possibilities of processing crude oil for export markets in mind and is capable of receiving VLCCs. The decline in international trade in oil products has left Portugal with a large amount of spare capacity, and as a result the old refinery at Lisbon is to be converted to a secondary processing plant. The remaining refinery is in the northern city of Oporto.

Several of the international oil companies have marketing operations in Portugal, although they are dependent for supplies on Petrogal, which is also building up a major market position itself. Exploration has been taking place to only a limited extent and is also primarily undertaken by Petrogal. Licences are held for onshore exploration in the Lisbon area around the mouth of the river Tagus. Shell is involved in some of these areas.

## Coal

*Coal Production and Consumption*

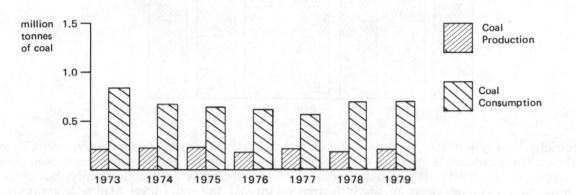

Coal plays a very small part in the energy economy of Portugal. In the north of the country, near Porto, low-grade coal is mined, with production of around 200,000 tonnes per annum. This is used as fuel by Electricidade de Portugal, the state electricity supply undertaking, in its Tapada do Outeiro power station. Other requirements for hard coal and coke for industrial purposes have to be imported.

## Gas

*Gas Production*

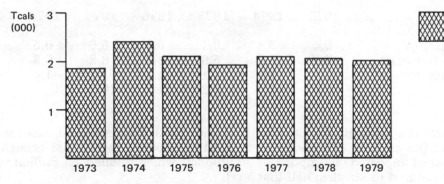

Portugal has no indigenous production of natural gas, either onshore or offshore. So far there has been no move towards the development of a system based on imported liquefied natural gas as is the case in Spain. The scale of economic activity and distribution of population in Portugal are unlikely to be sufficient to justify such a project, although it is possible that a link to the Spanish distribution network may be worthwhile in due course as it is expanded to serve cities in the north and west of Spain.

Production of manufactured gas is annually of the order of 2,000 teracalories, equivalent to only about 220 million cubic metres of natural gas. This is mainly produced by certain industries such as oil refining and used within the industrial sector. There is only a very limited amount of towns gas produced in the Lisbon area. Production and distribution is undertaken by Electricidade de Portugal.

**Electricity**

*Electricity Production*

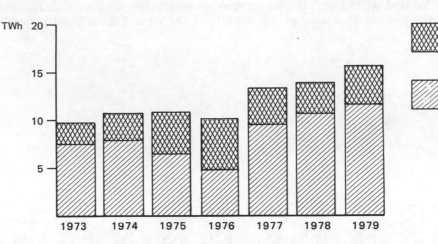

The electricity supply industry, as one of the country's basic industries, is now the responsibility of a state undertaking, Electricidade de Portugal (EDP). EDP is responsible for the national transmission system and overall supply of electricity. It handles almost all of the electricity for public supply, but there are also several important auto-producers in the industrial sector. At the retail level EDP sells approximately 40 per cent of the total and municipal authorities handle a significant quantity. EDP has particular responsibility for increasing the electrification of rural areas.

Hydro-electricity, obtained from the mountain areas of northern and eastern Portugal, is the main indigenous energy resource, and it makes a valuable contribution to the country's energy budget. Over 75 per cent of electricity is produced in this way, equivalent to over one-quarter of total energy supply. The remaining quantity of electricity is produced mainly from oil-fired power stations. There has been some consideration of building a nuclear power station but this is not as yet a firm project.

**ENERGY TRADE**

*Net Imports/(Exports) 1973-79*

|                              | 1973 | 1974 | 1975 | 1976 | 1977  | 1978 | 1979 |
|------------------------------|------|------|------|------|-------|------|------|
| Coal (million tonnes)        | 0.4  | 0.4  | 0.4  | 0.4  | 0.5   | 0.5  |      |
| Crude Oil (million tonnes)   | 4.3  | 5.8  | 5.6  | 6.0  | 6.2   | 6.3  | 8.5  |
| Oil Products (million tonnes)| 1.7  | 1.0  | 1.1  | 1.3  | 1.2   | 1.0  | 0.8  |
| Electricity (TWh)            | 1.7  | 1.0  | 0.2  | 1.7  | (0.5) |      |      |

Imports of crude oil have risen steadily and have doubled since 1973. To some extent the increase in crude oil imports has been at the expense of imports of finished oil products, which has brought about some saving in the overall cost of imported oil. Imports of oil products which totalled 1.7 million tonnes in 1973 have been progressively reduced to less than half that level.

The amount of coal imports has remained almost constant at 400-500,000 tonnes per annum. Unlike most other countries which are heavily dependent on imported oil there has been no significant move so far towards substituting coal for oil.

*Sources of Imported Crude Oil*

| (percentage) | | |
|---|---|---|
| Middle East | | 88.7 |
|   Iraq | 39.0 | |
|   Saudi Arabia | 25.2 | |
|   Iran | 20.1 | |
|   Other | 4.4 | |
| Eastern Europe | | 10.1 |
| Other | | 1.2 |
| TOTAL | | 100.0 |

Portugal imports almost 90 per cent of its crude oil requirements from the Middle East and is well placed both for terminals on the Eastern Mediterranean coast and for long-haul shipments in large crude carriers rounding Africa from the Persian Gulf. Saudi Arabia, the largest Middle East exporter, provides about one-quarter of imports, but the leading position is occupied by Iraq, which supplies a much greater proportion. Iraq is one of the countries with which Petrogal has sought close links to ensure crude oil supplies.

Outside the Middle East the only other source of significance is the Soviet Union, which is able to supply crude oil from its Black Sea terminal. This crude is of the heavier variety, as are the grades imported from the Middle East, and suited to Portugal's high demand for fuel oil. African crude oil, which, although closest to Portugal geographically, is light and relatively expensive, has been imported in only very small quantities.

## ENERGY POLICIES

Given the turmoil of political and social change which has taken place in Portugal over the last four years, and the almost concurrent difficulties in the international economy, it is not surprising that successive governments have been preoccupied with questions of general economic and industrial policy. However, there has been a consensus that the country's basic industries should be under state control. State undertakings have been set up in the oil sector and in the gas and electricity supply industries.

### Energy Supply

The main concern of government policy in relation to energy has been to assure the growing economy of adequate supplies. As far as internal distribution is concerned this has led to the nationalisation of the oil refineries and tighter control of product marketing, although this action was also taken partly for political reasons and because of operating and financial difficulties in the oil and petrochemicals industries. Petrogal, the integrated state oil company, now occupies a central role. In addition the transportation of crude oil must usually be carried out by the national tanker fleet.

Outside Portugal Petrogal is the agency through which the government is seeking to secure crude oil supplies. This approach recognises the role of producer-country governments and the main objective is to conclude additional supply agreements with state oil companies, as has been the case with Iraq, Abu Dhabi and Nigeria. The main policy area tackled, other than oil supply, is the possibility of developing nuclear power. However, a White Paper of 1979, suggesting the construction of at least one station, proved highly controversial and the government is in the process of reviewing its approach to nuclear power.

### Energy Conservation

So far little has been achieved in the field of energy conservation, with energy consumption rising at a rapid rate. The government in any case has considerable problems to cope with concerning the structure of industry and the economy in general, and undoubtedly part of the problem of reducing the rate of growth of energy consumption in relation to GDP must lie in this area. But it seems unlikely that the country can continue to base its economic development on intensive use of energy. In the existing circumstances the main thrust towards energy conservation lies in the action of market forces as prices and taxes on energy increase, although government measures in this respect are concerned primarily with financial and fiscal objectives.

# Spain

## KEY ENERGY INDICATORS

Energy Consumption
—million tonnes oil equivalent     73.7

Consumption Per Head
—tonnes oil equivalent     2.0
—percentage of West European average     55%

Net Energy Imports     70%

Oil Import-Dependence     98%

*Spain is one of the more populous countries of Western Europe, with nearly 37 million people. But it is only partially industrialised and has a rapidly rising requirement for energy. There are substantial indigenous resources in the form of coal and hydro-electric power and some prospects for offshore oil or gas. But development of the economy remains very dependent on oil imports. With this in mind, as well as the expectation of continually increasing demand for energy in total, and electricity in particular, a programme of nuclear power plant construction is under way. However, such is the country's need for energy that conservation will become an increasingly important issue.*

## ENERGY MARKET TRENDS

*Trend of Energy Consumption*

Energy Consumption
+4.4% p.a.

Gross Domestic Product
+2.6% p.a.

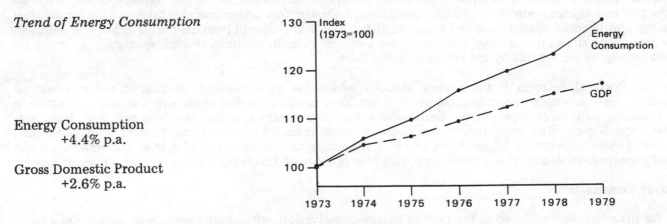

The trend in consumption of energy in Spain has shown remarkably little effect of the oil supply crisis in 1973. The upward trend in consumption has been unbroken since 1973 and has not been less than three per cent in any individual year. The economy in general has also experienced continuous growth and suffered no real decline in Gross Domestic Product in any year, reflecting the continuing process of industrial development. The nearest the country came to a halt in economic growth was in 1975 when GDP rose by only just over one per cent. As is usually the case with countries which are in the process of industrialisation there is a tendency for the rate of growth of energy consumption to exceed that of GDP. However, there must be increasing concern that energy consumption should be rising as quickly as it is and there has clearly been little achieved so far in terms of energy conservation.

*Pattern of Energy Supply and Consumption*

| Primary Fuel Supply (percentage) | | Final Consumption (percentage) | |
|---|---|---|---|
| Oil | 69 | Industry | 47 |
| Solid Fuel | 15 | Residential | 12 |
| Natural Gas | 2 | Transport | 28 |
| Primary Electricity | 14 | Other | 13 |
| TOTAL | 100 | TOTAL | 100 |

Spain has significant indigenous production of coal and primary electricity, but relies for over two-thirds of its primary fuel input on oil, almost all of which is imported. Output of coal has been increasing and the government is pressing ahead with a programme of nuclear power plant construction. However, until this materialises, growing consumption of energy, associated with the developing economy, will continue to be based on oil. Natural gas, which is also imported, is still only making a very small contribution to total energy input. The distribution system is being extended, but consumption is likely to increase only slowly.

The pattern of final energy consumption shows industry consuming a proportion well above the average for West European countries. This reflects the state of industrialisation in Spain and its concentration on energy-intensive industries. The general level of development is reflected by the very low share consumed in the residential sector, only 12 per cent compared with 28 per cent on average.

## ENERGY SUPPLY INDUSTRIES

Supply and distribution of all forms of energy is under close control by the state, particularly through the agency of the Instituto Nacional de Industria, which is responsible to the Ministry of Finance. Provincial and municipal authorities are involved in distributing electricity and gas to the public. In the oil sector, where private companies are able to operate, their activities are subject to licensing by the state authorities.

## Oil

*Oil Consumption*

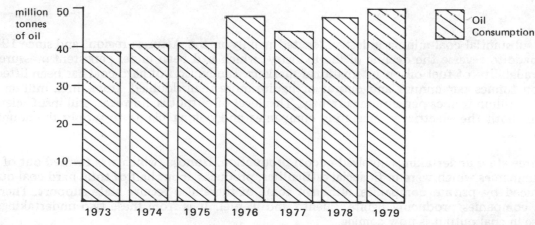

For some years there has been production of crude oil from an onshore field at Ayoluengo, near Burgos, but this field is now almost exhausted. About 200,000 tonnes per annum is obtained from fields at Castellon and Casablanca. Since 1974 indigenous output has been boosted by development of the offshore Amposta field, near the mouth of the river Ebro, although the total of indigenous production is less than one million tonnes per annum. These fields do however provide hope for additional discoveries, especially in offshore areas. Efforts are being concentrated on the areas near to the Amposta field and off Cadiz in the south of the country. Onshore exploration is continuing in the Burgos area and around Cardona.

The oil industry is subject to a state monopoly. The monopoly is delegated to the Compania Arrendataria del Monopolio de Petroleos (CAMPSA) which in turn licences private, including foreign, companies to participate in various stages of the industry. CAMPSA is controlled by the Ministry of Finance, but 49 per cent of its shares are held by private Spanish interests. CAMPSA assumes responsibilities in the supply and marketing of oil products and in exploration in Spanish territory. Hispanoil, a subsidiary of INI, is primarily concerned with securing overseas supplies of crude oil.

There are refineries at Tarragona, Castellon, Cartagena, Algeciras and Huelva on the south and east coasts, and at Bilbao and Corunna on the north-west coast. There is also an inland refinery at Puertollano, approximately half-way between the south coast and the capital, Madrid. A system of pipelines for transporting finished products from refineries to Madrid and other inland centres of consumption is being developed. One pipeline runs from Bilbao to serve Vitoria, Burgos, Valladolid and Salamanca in the north-west of the country. This pipeline is being extended to Madrid. A second pipeline links Cadiz and Madrid with the refinery at Puertollano. This pipeline continues to Saragossa in the north-east and construction of a final leg between Saragossa and Tarragona is under way.

INI controls directly or indirectly the larger part of Spanish refining capacity, which totals 60 million tonnes per annum. Spanish industrial or banking interests are involved in many of the refineries. Several of the major international companies hold minority interests in Spanish refineries.

## Coal

### Coal Production and Consumption

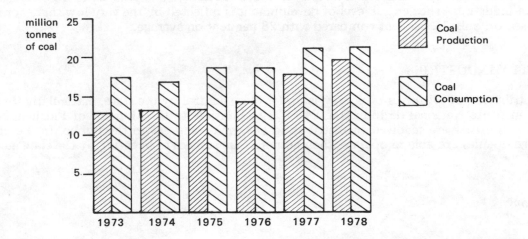

Spain has a substantial coal-mining industry, located mainly in the Asturias region, and since 1973 efforts have been made to reverse the decline of the industry, which had been under persistent pressure owing to the ready availability of fuel oil on international markets. Production of hard coal has been lifted from 10 to 12 million tonnes per annum and output of lignite more than doubled, from three million tonnes in 1973 to eight million tonnes per annum currently. This level of output is, however, still insufficient to meet demand from both the electricity generating companies and coking plants to supply the country's steel industry.

There are three state undertakings involved in coal production. Hunosa, which was formed out of a number of private companies which were in financial difficulties, produces about half of total hard coal output. The rest is produced by private companies, although some of these also receive state support. There are two nationalised companies producing lignite, Puento and Teruel. It is from these two undertakings that the main increase in coal output is now coming.

The current long-term energy plan envisages a doubling of coal production by the late 1980s, to around 40 million tonnes per annum. While this may be justifiable, given the country's extensive reserves, it will nevertheless involve considerable investment following a period of decline and poor profitability. But, in the absence of a major oil or gas find, it remains the only indigenous resources capable of meeting rising levels of energy consumption, and of substituting for fuel oil in power station and industrial boilers.

## Gas

### Gas Production and Consumption

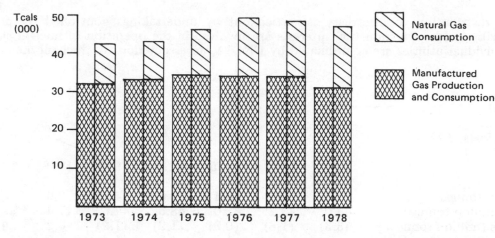

Production of natural gas in Spain is of negligible proportions, but during the 1970s facilities were developed to import liquefied natural gas as one of the key elements in the primary fuel balance. The state agency Empresa Nacional del Gas (ENAGAS) imports gas from Algeria and Libya, currently into its terminal in Barcelona. Distribution of natural gas remains limited to the Barcelona and Tarragona areas, but two additional trunk lines are being built, to supply other cities in the north, including Bilbao and Saragossa and to serve Castellon and Valencia. Consideration is being given to constructing a pipeline from Algeria and this project may depend on the further development of the natural gas supply system in Spain as well as the scope for transporting additional quantities across the border into France.

The use of natural gas is largely confined to industry. Of greater significance at this stage, and particularly in the residential sector, is the use of liquefied petroleum gases (LPG). The use of LPG is virtually ubiquitous, and is distributed by a specialist company Butano SA, which is controlled by INI and CAMPSA. In many individual towns, manufactured gas remains the basis for public gas supply.

## Electricity

### Electricity Production

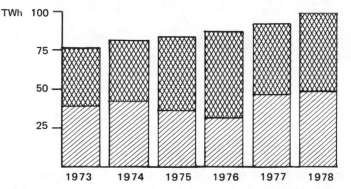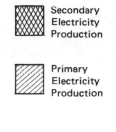

The extensive mountain and high-lying areas of Spain have provided significant hydro-electric potential, and it is only in the last two years that coal has displaced hydro-electricity as the largest indigenous source of primary energy. Under favourable conditions of rainfall hydro-electric plant has been capable of supplying up to 14 per cent of total energy requirements, and nearly half of electricity requirements.

There are three nuclear power plants in operation at present, contributing around two per cent of total energy requirements and nearly eight per cent of electricity. A number of other nuclear stations are under construction and in 1979 approval was given for a start on three more. Current plans envisage a total capacity of 11,000 MW by 1987 enabling nuclear power to provide 15 per cent of all energy. However, such has been the rate of growth in the Spanish economy that this might still involve an increase in the amount of oil, as well as coal, used in power stations.

Production and distribution of electricity is carried out by undertakings controlled by provincial or municipal authorities, although industrial interests are involved in the operation of nuclear stations. The operations of individual utilities are co-ordinated by UNESA, an association to which all the main utilities belong.

## ENERGY TRADE

*Net Imports/(Exports) 1973-79*

|  | 1973 | 1974 | 1975 | 1976 | 1977 | 1978 | 1979 |
|---|---|---|---|---|---|---|---|
| Coal (million tonnes) | 3.6 | 3.6 | 4.4 | 5.0 | 4.5 | 3.6 | 4.7 |
| Crude Oil (million tonnes) | 43.0 | 43.7 | 42.0 | 48.5 | 47.6 | 47.4 | 48.4 |
| Oil Products (million tonnes) | (3.3) | (1.8) | (0.9) | (1.2) | (1.2) | 0.2 | 2.4 |
| Natural Gas (000 million M$^3$) | 1.0 | 1.0 | 1.2 | 1.5 | 1.4 | 1.5 | 1.7 |
| Electricity (TWh) | (1.0) | (1.1) | (0.6) | (1.0) | (0.9) | (1.5) | |

Crude oil, almost all of which must be imported, is the major component in Spanish energy trade. Imports have continued to rise throughout the period since 1973. The increase in net imports of oil is all the greater if account is taken of the reduction in exports of finished products from Spanish refineries. Until the mid 1970s refiners were able to use some of their capacity to meet import requirements of northern European countries and the United States. But the extent of this trade has fallen considerably since 1973. Overall Spain's net imports of oil have risen from under 37 million tonnes in 1973 to over 50 million tonnes per annum. Quantities of natural gas and coal have to be imported, and these are expected to rise, particularly in the case of natural gas, as the internal distribution system is developed. In the case of electricity there is regularly a small net export.

*Sources of Imported Crude Oil*

| (percentage) | | |
|---|---|---|
| Middle East | | 73.7 |
|    Saudi Arabia | 35.6 | |
|    Iraq | 12.3 | |
|    United Arab Emirates | 10.3 | |
|    Iran | 9.2 | |
|    Other | 6.3 | |
| | | |
| Africa | | 15.3 |
|    Libya | 11.4 | |
|    Other | 3.9 | |
| | | |
| Western Hemisphere | | 4.4 |
| Other | | 6.6 |
| | | |
| TOTAL | | 100.0 |

Over 70 per cent of Spain's imports of crude oil are from the Middle East, with Saudi Arabia accounting for one-third. Iran and Iraq are also important sources. Lighter crude oils are imported from the United Arab Emirates and from Libya. There is also a relatively large proportion from the Caribbean. These tend to be of the heavier grades, particularly useful to meet high fuel oil requirements. Efforts are being made by the state oil agencies to diversify the availability of crude oil, including increased quantities from Mexico.

## ENERGY POLICIES

In the last year or two the Spanish government has been paying attention to both of the main areas of policy on energy, concerning questions of supply and conservation. A ten-year plan has been adopted and consideration has been given to more definite constraints on consumption.

**Energy Supply**

In 1979 the government adopted a basic long-term energy policy which involves emphasis on indigenous resources, diversification to limit the extent of crude oil imports and increased security of supply. The key element was the approval of a major programme of nuclear power development. This meant completion of a number of power stations in the course of construction and construction of a further three. When all of these plants are in operation, they are expected to meet 15 per cent of energy requirements, and a high proportion of electricity production. Output of coal is intended to be doubled, also requiring a large investment programme because of the long period of declining fortunes in that industry.

The use of natural gas will also be boosted, so as to meet around seven per cent of energy requirements. This may be accomplished through the construction of a gas pipeline from Algeria. Lastly, efforts will be made to prove new reserves of indigenous uranium. But if energy consumption continues to grow at anything like past rates, the economy will still need to import a high proportion of energy in the form of oil. Accepting this situation the government is keen to encourage greater exploration and is making strenuous efforts to conclude supply deals with Libya, Iraq and other oil exporting countries.

**Energy Conservation**

As a country which is still in the process of industrialising, economic growth has been gained only through a rapid rise in energy consumption. Countries such as Spain have thus been caught by the 1973 crisis with unfortunately large commitments in energy-intensive industries. The government has proposed taking a tough line with industry by setting targets for energy consumption, backed up by penalties for exceeding them. At the same time, it provides special tax allowances and loan schemes for investment in energy-saving equipment. Energy audits attract a 50 per cent cost subsidy. The government encourages the development of schemes to use waste heat or waste as a fuel and is supporting demonstration plants based on solar energy.

# Sweden

## KEY ENERGY INDICATORS

| | |
|---|---|
| Energy Consumption | |
| —million tonnes oil equivalent | 51.6 |
| Consumption Per Head | |
| —tonnes oil equivalent | 6.2 |
| —percentage of West European average | 177% |
| Net Energy Imports | 55% |
| Oil Import-Dependence | 100% |

*Sweden is an advanced industrial country with a high standard of living. Taken together with the severity of the climate in winter this gives rise to a very high consumption of energy per head—more than 70 per cent above the West European average. The historic base of energy supply has been hydro-electric power supplemented by the use of wood. But in recent decades economic growth has been founded on oil, although the country lacks indigenous resources of it. As a result it has become highly dependent on imported energy. In principle Sweden is well placed to expand the contribution of nuclear power as it has a number of plants in operation, a well-developed nuclear engineering industry and extensive reserves of uranium. However, the development of nuclear power is subject to fierce political debate and strong opposition on environmental grounds.*

## ENERGY MARKET TRENDS

*Trend of Energy Consumption*

Energy Consumption
+1.6% p.a.

Gross Domestic Product
+1.6% p.a.

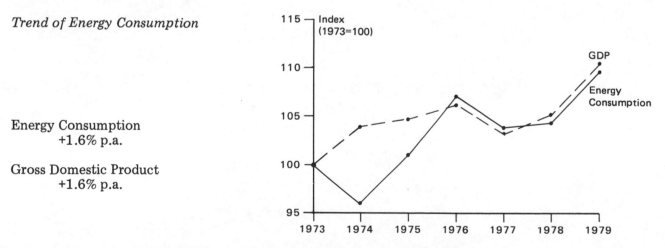

The oil supply crisis of 1973-74 had an immediate impact on energy consumption, which fell back by nearly five per cent in 1974. There was then a resurgence in consumption in 1975 and 1976. Economic growth was not affected severely in 1974 and the impact of the situation in world trade and international energy markets was not felt until 1975. Since that time the country has experienced mixed fortunes in terms of economic growth. Gross Domestic Product has risen at a relatively modest rate, and energy consumption has risen at the same rate. This may be partly attributable to activity levels in energy-intensive industries, which offset gains made in energy conservation.

*Pattern of Energy Supply and Consumption*

| Primary Fuel Supply (percentage) | | Final Consumption (percentage) | |
|---|---|---|---|
| Oil | 53 | Industry | 40 |
| Solid Fuel | 9 | Residential | 37 |
| Natural Gas | – | Transport | 17 |
| Primary Electricity | 38 | Other | 6 |
| TOTAL | 100 | TOTAL | 100 |

Oil provides over half of basic energy supply, although at 53 per cent the proportion is below the average for Western Europe. The balance of primary energy is largely attributable to hydro-electricity and nuclear power. The contribution of hydro-electric plant remains important, but Sweden has a number of major nuclear power plants which supply around 25 per cent of total electricity. A relatively small amount of electricity is generated by oil-fired plant, taking the overall use of electricity to a very high level.

The pattern of final energy consumption is characterised by a high proportion used in the residential sector. This is a reflection of both the climate and a high standard of living. On the other hand industry is a heavy user of energy and Sweden has a number of energy-intensive industries, such as iron and steel and pulp and paper manufacture.

## ENERGY SUPPLY INDUSTRIES

The state has long had a major direct involvement in the electricity supply industry. During the last decade, which has seen the emergence of serious issues affecting the supply of oil, the state has become pro-gressively involved in all phases of this industry, either directly or in support of private Swedish companies. Swedish enterprises, including the consumers' co-operatives, play an important part in the supply of oil products. Industrial companies produce a significant quantity of electricity, for their own use and for public supply. Sweden has no apparent commercial resources of oil or natural gas, but has important uranium reserves to back up its long-term energy situation.

## Oil

*Oil Consumption*

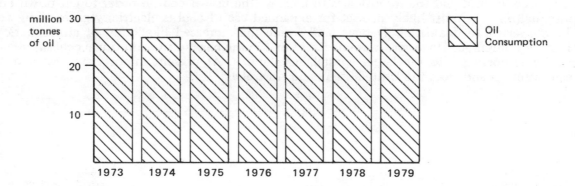

Oil plays a key role in Sweden's energy supply, total consumption of finished products being well over 25 million tonnes per annum. Despite continuing exploration efforts by Olje Prospektering AB, which is a state-owned company, no significant indigenous oil resources have been found. What success there has been is limited to minor oil shows on the island of Gotland.

International oil companies play a major role in the supply of crude oil and finished products from their overseas resources. British Petroleum, Shell, Exxon, Texaco and Gulf have sizeable operations and Mobil is also represented. BP and Shell operate refineries in the Gothenburg area and Gulf's refinery in Denmark is well placed for its Swedish operations. Texaco also acquired refining capacity on the west coast as a result of partnering OK, the cooperatives' oil company, in the construction of a refinery in the early 1970s. This refinery is currently being expanded to a capacity of ten million tonnes per annum, and is the largest in Sweden.

Swedish companies also occupy an important role in the supply of oil. OK is a leading marketer as well as refiner. The Axel Johnson group also has extensive interests, through Nynäs Petroleum, which operates the country's oldest refinery south of Stockholm, and through other importing and distribution companies. Other Swedish distributors, such as ARA, are involved in oil supply, especially the importation of bulk supplies of heating oil and fuel oil.

The state has been taking an increasing direct involvement in oil supply, through the agency of the state oil company Svenska Petroleum. Svenska Petroleum negotiates supply contracts, particularly with oil-exporting countries and will have a share of the capacity in the expanded OK/Texaco refinery. It is also possible that the state company may obtain a share of BP's refinery as part of a long-term crude oil supply arrangement.

## Coal

### Coal Consumption

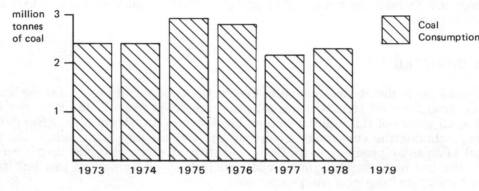

Production of coal in Sweden is negligible. There are deposits of low-grade coal in the south of the country which could be worked and the intention is to increase the use of coal in order to cut down on the need to import fuel oil. The most likely market for expanded use of coal is electricity generation, where plant could be converted to dual-firing systems, and where the increased likelihood of atmospheric pollution could best be minimised. However, it seems likely that in the near future additional coal supplies would be obtained by importing into the larger coastal installations. At present imports are drawn from various European countries and from the United States and Australia.

## Gas

### Gas Production

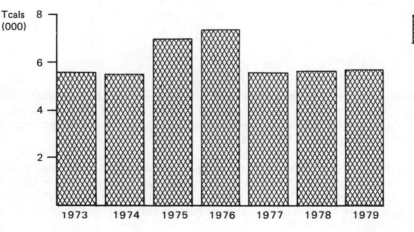

There is currently no system for distributing natural gas in Sweden and the results of the search for hydrocarbon reserves in Sweden have so far been even less promising than for oil. Towns gas has been manufactured at numerous local plants for many years, but its use has declined as a result of the development of new housing schemes and the declining cost-competitiveness of manufactured gas based on increasingly expensive imported oil.

A project exists for establishing a small regional network based on natural gas in the south-west. The expectation is that the area between Halmstad and Trelleborg, which includes Helsingborg and Malmö, will be linked to the proposed distribution system for Denmark, which would utilise that country's recently discovered offshore gas resources. The Danish government's decision to press ahead with this project, which would automatically involve supplying the Copenhagen area, has made the introduction of natural gas into Sweden more likely.

## Electricity

### Electricity Production

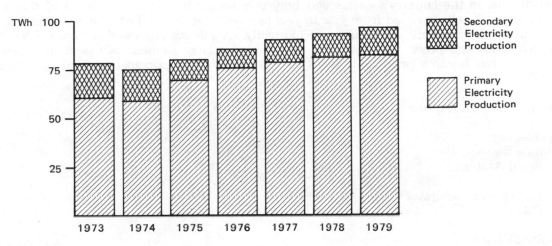

Total production of electricity now exceeds 90 TWh, representing the most significant source of energy for the economy. Of this total well over 60 per cent is produced from the country's extensive hydro-electric resources. But around 25 per cent is provided by the four large nuclear power stations. This means that only some ten per cent is generated by conventional thermal plant, based mainly on the use of heavy fuel oil.

The bulk of electricity supply is provided by a limited number of public undertakings and industrial companies, often participating in various combinations in particular major plants. A key role is also played by the state agency Vattenfallsverk (Water Falls Board), the name of which derives from the historic importance of hydro-electric power, although today the agency is preoccupied with the development of nuclear plant. The other leading public undertaking is Sydkraft AB, which is owned by five local authorities and the consumers' co-operative organisation Kooperativa Förbundet. Major private producers include Gullspångs Kraft AB, Krångede AB, Stora Kopparbergs Bergslags AB and AB Svarthalsforsen, which is owned by the Stockholm city council. All of these generate at least 4 TWh per annum. In the case of some of these energy-intensive industrial consumers, production of electricity for the surrounding region is integrated with production for their own use.

Nuclear power stations are being developed at four locations. The first unit came into operation in 1972 at Oskarshamn. Subsequently plant has been built at Barsebäck, near Malmö, at Ringhals, south of Gothenburg and at Forsmark, to the north of Stockholm. Total capacity of the four stations, comprising 12 units, is 9,500 MW. Vattenfallsverk and Sydkraft are solely responsible for the Ringhals and Barsebäck stations respectively. These two organisations are also leading participants in the consortia owning the Forsmark and Oskarshamm stations.

**ENERGY TRADE**

*Net Import/(Exports) 1973-79*

|                              | 1973 | 1974 | 1975 | 1976 | 1977  | 1978  | 1979 |
|------------------------------|------|------|------|------|-------|-------|------|
| Coal (million tonnes)        | 2.5  | 3.0  | 2.7  | 3.0  | 2.1   | 1.9   | 2.6  |
| Crude Oil (million tonnes)   | 10.6 | 10.0 | 12.3 | 13.4 | 14.2  | 15.6  | 16.0 |
| Oil Products (million tonnes)| 17.2 | 17.8 | 16.6 | 15.2 | 14.1  | 9.7   | 12.4 |
| Electricity (TWh)            | 0.7  | 2.9  | 0.9  | 2.1  | (1.9) | (1.0) | 1.1  |

Sweden is dependent on imports for all of its oil requirements. Since 1973 the total level of net imports has been around 28 million tonnes in most years, but there has been a marked change in the composition of imports. In 1973 over 60 per cent of oil imports were as crude oil, and the balance as finished products. But by 1978 these proportions had been reversed as domestic refining capacity was increased and utilised at a higher rate in order to reduce the overall cost of oil imports.

The use of coal in the country's energy economy is quite limited, but virtually all of this requirement is imported. Quantities have varied from year to year as a result of the level of activity in the industrial sector, as coal is used either directly by industry or indirectly after being processed for coke. The country's firm base of hydro-electric power, to which has been added a large element of base-load nuclear power, has meant that it has become practicable to export electricity. The principal flow of exports is usually to Denmark.

*Sources of Crude Oil Imports*

| (percentage)         |      |       |
|----------------------|------|-------|
| Middle East          |      | 49.1  |
|   Saudi Arabia       | 30.6 |       |
|   Iran               | 8.1  |       |
|   United Arab Emirates | 7.0  |       |
|   Other              | 3.4  |       |
|                      |      |       |
| United Kingdom       |      | 25.4  |
|                      |      |       |
| Africa               |      | 12.3  |
|   Nigeria            | 8.7  |       |
|   Other              | 3.6  |       |
|                      |      |       |
| Eastern Europe       |      | 9.1   |
| Other                |      | 4.1   |
|                      |      |       |
| TOTAL                |      | 100.0 |

With the development of North Sea oil reserves the United Kingdom has become a leading source of crude oil imports. Middle East countries nevertheless account for nearly 50 per cent of the total, a high proportion coming from that region's principal producer Saudi Arabia. But other sources are also drawn upon. The use of crude oil from the United Arab Emirates, to which must be added a further 12 per cent from African countries, testifies to the requirement for light low sulphur crude oil in order to meet stringent product specifications. The Soviet Union exports about 700,000 tonnes per annum of crude oil to Sweden.

Sweden's extensive imports of oil products are brought in from all the main refining centres of Western Europe and the Western Hemisphere. The practice of purchasing large quantities on the international market also draws in cargoes from Middle East and African oil-exporting countries. Substantial contracts for product imports, mainly heating and fuel oils, from the Soviet Union exist, and this country is in fact the largest individual source of imports, accounting for over 20 per cent of the total. The United Kingdom is the next largest source, supplying upwards of 15 per cent.

## ENERGY POLICIES

The state has for some time been involved in the consumer impact of the energy industries. There are stringent controls on pollution and the Price and Cartel Office has taken a close interest in prices of oil products. Developments in the world energy scene have drawn the state into more direct concern with the supply of imported energy and have led to the establishment of a wide-ranging programme of expenditure on research and development and the application of a variety of energy conservation measures. The overall aim of Sweden's energy policy is to stabilise energy consumption by 1990.

### Energy Supply

One principal objective is to reduce the country's dependence on oil as an energy form in view of the poor prospects for any indigenous production. Alternatively the state agency is seeking a direct stake in oil production resources, particularly in the North Sea. Diversification to use a greater proportion of coal is accepted, although this is nevertheless likely to be imported. The main form of energy which could continue to be expanded is nuclear power, and further units are awaiting completion. Over the last two years however the role of nuclear power has been a key political issue and this has not yet been resolved, despite the holding of a referendum on the subject in March 1980.

However, a great deal of effort is being devoted to alternative forms of energy and to energy conservation. The current three-year programme of research and development (1978-81) envisages expenditure of 842 million kronor, more than double the amount under the previous three-year programme. Within the total programme work on applying renewable resources, notably wind and biomass, figure prominently, and attention is being paid to the potential of Sweden's other indigenous energy resource, peat.

### Conservation

There are in force a number of schemes to encourage energy conservation. Grants of up to 35 per cent for conservation investment in buildings and industrial processes are made and up to 55 per cent is obtainable for demonstration projects in either of these fields. The 35 per cent grant is applicable to developments making use of combined heat and power schemes and those which utilise waste heat. This will complement existing work being done in the energy supply industries and by local authority undertakings to increase the role of district heating, such as through longer distance transmission of heat.

The current research and development programme places a high priority on energy conservation. Principal programme areas cover industrial processes, transportation and buildings. The ability of industry to reduce specific rates of energy consumption are important in certain energy-intensive industries, where additional capacity has to be sanctioned by the government. Energy conservation in buildings is also important in Sweden, where the residential sector absorbs a high proportion of final energy and many units are oil-fired. The objective of policy in this field, which is implemented by local authorities, is to reduce energy consumption in housing by an average of 3.5 TWh per annum over the decade 1978-88.

### Environment

There are strict controls on environmental pollution of all kinds in Sweden. Regulations are implemented by the National Swedish Environment Protection Board. Energy industries are particularly affected by anti-pollution measures. Sweden has set high standards for emission of sulphur dioxide and for content of lead-alkyl in motor gasoline. Environmental protection also affects the circumstances in which the mining of coal and uranium could take place.

# Switzerland

## KEY ENERGY INDICATORS

Energy Consumption
  —million tonnes oil equivalent                          23.7
Consumption Per Head
     —tonnes oil equivalent                        3.7
     —percentage of West European average    105%
Net Energy Imports                            60%
Oil Import-Dependence                       100%

*Switzerland has a high standard of living and corresponding demands for energy because of its climate. As a result its consumption of energy per head is above the West European average. Its energy economy rests on primary electricity, of which it is a net exporter, and oil, for which it is entirely dependent on imports. This means that overall Switzerland is highly dependent on imported energy. After wide-ranging deliberations an advisory commission has provided a comprehensive survey of the outlook for the Swiss energy economy. However, it remains to be seen whether market incentives and indirect measures taken by the federal government will suffice to make an impression on existing trends in consumption, or whether more direct action is called for, necessitating some loss of power by the cantons.*

## ENERGY MARKET TRENDS

*Trend of Energy Consumption*

Energy Consumption
  +0.2% p.a.

Gross Domestic Product
  −0.7% p.a.

In the period since 1973 the Swiss economy has been slow to recover. By 1979 Gross Domestic Product was still showing a net decline compared with 1973. However, the average standard of living has not followed this path, as the financial standing of the country has been reflected in a rising exchange rate. This has meant lower real costs for imports, amongst which energy is prominent. As a result, energy consumption, which is particularly high in the residential and transport sectors, has increased.

*Pattern of Energy Supply and Consumption*

| Primary Fuel Supply (percentage) | | Final Consumption (percentage) | |
|---|---|---|---|
| Oil | 55 | Industry | 23 |
| Solid Fuel | 2 | Residential | 43 |
| Natural Gas | 3 | Transport | 25 |
| Primary Electricity | 40 | Other | 9 |
| TOTAL | 100 | TOTAL | 100 |

Hydro-electric power has formed the basis for development of the Swiss economy. But growth in recent times has been fuelled by oil, which has been the cheapest available on world markets and the easiest to transport to Switzerland. The role of hydro-electricity remains important, but of greater significance in producing electricity nowadays is the growing capacity of the country's nuclear power stations. At present coal and natural gas contribute relatively little to total energy input, but the share of both, particularly of the latter, is expected to rise.

The high level of personal living standards is reflected by the very high proportion of final energy consumed in the residential sector. At 43 per cent the share is 55 per cent higher than the European average. The transport sector too consumes a relatively high proportion, 25 per cent as against the European average of less than 21 per cent. The obverse of the situation in the residential and transport sectors is that industry is the smallest energy-consuming sector of the three. Apart from the activities of Alusuisse there are not many energy-intensive operations.

## ENERGY SUPPLY INDUSTRIES

The federal government has very little direct involvement in the energy supply industries. Supply of oil products, whether by importation or from refining crude oil, has been left to private companies, and electricity has continued to be produced and supplied by the established undertakings, which have combined as necessary in consortia to build new plant, whether hydro-electric or nuclear.

## Oil

*Oil Consumption*

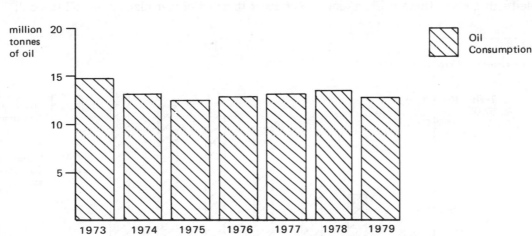

There is no indigenous production of crude oil, and continuing exploration activity has revealed no significant shows of either oil or natural gas. Oil is nevertheless one of the two pillars of the country's energy economy, and is brought in by a combination of pipeline, barge, rail and road systems. Crude oil is piped from the Mediterranean terminal of Genoa through a branch of the Central European Pipeline which carries crude oil to refineries in southern Germany, and through a spur line linked to the South European Pipeline which runs from Marseilles to eastern France and the Rhineland. Basle is the terminal for oil products brought up the Rhine.

There are two refineries in Switzerland. Shell operates a refinery at Neuchâtel, with a capacity of three million tonnes per annum and a consortium of companies, mainly other international companies, operates one at Aigle, at the eastern end of Lake Geneva. The Aigle refinery has a capacity of 3.5 million tonnes per annum. The total capacity for refining crude oil is thus well short of the capability to meet all of the country's requirements, even nominally. In practice, the predominance of requirements for motor gasoline, diesel and heating oil would involve either great investment in sophisticated processing capacity or else expensive movements of surplus products out of the refinery supply areas.

International oil companies play a leading part in the importation and distribution of crude oil and oil products. There are however independent importers whose operations are based on access to bulk market supplies, and on the marketing side independent companies such as Migros, the national supermarket chain, and AVIA, which is a grouping of numerous individual retailers, take important shares of the market.

## Coal

### Coal Consumption

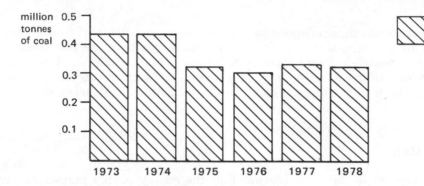

There is no domestic mining industry, and what requirements of coal there are have to be met by import either from Germany or Austria. Imports are of the order of 300,000 tonnes per annum, a combination of hard coal, lignite and coke for industrial purposes. The importation of coal is likely to remain small for the foreseeable future, since there is little scope to convert thermal power plant from oil to coal.

## Gas

### Gas Production and Consumption

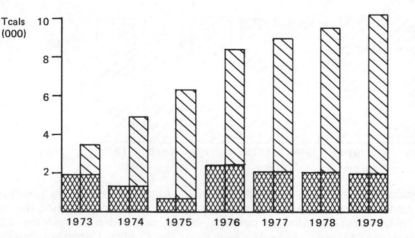

Switzerland has not so far identified any significant indigenous resources of natural gas, and as it is not close to major reserves in neighbouring countries, natural gas has not developed as a main energy carrier. Only limited amounts of gas are manufactured and much of the gas produced is derived from the oil refineries. With increasing concern for energy conservation refinery gas is now usually consumed within the refineries.

However, Switzerland has been developing a network for distributing natural gas based on supplies transported via the West German system from the Netherlands. Although still small in its contribution to the total energy balance, the share of natural gas has been rising more quickly than other energy forms. The gas system of the capital, Bern, has itself been converted to using natural gas and industry is seeking to expand its use of natural gas as a measure of diversification. There are several possibilities open to Switzerland in developing additional natural gas supplies, as trunklines are being developed in Italy, Austria and Southern Germany to draw upon gas from the Soviet Union, North Africa and other sources involving long-haul importation of liquefied natural gas into southern or northern European terminals.

## Electricity

### Electricity Production

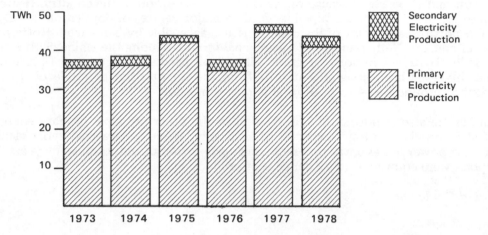

Power for the Swiss economy has traditionally been derived from the country's very large hydro-electric potential. Electricity remains a most important energy form in all sectors of the economy and 80 per cent of electricity is generated by hydro-electric stations. The country has however been developing the use of nuclear power during the 1970s, such that this form of primary electricity accounts for 17 per cent of electricity production. Switzerland has thus met rising demand for electricity from nuclear plant, more so than any other country.

There are three nuclear power stations in operation and a fourth one is expected to be commissioned in 1981. These are all to be found in the northern or north-western part of the country, close to the main centres of electricity demand, as well as to the grids of neighbouring countries. The first station, at Beznau, in Aargau canton, came into operation in 1970 and a second, at Muehleberg, in the Bern area, in 1972. Latest to commission is a 950 megawatt station at Gösgen, in Solothurn canton, and this is to be followed by a 1,000 megawatt station at Leibstadt, also in Aargau. Under construction is a 1,100 megawatt station at Kaiseraugst, which will be the third in Aargau, to come into operation in 1984. At a much earlier stage of construction is Switzerland's sixth station, at Graben, in Bern canton. Eventually these will provide a total capacity of over 5,000 megawatts.

The supply of electricity is in the hands of a limited number of undertakings, representing cantons or major towns and cities. Individual power plants are often owned by consortia of municipalities and production companies. The largest of these are all involved to some extent in the country's nuclear power stations, since each area has had to cater for additional electricity demand from this source. Shares have also been taken by Alusuisse (in Kaiseraugst) and by Swiss Federal Railways (in Leibstadt and Gösgen), two of the country's largest individual consumers of electricity. West German utilities, notably Badenwerk and Rheinisch-Westfälisches Electrizitätswerk, and Electricité de France have interests in the Kaiseraugst plant. On the other hand the extent of cross-border transfers of electricity has led to the involvement of a consortium of Swiss electricity suppliers and the Federal Railways in the Bugey nuclear power plant of Electricité de France.

## ENERGY TRADE

*Net Imports/(Exports) 1973-79*

|                              | 1973  | 1974  | 1975  | 1976  | 1977   | 1978  | 1979 |
|------------------------------|-------|-------|-------|-------|--------|-------|------|
| Coal (million tonnes)        | 0.3   | 0.5   | 0.3   | 0.3   | 0.3    | 0.3   | 0.3  |
| Crude Oil (million tonnes)   | 6.2   | 6.0   | 4.7   | 4.9   | 4.6    | 4.2   | 4.6  |
| Oil Products (million tonnes)| 8.3   | 7.7   | 7.9   | 8.4   | 9.0    | 9.4   | 8.7  |
| Natural Gas (000 million M$^3$) | 0.2 | 0.4 | 0.6   | 0.7   | 0.8    | 0.8   | 0.9  |
| Electricity (TWh)            | (3.5) | (4.0) | (9.7) | (1.9) | (10.2) | (5.2) |      |

Oil is the most significant primary source of energy for Switzerland. It must be entirely imported, which is all the more difficult and expensive because of the land-locked position of the country. However, not only is Switzerland close to, or on, oil or gas pipelines feeding major centres of population in Italy, France and West Germany. The north-western part of the country is also accessible by barge from Rotterdam, the canal network of Belgium and the Netherlands, and oil and coal terminals along the Rhine. This traffic is centred on the port of Basle. Total net imports of crude oil and oil products are around 14 million tonnes per annum. There has however been a significant shift from the importation of crude oil to products, the latter now representing around 65 per cent of total import tonnage.

Coal and natural gas are also imported, but production of the other principal primary energy form, electricity, is such that Switzerland is a net exporter of electricity. Based on low-cost hydro-electric resources and base-load nuclear power net exports represent a high proportion of output in some years. Thus in 1975 and 1977 net exports were equivalent to 22 per cent of production.

*Sources of Imported Crude Oil*

| (percentage)   |      |       |
|----------------|------|-------|
| Middle East    |      | 50.4  |
|   Abu Dhabi    | 31.7 |       |
|   Saudi Arabia | 14.3 |       |
|   Other        | 4.4  |       |
|                |      |       |
| Africa         |      | 43.8  |
|   Libya        | 23.0 |       |
|   Nigeria      | 10.5 |       |
|   Algeria      | 10.3 |       |
|                |      |       |
| Other          |      | 5.8   |
|                |      |       |
| TOTAL          |      | 100.0 |

Middle East sources supply around half of Switzerland's imports of crude oil but African countries are also very important. This is largely a reflection of the pattern of products required in the Swiss market, as well as the proximity of North African sources to the pipeline terminals at Genoa and Marseilles. This unusual pattern of demand is also reflected in the high proportion of crude oil from Abu Dhabi, the largest individual source of crude oil. Abu Dhabi has supplied more than twice the amount imported from Saudi Arabia, although the latter is a much larger exporter of crude oil on world markets.

The most significant source of imported oil products is France, owing to the proximity of the Strasbourg refinery. Belgium, Netherlands and West Germany also provide important quantities of product, either shipped up the Rhine or moved in overland from refineries in southern Germany. Refineries in northern Italy are an additional source of products. The accessibility of some main consuming areas to barge-borne imports from Rotterdam, and the important role played by independent importers and distributors means that up to a quarter of product imports originate from Eastern European sources.

## ENERGY POLICIES

In general the federal government has occupied a very limited role in the development of the energy sector. This is in part a reflection of the constitutional arrangements within the confederation which provides for limited powers at the federal level and the maintenance of strong cantonal powers. But up to the present time private and local initiatives combined with the general international economic standing of the country have kept Switzerland adequately provided with energy. The indications are, however, that greater initiative may be called for from the central government.

**Energy Supply**

In practice electricity supply undertakings have advanced the contribution from nuclear power stations throughout the 1970s. The development of nuclear power was the subject of a referendum in early 1979, the result of which was to accept the contribution made from this source. The federal parliament had previously recommended rejection of the 'anti-nuclear' referendum initiative, although legislation has been tightened to ensure detailed public scrutiny of each individual application for nuclear plant.

At the end of 1978 a commission set up by the federal parliament gave its report and recommendations on the Swiss energy situation. The strategy recommended by the commission envisages an expansion of nuclear capacity to over 6,000 megawatts, some further exploitation of hydro-electric potential, although the extent of this has been estimated as sufficient only to provide 3.5 TWh per annum, and increased use of coal and natural gas. It is particularly the latter which is expected to grow in use, supplanting oil products.

**Conservation**

The federal government has played a very limited direct role in energy conservation. Up to the present its activities have been confined to information and advisory work. Switzerland does however participate in a number of the cooperative programmes coordinated by the International Energy Agency, particularly those concerned with research, development and demonstration projects in solar energy and the use of hydrogen, as well as most of the projects concerned with energy conservation.

# United Kingdom

## KEY ENERGY INDICATORS

Energy Consumption
 million tonnes oil equivalent      220.8
Consumption per head
    —tonnes oil equivalent      4.0
    —percentage of West European average      111%
Net Energy Imports      18%
Oil Import-Dependence      45%

*As a highly industrialised country of 54 million people the United Kingdom is one of the largest individual consumers of energy. But the country is well placed for energy resources by comparison with other European countries. It possesses very large reserves of coal, supporting one of Europe's major mining industries, and exploration in the North Sea and other parts of the continental shelf has revealed an important oil and gas province. The exploitation of these resources has brought about a rapid reduction in the amount of energy which needs to be imported, and the country will be approximately self-sufficient in energy, at least for a short period during the mid 1980s.*

## ENERGY MARKET TRENDS

*Trend of Energy Consumption*

Energy Consumption
 -0.2% p.a.

Gross Domestic Product
 +1.4% p.a.

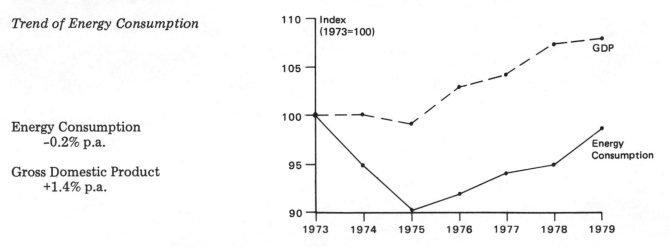

Following the 1973 oil supply crisis United Kingdom energy consumption continued on a downward path for the next two years, not turning upwards until 1976. Since that time there has been limited growth in energy consumption. One factor in this situation is the relative stagnation of the economy, particularly in sectors of industry which are significant consumers of energy. Growth in Gross Domestic Product has come about as much as a result of expansion in energy-producing industries as in energy-consuming manufacturing industries. Furthermore, growth in service sector activity, which is also reflected as growth in GDP statistically, tends to involve less intensive use of energy.

Another factor in evidence over the period since 1973 is the increase in both nominal and real prices of energy. Higher prices, combined with efforts at conservation, at least in some sectors, have brought about a slightly lower rate of growth in energy consumption than would otherwise have been the case.

Also of some importance in giving rise to a lower profile of energy consumption has been the changing mix of fuels used. In the period since 1973 the use of natural gas has risen sharply. Use of this fuel involves less wastage and loss between production and use than in the case of other fuel types. There has thus been an increase in the overall efficiency with which energy has been used.

*Pattern of Energy Supply and Consumption*

| Primary Fuel Supply (percentage) | | Final Consumption (percentage) | |
|---|---|---|---|
| Oil | 44 | Industry | 38 |
| Solid Fuel | 33 | Residential | 26 |
| Natural Gas | 18 | Transport | 23 |
| Primary Electricity | 5 | Other | 13 |
| TOTAL | 100 | TOTAL | 100 |

As in almost all industrial countries oil is the single largest source of energy, but in the United Kingdom the proportion, while approaching half of total primary fuel supply, is lower than in almost all other West European countries. Coal, the resource which fuelled the country's original industrial revolution, has retained a key role in energy supply, accounting for one-third of the total, and providing the bulk of the fuel used in electricity generation. The extensive role of manufactured gas in the energy spectrum has been successfully assumed by natural gas, derived from the country's extensive offshore resources. However, the share is unlikely to rise much further, unless substantial new reserves are discovered in either the United Kingdom or Norwegian sectors of the North Sea.

Consumption of energy by industry and the residential sector is below the average for Western Europe. In the industrial sector this reflects the relative stagnation of manufacturing industry, and, in particular, problems in energy-intensive industries.

In the residential sector the temperate climate and relatively low level of central heating installations combine to give a lower requirement for space heating. On the other hand the transport sector takes an above-average share of final energy consumption, reflecting both the facts of geography and the distribution of population and economic activity, as well as the low proportion of goods traffic carried by rail.

## ENERGY SUPPLY INDUSTRIES

State-controlled enterprises occupy a central role in the supply of energy in the United Kingdom. Production of coal and electricity is the responsibility of nationalised bodies, as is the distribution and sale of gas and electricity. Oil and gas are produced almost entirely by private companies, but gas must be sold to the state corporation for public supply. Distribution of coal and oil products is made by private industry.

## Oil

*Oil Production and Consumption*

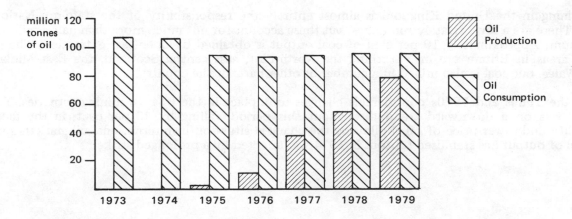

The oil market is dominated by a small number of major companies. This is in part a reflection of the presence of two of the leading international companies, BP and Shell. But Exxon is also long-established as one of the main supply companies. Texaco and Mobil occupy second-rank positions, but Gulf and Chevron have much more limited involvement.

A number of other companies have developed operations in the United Kingdom, although usually with limited geographic coverage. CFP, Petrofina and Continental have built refinery capacity on the east coast of England. Phillips, in partnership with Imperial Chemical Industries, has a refinery on Teesside. ICI is a major consumer of oil products and along with Phillips has become progressively involved in North Sea activity.

For more than 60 years the state has had a major interest in BP. For much of the time this has involved a majority shareholding. The company has not however been used as a state agency. It was only in 1976 that such an entity was set up in the form of the British National Oil Corporation. BNOC has two main areas of involvement in the United Kingdom oil picture. Firstly, private companies involved in offshore production have had to negotiate agreements with BNOC, giving it a 51 per cent participation right. Technically this gives the state company a right to a corresponding amount of production, added to which it also handles the state's royalty crude. In practice a large proportion is sold back to the companies as BNOC currently has no refining or marketing interests. Secondly, BNOC is directly involved in exploration and development offshore. It is a main participant in, and operator for, the Ninian field, to the north-east of Shetland.

The oil industry has changed dramatically over the last few years from being virtually entirely dependent on imports to near self-sufficiency. In 1975 production of North Sea oil was less than two million tonnes. In 1980 production is likely to exceed 80 million tonnes. The leading oil companies are all heavily involved in exploration and production. BP has the Forties Field, which is producing crude oil at the rate of 500,000 barrels per day (equivalent to 25 million tonnes in a year). Shell and Esso are joint holders of the license for the Brent, Cormorant and Dunlin fields, also north-east of Shetland. These fields in total will be capable of a much higher level of output.

## Coal

### Coal Production

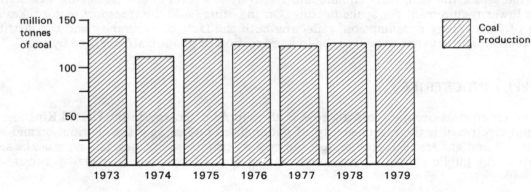

Coal mining in the United Kingdom is almost entirely the responsibility of the state-run National Coal Board. There are a few privately run mines, but these account for not much more than half a million tonnes per annum. Approximately 10 per cent of coal output is obtained by open-cast extraction. The principal mining areas in Britain are in Yorkshire, the North-East, east central Scotland, the East Midlands and South Wales, but coal is also mined in a number of other parts of the country.

During the 1960s and 1970s considerable changes took place in the Board's mining activities. Total production was on a downward trend throughout this period, falling by 30 per cent, in the face of the availability and lower price of oil. Following the changed situation in international oil markets since 1973 the level of output has stabilised (output in 1974 was affected by a prolonged strike).

Mining declined particularly sharply in South Wales and in Ayrshire, in west central Scotland. Employment fell correspondingly as high-cost mines were closed. On the other hand the Board's current programme envisages an expansion of output to at least 150 million tonnes per annum during the 1980s. This programme entails a much larger amount of new production capacity than is apparent as other existing high-cost mines are closed and others are worked out. The Board has very large reserves potentially available to it, in areas which could be mined economically. In some cases, such as at Selby in Yorkshire this involves only an extension to a traditional mining area and development is not difficult to proceed with. But the Board has also proved up reserves in other parts of the country where the time-scale for development is very uncertain.

The coal industry relies very heavily on the use of coal in electricity generation. The generating boards take 70 per cent of production. Commerce, industry and domestic consumers take relatively small amounts. The National Coal Board has devoted much effort therefore to research and development work to make the use of coal by these sectors more convenient and efficient. But the Board is also looking to new markets in the long term with use of coal as a feedstock for chemicals or synthetic natural gas.

## Gas

*Gas Production and Consumption*

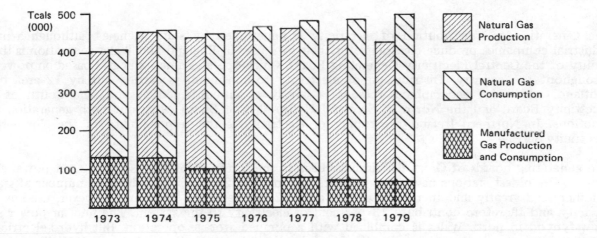

The supply of gas is the responsibility of the nationalised undertaking, British Gas Corporation. With the exception of limited quantities of gas used directly by some producing companies for petrochemical operations, all gas must be sold to the Corporation. The local supply of gas in Northern Ireland is undertaken by municipally run plant based on oil or coal.

The gas industry has undergone a rapid transformation. In a matter of only 10 years the system has been converted completely to the use of natural gas, which is almost entirely derived from the North Sea. In the mid 1960s British Gas Corporation pioneered the ocean transportation of liquefied natural gas from Algeria. This import is likely to continue, but at a modest level as additional supplies for the gas market are expected to come from imported gas from the Norwegian sector of the North Sea. Already, increasing quantities of gas from the Frigg field are being absorbed into the system via the treatment terminal at St Fergus in north-east Scotland.

The conversion from a multitude of localised gas manufacturing plants to the use of natural gas has meant that British Gas Corporation has developed a national supply grid. This is complemented by the existence of several major fields supplying the system and storage terminals for LNG.

British Gas Corporation is involved in exploration and development offshore and is to develop a recent find in Morecambe Bay. Not only is this field close to a concentration of population and industry in north-west England, but it also adds supply capacity at a strategic location in the system.

## Electricity

*Electricity Production*

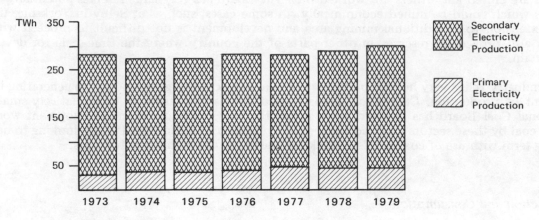

The generation and distribution of electricity is undertaken by state agencies, although a number of industrial companies produce electricity for their own use. In England and Wales generation is the responsibility of the Central Electricity Generating Board, which operates a national grid based on power stations throughout the country. Distribution of electricity to consumers is carried out by 12 area boards. In Scotland, which for geographical reasons is largely a self-contained system, the South of Scotland Electricity Board and the North of Scotland Hydro-Electric Board carry out both generation and sales functions. In Northern Ireland the supply of electricity is the responsibility of the Northern Ireland Electricity Service.

The generating boards of Great Britain have been in the forefront of the use of nuclear power for public supply. The oldest stations have been in operation for over 20 years. But the total number of stations has not increased greatly and there are to date only 12 in operation. They are, however, used as base-load capacity and therefore contribute 13 per cent of electricity to the system. The nuclear power station at Trawsfynydd in north Wales is combined with a pumped storage operation. But hydro-electric power is otherwise almost entirely generated in the Scottish mountains under the aegis of the NSHEB.

Over half of total electricity generating capacity is coal-fired, and a further 20 per cent oil-fired. In fact, as a result of the long lead-times involved in planning and constructing power stations a substantial amount of new oil-fired capacity has been commissioned over the last few years. But new plant is almost certain to be coal-fired or nuclear, and some of the oil-fired plant may remain idle for a long time.

## ENERGY TRADE

*Net Imports/(Exports) 1973-79*

|  | 1973 | 1974 | 1975 | 1976 | 1977 | 1978 | 1979 |
|---|---|---|---|---|---|---|---|
| Coal (million tonnes) | (1.1) | 1.9 | 3.1 | 1.6 | 0.5 | 0.1 | 2.1 |
| Crude Oil (million tonnes) | 112.3 | 111.4 | 89.9 | 86.2 | 54.0 | 43.2 | 20.5 |
| Oil Products (million tonnes) | 0.9 | (0.1) | 1.1 | 5.3 | 1.2 | 1.9 | 1.3 |
| Natural Gas (000 million M³) | 0.8 | 0.7 | 0.9 | 1.1 | 1.8 | 5.2 | 9.4 |

Since 1975 the United Kingdom has progressed towards virtual self-sufficiency in energy. Net imports of crude oil have declined rapidly as production from the North Sea has built up. In 1980 net imports are expected to be well below 20 million tonnes. Net imports of coal and oil products are relatively small.

However imports of natural gas are now on a rising trend as gas from the Frigg field in the Norwegian sector of the North Sea is piped ashore in north-east Scotland. So far the United Kingdom has been considered the most suitable disposal for Norwegian gas despite having to sell to a monopoly buyer. Trade in coal is limited but the Central Electricity Generating Board has plans to install facilities which would enable it to import larger quantities if desired.

*Sources of Imported Crude Oil*

| (percentage) | | |
|---|---|---|
| Middle East | | 83.3 |
| Saudi Arabia | 32.8 | |
| Kuwait | 22.1 | |
| Iraq | 12.3 | |
| Iran | 9.0 | |
| United Arab Emirates | 6.4 | |
| Other | 0.7 | |
| Norway | | 6.7 |
| Eastern Europe | | 3.9 |
| Other | | 6.1 |
| TOTAL | | 100.0 |

Imported crude oil comes overwhelmingly from the Middle East, particularly from Saudi Arabia. Although actual quantities have declined, the relative importance of this area has increased as North Sea production has built up. This is due to the quality of North Sea crude oil which has meant that it has displaced mainly African oil.

Teesside is the landfall for crude oil from the Ekofisk and other fields in the Norwegian sector. The major part of this output is re-exported but some is used as main feedstock at the Teesside refinery of Phillips, the main participant in, and operator of, the Ekofisk field.

## ENERGY POLICIES

Governments have had an important role in the energy sector since the war, following the nationalisation of coal mining and the supply and distribution of gas and electricity. Latterly governments have been obliged to take an active part in offshore oil and gas development on account of the scale of reserves being discovered and developed. This led to the setting up of the British National Oil Corporation and the establishment of a special tax regime covering offshore operations. The award of licenses has also necessitated periodic reviews of policy.

Only in the oil sector is there competition within the industry but the extent of competition has been limited by the market positions and supply networks developed by the major companies. Their position has been reinforced by the geographical situation of the United Kingdom, which requires coastal terminals for access to the market. The main instrument of policy towards market competition is the Monopolies Commission, which has on occasions carried out investigations into oil industry activities. The Commission operates independently of the government but can only look into subjects referred to it.

### Energy Supply

Changes in government, combined with rapid changes in price and availability of fuels in international markets, have meant that policies on licensing and taxation have been seen in turn as restrictive or easy. But in any event the country is now approaching approximate self-sufficiency in oil and gas.

The government has nevertheless maintained support for the general stance of the National Coal Board, namely the development of new, lower cost capacity, albeit with a high investment cost. Coal continues to be favoured at the expense of oil as a principal fuel for electricity generation.

However, the present government has moved towards backing nuclear power as the main source of electricity supply in the future. In order to meet the various objectives of policy this involves supporting both the home-designed Advanced Gas Cooled Reactors and the Pressurised Water Reactor of the United States firm of Westinghouse.

Other 'benign' sources of energy are not considered to have much potential at their current stage of development. The government is however supporting R and D work on the project for a barrage across the Severn estuary.

## Conservation

Pricing has been used as a principal instrument of policy to encourage conservation of energy. In the case of nationalised undertakings pressures towards higher charges have been reinforced by strict financial guidelines laid down by the government. There has however been no movement towards a consistent policy on taxes from a conservation point of view. Duties are levied on oil products, especially motor gasoline and diesel oil, but coal, gas and electricity are free of duty.

The main thrust of conservation policy has been through public awareness campaigns and providing assistance with conservation surveys. In government buildings economy measures have been implemented. Support has been given by the Department of Energy in the form of incentives to industrial firms to re-equip with more efficient boilers and in grants for insulation in housing. Reports on district heating and combined heat and power systems have been prepared, but no action has yet been taken.

# West Germany

## KEY ENERGY INDICATORS

Energy Consumption
    —million tonnes oil equivalent            287.8
Consumption Per Head
    —tonnes oil equivalent                 4.7
    —percentage of West European average    132%
Net Energy Imports                    59%
Oil Import-Dependence              96%

*West Germany is the most populous country in Western Europe, a major industrial country, with a high standard of living. It is therefore the largest consumer of energy in Western Europe, with a per capita consumption more than 30 per cent above the average. A large domestic coal-mining industry has been maintained but oil and natural gas have met rising energy needs. Indigenous oil and gas resources are limited, so that the country is highly dependent on energy imports. Growth of nuclear power has been inhibited by political and environmental constraints and much effort is being put into developing new technologies, especially those which would utilise indigenous coal resources.*

---

## ENERGY MARKET TRENDS

*Trend of Energy Consumption*

Energy Consumption
  +1.3% p.a.

Gross Domestic Product
  +2.4% p.a.

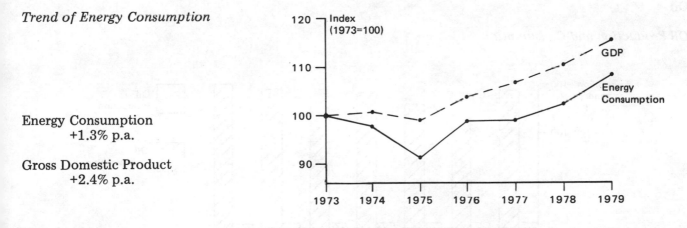

Reaction to the 1973 oil supply crisis led to a fall in energy consumption of two per cent in 1974 and of 6.6 per cent in 1975. This was associated with a check to economic growth in 1974, when Gross Domestic Product rose by less than one per cent, and in 1975, when GDP fell by nearly two per cent. Thereafter the country has enjoyed a continuation of economic growth, albeit not at the same levels as prior to 1973. But this growth has been associated with a reduced rate of energy consumption. In the period since 1973 energy consumption has risen at little more than half the rate of growth of Gross Domestic Product.

*Pattern of Energy Supply and Consumption*

| Primary Fuel Supply (percentage) | | Final Consumption (percentage) | |
|---|---|---|---|
| Oil | 54 | Industry | 37 |
| Solid Fuel | 27 | Residential | 28 |
| Natural Gas | 15 | Transport | 18 |
| Primary Electricity | 4 | Other | 17 |
| TOTAL | 100 | TOTAL | 100 |

Oil represents by far the most important source of energy, and economic growth in West Germany has been fulled largely from this source. Coal output has remained a major provider of energy, although only with extensive financial support which has maintained its markets in electricity generation and industry. However, a rising share of total energy supply has been furnished by natural gas, which has helped to curb the growth in demand for oil. Because of its geographical location West Germany is well placed to link into the East European gas trunkline system fed with Soviet natural gas. Primary electricity production makes only a small contribution to the total balance at this stage. Hydro-electric potential is limited and construction of nuclear power plant has been slow to develop, although the country is well equipped to build and operate such plants.

The pattern of final energy consumption shows that the shares of industry, residential use and transport are at, or not much below, average levels for Western Europe. However, consumption in commerce and public services is well above-average. Here, as well as in the residential sector, use of energy for space heating is a major factor. In the economy as a whole space heating is estimated to take up 40 per cent of final energy consumption. As a result, the government's research and development programme treats this area as a high priority, with particular attention being paid to use of district heating and solar energy.

## ENERGY SUPPLY INDUSTRIES

Successive governments in the Federal Republic have applied the principles of laissez-faire to the energy industries as far as practicable, in common with the approach to the industrial and commercial sectors. This has led to a situation in which there is considerable competition between fuels and a diversity of sources of supply have been established, encouraged by the country's geographical position. The government is however inevitably drawn into the operations of the sector, not only because of the need to ensure adequate energy supply but also to monitor the activities of utilities operating under monopoly supply conditions.

## Oil

*Oil Production and Consumption*

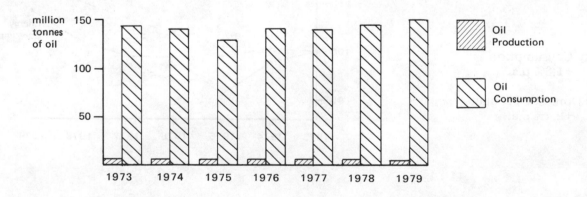

Indigenous production of crude oil is now less than five million tonnes per annum, having fallen steadily from the peak level of nearly 8 million tonnes in the mid 1960s. Production is obtained almost entirely from fields in the North German Plain. So far no significant traces of oil have been found offshore, and the total area of the North Sea falling under West German jurisdiction is quite small. Both in the North Sea and in other parts of the world exploration by German companies, including affiliates of foreign companies, is carried out by the DEMINEX consortium.

With domestic production amounting to less than five per cent of the country's oil requirements West Germany has become reliant on international supply arrangements. The policy of laissez-faire adopted by successive Federal governments has been applied as much to the energy sector as to the rest of industry and commerce. This is evident in the strong representation of the international oil companies and the role played by independent distributors and importers, which have been protected by the strong competition laws designed to prevent excessive vertical and horizontal integration by companies. Exxon, Shell, BP, Texaco and Mobil all have major operations in refining and marketing and other international oil companies such as Occidental and Continental have also become established in the market.

Domestically owned interests in the sector are now concentrated in VEBA OEL which has refining capacity of 23 million tonnes per annum, controls several leading distributors of fuels and has a share in the country's leading motor gasoline retailer ARAL. VEBA also holds a majority share in DEMINEX, through which it obtains crude oil from the Thistle field in the UK sector of the North Sea.

## Coal

*Coal Production and Consumption*

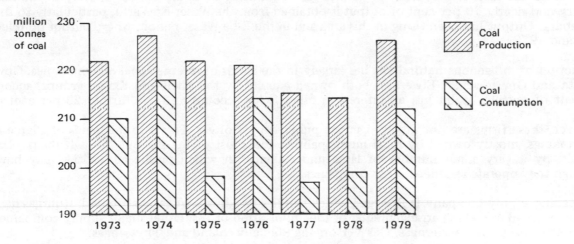

The West German coal-mining industry is the largest in Europe in terms of tonnage produced. There is important production of both hard coal and lignite. Output of the latter is over 120 million tonnes per annum and has been on a rising trend. Output of hard coal on the other hand has declined to around 90 million tonnes per annum. The reason for this divergence is the great difference in the cost of production, as lignite is mined by open-cast operation, whereas hard coal is obtained by deep mining, often in old or difficult pits. The difference is such as to render lignite competitive as a fuel for electricity generation, whereas hard coal requires protection, in the form of import controls and subsidies to users, in order to maintain its markets.

The major area for coal production is in north-west Germany, particularly in the Ruhr and the Rhineland. There are two principal producing companies. Ruhrkohle is responsible for producing over 70 million tonnes per annum of hard coal and coke, and Rheinische Braunkohlenwerke produces 110 million tonnes per annum of lignite. Other important producers of coal are Saarbergwerke, in Saarland, and Bayernwerk, in Bavaria. In all of these companies provincial and local authorities have significant interests, either directly or through electricity supply undertakings.

The electricity utilities form the most important market for coal output. But other industries are also important, particularly the iron and steel sector. Nowadays the commercial and residential sectors take very little of total output, having converted to the use of oil or natural gas.

## Gas

*Gas Production and Consumption*

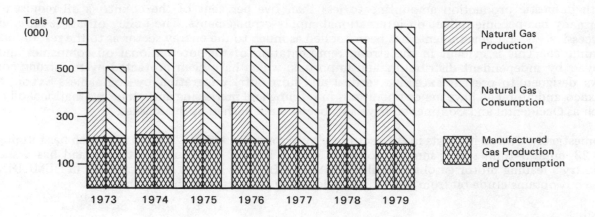

Natural gas has come to assume a growing importance in the West German energy supply pattern. Domestic production of natural gas has more than doubled in the last ten years and is continuing to rise, meeting 37 per cent of the total requirement of natural gas. Producing areas are almost entirely in the north of the country and nearly 70 per cent of output is obtained from the Weser-Ems area, particularly to the south of Oldenburg. Output has been rising in this area and in the Elbe-Weser region, where output doubled between 1976 and 1978.

Production of indigenous natural gas lies largely in the hands of international oil companies. Gewerkschaft Brigitta and Gewerkschaft Elwerath, both owned equally by the Shell and Exxon groups, account for 60 per cent of output. Mobil has an interest in other fields accounting for a further 20 per cent of output.

However, these firms are not involved in the public supply of gas. This is in the hands of a large number of undertakings, mostly owned by local municipalities. But most of the gas put through the public system is handled by a very small number of large undertakings, in which public authorities may have a share, although they operate as independent companies.

The leading supply company is Ruhrgas, which handles two-thirds of gas distributed. Ruhrgas has also been most concerned in making arrangements for the importation of gas. Other major supply companies involved in import projects are Saarferngas, Gas Versorgung Süddeutschland and Thyssengas.

## Electricity

*Electricity Production*

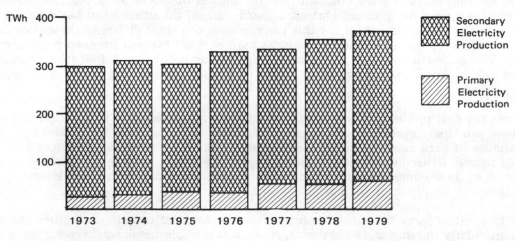

Electricity supply is in the hands of a large number of local undertakings, usually municipally owned. But some 95 per cent of total supply is generated by no more than ten companies. Public authorities have a major interest in the companies, although they operate as independent undertakings. The Federal authorities do not have any participation.

The largest electricity company is Rheinisch-Westfälisches Elektrizitätswerk AG, in which local authorities hold a 56 per cent interest. RWE supplies 40 per cent of total electricity in the Federal Republic, concentrated in the heavily populated and industrialised Rhineland. Other leading electricity supply companies are Vereinigte Elektrizitätswerke Westfalen, Nordwestdeutsche Kraftwerk, Badenwerk, Bayernwerk, Energie-Versorgung Schwaben, Hamburgische Electricitäts-Werke, Isar-Amperwerke and Preussische Elektrizitäts AG. These larger companies are involved in all aspects of electricity generation and supply, including much of the research and development work associated with nuclear power plant. The state is involved in research and development work primarily in so far as safety questions are concerned. Many of the larger industrial companies generate electricity for their own use. This capacity has now been officially called on in order to supplement the public supply companies' capacity. This enables a greater proportion of total energy requirements to be met from indigenous resources and also helps to postpone the time when further generating capacity is required. Currently, construction of either nuclear or coal-fired capacity is constrained by environmental questions.

## ENERGY TRADE

*Net Imports/(Exports) 1973-1979*

|  | 1973 | 1974 | 1975 | 1976 | 1977 | 1978 | 1979 |
|---|---|---|---|---|---|---|---|
| Coal (million tonnes) | (14.0) | (20.5) | (12.5) | (10.3) | (10.8) | (17.1) | (13.0) |
| Crude Oil (million tonnes) | 112.7 | 104.5 | 91.9 | 105.3 | 102.5 | 102.5 | 115.5 |
| Oil Products (million tonnes) | 32.1 | 27.6 | 30.7 | 34.1 | 31.5 | 35.8 | 29.6 |
| Natural Gas (000 million $M^3$) | 17.6 | 25.2 | 29.6 | 31.8 | 33.9 | 34.3 | 40.4 |
| Electricity (TWh) | 10.3 | 5.9 | 7.8 | 1.0 | 6.0 | 3.1 | 0.6 |

The Federal Republic has substantial trade in all of the main forms of energy. It is almost entirely dependent on imported crude oil for its refineries, but in addition it has a large net import of oil products which are transported by pipeline or barge, principally from the Rotterdam area. There has developed a natural economic relationship between Rotterdam, as a refining centre and important import terminal, and the major oil consuming area of the Rhineland.

Nearly 70 per cent of the country's requirement for natural gas is imported. Half of this amount is met by the large reserves of natural gas available in the Netherlands and the remaining quantities from a variety of sources. Mainly this comes from the Soviet Union, either directly, or indirectly as a result of a three-way arrangement with Iran—the Iranian gas being exchanged for Soviet supplies. Smaller quantities are imported via the liquefied natural gas terminals at Fos, near Marseilles, and Trieste.

Future increases in the supply of natural gas are not expected to come from the Netherlands, which may indeed reduce supplies in the longer term. Instead the gas supply companies are looking towards additional sources of liquefied natural gas, and both Ruhrgas and Thyssengas are involved in a project to bring in substantial quantities of LNG via a terminal in the Netherlands in the late 1980s.

*Sources of Imported Crude Oil*

| (percentage) | | |
|---|---|---|
| Middle East | | 37.0 |
| Saudi Arabia | 15.6 | |
| Iran | 10.1 | |
| United Arab Emirates | 6.6 | |
| Other | 4.7 | |
| Africa | | 37.5 |
| Libya | 15.6 | |
| Nigeria | 12.7 | |
| Algeria | 8.5 | |
| Other | 0.7 | |
| United Kingdom | | 10.5 |
| Eastern Europe | | 5.8 |
| Other | | 9.2 |
| TOTAL | | 100.0 |

The Middle East is the most significant area of supply for imported crude oil, and this significance increases if account is taken of the sources of crude oil for the large quantities of products imported. However, West Germany absorbs large quantities of African crude oil and is one of the principal destinations for North Sea oil. A particularly high proportion of such oil has to be used in order to meet the low sulphur content required in oil products in the West German market. Oil products are imported from a number of countries. The Netherlands is by far the most important, accounting for some 40 per cent, and East European sources account for over 20 per cent.

## ENERGY POLICIES

In general Federal government policy has been to rely on private companies, whether domestic or foreign, and the individual supply undertakings to meet the country's energy needs. However in some areas legislation plays an important role and Federal agencies are correspondingly active.

### Energy Supply

In years when there was a ready supply of oil on international markets the government's laissez-faire policy meant that West Germany benefited from competitively priced products. Increasing problems in the supply of oil has led to concern on the part of the government to retain significant domestically owned operations and step up the search for access to crude oil reserves. Thus it has encouraged the consolidation of German oil activities in VEBA and supported the activities of DEMINEX.

External events have also increased the justification for supporting the level of coal production, which has been achieved through import controls and various financial measures. The expansion of natural gas imports, in particular from the Soviet Union, must also be underwritten by the government's policies.

The government's role in research and development tends to be confined to safety aspects and much of the work on new processes is left to individual companies. The current federal programme for research and development 1977-80 involves expenditure of over DM6.5 billion of which 70 per cent is attributable to nuclear safety and waste management problems.

### Conservation

The policy of free market pricing should mean that prices have a significant impact in terms of conservation, in contrast with the period up to 1974 when a ready supply of energy encouraged consumption. However, the levels of international oil prices has been undermined by the relatively buoyant exchange rate for the Mark.

Specific measures have been adopted to enforce lower levels of energy consumption, mainly in respect of permitted temperature levels in public places. Speed restrictions have been in force, although not as yet applied to the motorways.

With market prices in force the government has not levied any taxes as a means towards conservation. Specific duties on oil products have been in effect for many years, either in order to raise revenue or to protect domestic coal production.

### Environment

The Federal government has established tight restrictions on pollution which have an impact on all types of energy. Most significant are controls on the emission of sulphur dioxide, affecting the investment costs of electricity generating capacity and prospects for coal gasification, and involving tight specifications on oil products and the scope for burning coal. West Germany has also been one of the leading countries in trying to reduce the amount of lead alkyl in motor gasoline.

# Part Three:
# Energy Organisations

# International

## INTER-GOVERNMENTAL AUTHORITIES AND AGENCIES

### COMMISSION OF THE EUROPEAN COMMUNITIES

*Address:* 200 Rue de la Loi, B-1049 Bruxelles, Belgium
Telephone (02) 735 00 40  Telex 21877

The Commission is the central administrative and policy-formulating body of the European Communities. It is concerned with the whole range of economic and social matters, including trade restrictions, commercial practices, competition, pricing and taxation.

Specific energy matters are usually dealt with by Directorate-General XVII in Brussels, which has sections for: energy-saving and forecasting; coal; oil and natural gas; nuclear energy and other primary sources of electricity. The Commission incorporates responsibilities and activities of the European Atomic Energy Community (EURATOM) and the European Coal and Steel Community.

### INTERNATIONAL ATOMIC ENERGY AGENCY

*Address:* Kärntner Ring 11, PO Box 590, A-1011 Wien, Austria
Telephone (0222) 52 45 11  Telex 112645

The IAEA is a specialised agency of the United Nations concerned with the development of nuclear power for peaceful purposes. Its main objectives are to increase the contribution of atomic energy to peace, health and prosperity throughout the world. A key aspect of its work is the promotion of proper standards of safety and operating procedure for nuclear facilities. This extends to the operation of non-proliferation safeguard arrangements under which research facilities operate in member countries.

### INTERNATIONAL ENERGY AGENCY

*Address:* 2 Rue André Pascal, F-75775 Paris, Cedex 16, France
Telephone (1) 524 82 00

The International Energy Agency (IEA) was established in 1974 as an independent organisation within OECD, specifically to deal with the issues which became apparent as a result of the oil supply crises of 1973-74. Initially these centred on contingency planning in the event of a subsequent sudden shortfall or disruption in crude oil supplies. Latterly, however, questions of general availability of energy and the role of energy conservation have become more important. The IEA carries out analyses of developments in member countries and co-ordinates programmes of energy conservation and research and development of additional energy resources.

Membership of the IEA is similar to that of OECD, but does not include France, Finland, Iceland or Portugal.

### NUCLEAR ENERGY AGENCY

*Address:* 2 Rue André Pascal, F-75775 Paris, Cedex 16, France
Telephone (1) 524 82 00

The Nuclear Energy Agency is a semi-autonomous organisation within the OECD. In addition to OECD members the European Commission also participates in NEA activities.

The main purpose of the NEA is to promote co-operation on safety and regulatory aspects of nuclear development and to assess its future role as contributor to economic progress. The NEA co-ordinates international programmes of R & D and monitors technical and economic aspects of the nuclear fuel cycle.

### ORGANISATION FOR ECONOMIC CO-OPERATION AND DEVELOPMENT

*Address:* 2 Rue André Pascal, F-75775 Paris, Cedex 16, France
Telephone (1) 524 82 00

The OECD is the principal inter-governmental organisation in Western Europe, including also other leading industrial nations in the western world, 24 nations in all. The two principal objectives of OECD are to help member countries promote economic growth, employment and improved standards of living, and, secondly, to promote sound and harmonious development of the world economy and improve the condition of the poorest economies.

In view of the important role of energy in economic development the OECD monitors closely developments in this sphere. In addition two semi-autonomous agencies have been established within the overall structure of OECD: the Nuclear Energy Agency and the International Energy Agency.

## ORGANISATION OF ARAB PETROLEUM EXPORTING COUNTRIES

*Address:* PO Box 20501, Kuwait

OAPEC is an association representing the Arab States within OPEC, the Organisation of Petroleum Exporting Countries. It includes a majority of OPEC members and countries which account for a high proportion of total OPEC reserves and production. Member countries are Algeria, Bahrain, Egypt, Iraq, Kuwait, Libya, Qatar, Saudi Arabia, Syria and the United Arab Emirates.

## ORGANISATION OF PETROLEUM EXPORTING COUNTRIES

*Address:* Obere Donaustrasse 93, A-1020 Wien, Austria
Telephone (0222) 26 55 11   Telex 134474

OPEC was set up in 1960 as an association of states for which the export of petroleum was an important economic activity. Membership is basically open to countries with a substantial net export of crude oil and similar interests to those of existing members. Initial membership comprised Iran, Iraq, Kuwait, Saudi Arabia and Venezuela. Subsequently it has expanded to include Algeria, Ecuador, Gabon, Indonesia, Libya, Nigeria, Qatar and the Union of Arab Emirates.

The main concern of OPEC is co-ordination of policies on the availability and price of crude oil, but it also operates a fund to channel a proportion of member countries' revenues towards poorer developing countries.

## STATISTICAL OFFICE OF THE EUROPEAN COMMUNITIES

*Address:* 5 Rue du Commerce, Boîte 1003, Luxembourg
Telephone 49 00 81   Telex 1325

The Statistical Office is responsible for the collection of statistics relevant to all the functions of the European Commission in Brussels. In the field of energy these include trade, production indicators, energy balances and input-output analyses. Regular statistics are produced on electrical energy, hydrocarbons and coal.

## UNITED NATIONS ECONOMIC COMMISSION FOR EUROPE

*Address:* Palais des Nations, CH-1211, Genève 10, Switzerland
Telephone  (022) 34 60 11   Telex 289696

The Economic Commission for Europe is a regional body under the Economic and Social Council of the United Nations. It provides a forum for all European countries to discuss general economic issues and seeks to provide basic information and analysis about the economic situation of Europe. This includes regular publications of reports and statistics on the coal, gas and electricity industries of member countries.

## ENTERPRISES (INTERNATIONAL ENERGY COMPANIES)

### BRITISH PETROLEUM COMPANY LIMITED

*Address:* Britannic House, Moor Lane, London EC2Y 9BU, England
Telephone (01) 920 8000
*Gross Revenue:* £22,705.7 million (1979)
*Total Assets:* £9,805.0 million
*Energy Sectors:* Oil, gas, coal, uranium, petrochemicals

BP is one of the major international oil companies. From the position of being a key seller of crude oil the group became during the 1970s deficient in crude oil in relation to its product market requirements, despite making significant discoveries of oil in many different parts of the world. BP is involved in intensive exploration activity, including offshore areas in north-west Europe. The company exploited the first major North Sea oil field, Forties.

Although North American operations have become important within the group, the bulk of its refining and marketing activity is centred on Western Europe. Refinery production is around 75 million tonnes per annum. Product output includes feedstock for the group's large-scale petrochemical operations.

While continuing to search for and exploit new oil resources BP has diversified into other energy sectors, acquiring a 25 per cent interest in the West German gas supplier Ruhrgas and building up coal resources worldwide which have made it the eighth largest private producer of coal.

### BURMAH OIL COMPANY

*Address:* Burmah House, Pipers Way, Swindon, Wiltshire SN3 1RE, England
Telephone (0793) 30151   Telex 449225
*Gross Revenue:* £1,086.6 million (1979 excl taxes)
*Total Assets:* £631.5 million
*Energy Sectors:* Oil, gas

Burmah Oil Company is engaged in exploration for oil and gas in many parts of the world. In the North Sea its main interest is an eight per cent share of the Thistle field, but it is involved in exploration in a number of other areas. Product marketing operations exist in several European countries in addition to the United Kingdom. These are primarily engaged in the sale of lubricating oils, under the Castrol brand name, and automotive fuels.

The Burmah group includes international transportation of liquefied natural gas in the Far East, for which it operates a fleet of seven large LNG carriers.

## COMPAGNIE FRANCAISE DES PETROLES

*Address:* 5 Rue Michel-Ange, F-75781 Paris,
    Cedex 16, France
    Telephone (1) 524 46 46  Telex 611992
*Gross Revenue:* F73,586.0 million (1979)
*Total Assets:* F57,400 million
*Energy Sectors:* Oil, gas, uranium, petro-
    chemicals

Compagnie Française des Pétroles (CFP) has developed into an important international company with extensive involvement in exploration, processing and marketing in many parts of the world. The French government has a substantial shareholding with an effective 40 per cent voting right.

CFP has subsidiary companies operating under the TOTAL name in most West European countries. It occupies a prominent position in the North Sea, through participation in consortia which have been successful in a number of areas, including the Ekofisk and Frigg fields.

The group has uranium mining capacity in central France and is engaged in further exploration work. It is also looking to expand its activities into the coal trade, in conjunction with Charbonnages de France.

## ENTE NAZIONALE IDROCARBURI

*Address:* Piazzale Enrico Mattei 1, 00144 Roma,
    Italy
    Telephone (06) 59001  Telex 610082
*Gross Revenue:* $28,518.7 million (1978)
*Total Assets:* $16,154.1 million
*Energy Sectors:* Oil, gas, electricity, uranium,
    petrochemicals

ENI is the Italian state hydrocarbons agency and one of the key industrial groupings in the Italian economy. It has become involved in exploration on a wide scale internationally and has refining or marketing operations in many West European countries. These usually operate under the AGIP name.

ENI subsidiaries are also involved in construction and engineering work associated with energy developments, including refinery construction and pipeline laying.

## ESSO EUROPE INC

*Address:* 50 Stratton Street, London W1, England
    Telephone (01) 493 7030
*Energy Sectors:* Oil, gas

Esso Europe is a company of the Exxon group responsible for the co-ordination of group activities in Europe. Esso subsidiaries are to be found throughout Europe. Esso Europe is not involved in any operational activities itself.

## EXXON CORPORATION

*Address:* 1251 Avenue of the Americas, New
    York, NY-10020, USA
    Telephone (212) 398 3000
*Gross Revenue:* $83,555.5 million (1979)
*Total Assets:* $49,490.0 million
*Energy Sectors:* Oil, gas, coal, uranium, petro-
    chemicals

Exxon is the largest of the major international oil companies with exploration, production, processing and marketing operations throughout the world. It is a participant in Aramco, the key Saudi Arabian production company.

Sales of petroleum products in Europe exceed 100 million tonnes per annum, representing nearly 40 per cent of group total sales. European refineries of the group supply 85 per cent of requirements. Part of the product output goes to feed the group's petrochemical operations.

Exxon subsidiary companies play a leading role in exploration for oil and gas in Europe. In partnership with Shell significant resources are being exploited in the North Sea, including the Brent area complex of oil and gas fields and Dutch natural gas fields.

## GULF OIL CORPORATION

*Address:* PO Box 1166, Pittsburgh,
    Pennsylvania 15230, USA
    Telephone (412) 263 5000
*Gross Revenue:* $25,893 million (1979)
*Total Assets:* $17,265 million
*Energy Sectors:* Oil, gas, coal, uranium, nuclear
    power

Gulf Oil is one of the largest international oil companies, although its operations in Europe are limited by comparison with groups such as BP, Shell and Exxon. Sales of oil products in Europe are approximately 15 million tonnes per annum. The group has nearly 4,000 sales outlets in Europe.

Gulf's crude oil supply operations are based on the transhipment terminal at Bantry Bay in Ireland, from which long-haul crude is moved to refineries in Wales, Denmark and the Netherlands. Total capacity amounts to 18 million tonnes per annum.

## NV KONINKLIJKE NEDERLANDSCHE PETROLEUM MAATSCHAPPIJ

*Address:* 30 Carel van Bylandtlaan, Den Haag, Netherlands
Telephone (070) 77 66 55
*Energy Sectors:* Oil, gas, coal, nuclear power, petrochemicals

Royal Dutch Petroleum Company is a Dutch based company and principal parent company of the Royal Dutch/Shell group. Royal Dutch Petroleum Company holds 60 per cent of the shares in the two holding companies Shell Petroleum NV and Shell Petroleum Company Limited. The two holding companies control the many operating and service companies of the Royal Dutch/Shell group.

## MOBIL CORPORATION

*Address:* 150 East 42nd Street, New York, NY-10017, USA
Telephone (212) 833 4242  Telex 232561
*Gross Revenues:* $48,241 million (1979)
*Total Assets:* $27,506 million
*Energy Sectors:* Oil, gas, petrochemicals

Mobil is one of the leading international oil companies. Total product sales in Europe are over 35 million tonnes per annum, which is around 30 per cent of the group's sales worldwide. The group has important subsidiary companies in the principal markets, backed up by refining capacity of nearly 50 million tonnes per annum. Mobil group companies operate large modern refineries in France, Netherlands, West Germany and the United Kingdom.

Mobil is involved in exploration and development of oil and gas. In the UK sector of the North Sea it operates the Beryl field and in West Germany it has oil and gas production interests.

## MOBIL EUROPE INC

*Address:* Mobil Court, 3 Clements Inn, London WC2A 2EB, England
Telephone (01) 831 7171  Telex 8812411
*Energy Sectors:* Oil, gas

Mobil Europe is a subsidiary company of Mobil Corporation. It is not engaged in operational activities, but occupies a co-ordinating and advisory role for operational Mobil companies in Europe.

## PETROFINA SA

*Address:* Rue de la Loi 33, B-1040 Bruxelles, Belgium
Telephone (02) 513 69 00  Telex 21556
*Gross Revenue:* BF202,648.9 million (1979)
*Total Assets:* BF279,463.5 million
*Energy Sectors:* Oil, gas, petrochemicals

Petrofina is one of the largest Belgian companies and a substantial company in the international oil business. It has marketing operations in most European countries and refinery operations in several of the main markets. Refining activity is backed up by exploration and development activity particularly in the North Sea.

Main involvement is in the Ekofisk complex, where Petrofina holds a 30 per cent share. Also in the southern part of the North Sea the group has a 16 per cent interest in the Hewett gas field. Further north Petrofina has interests of around 30 per cent in several discoveries.

## ROYAL DUTCH/SHELL GROUP

*Addresses:* Shell International Petroleum Co Ltd
Shell Centre, London SE1 7NA, England
Telephone (01) 934 1234  Telex 919651

Shell Internationale Petroleum Mij BV
30 Carel van Bylandtlaan, Den Haag, Netherlands
Telephone (070) 77 66 55
*Gross Revenue:* £34,830.0 million (1979)
*Total Assets:* £18,482.0 million
*Energy Sectors:* Oil, gas, coal, nuclear power, petrochemicals

The Royal Dutch/Shell companies form part of a group owned by the Royal Dutch Petroleum Company and Shell Transport and Trading Company. Activities are carried out worldwide under the 'Shell' name. Of the international oil companies turnover of the Royal Dutch/Shell group is second only to that of Exxon.

Shell produces around 300,000 barrels per day of oil in Europe and is one of the leading firms involved in exploration in the North Sea. Sales of petroleum products in Europe are over 85 million tonnes per annum, including feedstocks made available to the petrochemicals producing subsidiaries of the group. Shell, jointly with Esso, is one of the key producers of natural gas in the Netherlands.

## SHELL TRANSPORT AND TRADING COMPANY LIMITED

*Address:* Shell Centre, London SE1 7NA, England
Telephone (01) 934 1234  Telex 25781 (overseas) 25733 (inland)
*Energy Sectors:* Oil, gas, coal, nuclear power, petrochemicals

Shell Transport and Trading is a British company eith a 40 per cent interest in the two holding companies of the Royal Dutch/Shell group, viz Shell Petroleum NV and Shell Petroleum Company Limited, which in turn own the operational companies of the group.

## STANDARD OIL COMPANY OF CALIFORNIA

*Address:* 225 Bush Street, San Francisco,
   California CA-94104, USA
   Telephone (415) 894 7700
*Gross Revenue:* $30,938.4 million (1979)
*Total Assets:* $18,102.6 million
*Energy Sectors:* Oil, gas, petrochemicals

Standard Oil Company of California is one of the world major international oil companies with operations in all phases of oil and gas production and supply throughout the world. In Europe affiliate companies are involved in exploration, refining and marketing in almost all countries. These include a share in the Ninian field in the UK sector of the North Sea and in Danish oil and gas finds.

Refining and product marketing operations are usually carried on under the Chevron brand name, but also sometimes jointly with Texaco through Caltex companies. The group has a major refinery at Rotterdam supported by the group's extensive crude oil resources. Gross production of crude oil by the group is 3.2 million barrels per day, including a share in the main Saudi Arabian production company Aramco.

## TEXACO INC

*Address:* 200 Westchester Avenue, White
   Plains, New York NY-10650, USA
   Telephone (914) 253 4000
*Gross Revenue:* $38,350.4 million (1979)
*Total Assets:* $22,992.0 million
*Energy Sectors:* Oil, gas,

Texaco is a major international oil company with extensive involvement in exploration, refining and marketing in Western Europe.

The Texaco group is involved in exploration in the North Sea and offshore Spain. It has important refining and marketing interest in the UK, West Germany, the Benelux countries and Sweden, and associated interests in supply facilities, including crude oil and products pipelines.

## PROFESSIONAL INSTITUTIONS AND TRADE ASSOCIATIONS

## ASSOCIATION EUROPEENNE DES GAZ DE PETROLE LIQUEFIES

*Address:* 4 Avenue Hoche, F-75008 Paris, France
   Telephone (1) 227 48 12  Telex 650436
*Energy Sector:* Gas

The European LPG Association represents at European level the interests of distributors of liquefied petroleum gas. Its members are the national industry associations of individual European countries, totalling 16 in all. The main concern of these associations is the setting of codes of practice and standards in distribution and consumption of LPG. The European LPG Association is concerned with European standards and Directives of the European Commission.

## CEPCEO

*Address:* c/o Hobart House, Grosvenor Place,
   London SW1X 7AE, England
   Telephone (01) 235 2020
*Energy Sector:* Coal

CEPCEO is the association of European coal producers. It provides a common voice in dealings with the European Commission and other international and governmental bodies. Analyses of the general energy situation and the coal industry are produced from time to time.

## CIGRE

*Address:* 112 Boulevard Haussmann, F-75008
   Paris, France
   Telephone (1) 522 65 12
*Energy Sector:* Electricity

CIGRE, the International Conference on Large High-Voltage Electric Systems, is an organisation bringing together electricity producers, plant manufacturers and consultants involved in the problems of generation and transmission of high voltage electricity. Conferences are held in alternate years at which a wide range of issues are discussed, building on the work of permanent working groups.

## CIRED

*Address:* IEE Conference Department, Savoy
   Place, London WC2R 0BL, England
   Telephone (01) 240 1871  Telex 261176
*Energy Sector:* Electricity

CIRED is the international Conference on Electricity Distribution. Its main activity is a conference every two years for representatives of all organisations concerned with the distribution of electricity. Twelve European countries are involved in its activity.

## COMETEC-GAZ

*Address:* 4 Avenue Palmerston, B-1040
   Bruxelles, Belgium
   Telephone (02) 230 43 85
*Energy Sector:* Gas

The Comité d'Etudes Economiques de l'Industrie du Gaz consists of representatives of gas industries in Austria, Belgium, Denmark, France, Italy,

Netherlands, Spain, Switzerland, West Germany and the UK, and is concerned with economic and commercial issues of general interest. It provides a common voice for the industry in relation to international organisations.

## CONCAWE

*Address:* van Hogenhoucklaan 60, 2596 TE,
  Den Haag, Netherlands
  Telephone (070) 24 50 35
*Energy Sector:* Oil

CONCAWE is an organisation set up by the leading oil companies in Western Europe to provide a forum for the industry's general interests in environmental pollution questions, and to represent the industry's position on these issues. CONCAWE collates information on the extent of pollution arising from the oil industry's activities, the costs and other implications of reducing pollution and the state of anti-pollution measures.

## INTERNATIONAL COLLOQUIUM ON GAS MARKETING

*Address:* 23 Rue Philibert Delorme,
  F-75840 Paris, France
  Telephone (1) 766 52 62
*Energy Sector:* Gas

The Colloquium is a forum for representatives of national gas marketers to discuss all aspects of marketing. The gas industries of Austria, Belgium, Denmark, France, Italy, Netherlands, Portugal, Spain, Switzerland, West Germany and the UK are represented, along with Canada and the United States. Regular meetings are held and standing groups examine inter alia new uses of gas and customer relations.

## INTERNATIONAL GAS UNION

*Address:* Union Internationale de l'Industrie
  du Gaz (UIIG), 62 Rue de Courcelles,
  F-75008 Paris, France
  Telephone (1) 766 03 51
*Energy Sector:* Gas

The IGU is an organisation of the principal gas undertakings in each of 36 member countries. The concern of IGU is to study problems of the industry and its development and to promote communication between technical people in different countries.

Every three years the IGU organises a world congress on gas. At these conferences permanent working groups report on various economic and technical aspects of the gas industry.

## INTERNATIONAL INSTITUTE FOR APPLIED SYSTEMS ANALYSIS

*Address:* Schlossplatz 1, A-2361 Laxenburg,
  Austria
  Telephone (02236) 7115 21 0  Telex 079137
*Energy Sector:* Energy

The IIASA was set up with support from scientific institutions in 17 nations including eastern bloc countries. Its remit is the evaluation of long-term trends and the inter-relationships of systems. A five-year programme analysing the role of energy and long-term supply and demand prospects is being completed in 1980.

## MARCOGAZ

*Address:* 4 Avenue Palmerston, B-1040
  Bruxelles, Belgium
  Telephone (02) 230 43 85
*Energy Sector:* Gas

MARCOGAZ is an association of gas industries of the European Community. It is concerned with issues affecting the gas industry in general, but in particular the standardisation of equipment using gas. In addition MARCOGAZ acts as a representative organisation of the Community gas industries in discussions with the European Commission.

## NORDEL

*Address:* Jämtlandsgatan 99, S-16287 Vällingby,
  Sweden
  Telephone (08) 87 00 00
*Energy Sector:* Electricity

Nordel is an expression of Nordic co-operation in the field of public electricity supply. It is an association of people active in power supply industries in Denmark, Finland, Norway, Sweden and Iceland. It is an advisory and recommendatory organisation promoting co-operation in production, distribution and consumption.

The main continuing activities of Nordel are: to co-ordinate forecasts of electricity consumption in Nordic countries and related proposals for investment; and to monitor operational issues in production and transmission.

## UNIPEDE

*Address:* 39 Avenue de Friedland, F-75008
  Paris 8, France
  Telephone (1) 256 94 00  Telex 660471
*Energy Sector:* Electricity

The Union Internationale des Producteurs et Distributeurs d'Energie is an association including electricity undertakings or their representative organisations. It provides communication between members on all technical and technico-economic aspects of electricity generation and distribution.

## THE URANIUM INSTITUTE
*Address:* New Zealand House, Haymarket,
 London SW1Y 4TE, England
 Telephone (01) 930 5726  Telex 917611
*Energy Sector:* Uranium

The Uranium Institute brings together the various parties concerned with the development of uranium. It includes exploration, development and processing companies, fuel fabricators and electricity generating companies. The Institute provides a co-ordinated view of the uranium industry and an annual assessment of the supply and demand situation.

## WORLD ENERGY CONFERENCE
*Address:* 34 St James's Street, London SW1,
 England
 Telephone (01) 930 3960
*Energy Sector:* Energy

The World Energy Conference takes place every four years. At these conferences the full range of technical and economic aspects of energy development and use are considered. There is a permanent secretariat and organising committees in many countries work to prepare material for the conferences. Proceedings are published providing a survey of main energy issues.

## WORLD PETROLEUM CONGRESS
*Address:* 61 New Cavendish Street,
 London W1M 8AR, England
 Telephone (01) 636 1004
*Energy Sectors:* Oil, gas

The World Petroleum Congress takes place every four years. These conferences bring together expert opinion and synthesized information on all aspects of the petroleum sector. Work is carried on under a permanent secretariat based in London and the various national committees which are usually centred on industry professional associations in participating countries.

# Great Britain and Ireland

## United Kingdom

### GOVERNMENT DEPARTMENTS AND OFFICIAL AGENCIES

ADVISORY COUNCIL FOR APPLIED
RESEARCH AND DEVELOPMENT
*Address:* Cabinet Office, 70 Whitehall,
London SW1A 2AS
Telephone (01) 233 6139

The Advisory Council for Applied Research and Development (ACARD) was established to provide advice to the government on the state of research and development work in the UK and its application in both the public and private sectors.

ADVISORY COUNCIL ON ENERGY
CONSERVATION
*Address:* Department of Energy, Room 1689,
Thames House South, Millbank,
London SW1P 4QJ
Telephone (01) 211 3222 Telex 918777

The Advisory Council on Energy Conservation was set up in 1974 to provide information and advice to the Secretary of State for Energy on the efficient use of energy. There are working groups dealing with industry and commerce, transport, buildings, general policy and education. Numerous reports have been published identifying the scope for energy conservation and suggesting measures which could be instituted.

ADVISORY COUNCIL ON RESEARCH AND
DEVELOPMENT FOR FUEL AND POWER
*Address:* Department of Energy, Thames House
South, Millbank, London SW1P 4QJ
Telephone (01) 211 3000

ACORD is a specialist advisory group set up by the Department of Energy to examine and advise on the research and development programmes of the nationalised energy industries.

BUILDING RESEARCH ESTABLISHMENT
*Address:* Building Research Station, Garston,
Watford WD2 7JR
Telephone (092 73) 74040

The Building Research Establishment is state-funded and falls within the responsibility of the Department of the Environment. It is concerned with the whole range of technical aspects of buildings, carrying out research and tests on materials and structures. Part of this work deals with energy conservation. The Establishment has also done work on structures and construction techniques relating to offshore, e.g. sea-bed, developments.

DEPARTMENT OF ENERGY
*Address:* Thames House South, Millbank,
London SW1P 4QJ
Telephone (01) 211 3000 Telex 918777

The Department of Energy has wide-ranging responsibilities with policy-making, administrative and operational aspects. It is concerned with policy for all forms of energy, including the development of new sources. It is the sponsoring department for the British Gas Corporation, the National Coal Board, British National Oil Corporation and the Atomic Energy Authority. It also has a general responsibility for the oil industry and the nuclear construction and engineering industries. A detailed interest is taken in offshore oil and gas development, with control of licensing, exploitation and operational and safety procedures.

DEPARTMENT OF THE ENVIRONMENT
*Address:* 2 Marsham Street, London SW1P 3EB
Telephone (01) 212 3434 Telex 22221

The Department of the Environment has the responsibility in England and Wales for questions of land use planning and development, regional economic development and environmental matters. These responsibilities include monitoring and administration of controls on pollution, and the setting of standards in building design and materials.

## HEALTH AND SAFETY COMMISSION
*Address:* Regina House, 259-269 Old Marylebone Road, London NW1 5RR
Telephone (01) 723 1262

The Health and Safety Commission is responsible for administering the provisions of the Health and Safety Executive. The Commission is concerned with the protection of employees and the general public from health hazards arising from substances handled or environmental pollutants.

## NATIONAL ENGINEERING LABORATORY
*Address:* East Kilbride, Glasgow G75 0QU
Telephone (035 52) 20222  Telex 77588

The National Engineering Laboratory has built up extensive facilities for research, development and testing related to offshore engineering work. This work has covered: underwater tools; mooring and propulsion systems; structural testing; measurement of oil and gas flows. The laboratory falls under the general control of the Department of Industry.

## NATIONAL MARITIME INSTITUTE
*Address:* Faggs Road, Feltham, Middlesex TW14 0LQ
Telephone (01) 977 0933  Telex 263118

The Institute, which comes under the Department of Industry, carries out research and development work over a wide range of activities. These include the performance of offshore structures under various wind, wave and current conditions. The Institute has facilities to test new designs of vessels and structures.

## OFFSHORE ENERGY TECHNOLOGY BOARD
*Address:* Department of Energy, Thames House South, Millbank, London SW1P 4QJ
Telephone (01) 211 3000

The OETB was established by the Department of Energy with the specific task of defining the optimal programme for research and development work related to offshore energy exploitation. It is concerned with the efficient use of technology, as well as its economic performance, developing these resources and also the capacity of British Industry to provide the appropriate technology.

## OFFSHORE SUPPLIES OFFICE
*Address:* Alhambra House, 45 Waterloo Street, Glasgow G2 6AS
Telephone (041) 221 8777  Telex 779379

The Offshore Supplies Office is a division of the Department of Energy concerned particularly with encouraging the maximum involvement of British suppliers of products and services required in offshore oil and gas development. It provides information, advice and promotional facilities for British firms, including assistance with developing their potential to take advantage of markets for goods and services overseas.

## SCOTTISH OFFICE
*Address:* New St Andrew's House, St James Centre, Edinburgh EH1 3SX
Telephone (031) 556 8400  Telex 727301

The Scottish Office carries out a wide range of functions which in England and Wales fall under government ministries. Within the Scottish Office the principal departments concerned with energy developments are the Scottish Development Department (SDD) and the Scottish Economic Planning Department (SEPD). The SDD is responsible for general planning matters and environmental protection. The SEPD is responsible for regional development and energy policy within the overall framework for the UK. It also has specific responsibility for the Scottish electricity supply industry and the Scottish Development Agency.

## UNITED KINGDOM ATOMIC ENERGY AUTHORITY
*Address:* 11 Charles II Street, London SW1Y 4QP
Telephone (01) 930 5454  Telex 22565

The UKAEA is a state research and development establishment with responsibilities over the whole range of matters connected with nuclear power development. It has extensive research facilities. The largest of these is the Atomic Energy Research Establishment at Harwell (Oxfordshire). Other important establishments include the Culham Laboratory (Oxfordshire), the centre for research into nuclear fusion, and the Risley Nuclear Power Development Establishment (Cheshire); which is concerned with all stages of reactor component development.

The UKAEA operates two important nuclear facilities. At Dounreay (Highland Region) the Authority has an experimental reactor. This is also the location for work on fast-breeder reactors. At Windscale (Cumbria) it has laboratories, associated with the fuel-reprocessing plant, working on plutonium fuel and radiation products.

## WARREN SPRING LABORATORY

*Address:* Gunnels Wood Lane, Stevenage,
  Herts SG1 2BX
  Telephone (995) 3388  Telex 82250

The Warren Spring Laboratory falls under the responsibility of the Department of Industry. It is concerned with process engineering including chemicals and minerals. Associated with this is work on environmental pollution, and work concerned with materials handling, hydraulic behaviour and oil contamination at sea.

## ENTERPRISES (PUBLIC AND PRIVATE SECTOR COMPANIES)

### BP OIL LIMITED

*Address:* BP House, Victoria Street,
  London SW1E 5NJ
  Telephone (01) 821 2000  Telex 8811151
*Energy Sectors:* Oil, petrochemicals

BP Oil is a subsidiary company of British Petroleum Company, responsible for the refining and marketing activities of the group in the United Kingdom. As a marketer of oil products it is one of the principal suppliers in the UK market. Finished products are obtained almost entirely from the group's oil refineries in the UK, although some products are imported from other group-owned refineries, particularly Rotterdam.

BP Oil operates three major refineries. Largest is that on the Isle of Grain (Kent) which has a throughput capacity of 10.5 million tonnes per annum. At Grangemouth, on the Firth of Forth, the company operates one of the oldest established refineries. This refinery, of 8.6 million tonnes per annum capacity, is associated with an important petrochemical plant and is fed with Forties crude oil via the pipeline from Peterhead and with longer-haul crude oil imported through the deep-water ocean terminal at Finnart, on Loch Long.

The company's other principal refinery is at Llandarcy, in South Wales. This too is supplied by pipeline from the deep-water on Milford Haven, and is partly geared to producing feedstock for the BP Chemicals plant at Baglan Bay. BP Oil also operates the only refinery in Northern Ireland, at Belfast.

### BRITISH GAS CORPORATION

*Address:* Rivermill House, 152 Grosvenor Road,
  London SW1V 3JL
  Telephone (01) 821 1444  Telex 938529
*Gross Revenue:* £2,971.8 million (1979)
*Total Assets:* £2,180.8 million
*Energy Sector:* Gas

British Gas Corporation is a state undertaking with the monopoly for the public supply of gas in Great Britain. It has very extensive operations as gas is an important form of energy in most parts of the country. There are nearly 15 million customers altogether, of which 14.3 million are domestic consumers. Total supply is some 16,000 million therms per annum.

During the last ten years the whole of the public supply system has been converted from towns gas to natural gas. Since the mid 1960s small amounts of liquefied natural gas have been imported from Algeria for peak-shaving purposes. But the discovery of substantial gas resources in the North Sea led to a rapid phasing out of manufactured gas. The Corporation's 138,000 miles of gas mains are fed through a strategic high-pressure grid linking the LNG import terminal, southern North Sea gas, which is landed on the Norfolk coast, and northern North Sea gas which is landed at St Fergus in north-east Scotland.

The northern North Sea area is now the Corporation's principal supply source, including gas from the Norwegian sector for which the UK is a natural market. Two trunk lines are in operation and two more are planned. An additional source of gas, in Morecambe Bay, has been discovered by the Corporation and is to be developed, with landfall at Barrow (Cumbria).

### BRITISH NATIONAL OIL CORPORATION

*Address:* 150 St Vincent Street, Glasgow G2 5LJ
  Telephone (041) 204 2525  Telex 777633
*Gross Revenue:* £3,244.9 million (1979)
*Total Assets:* £968.5 million
*Energy Sector:* Oil

BNOC is the state oil company, set up in 1976 as the vehicle for state involvement in offshore oil operations. It is engaged in exploration and production activity in its own right and is operator for the important Thistle field. But, to date, the more extensive area of BNOC activity has arisen through the Participation Agreements which have been negotiated with private sector companies in the North Sea, and the equity interest which has been automatically accorded to the Corporation in the issue of new exploration licences.

Participation rights in fields in production have led to BNOC having access to a large proportion of North Sea oil, to which is added oil taken by the state as royalty in kind. As BNOC is not involved in downstream activity it has therefore established a large trading operation, either selling participation oil back to private sector companies or handling it on the open market.

### BRITISH NUCLEAR FUELS LIMITED

*Address:* Risley, Warrington WA3 6AS
  Telephone (0925) 35953  Telex 627581
*Gross Revenue:* £237.2 million (1979)
*Total Assets:* £284.7 million
*Energy Sectors:* Uranium, nuclear power

BNFL, formerly the Production Group of the UK Atomic Energy Authority, was incorporated as a private company in 1971, although the UKAEA owns the entire share capital.

The principal activities of BNFL are the provision of nuclear fuels services, including the conversion and enrichment of uranium, the manufacture of uranium or plutonium-based fuels and related fuel cycle services for all types of nuclear power stations, including reprocessing of fuel. BNFL is a participant in the Urenco uranium enrichment group.

BNFL operates two Magnox type nuclear power stations, at Calder Hall (Cumbria) and Chapelcross (Ayrshire) which are linked to the company's reprocessing activity.

## CENTRAL ELECTRICITY GENERATING BOARD
*Address:* Sudbury House, 15 Newgate Street, London EC1A 7AU
Telephone (01) 248 1202  Telex 883141
*Gross Revenue:* £4,047.3 million (1979)
*Total Assets:* £4,236.5 million
*Energy Sector:* Electricity

The CEGB is a state undertaking responsible for all generation of electricity for the public supply system in England and Wales. Output is sold to the 12 Area Boards which distribute electricity to final consumers.

The CEGB operates 131 power stations with a total capacity of more than 56,000 MW. Although the Board has been in the forefront of the commercial use of nuclear power, total nuclear generating capacity is little more than 4,000 MW. The bulk of the Board's capacity is steam plant of which 75 per cent is coal-fired. The CEGB consumes around 75 million tonnes per annum of coal in its power stations. However, the proportion of nuclear capacity which is under construction or planned is much higher.

## COALITE GROUP
*Address:* Buttermilk Lane, PO Box 21, Bolsover, Derbyshire S44 6AB
Telephone (0246) 822281  Telex 54250
*Gross Revenue:* £278.1 million (1979)
*Total Assets:* £63.8 million
*Energy Sectors:* Oil, coal

The principal activities of the Coalite Group are the production of solid smokeless fuel, refining and chemicals manufacture and fuel distribution. It is also involved in warehousing and shipping services and diverse other manufacturing or merchanting activities. Approximately 65 per cent of turnover is attributable to production and distribution of solid fuels, fuel oils and chemicals.

The group operates four plants in Yorkshire and Derbyshire manufacturing smokeless fuel, and an associated plant utilising coal based oil by-products. Both solid fuels and fuel oils are partly distributed by the subsidiary company Charringtons.

## THE ELECTRICITY COUNCIL
*Address:* 30 Millbank, London SW1P 4RD
Telephone (01) 834 2333  Telex 23385
*Gross Revenue:* £5,445.0 million (1979)
*Total Assets:* £6,801.0 million
*Energy Sector:* Electricity

The Electricity Council is a forum in which the general policy of the electricity supply industry in England and Wales is formulated. It is a quasi-federal body, comprising the Chairmen of the 12 Area Electricity Boards, which are themselves appointed by the Secretary of State for Energy, three members of the Central Electricity Generating Board and up to six independent members, also appointed by the Secretary of State.

The Council's special responsibilities lie in finance, investment planning, tariff policy, research and industrial relations. It is also the channel for consultation and advice on behalf of the Electricity distribution industry. Although each of the Area Boards makes an annual report on its activities, the Electricity Council is required to prepare the consolidated report for the distribution sector.

## ESSO PETROLEUM COMPANY LIMITED
*Address:* Esso House, Victoria Street, London SW1E 5JW
Telephone (01) 834 6677  Telex 24942
*Gross Revenue:* £3,112.5 million (1979)
*Total Assets:* £1,754.9 million
*Energy Sectors:* Oil, gas, petrochemicals

Esso Petroleum Company is a wholly owned subsidiary of Exxon Corporation, involved in all aspects of the oil industry in the United Kingdom. It is heavily involved in offshore oil exploitation, is the largest oil refining company in the country and supplies about 20 per cent of all product requirements.

In exploration and development Esso, in partnership with Shell, participates in the Brent, Auk and Cormorant fields east of the Shetlands. Esso Petroleum Company's associate company Esso Chemicals is planning to build an ethylene cracker in Fife based on gas liquids from these fields.

Esso Petroleum operates two of the country's largest refineries. At Fawley, on Southampton Water, it has a refinery of over 18 million tonnes per annum capacity, providing the full range of products, including chemical feedstock. The other refinery, of 15 million tonnes per annum capacity is at Milford Haven, where there are deep-water facilities. Distribution of products from these refineries includes the use of product pipelines, notably those carrying products from South Wales to the Midlands and aviation fuel from Fawley to Heathrow Airport.

## IMPERIAL CHEMICAL INDUSTRIES LIMITED

*Address:* Imperial Chemical House, Millbank,
    London SW1P 4QG
    Telephone (01) 834 4444  Telex 21324
*Gross Revenue:* £5,368.0 million (1979)
*Total Assets:* £4,453.0 million
*Energy Sectors:* Oil, petrochemicals

ICI is one of Europe's leading chemical companies with major petroleum-based operations. The UK accounts for 41 per cent of total sales and other European countries a further 20 per cent.

The centre of ICI's processing and manufacturing operations is Teesside, which has become one of the key petroleum centres of Europe. The company operates several cracking plants producing ethylene from oil components, principally naphtha. Its requirement for feedstock and fuel has led it towards integration upstream in refining and exploration activity.

ICI is joint owner with Phillips Petroleum in a refinery of five million tonnes per annum capacity on Teesside. The refinery is largely geared to meeting the requirements of ICI but other products including motor gasoline and heating oils are produced for direct distribution. ICI also produces a substantial amount of gasoline as a by-product from naphtha-cracking. The Teesside refinery is well placed to use Ekofisk crude oil, but ICI is involved in North Sea exploration and development too, with a share in the production from the Ninian field.

## MOBIL OIL COMPANY LIMITED

*Address:* Mobil House, 54-60 Victoria Street
    London SW1E 6QB
    Telephone (01) 828 9777  Telex 8812411
*Gross Revenue:* £889.0 million (1979)
*Total Assets:* £303.2 million
*Energy Sector:* Oil

Mobil Oil Company is a wholly owned subsidiary of Mobil Corporation of New York, one of the major international oil companies. Mobil Oil is an important refining and marketing company in the UK with a refinery on the Thames estuary. The refinery has a throughput capacity of over eight million tonnes per annum and supplies Mobil Oil's distribution network.

Crude oil for the refinery comes primarily from the Beryl field in the North Sea, which is operated by an associate company of the Mobil group. In order to take full advantage of the quality of the North Sea oil and to meet the company's market for

motor gasoline Mobil Oil is adding a large catalytic cracking complex to its refinery.

## NATIONAL COAL BOARD

*Address:* Hobart House, Grosvenor Place,
    London SW1X 7AE
    Telephone (01) 235 2020  Telex 882161
*Gross Revenue:* £2,989.4 million (1979)
*Total Assets:* £1,733.3 million
*Energy Sector:* Coal

The NCB is a nationalised undertaking producing almost all of the United Kindgom's coal output. The Board operates with a number of Area Boards concerned with deep-mined coal, and the Opencast Executive, which is responsible for opencast working. Total saleable output of the NCB is around 120 million tonnes per annum, of which approximately 14 million tonnes is produced by opencast working.

The mining activities of the NCB are concentrated in the north-east of England, Yorkshire, the East Midlands, South Wales and eastern Scotland. But, the Areas vary considerably in their content of workable reserves and average costs of production. At the same time the NCB has a major programme of investment geared to raising total output.

The NCB has an important research and development programme, the primary objectives of which are to improve the technologies of handling and firing and to establish the commercial viability of the use of coal for producing chemicals and substitute natural gas.

## NORTH OF SCOTLAND HYDRO-ELECTRIC BOARD

*Address:* 16 Rothesay Terrace,
    Edinburgh EH3 7SE
    Telephone (031) 225 1361  Telex 72480
*Gross Revenue:* £172.7 million (1979)
*Total Assets:* £547.8 million
*Energy Sector:* Electricity

The North of Scotland Hydro-Electric Board is an autonomous nationalised authority responsible for generation transmission and sale of electricity in Scotland north of a line between the Firth of Clyde and the Firth of Tay. This area includes the Western Isles and Orkney and Shetland.

Of the Board's total capacity of 2,000 MW, 1,750 MW consists of numerous hydro-electric plants throughout the highlands. A large thermal power station, of 1,320 MW is under construction at Peterhead, north of Aberdeen, and close to the landfall of North Sea oil and gas pipelines. Peterhead will be fired by oil or gas. In island areas the Board operates small turbine plants.

## NORTHERN IRELAND ELECTRICITY SERVICE

*Address:* Danesfort, 120 Malone Road,
Belfast BT9 5MT
Telephone (0232) 661100 Telex 747114
*Gross Revenue:* £165.8 million (1979)
*Total Assets:* £450.8 million
*Energy Sector:* Electricity

The Northern Ireland Electricity Service operates a self-contained electricity production and distribution system in Northern Ireland. It is responsible to the Department of Commerce of the Northern Ireland office.

Total sales of electricity are approximately 5,000 MWh per annum. Of this total 75 per cent is generated at Ballylumford on the Antrim coast near Larne. Other main stations are Coolkeeragh, near Londonderry, and Belfast. A new oil-fired station is being completed at Kilroot, on Belfast Lough. As a result the proportion of oil-fired capacity will rise above 75 per cent but will be under-utilised compared with coal-fired plant.

## SHELL UK LIMITED

*Address:* Shell-Mex House, Strand,
London WC2R 0DX
Telephone (01) 438 3701 Telex 22585
*Gross Revenue:* £3,003.4 million (1979)
*Total Assets:* £2,572.1 million
*Energy Sectors:* Oil, gas, petrochemicals

Shell UK is a subsidiary company of the Royal Dutch/Shell group, and is involved in all phases of the oil industry in the United Kingdom. It is the largest distributor and marketer of oil products and is one of the largest refiners of crude oil, with refineries at several strategic locations around the country. Total capacity of these refineries is 32 million tonnes of crude oil per annum.

The company's largest refinery is at Stanlow, in Cheshire. The refinery has a capacity of 18 million tons per annum and much sophisticated equipment, providing a wide range of products and basic feedstocks for the Group's extensive petrochemical activities in north-west England. Although situated on the river Mersey, the refinery is supplied via an offshore discharge buoy at Amlwch, in Anglesey, where the largest VLCCs can be accommodated. Other principal refineries are at Shellhaven, on the Thames estuary, and at Teesport at the mouth of the river Tees. Shell is a major participant in United Kingdom Oil Pipelines Ltd, which operates a products pipeline enabling the company to supply the Midlands from either Stanlow or Shell-haven.

Shell UK occupies a central role in the development of oil and gas in the North Sea. Operating in partnership with Esso it developed the important Leman Bank and Indefatigable gas fields in the southern part of the North Sea. In the northern sector, to the north-east of Shetland, Shell and Esso are jointly exploiting the large Brent field. Crude oil from Brent, and from other fields in the area, including Cormorant and Dunlin, in which Shell has an interest, is brought ashore at Sullom Voe in Shetland.

## SOUTH OF SCOTLAND ELECTRICITY BOARD

*Address:* Cathcart House, Spean Street,
Glasgow G44 4BE
Telephone (041) 637 7177 Telex 777703
*Gross Revenue:* £463.4 million (1979)
*Total Assets:* £712.6 million
*Energy Sector:* Electricity

The SSEB is a state authority responsible for generation, transmission and sale of electricity in southern Scotland, which includes the bulk of the country's population and economic activity. Total sales of electricity are running at around 19,000 GWh per annum.

The Board operates nuclear, coal and oil-fired power stations and five small hydro-electric plants in Galloway. Total capacity operated by the SSEB is 7,800 MW. Largest station is the coal-fired plant at Longannet in Fife with a capacity of 2,400 MW. Other main coal-fired stations are also in east central Scotland, at Kincardine and Cockenzie. In the western part of the Board's area are principal nuclear and oil-fired stations. respectively at Hunterston (Ayrshire) and Inverkip, on the Clyde. A second nuclear power station, of 1,320 MW initially has been authorised for construction near Dunbar on the east coast. Site work is commencing in 1980.

## TEXACO LIMITED

*Address:* 1 Knightsbridge Green,
London SW1X 7QJ
Telephone: (01) 584 5000 Telex 919430
*Energy Sector:* Oil

Texaco Ltd is a wholly owned subsidiary of the major US-based international oil company Texaco Inc. Texaco's operations in the United Kingdom include exploration, refining, distribution and marketing.

Product supplies originate principally from the Pembroke oil refinery, which has a capacity of nine million tonnes per annum. Distribution of products to main centres of consumption in England is facilitated by the Mainline pipeline running from South Wales to the Midlands and the North West.

In the North Sea, Texaco has an interest in several fields. Principally these are the Tartan field and an extension of the Brent field, but several other discoveries of hydrocarbons have also been made.

## PROFESSIONAL INSTITUTIONS AND TRADE ASSOCIATIONS

### CBMPE
*Address:* 178-202 Great Portland Street,
  London W1N 6DU
  Telephone (01) 637 8841  Telex 27273
*Energy Sectors:* Oil, gas, petrochemicals

The Council of British Manufacturers of Petroleum Equipment is a trade association representing United Kingdom based companies serving the oil, petrochemicals, natural gas and other process industries. It provides a forum for coordinating information on the industry, assistance in market development and representing industry's view to the government and other organisations.

### CHAMBER OF COAL TRADERS
*Address:* Victoria House, Southampton Row,
  London WC1
  Telephone (01) 405 8218
*Energy Sector:* Coal

The Chamber of Coal Traders comprises trade associations representing wholesalers, retailers and exporters of coal. The two principal trade associations are the National Association of Solid Fuel Wholesalers and the Coal Merchants Federation of Great Britain, although in fact most wholesalers are also retailers. There are some 6,000 members of the Federation. Imports of smokeless fuel and anthracite to supplement domestic supplies are handled by wholesalers. There is also a separate grouping for companies who handle export shipments of coal, the British Coal Exporters Federation.

Activities of the Chamber are concerned with the adequacy of supplies of solid fuel and their quality. There is a continuing dialogue with the National Coal Board and the Department of Energy on these matters and EEC developments affecting fuel specifications are also monitored. Also of concern are the arrangements made for stocking and transporting coal and issues affecting bulk road transport.

### INSTITUTE OF ENERGY
*Address:* 18 Devonshire Street, Portland Place,
  London W1N 2AU
  Telephone (01) 580 7124
*Energy Sector:* Energy

The Institute of Energy is a professional body for energy engineers and others concerned with economic aspects of energy production and utilisation. It is an examining body for professional chartered engineers and a member of the Council of Engineering Institutions.

### INSTITUTE OF PETROLEUM
*Address:* 61 New Cavendish Street,
  London W1M 8AR
  Telephone (01) 636 1004  Telex 264380
*Energy Sector:* Oil

The Institute of Petroleum is a professional association of oil industry personnel and others connected with the industry. It is concerned with the science, technology and economics of petroleum and its uses. The Institute provides a forum for discussion and analysis of oil industry matters, provides information about the industry and represents industry views to the government.

### INSTITUTION OF ELECTRICAL ENGINEERS
*Address:* Savoy Place, London WC2R 0BL
  Telephone (01) 240 1871  Telex 261176
*Energy Sector:* Electricity

The Institution of Electrical Engineers is a professional association of engineers in all branches of electrical and electronic engineering, including process control and automated systems.

### INSTITUTION OF GAS ENGINEERS
*Address:* 17 Grosvenor Crescent,
  London SW1X 7ES
  Telephone (01) 245 9811
*Energy Sector:* Gas

The IGE is a professional society for engineers, and a qualifying body for chartered engineers. It is a member of the Council of Engineering Institutions. Membership consists largely of practising engineers within the British gas industry but also includes engineers working in other areas of the industry. The IGE provides a forum, especially through its annual conference, for discussion of technical and economic aspects of gas production, transmission and utilisation.

### INSTITUTION OF MINING ENGINEERS
*Address:* Hobart House, Grosvenor Place,
  London SW1X 7AE
  Telephone (01) 235 3691
*Energy Sector:* Coal

The Institution of Mining Engineers is a professional association of engineers working in coal and minerals mining and in related industrial and service activities.

### INSTITUTION OF NUCLEAR ENGINEERS
*Address:* 1 Penerley Road, London SE6 2LQ
  Telephone (01) 698 1500
*Energy Sector:* Electricity

The Institution of Nuclear Engineers has been established as a professional body representative of engineers working in all areas of the peaceful use of nuclear energy technology. It provides a forum for discussion of issues in nuclear technology and participates in the European Nuclear Society.

## UK OFFSHORE OPERATORS ASSOCIATION
*Address:* Fifth Floor, 192 Sloane Street,
   London SW1X 9RB
   Telephone (01) 235 0762
*Energy Sectors:* Oil, gas

The UKOOA is a' trade association representing companies directly involved in development of offshore oil and gas resources. It was established in order to present a coordinated view by the industry to government on matters of operations, safety, technology, commerce and taxation.

## THE WATT COMMITTEE ON ENERGY LIMITED
*Address:* 75 Knightsbridge, London SW1X 7RB
   Telephone (01) 245 9238
*Energy Sector:* Energy

The Watt Committee is an organisation of 62 member institutions relevant to energy. Its main objects are to promote research, development and other scientific and technological work on energy and to disseminate information about energy for the benefit of the general public.

The Watt Committee draws upon the expertise of members of its component institutions, concentrating on the aspects of winning, conversion, transmission and utilisation of energy in the United Kingdom with a view to promoting public discussion and influencing government policy. It also seeks to identify areas in need of additional research and development work.

# Republic of Ireland

## GOVERNMENT DEPARTMENTS AND OFFICIAL AGENCIES

## DEPARTMENT OF ENERGY
*Address:* Kildare Street, Dublin 2
   Telephone (01) 78 94 11  Telex 4651

The Department of Energy was established in 1980, energy matters previously being handled within the Department of Industry, Commerce and Energy. The Department is responsible for the development of energy policy, particularly the security and adequacy of supplies. Exploration and development licencing is carried out by the Department in conjunction with the Geological Survey of Ireland.

## DEPARTMENT OF THE ENVIRONMENT
*Address:* Custom House, Dublin 1
   Telephone (01) 74 29 61

The Department of the Environment has general responsibility for environmental protection and the setting of standards for environmental pollution. It is assisted in carrying out these functions by the Inter-Departmental Environment Committee and the Environment Council.

## ENVIRONMENT COUNCIL
*Address:* c/o Department of the Environment,
   Custom House, Dublin 1
   Telephone (01) 74 29 61

The Environment Council was set up as an expert body to advise the Minister of the Environment. Its functions are to prepare a national environment policy, to monitor the state of the environment and issue reports on it as necessary.

## INTERDEPARTMENTAL ENVIRONMENT COMMITTEE
*Address:* c/o Department of the Environment,
   Custom House, Dublin 1
   Telephone (01) 74 29 61

The Inter-Departmental Committee was set up in 1974 to coordinate the activities of 13 relevant departments. It has particular responsibilities for assessing the impact of actions proposed by the European Commission and developments at international level. It also provides input to the Environment Council.

## NATIONAL BOARD FOR SCIENCE AND TECHNOLOGY
*Address:* Shelbourne House, Shelbourne Road,
   Dublin 4
   Telephone (01) 68 33 11

The National Board for Science and Technology coordinates the programme of research on a number of energy subjects. These include research on alternative energy sources, solar, wave, tidal and wind power. The Board provides advice on future projects · for research and development work.

## NUCLEAR ENERGY BOARD
*Address:* Lower Hatch Street, Dublin 2
   Telephone (01) 76 43 75  Telex 30610

The Nuclear Energy Board was set up under the Nuclear Energy Act to advise on all matters concerning nuclear power. It is responsible for the regulation and control of the use, transportation and disposal of radioactive materials to ensure the safety of the public and protection of the environment. The Board assesses all proposals for nuclear power development and must prepare and administer the appropriate safety regulations. In the event of construction of a nuclear plant, the Board will be responsible for proper operation and management of it.

## ENTERPRISES (PUBLIC AND PRIVATE SECTOR COMPANIES)

### ALLIANCE AND DUBLIN CONSUMERS' GAS COMPANY

*Address:* D'Olier Street, Dublin 2
　　Telephone (01) 78 71 11
*Gross Revenue:* IR£20.6 million (1979)
*Total Assets:* IR£17.6 million
*Energy Sector:* Gas

Alliance and Dublin is a gas utility established under public statute. In 1979 total sales amounted to 29 million therms. Sales have been on a downward trend since the year of peak sales in 1973 when supply totalled 36 million therms. During the last few years, however, the rate of decline in sales of gas has become much less marked.

At present the company produces gas from naphtha but is actively looking at the possibility of producing gas from liquefied petroleum gas or of changing over to natural gas. Following the development of the Kinsale Head gas field the Irish Gas Board has been asked by the government to examine in detail the possibility of bringing natural gas to the Dublin area.

### CORK GAS COMPANY

*Address:* 71-72 Patrick Street, Cork
　　Telephone (021) 2 52 52
*Gross Revenue:* IR£4.0 million (1979)
*Total Assets:* IR£3.8 million
*Energy Sector:* Gas

The Cork Gas company is a publicly owned distributor of gas in the Cork area. At present it produces gas from naphtha feedstock, which is obtained either from the Whitegate refinery of Irish Refining Company or by direct importation. In the near term the company's gas-making plant is to utilise natural gas from the Kinsale Head field, which it will convert to a lower calorific value for use in the existing distribution system. However, the company will be obliged in due course to distribute the natural gas directly, involving conversion of its distribution facilities and the appliances of its commercial and domestic consumers.

### ELECTRICITY SUPPLY BOARD

*Address:* Lower Fitzwilliam Street, Dublin 2
　　Telephone (01) 76 58 31  Telex 5313
*Gross Revenue:* IR£237.5 million (1979)
*Total Assets:* IR£515.7 million
*Energy Sector:* Electricity

The ESB is a public undertaking responsible for the generation, transmission and distribution of electricity. In 1978-79 total production amounted to 9,600 GWh.

The ESB has a total generating capacity of 2,900 MW of which 1,700 MW is oil-fired. Other main sources of power are 450 MW of peat-fired and 510 MW of hydro-electric plant.

However, given the high rate of utilisation of peat and hydro-electric plant, indigenous sources are of greater significance in terms of output. Future capacity is likely to concentrate on the use of coal and the ESB is seeking permission in principle to build a nuclear power station.

### ESSO EXPLORATION AND PRODUCTION IRELAND INC

*Address:* Block 5, The Centre, Walton-on-Thames, Surrey, England
　　Telephone (093 22) 40331  Telex 917278
*Energy Sectors:* Oil, gas

Esso Exploration and Production is a subsidiary company of Exxon Corporation of New York. It is engaged in exploration and development activity in Irish offshore areas. It is a partner with Marathon in 52 blocks off the south coast of Ireland.

### ESSO TEORANTA

*Address:* Stillorgan, Blackrock, Co Dublin
　　Telephone (01) 88 16 61  Telex 5893
*Gross Revenue:* IR£208.1 million (1979)
*Total Assets:* IR£14.9 million
*Energy Sector:* Oil

Esso Teoranta is a subsidiary company of the Exxon group. Its immediate holding company is Esso Petroleum Company, the refining and marketing company for the United Kingdom.

Esso Teoranta is engaged in refining and marketing in Ireland. It is the largest marketer and as a result is operator of the industry refinery at Whitegate, near Cork. The refinery supplies much of Esso Teoranta's product requirements, but other group refineries in the UK are also important sources.

### IRISH GAS BOARD

*Address:* Little Island, Cork
　　Telephone (021) 50 90 99  Telex 32087
*Energy Sector:* Gas

The Irish Gas Board is a state-owned undertaking set up under the Gas Act of 1976 to handle the acquisition and distribution of natural gas in Ireland. The specific impetus to establish the Board was the development of the Kinsale Head gas field by Marathon Petroleum Ireland.

Initial activities of the Board have been the arrangement of supply contracts with ESB, Nitrigin Eireann Teoranta and other industrial consumers of gas in the Cork area and construction of the necessary pipelines. Future activity is expected to concentrate on use of natural gas in the residential and commercial sectors and the possibility of extending the distribution area.

## IRISH NATIONAL PETROLEUM CORPORATION
*Address:* Harcourt House, Harcourt Street,
   Dublin 2
   Telephone (01) 75 79 11  Telex 4491
*Energy Sector:* Oil

The Irish National Petroleum Corporation is a state oil company, established only in 1979. It has general powers to engage in the supply and distribution of petroleum products. At this stage it does not have any refining capacity.

## IRISH REFINING COMPANY LIMITED
*Address:* Whitegate, Midleton, Co Cork
   Telephone (021) 2 51 44  Telex 6058
·*Energy Sector:* Oil

Irish Refining Company operates the only refinery in the Republic of Ireland, at Whitegate, near Cork. The refining company is owned by the principal marketers of oil products in Ireland, Esso Teoranta, Irish Shell, BP Ireland and Texaco Operations Europe, all subsidiary companies of major international oil companies. Esso Teoranta acts as operator of the refinery.

The Whitegate refinery produces all main oil products but its throughput capacity is less than three million tonnes per annum. This has meant that increasing amounts of products have been imported by participating companies from other group refineries or from international bulk markets.

## IRISH SHELL LIMITED
*Address:* 20-22 Hatch Street, Dublin 2
   Telephone (01) 68 74 11  Telex 5161
*Gross Revenue:* IR£199.6 million (1979)
*Energy Sector:* Oil

Irish Shell is a subsidiary company of Royal Dutch/Shell, and one of the leading marketers of petroleum products in the Republic of Ireland. The major proportion of supplies of finished products is obtained from the industry refinery at Whitegate,

in which Irish Shell has a 24 per cent interest. Additional quantities of products are brought in from other group refineries, particularly those in the UK and Netherlands.

## MARATHON PETROLEUM IRELAND LIMITED
*Address:* Canada House, 65 St Stephen's Green,
   Dublin 2
   Telephone (01) 78 19 55  Telex 4455
*Energy Sectors:* Gas, oil

Marathon Petroleum Ireland is one of the companies most prominent in the field of exploration in Ireland. It is a subsidiary company of Marathon Oil Company of Ohio.

Marathon Petroleum is the only company to have successfully exploited hydrocarbon resources in Irish offshore waters. Its Kinsale Head gas field was brought into production in 1978 and is to supply an average 1,300 million cubic metres per annum of natural gas to the Irish Gas Board.

Marathon holds altogether 49 blocks in the offshore areas to the south and south-east of the country, and is partner with Esso in a further 52 blocks.

## PEAT DEVELOPMENT AUTHORITY
*Address:* 76 Lower Baggot Street, Dublin 2
   Telephone (01) 68 85 55  Telex 30206
*Energy Sector:* Peat

The Peat Development Authority (Bord na Mona) has been in existence since 1946. From its initial responsibilities for draining and developing bogs, its operations have extended to include the sale of peat products. It is engaged in the mechanical production of peat fuel for power stations and also produces peat products for industrial and commercial use.

The Peat Authority operates over an area of 130,000 acres and is developing a further 61,000 acres. Total output from its workings amounts to four million tonnes per annum, two-thirds of which is used by the ESB in its specially equipped power stations.

## PHILLIPS PETROLEUM COMPANY IRELAND
*Address:* Portland House, Stag Place,
   London SW1, England
   Telephone (01) 828 9766  Telex 913101
*Energy Sectors:* Oil, gas

Phillips Petroleum Co Ireland is a subsidiary of Phillips Petroleum of Oklahoma. The Phillips group has been one of the most successful in offshore exploration in north-west Europe and the Irish company has had some significant success in Irish waters. It has a 37.5 per cent interest in four blocks in the Porcupine Trough area to the west of Ireland and has options on nine other blocks. Wells drilled in this area have discovered hydrocarbons, although distance and water depth mean that very large quantities will need to be proved to ensure commercial viability.

## PROFESSIONAL INSTITUTIONS AND TRADE ASSOCIATIONS

### CONFEDERATION OF IRISH INDUSTRY
*Address:* Confederation House, Kildare Street, Dublin 2
Telephone (01) 77 98 01  Telex 4711
*Energy Sectors:* Oil, gas

The Confederation of Irish Industry is a representative organisation for Irish industrial firms. Within the CII there are sections with particular interest in energy matters. The Irish Mining and Exploration Group includes companies holding some 80 per cent of prospecting licences, and includes exploration and operating companies. There is also a group representing suppliers of goods and services for the offshore industry.

### INSTITUTE OF PETROLEUM
*Address:* c/o Bank of Ireland, Lower Baggot Street, Dublin 2
Telephone (01) 78 57 44
*Energy Sector:* Oil

The Institute of Petroleum is a professional association for those engaged in the oil industry. It acts as a forum for the discussion of industry issues and represents industry views to the government. It also sets out agreed standards for operations of the industry.

# Scandinavia

## Denmark

### GOVERNMENT DEPARTMENTS AND OFFICIAL AGENCIES

#### ELEKTRICITETSRÅDET
*Address:* Gothersgade 160, DK-1123
København
Telephone (01) 11 65 82

The Electricity Council is responsible for the general planning and operation of the electricity supply industry in Denmark and the provision of advice to the government on matters affecting the industry. The Council is an administrative body reporting to the Ministeriet for Offentlige Arbejder (Ministry of Public Works). It administers regulations on the operation and management of electricity stations and is concerned with general issues of safety.

#### ENERGIMINISTERIET
*Address:* Strandgade 29, DK-1401 København K
Telephone (01) 57 61 60

The Ministry of Energy was established in late 1979 reflecting the increasing concern of the Danish government in energy matters, decisions to develop oil and gas fields in the Danish sector of the North Sea and the policy of landing natural gas in Denmark, which entails development of a natural gas supply system.

The Ministry was constituted from the energy sections of the Ministry of Industry, and deals with matters of offshore licensing, exploration and development, pricing and energy policy.

#### FORSØGSANLAEG RISØ
*Address:* DK-4000 Roskilde
Telephone (03) 37 1212

The Risø Research Station is a state institute concerned with research and development work relating to the peaceful uses of nuclear energy. It is an official source of advice on issues of safety and security. The station can initiate research and development work on nuclear power and on wider energy issues.

#### INDUSTRIMINISTERIET
*Address:* Slotholmsgade 12, DK-1216
København
Telephone (01) 12 11 97

With the establishment of the Ministry of Energy the Ministry of Industry lost most of its responsibilities in the field of energy. It retains, however, two principal responsibilities: the use of energy in industry, including energy conservation measures and investment in more energy-efficient plant and processes; responsibility for the general activities of the Monopolies Board (Monopoltylsynet).

#### MILJØMINISTERIET
*Address:* Slotholmsgade 12, DK-1216
København K
Telephone (01) 12 76 88

The Ministry of the Environment is concerned with developments in the energy sector from a number of different aspects. Three of its divisions are most closely concerned: the Conservation Division (Fredningsstyrelsen), responsible for the exploitation of natural resources; the Environment Division (Miljøstyrelsen), concerned with pollution of water, pollution in the production and use of energy, product qualities, especially lead alkyl in motor gasoline and suphur content of fuels; the Planning Division (Planstyrelsen), concerned with the use of energy in transport and buildings. The Ministry of the Environment is also generally responsible for questions of nuclear safety and inspection.

## MONOPOLTILSYNET
*Address:* Norregade 49, DK-1165 København
   Telephone (01) 12 19 08

The Monopolies Board is an administrative body under the Ministry of Industry. It is responsible for surveillance and investigation of monopoly situations in industry. The oil industry has been one of the key industries subject to scrutiny by the board.

## ENTERPRISES (PUBLIC AND PRIVATE SECTOR COMPANIES)

### BP OLIE-KOMPAGNIET A/S
*Address:* Amaliegade 3, DK-1294 København K
   Telephone (01) 15 54 55  Telex 15022
*Gross Revenue:* Kr 2031.1 million (1978)
*Energy Sector:* Oil

BP Olie-Kompagniet is a wholly owned subsidiary of the major international oil company British Petroleum Company. It is one of Denmark's leading marketers of oil products, but does not have any refining capacity within the country. The BP group does however operate a refinery at Gothenburg which is well placed for supplying the Danish market. Other products are imported from the group's main export refineries in the United Kingdom and the Benelux countries, or obtained under exchange arrangements from other companies with refineries in Denmark.

### DANSK ESSO A/S
*Address:* Sankt Annae Plads 13, DK-1298
   København K
   Telephone (01) 14 28 90  Telex 27090
*Gross Revenue:* Kr 2867.1 million (1978)
*Total Assets:* Kr 1744.0 million
*Energy Sector:* Oil

Dansk Esso is a wholly-owned subsidiary of the US-based international oil company Exxon. Its operations in Denmark include transportation and refining of crude oil and the distribution and marketing of oil products.

The company operates a refinery at Kalundborg on the north-west coast of Zealand. The refinery has a capacity of 3.5 million tonnes per annum of crude oil. This refinery produces almost all of Dansk Esso's product requirements which amount to around 2.6 million tonnes per annum. This represents a market share of 18 per cent, making Dansk Esso one of the country's largest suppliers of oil.

### DANSK OLIE OG NATURGAS A/S
*Address:* Kristianiagade 8, DK-2100 København
   Telephone (01) 14 28 90  Telex 22461
*Energy Sectors:* Oil, gas

Dansk Olie og Naturgas is a state-owned company which is only now moving into a stage of significant operational activity. It has contracted to purchase natural gas discovered in the Danish sector of the North Sea by the Dansk Undergrund Consortium and develop the necessary trunk pipeline system to distribute the gas. The company has also entered into arrangements with the West German gas supply company Ruhrgas whereby the Danish system will be linked to the main north German gas grid and additional supplies obtained through this channel.

### DANSK SHELL A/S
*Address:* Shellhuset, Kampmannsgade 2,
   DK-1604 København V
   Telephone (01) 12 53 40  Telex 22242
*Gross Revenue:* Kr 4552.5 million (1979)
*Total Assets:* Kr 2346.1 million
*Energy Sector:* Oil

Dansk Shell is a wholly owned subsidiary company of the Royal Dutch/Shell group. It is the leading distributor and marketer of oil products in Denmark. The company's supplies are obtained primarily from the refinery at Fredericia, in southern Jutland. The refinery has a crude oil throughput capacity of three million tonnes per annum. The eastern part of the country, including the major conurbation of Copenhagen, can equally well be supplied from the Gothenburg refinery of Svenska Shell.

### ELEKTRICITETSSELSKABET ISEFJORD-VAERKET INTERESSENTSKAB (IFV)
*Address:* Strandvejen 102, DK-2900 Hellerup
   Telephone (01) 62 71 00  Telex 37500
*Gross Revenue:* Kr 1219.0 million (1978)
*Total Assets:* Kr 2175.9 million
*Energy Sector:* Electricity

IFV is a company set up by three major electricity distributors to provide supplies of power to their supply areas. The distributors are Frederiksberg commune, NESA, which distributes electricity in north-east Zealand, and NVE Svinninge, which supplies north-west Zealand.

IFV operates the key generating stations at Kyndby and Asnaes. Kyndbyvaerket has a capacity of 940 MW and Asnaesvaerket is being expanded to 1400 MW, making it the largest power station in Denmark. IFV is the majority participant in Elkraft, the co-ordinating organisation for electricity supply in eastern Denmark.

ELKRAFT AMBA
*Address:* Parallelvej 19, DK-2800 Lyngby
  Telephone 88 33 88  Telex 37500
*Gross Revenue:* Kr 984.8 million (1978)
*Energy Sector:* Electricity

Elkraft was established in 1978 by the major electricity producers in Zealand, Falster and Lolland, with powers to act for them in the interests of more economic and efficient planning and operation of the public electricity supply system on the eastern side of the Great Belt, as well as handling power exchanges with Sweden and West Germany, which had already previously been done on a co-ordinated basis. Elkraft also has responsibilities for planning the construction and operation of district heating systems.

Participants in Elkraft are Elektricitetsselskabet Isefjordvaerket (IFV), Copenhagen commune, and Sydøstsjaellands Elektricitets A/S (SEAS).

ELSAM
*Address:* DK-7000 Fredericia
  Telephone (05) 56 25 00  Telex 51151
*Gross Revenue:* Kr 1,541.8 million (1979)
*Total Assets:* Kr 719.7
*Energy Sector:* Electricity

ELSAM is a partnership of the public electricity supply undertakings in Funen and Jutland. Its role is the overall co-ordination of operations, planning and investment west of the Great Belt which divides east and west Denmark. Partners in ELSAM are Fynsvaerket, Midtkraft, Nordjyllands Elektricitetsforsyning, Nordkraft, Skaerbaekvaerket, Sønderjyllands Højspaendingsvaerk and Vestkraft.

The major part of ELSAM's turnover consists of electricity and fuel supplies for participating electricity producers, as ELSAM is not intended to make a profit itself. Turnover related to purchased fuel supplies totalled Kr 1,187 million in 1979. Most of the balance represents exchanges of electricity between partners and the networks in Norway, Sweden and Germany. In 1979 15 per cent of ELSAM's load was met by imports.

ELSAM is responsible for initiating research and development activity on behalf of its partners. This includes currently studies on nuclear power, electric heating, district heating and the further conversion of plant to coal-firing.

GULF OIL A/S
*Address:* Kvaesthusgade 3, DK-1003 København K
  Telephone (01) 13 50 21  Telex 27048
*Gross Revenue:* Kr 1,949.0 million (1978)
*Total Assets:* Kr 1,329.2 million
*Energy Sector:* Oil

Gulf Oil A/S is a subsidiary of the United States based international oil company Gulf Oil. In Denmark it is a leading distributor and marketer of oil products. Most of Gulf Oil A/S's product supplies are obtained from the company's refinery at Stigsnaes on the south-west coast of Zealand. Although only capable of taking smaller sized VLCC's crude oil supply for long-haul crude oil is effected by trans-shipment of oil at the deepwater terminal at Bantry Bay on the west coast of Ireland.

HOVEDSTADENS KULIMPORT A/S
*Address:* HC Andersens Boulevard 44-46,
  DK-1553 København V
  Telephone (01) 15 16 44
*Gross Profits:* Kr 20.0 million (1978)
*Total Assets:* Kr 88.3 million
*Energy Sectors:* Oil, coal

Hovedstadens Kulimport is an undependent trading company dealing in oil products and solid fuels. It has interests in shipping, transport and distribution facilities.

KKKK A/S
*Address:* Islands Brygge 22, DK-2300
  København S
  Telephone (01) 57 44 44  Telex 31163
*Gross Revenue:* Kr 214.0 million (1978)
*Total Assets:* Kr 107.8 million
*Energy Sectors:* Oil, coal

Formerly the Københavns Kul og Koks Kompagnie, KKKK A/S carries on import, transport and distribution activities in oil products, particularly motor gasoline, and solid fuels.

KØBENHAVNS BELYSNINGSVAESEN
*Address:* Vognmagergade 8, DK-1149
  København K
  Telephone (01) 12 72 90  Telex 15996
*Energy Sectors:* Electricity, gas, heat

Københavns Belysningsvaesen is a municipal undertaking and one of the largest suppliers and distributors of electricity in Denmark. Electricity sales amount to ten per cent of the national total.

The authority has six power stations producing electricity. There are also a number of plants supplying district heat amounting to some two million teracalories per annum. At Sundby the municipality operates a gas plant sending out around 160 million cubic metres of gas per annum.

MOBIL OIL A/S
*Address:* HC Andersens Boulevard 1, DK-1553
  København V
  Telephone (01) 12 66 33
*Gross Revenue:* Kr 886.1 million (1979)
*Total Assets:* Kr 382.9 million
*Energy Sector:* Oil

Mobil Oil is a wholly owned subsidiary of the major international oil company Mobil Corporation of New York. Mobil Oil's sales of petroleum products total 500,000 cubic metres per annum, equivalent to around seven per cent of the whole market. Products sales are concentrated in automotive fuels and heating oils. The company imports most of its requirements as it does not own refining capacity in Denmark, using the terminal facilities of Nordisk Tanklager A/S at Copenhagen, Fredericia and Ålborg. Mobil Oil is a 50 per cent shareholder in Nordisk Tanklager.

## NESA A/S
*Address:* Strandvejen 102, DK-2900 Hellerup
   Telephone (01) 62 41 41  Telex 37500
*Gross Revenue:* Kr 1,302.5 million (1978)
*Total Assets:* Kr 892.6 million
*Energy Sector:* Electricity

NESA is the largest individual distributor of electricity in Denmark accounting for over 20 per cent of units sold. Its supply area covers north Zealand including parts of the Copenhagen city area. Power supplies for NESA are obtained from IFV, the partnership company which operates two of the country's largest power stations, at Kyndby and Asnaes on the northern and north-western parts of Zealand.

## NORSK HYDRO OLIE A/S
*Address:* Vester Søgade 10, DK-1601
   København V
   Telephone (01) 13 19 09  Telex 19466
*Gross Revenue:* Kr 357.8 million (1979)
*Total Assets:* Kr 180.7 million
*Energy Sector:* Oil

Norsk Hydro Olie is a subsidiary company of the Norwegian state-owned industrial and energy concern Norsk Hydro A/S. The Danish subsidiary is involved in trade in oil products. These are supplied from the parent company's refinery on the west coast of Norway and are underpinned by the group's availability of North Sea crude oil.

## OLIESELSKABET DANMARK AMBA
*Address:* Rådhuspladsen 3, DK-8100 Århus C
   Telephone (06) 12 38 88  Telex 64588
*Gross Revenue:* Kr 528.7 million (1978)
*Total Assets:* Kr 335.0 million
*Energy Sector:* Oil

Olieselskabet Danmark is an associate company of the Swedish oil consumers' co-operative Oljekonsumenternas Forbund. Members of the Danish oil consumers' co-operative include companies, institutions and individual consumers of oil products. Sales to members in 1979 comprised 135,000 cubic metres of motor gasoline and 470,000 cubic metres of heating oil.

## SYDØSTSJAELLANDS ELECTRICITETS A/S
*Address:* Tingvej 7, DK-4690 Haslev
   Telephone (03) 69 27 00  Telex 40234
*Gross Revenue:* Kr 443.2 million (1978)
*Total Assets:* Kr 682.4 million
*Energy Sector:* Electricity

SEAS is the third largest distributor of electricity in Denmark, selling over 1,300 GWh per annum in the southern half of Zealand. SEAS operates two power stations, at Stigsnaes, close to the Gulf Oil refinery, and at Masnedø. The balance of SEAS' electricity requirements are met from the plants at Kyndby and Asnaes operated by IFV, the electricity production partnership of Frederiksberg commune, NESA and NVE.

## TEXACO A/S
*Address:* Holmens Kanal 5, DK-1060
   København K
   Telephone (01) 12 02 11  Telex 19462
*Gross Revenue:* Kr 1,769.5 million (1978)
*Total Assets:* Kr 626.8 million
*Energy Sectors:* Oil, coal

Texaco A/S is a subsidiary company of the major international oil company Texaco Inc. It is a leading marketer of oil products and has subsidiary companies in Denmark involved in coal distribution. Some of the company's installations are capable of handling coal.

Texaco A/S does not have any oil refining capacity in Denmark, but there are associate companies in the Texaco group which operate refineries in Schleswig-Holstein, close to the Jutland border, and on the west coast of Sweden.

## PROFESSIONAL INSTITUTIONS AND TRADE ASSOCIATIONS

## DANATOM
*Address:* Allegade 2, DK-3000 Helsingør
   Telephone (03) 36 00 22
*Energy Sector:* Nuclear power

DANATOM is an independent institution within the Academy of Technical Sciences, set up by electricity companies and other commercial companies with the general remit of analysis and development of nuclear energy in the industrial sector. It also carries out a role of providing general information about nuclear power.

## DANSK ELVAERKERS FORENING
*Address:* Rosenørns Allé 9, DK-1970
   København V
   Telephone (01) 39 01 11
*Energy Sector:* Electricity

The Danish Association of Electricity Supply Undertakings has come to occupy a key role in the electricity supply industry. Since 1978 the Association's position has been reinforced by statute in order to ensure efficient overall co-ordination of electricity production and supply.

Because of the geography of electricity production and consumption, which so far has not necessitated a high-voltage link across the Great Belt, the roles of ELKRAFT and ELSAM remain great, and indeed have gained in importance relative to individual-member undertakings.

## DANSK GASTEKNISK FORENING

*Address:* Strandvejen 72, DK-2900 Hellerup
  Telephone (01) 48 12 00
*Energy Sector:* Gas

The Danish Gas Engineers' Association is a professional organisation which provides a forum for consideration of technical as well as economic and political matters affecting the gas industry. It is an advisory body for technical and safety purposes and a member of the International Gas Union.

## FORENING AF KOMMUNALE ELVAERKER

*Address:* Gyldenløvesgade 11, DK-1600 København
  Telephone (01) 12 27 88
*Energy Sector:* Electricity

The Association of Municipal Electricity Producers is a representative association of local authorities involved in the production and distribution of electricity.

## FORENING AF KOMMUNALE GASVAERKER

*Address:* Gyldenløvesgade 11, DK-1600 København'
  Telephone (01) 12 27 88
*Energy Sector:* Gas

The Association of Municipal Gas Producers is an organisation representing the many authorities involved in local supply of manufactured gas.

## OLIEBRANCHENS FAELLESREPRAESEN-TATION

*Address:* Amaliegade 10, DK-1256 København K
  Telephone (01) 11 30 77
*Energy Sector:* Oil

The Danish Petroleum Industry Association is a trade association representing importers, producers, refiners and wholesalers of oil products. The objective of the Association is to provide information and advice about the oil sector to the government, official bodies and the public, and to contribute to committees and institutions affecting the oil industry. This includes questions of product specifications, standards, safety and environmental matters and other issues of a technical nature.

# Finland

## GOVERNMENT DEPARTMENTS AND OFFICIAL AGENCIES

### KAUPPA- JA TEOLLISUUSMINISTERIÖ

*Address:* Aleksanterinkatu 10, SF-00170
  Helsinki 17
  Telephone (90) 16 01

The principal state authority in the field of energy is the Energy Department (Energiaosasto) of the Ministry of Trade and Industry. It is responsible for: formulation and implementation of general energy policies; support of research and development; planning of energy supply, production and conservation; energy investment; international co-operation; technical aspects of nuclear power; the electricity grid.

Public funds for energy research projects are largely channelled through the Ministry. These constitute a high proportion of the available finance, including finance for research work carried out in private companies. Ministry funds are also given towards product development.

### SISÄASIAINMINISTERIÖ

*Address:* Hallistuskatu 4E, Helsinki
  Telephone (90) 16 01

The Ministry of the Interior is concerned with developments in the energy sector through its responsibilities for environmental matters. The Department of Environmental Protection (Ympäristönsuojeluosasto) deals with water and atmospheric pollution, product qualities and other planning aspects.

## ENTERPRISES (PUBLIC AND PRIVATE SECTOR COMPANIES)

### OY ESSO AB

*Address:* Kuunkehra 1, PL 37, SF-02211 Espoo 21
  Telephone (90) 86 77 1  Telex 124711
*Gross Revenue:* $386.0 million (1978)
*Energy Sector:* Oil

OY ESSO AB is a leading private sector distributor and marketer of oil and petrochemical products. It is a wholly owned subsidiary company of the major United States based international oil company Exxon. Product supplies are obtained almost entirely from the state oil company's refineries at Naantali and Porvoo, which can provide a full range of products.

## HELSINGIN KAUPUNGIN ENERGIALAITOS
*Address:* Kampinkuja 2, PL 469, SF-00101
  Helsinki 10
  Telephone (90) 61 71  Telex 122290
*Gross Revenue:* Mk 785.2 million (1979)
*Total Assets:* Mk 1,527.6 million
*Energy Sectors:* Electricity, gas, heat

The Helsinki Energy Board was formed in 1978 through combining the operations of the electricity and gas works within the city. The municipally owned operation is one of the largest distributors of electricity in Finland, with total turnover of 2,300 GWh and has important operations providing production, transmission and sales of district heat. The connected load for district heat is over 1,800 MW, with sales of 4,700 GWh.

Approximately 90 per cent of the Board's electricity and all of the district heat is produced in plant within the city area. The balance is largely obtained from other producing companies in which the Board holds an interest, including Oulujoki Oy, Kemijoki Oy and, indirectly, Teollisuuden Voima, which has begun to produce electricity from its nuclear power station at Olkiluoto. The Helsinki Energy Board's production of gas amounts to nearly 25 million cubic metres per annum, based on the use of butane as feedstock.

## IMATRAN VOIMA OY
*Address:* Malminkatu 16, PL 138, SF-00101
  Helsinki 10
  Telephone (90) 64 78 11  Telex 124608
*Gross Revenue:* Mk 1,999.0 million (1978)
*Total Assets:* Mk 5,856.9 million
*Energy Sector:* Electricity

Imatran Voima Oy (IVO) is a state-owned undertaking engaged in production and distribution of electricity. It is by far the largest producer of electricity, with output of over 16,000 GWh per annum and its role in distribution is a key one as it operates the national grid system. Its position is reinforced by statute and government policy giving it a dominant role in the planning, development and operation of the country's electricity supply system.

Apart from its own production operations, Imatran Voima has interests in a number of other important producing companies, notably Kemijoki Oy and Oulujoki, which operate hydro-electric plants in the north of the country. Although development of hydro-electric plant has continued, Imatran Voima has become heavily involved in thermal power production. It operates a 345 MW oil-fired station at Naantali and in 1978 completed a 1,000 MW coal-fired station at Inkoo. IVO owns the Loviisa nuclear power station (840 MW) and is a participant in Teollisuuden Voima Oy, which operates the 1,320 MW nuclear station being completed at Okiluoto.

## KEMIJOKI OY
*Address:* Valtakatu 9-11, SF-96100 Rovaniemi 10
  Telephone (991) 14141  Telex 37220
*Energy Sector:* Electricity

Kemijoki is a producer and distributor of electricity, operating in the Kemi river area of northern Finland. Kemijoki operates eight hydro-electric stations which produce some 3,000 GWh per annum. This makes it the largest producer of electricity, aside from the state-owned company Imatran Voima. Only part of Kemijoki's production is distributed in the Kemi area and the net surplus is transferred to other areas of industry and population further south.

## NESTE OY
*Address:* Keilaniementie 1, SF-02150 Espoo 15
  Telephone (90) 45 01  Telex 124641
*Gross Revenue:* Mk 11,572.7 million (1979)
*Total Assets:* Mk 5,219.8 million
*Energy Sectors:* Oil, gas

Neste is the state-owned oil company and the largest industrial enterprise in Finland. It has a monopoly of oil refining and operates two refineries, at Porvoo to the east of Helsinki and at Naantali, to the north of Turku on the south-west coast. The total capacity of these refineries is 15 million tonnes of crude oil per annum.

Distributors and marketers of oil products must buy products from Neste if available. Neste itself owns 50 per cent of two of the leading marketers, E-Öljyt and Kesoil. Nearly 90 per cent of Neste's product output is sold directly or indirectly to the domestic market, but Neste is also refining three million tonnes of crude oil for the Swedish state oil company Svenska Petroleum.

Neste acts as the agency for the importation of natural gas from the Soviet Union. This is brought in via Lappeenranta in south-east Finland. Neste uses some of the gas itself and supplies the rest to industrial companies close to the trunkline.

## POHJOLAN VOIMA OY
*Address:* Isokatu 14, PL 229, SF-90101 Oulu 10
  Telephone (981) 22 44 66  Telex 32250
*Total Assets:* Mk 446.2 million
*Energy Sector:* Electricity

Pohjolan Voima is one of the key producers of electricity in the northern part of Finland where a high proportion of the country's hydro-electric power potential is to be found. The company is itself owned by a group of eight electricity distribution and consuming companies including important industrial enterprises such as Enso-Gutzeit and Rauma-Repola.

Total production capacity is some 900 MW. The important base-load of output comes from hydro-electric plant. The balance is produced at thermal stations, notably the 220 MW oil-fired plant at Kristiina, or alternatively purchased from other undertakings. Total sales of electricity approach 3,000 GWh per annum.

## SÄHKÖNTUOTTAJIEN YHTEISTYÖVALTUUS KUNTA

*Address:* Lönnrotinkatu 4, Helsinki
  Telephone (90) 64 84 35
*Energy Sector:* Electricity

STYV, the Power Producers' Co-ordinating Council was set up in 1974 and is the organisation responsible for development and operation of an efficient electricity supply system in Finland. It is concerned with the general planning of electricity production, the national transmission network, international cable links and joint-operating arrangements. It is also the main channel of advice and information to the government on matters affecting the electricity industry.

STYV consists of Imatran Voima, the state-owned power producer and distributor, and the organisations representing public supply undertakings, (Suomen Sähkölaitosyhdistys) and industrial electricity producers (Teollisuuden Sähköntuottajien Liitto.)

## OY SHELL AB

*Address:* Ulappasaarentie 4, PL 33, SF-00980
  Helsinki 98
  Telephone (90) 31 90 1  Telex 124718
*Gross Revenue:* Mk 2,007.0 million (1979)
*Total Assets:* Mk 792.8 million
*Energy Sector:* Oil

Oy Shell AB is a wholly owned subsidiary company of the Royal Dutch/Shell group. It is only engaged in distribution and marketing operations as its product supplies are almost entirely purchased from the state-owned refining company Neste. Shell is the largest private sector marketer, with sales of 1.6 million tonnes per annum of all petroleum products.

## TEOLLISUUDEN VOIMA OY

*Address:* Kutojantie, SF-02630 Espoo 63
  Telephone (90) 52 35 22  Telex 122065
*Energy Sector:* Electricity

Teollisuuden Voima is a company which has been established to operate the nuclear power station which is nearing completion at Olkiluoto on the west coast of Finland. Ownership of the company lies between 16 major industrial companies, including Enso-Gutzeit and Rauma-Repola, and on the other hand six power companies, including the state-owned Imatran Voima and Pohjolan Voima.

The two power companies have the largest individual shareholdings. Pohjolan Voima owns 15.4 per cent of Teollisuuden Voima and Imatran Voima 13.6 per cent. The state power company does however have a leading role in management of the company by virtue of its control of the national grid and its general responsibilities for electricity supply. Directly or indirectly the state has a 50 per cent interest in the company.

The first 660 MW unit at Olkiluoto was brought into operation in 1979 to be followed by the second unit in 1980. When in full operation Teollisuuden Voima will generate around 20 per cent of the country's electricity requirements.

# PROFESSIONAL INSTITUTIONS AND TRADE ASSOCIATIONS

## ÖLJYALAN KESKUSLIITTO

*Address:* Fabianinkatu 8, SF-00130 Helsinki 13
  Telephone (90) 65 58 31
*Energy Sector:* Oil

The Finnish Petroleum Federation is a trade organisation representing the oil companies operating in Finland. There are 11 member companies altogether, including the state oil company Neste Oy.

The Federation covers all matters of interest to the oil industry. Principally these are concerned with energy policy, commercial economics, environmental issues, technical standards and safety, training, and marketing services for the whole industry. The Federation acts as the link between the industry and government and is represented on numerous public committees.

## SUOMEN ATOMITEKNILLINEN SEURA RY

*Address:* Valtion Teknillinen Tutkimuskeskus,
  Ydinvoimatekniikan Laboratorio,
  Lönnrotinkatu 37, SF-00180 Helsinki 18
*Energy Sector:* Nuclear power

The Finnish Nuclear Society is concerned with the general state of information and understanding about nuclear power, by government, industry, institutions and the general public. In the recent past it has examined the alternatives to nuclear energy, nuclear technology and issues of safety.

## SUOMEN BENSIINIKAUPPIAITTEN LIITO RY

*Address:* Mannerheimintie 40, SF-00100
  Helsinki 10
  Telephone (90) 49 93 48
*Energy Sector:* Oil

The Federation of Finnish Gasoline Marketers is a trade association representing importers, distributors and dealers in the motor fuel trade.

SUOMEN SÄHKÖLAITOSYHDISTYS RY
*Address:* Mannerheimintie 76, PL 100, SF-00260
  Helsinki 26
  Telephone (90) 40 81 88
*Energy Sector:* Electricity

The Finnish Association of Electricity Supply
Undertakings brings together public and private
electricity producers. It is a representative organisation concerned with matters affecting the
management and general development of electricity supply. It provides information and advice
to government and the general public, monitors
activities within the industry and is concerned with
training. It undertakes research and development
work regarding network construction and
operation, and efficient operation of generating
plant. It also provides a consulting service in plant
planning.

# Norway

## GOVERNMENT DEPARTMENTS AND OFFICIAL AGENCIES

INDUSTRIDEPARTEMENTET
*Address:* Akersgaten 42, Oslo 1
  Telephone (02) 11 90 90

The Ministry of Industry has an important interest
in energy developments in Norway. It is concerned
with the supply of energy to industry, the pattern
and efficiency of energy utilisation in industrial
plant and processes, mining activity and onshore
exploration activity. It has particular responsibilities for activities in Svalbard.

The Ministry has a general responsibility for the
activities of two of Norway's major industrial
companies which are involved in energy, as producers and consumers. Norsk Hydro is the country's
largest industrial concern. The Ministry exercises
the state's rights as a 51 per cent shareholder, and
plays a similar role in relation to Årdal og Sunndal
Verk, the leading aluminium producer.

MILJØVERNDEPARTEMENTET
*Address:* Myntgaten 2, Oslo 1
  Telephone (02) 11 90 90

The Ministry of the Environment has a wide range
of responsibilities relevant to energy production
and consumption. It is concerned with local energy
planning matters, the regional economic impact of
major developments, energy conservation,
pollution, alternative energy sources and research
and development work in the energy sector.

NORGES VASSDRAGS- OG
ELEKTRISITETSVESEN
*Address:* Middelthunsgate 29, Oslo 3
  Telephone (02) 46 98 00  Telex 11912

The Norwegian State Watercourse and Electricity
Administration is the government body responsible for the planning, development and management of the country's hydro-electric power
production and associated matters. The NVE falls
under the general control of the Ministry of
Industry.

The NVE has administrative, policy and operational responsibilities. Divisions of the Administration determine overall exploitation of water
resources, the efficiency of the national electricity
supply system and the operation of the many state-
owned electricity production plants.

OLJE- OG ENERGIDEPARTEMENTET
*Address:* Tollbugaten 31, Oslo 2
  Telephone (02) 11 90 90

The Ministry of Petroleum and Energy has responsibilities for the development and implementation
of government policies over the whole range of
energy matters. These responsibilities include
energy supply and pricing, the organisation and
administration of energy research, and research
in relation to the continental shelf. The role of
electricity in the energy economy of the country
and issues of nuclear power policy fall under its
responsibility.

The Ministry is responsible for several key state
energy undertakings, including Statoil, the state oil
and gas development company, and Norsk Olje,
which has been established as a leading oil refining
and marketing company.

OLJEDIREKTORATET
*Address:* Lagårdsveien 80, PB 600, N-4000
  Stavanger
  Telephone (045) 33 160  Telex 33100

The Petroleum Directorate was set up as a self-
contained administration under the general supervision of the Ministry of Oil and Energy to deal
with the government's interest in the important
issues arising from development of offshore oil
and gas resources.

The responsibilities of the Petroleum Directorate
cover licensing, exploration programmes, development programmes, production pricing, safety and
technical standards. On questions of safety and the
work environment for people in offshore exploration and development the Directorate reports to
both the Ministry of Petroleum and Energy and the
Ministry of Local Government and Labour.

## ENTERPRISES (PUBLIC AND PRIVATE SECTOR COMPANIES)

### BERGENSHALVØENS KOMMUNALE KRAFTSELSKAP

*Address:* Midthunhaugen 10, Bergen
. Telephone (05) 10 15 20
*Energy Sector:* Electricity

The Bergen municipal authority owns one of the country's largest individual electricity production systems, capitalising on the immense hydro-electric potential of the region. Annual electricity output is around 3,200 GWh, meeting the electricity requirements of the important regional centre of Bergen.

### NORSK HYDRO A/S

*Address:* Bygdøy Allé 2, Oslo 2
Telephone (02) 56 41 80 Telex 18350
*Gross Revenue:* Kr 9,104 million (1979)
*Total Assets:* Kr 15,339.0 million
*Energy Sectors:* Oil, gas, electricity

Norsk Hydro is Norway's largest industrial company. The state owns 51 per cent of the shares. The company has interests in minerals, mining and processing and has a high requirement for energy products as fuels and feedstocks and is one of the largest producers of electricity, which is generated mainly for its own internal use, notably in aluminium manufacture. Norsk Hydro's operations are spread throughout Norway, as is its production of electricity.

Turnover in the Petroleum Division of the company totalled Kr 2,900 million in 1979. This is derived mainly from its share in output from the Ekofisk and Frigg fields and the sale of finished products refined at the Mongstad refinery north of Bergen. This refinery has a throughput capacity of 4.5 million tonnes per annum, 30 per cent of which is owned by Norsk Hydro. Of the 1.1 million tonnes per annum obtained from Mongstad about half is sold through group companies in Sweden and Denmark. The other half is absorbed as fuel or feedstock in fertiliser, petrochemicals and other manufacturing plants.

### NORSKE ESSO A/S

*Address:* Haakon VII's gate 9, PB 1369, Oslo 1
Telephone (02) 41 26 20 Telex 11286
*Gross Revenue:* Kr 2,724.7 million (1978)
*Total Assets:* Kr 1,256.6 million
*Energy Sector:* Oil

Norske Esso is a wholly owned affiliate of the United States based international oil company Exxon, and is involved in all aspects of the oil industry in Norway. It has participated in all offshore licensing rounds, often as operator, and has interests in the Statfjord, Odin, Balder and Sleipner discoveries.

Norske Esso is one of the country's leading marketers of oil products, with an average market share of 28 per cent. Almost all of the company's oil products are obtained from the refinery at Slagen on Oslofjord. This refinery has a throughput capacity of 5.5 million tonnes per annum, producing the range of main products. There is a small specialist bitumen-producing refinery at Valløy, also on Oslofjord. In order to reduce its reliance on the heavy fuel oil market new upgrading equipment has been installed in the Slagen refinery.

### A/S NORSKE SHELL

*Address:* Tullinsgaten 2, Oslo 1
Telephone (02) 20 02 50 Telex 11224
*Gross Revenue:* Kr 2,412.7 million (1978 excl VAT)
*Total Assets:* Kr 1,386.4 million
*Energy Sector:* Oil

A/S Norske Shell is a wholly owned subsidiary company of the international Royal Dutch/Shell oil group. It is one of Norway's leading oil companies with refining, distribution and marketing interests. Norske Shell supplies the whole range of main oil products and its marketing network includes over 600 service stations throughout the country. In total the company supplies nearly one-quarter of all product requirements. Supply of products is based on the company's refinery at Sola, near Stavanger, which has a throughput capacity of three million tonnes per annum.

As in other sectors of the North Sea, Shell is involved in exploration and development work. Norske Shell holds a 50 per cent interest in the Albuskjell gas/condensate field, which has been brought into operation using the Ekofisk production and pipeline complex. The company has an interest of just under nine per cent in the large Statfjord oil and gas field, which commenced production in late 1979.

### OSLO LYSVERKER

*Address:* Sommerrogate 1, Oslo 2
Telephone (02) 56 41 60 Telex 18715
*Gross Revenue:* Kr 831.0 million (1978)
*Total Assets:* Kr 5,171.0 million
*Energy Sector:* Electricity

Oslo Lysverker is the municipally owned undertaking responsible for the supply and distribution of electricity to the Oslo city area. Aside from the state-owned plants of NVE-Statskraftverkene, it is the largest producer of electricity in Norway, with output of 5,500 GWh per annum.

The municipality owns water resources in several parts of the country and operates a number of hydro-electric plants. These are located primarily in the Hallingdal and Aurland area in south central Norway. Oslo Lysverker also has interests in generating plant in other areas which has been built in participation with the state, other local authorities or private companies.

## PHILLIPS PETROLEUM COMPANY NORWAY

*Address:* Munkedamsveien 3B, Oslo
    Telephone (02) 42 38 60  Telex 18235
*Energy Sectors:* Oil, gas

Phillips Petroleum Company Norway is a wholly owned subsidiary of Phillip's Petroleum Co of Oklahoma. Although the company is not involved in oil refining in Norway and is not a significant marketer of products, it has become an important part of the oil industry through its role as operator of the Ekofisk area system and participation in other exploration activity in the Norwegian sector of the North Sea.

Phillips Norway discovered the Ekofisk field and other deposits of oil and gas in that area and is operator of the field and the related oil and gas pipelines on behalf of a number of other companies. The Phillips group also has a share of an oil refinery on Teesside where Ekofisk crude oil is landed.

## SAMKJØRINGEN AV KRAFTVERKENE I NORGE

*Address:* Husebybakken 28B, Oslo
    Telephone (02) 46 19 30  Telex 11911
*Energy Sector:* Electricity

The Norwegian Power Pool is an organisation of electricity producers to which a substantial degree of overall control and co-ordination of the public electricity supply system is accorded. Membership of the Power Pool, which is 116, includes all the major producers of electricity and covers virtually all of the country's production.

The Power Pool operates a national electricity grid, which is subdivided into four regions, Oslo, Bergen, Trondheim and Narvik. Inter-region movements as well as exchanges with Sweden, Denmark and Finland are carried out by the Power Pool.

## STATOIL—DEN NORSKE STATS OLJESELSKAP A/S

*Address:* Lagårdsveien 78, PB 300, N-4001
    Stavanger
    Telephone (045) 33 180  Telex 33326
*Gross Revenue:* Kr 3,308.2 million (1979)
*Total Assets:* Kr 10,159.1 million
*Energy Sectors:* Oil, gas

Statoil, the Norwegian state oil company, has developed rapidly into all stages of the oil industry during the last few years. Principally its concern is exploration and development activity in the Norwegian sector of the North Sea. Since the early rounds of licensing Statoil has become automatically a holder of 50 per cent rights. In addition

to this it handles the state's oil and gas taken as royalty. It is into the exploration and development of oil and gas that most investment is channelled, notably in the major Statfjord field, which came into production in late 1979.

Statoil also has a 50 per cent share in the Murchison field, a 40 per cent share in Heimdal and a small interest in the large Frigg gas field. Statoil holds a 50 per cent interest in Norpipe which operates the oil and gas pipelines from the Ekofisk complex.

In the Norwegian market Norske Olje, which has been built up on the basis of distribution and marketing assets originally transferred from Norsk Hydro, supplies approximately 25 per cent of Norway's product requirements. These are met from the Mongstad refinery on the west coast. Statoil owns 74 per cent of Norsk Olje and directly or through Norsk Olje Statoil owns 70 per cent of the Mongstad refinery, the balance being in the hands of Norsk Hydro.

## STATSKRAFTVERKENE

*Address:* Middelthunsgate 29, Oslo 3
    Telephone (02) 46 98 00  Telex 11912
*Energy Sector:* Electricity

Statskraftverkene is the operating group within the Norges Vassdrags- og Elektrisitetsvesen responsible for the many state-owned power stations. Annual production from NVE's power stations is around 22,000 GWh, equivalent to 30 per cent of the country's total electricity production.

Statskraftverkene has electricity production capacity in each of the four regions into which Norway is divided for purposes of grid administration. However the largest element of its capacity is to be found in the Trondheim region where it produces half of all electricity output. State-owned plant also produces over half of the electricity in the northern region of the country (Narvik) although this involves output of only 2,000 GWh per annum.

## PROFESSIONAL INSTITUTIONS AND TRADE ASSOCIATIONS

### NORSK PETROLEUMSINSTITUTT

*Address:* Bygdøy Allé 8, Oslo
    Telephone (02) 55 00 07
*Energy Sector:* Oil

The Norwegian Petroleum Institute is a professional organisation for the oil industry. It provides a forum for discussion of matters of interest to the industry and provides advice on behalf of the industry to government and other official bodies. It also monitors activities within the industry, providing information and semi-technical services.

## NORSKE ELEKTRISITETSVERKERS FORENING

*Address:* Gaustadalléen 30, Oslo
   Telephone (02) 69 58 70
*Energy Sector:* Electricity

The Norwegian Association of Electricity Producers is an organisation representing the interests of private and public owners of generating plant and transmission systems. It is concerned with matters affecting the construction and operation of plant and facilities, including economic, technical and safety issues.

# Sweden

## GOVERNMENT DEPARTMENTS AND OFFICIAL AGENCIES

### DELEGATIONEN FÖR ENERGIFORSKNING

*Address:* Sveavägen 9-11, 9 tr, S-11157 Stockholm
   Telephone (08) 763 10 00

The Energy Research and Development Commission is responsible for planning and co-ordinating the programme of research and development. A principal area of interest in the Commission's activity is the programme of study on total energy systems.

### ENERGISPARKOMMITTEN

*Address:* Kungsgatan 56, 2 tr, S-11122 Stockholm
   Telephone (08) 24 07 20

The Energy Conservation Committee has the responsibility of co-ordinating information output on energy conservation and carrying out its own publicity and advice. It also advises the government on the scope for new measures.

### HANDELSDEPARTMENTET

*Address:* Rosenbad 2, Fack, S-10310 Stockholm
   Telephone (08) 763 10 00  Telex 17920

The Ministry of Commerce is concerned with internal and external trade in energy products. It administers regulations on stocks, taxes and duties and those affecting distribution and marketing of fuels.

### INDUSTRIDEPARTMENTET

*Address:* Storkyrkobrinken 7, Fack, S-10310
   Stockholm
   Telephone (08) 763 10 00  Telex 14180

The Ministry of Industry is responsible for general industrial matters and regional planning. The Energy Division of the department is concerned with energy planning, energy use, the production and distribution of energy including the relevant permits and safety issues, and international co-operation on energy matters. The tasks of the department are carried out by a number of state agencies and companies including the State Power Board, the Nuclear Power Inspectorate and Svenska Petroleum AB.

### NÄMNDEN FÖR ENERGIPRODUKTIONS-FORSKNING

*Address:* Kistagången 4, Box 1103, S-16312
   Spånga
   Telephone (08) 752 03 60  Telex 12992

The National Swedish Board for Energy Source Development is responsible for the energy production aspects of the energy research programme. The range of energy sources being looked at in this section of the programme includes: peat, biomass, solar, wind and geothermal energy; total energy systems; combustion techniques; coal technology; fission and fusion power; synthetic fuels, fuel cells, ocean energy.

### STATENS INDUSTRIVERK

*Address:* Fredsgatan 4, Box 16315, S-10326
   Stockholm 16
   Telephone (08) 24 06 00  Telex 12072

The National Swedish Industrial Board administers government policies in the industrial sector under the supervision of the Ministry of Industry. The Board is responsible for information and training in the field of conservation technologies and support for prototype and demonstration plants. It also handles state grants to promote utilisation of more energy-efficient technologies or the substitution of solid fuels for oil in industrial facilities.

The Industrial Board carries out detailed analysis and forecasting of energy requirements and is involved in the planning of local authority energy systems and the development of district heating.

### STATENS INSTITUT FÖR BYGGNADS FORSKNING

*Address:* Box 785, S-80129 Gävle
   Telephone (026) 10 02 20

The National Swedish Institute for Building Research has the role of undertaking research and experimental work to advance the rational use of energy in buildings. The Institute is particularly involved in work on heating and ventilation systems, the required levels of heating in homes and the energy-saving potential of altering existing buildings.

STATENS KÄRNKRAFTSINSPEKTION
*Address:* Sehlstedtsgatan 11, Box 27106,
   S-10252 Stockholm
   Telephone (08) 67 00 10  Telex 11961

The Swedish Nuclear Power Inspectorate is responsible for testing and supervising in questions of
technical safety and security of fissile material. It
has the authority to initiate and direct research
and development work to ensure safety levels.


STATENS NATURVÅRDSVERK
*Address:* Smidesvägen 5, Fack, S-17120
   Solna
   Telephone (08) 98 18 00  Telex 11131

The National Swedish Environment Protection
Board is responsible for administration of legislation on a wide variety of matters affecting the
environment. In the energy sector it is concerned
with the effects of consumption of energy and
existing energy production centres, excluding
the radiological aspects of nuclear power developments.


STATENS PRIS- OCH KARTELLNÄMND
*Address:* Vasagatan 7, Box 1115, S-11181
   Stockholm
   Telephone (08) 14 20 80  Telex 17129

The National Price and Cartel Office is responsible
for monitoring and investigating prices and competition in Swedish industry and commerce. It is
concerned with prices of crude oil and products
imported into Sweden and the freight charges
made to Swedish affiliates of international companies. Enquiries into the relationship of affiliates
to parent companies have been carried out.

SPK monitors costs of refining in Sweden and the
prices and cost structures of electricity undertakings.


STYRELSEN FOR TEKNISK UTVECKLING
*Address:* Liljeholmsvagen 32, Fack, S-10072
   Stockholm 43
   Telephone (08) 744 51 00  Telex 10840

The National Swedish Board for Technical
Development is the channel for official support for
technical research and further development work
in industry. A primary objective of the STU is
that research projects should lead to practical uses.
Within the overall energy development programme
the STU is responsible for sections dealing with the
use of energy in industrial processes, in motive
power systems and in industrial buildings.

## ENTERPRISES (PUBLIC AND PRIVATE SECTOR COMPANIES)

ARA-BOLAGE AB
*Address:* Jakobsgatan 6, Box 16144, S-10323
   Stockholm
   Telephone (08) 22 64 80  Telex 19314
*Gross Revenue:* Kr 700.0 million (1978)
*Energy Sectors:* Oil, coal

ARA-Bolage is one of the largest importers of oil
products and solid fuels. It deals in coal and coke,
motor fuels, diesel and heating oil, fuel oils and
lubricants. A substantial amount of its product is
obtained from international bulk markets including Eastern European countries, particularly
for fuel oils.

ARA-Bolage has a turnover of Kr 700 million. It
is a subsidiary company of the United States
oil company Continental Oil.


ASEA AB
*Address:* Hamngatan 2, Box 7373, S-10391
   Stockholm
   Telephone (08) 24 59 50  Telex 17236
*Gross Revenue:* Kr 11,830.0 million (1979 excl
   VAT)
*Total Assets:* Kr 16,267.0 million
*Energy Sectors:* Electricity, nuclear power

ASEA AB is one of Sweden's leading industrial
companies, with extensive interests in many
branches of engineering. The group manufactures
and installs electricity generation and transmission
equipment, motive power units and lighting installations. Power equipment accounts for around
one-third of total sales.

ASEA, principally through ASEA ATOM, in which
it is a partner with the state, is involved in a
number of nuclear power station construction
projects. ASEA ATOM has built or has contracts
to build all the units at the Forsmark, Barsebäck
and Oskarshamn power stations and built the first
unit at the Ringhals station. The company is also
building Finland's second nuclear power station at
Olkiluoto on the west coast of the country.

ASEA has direct involvement in electricity production. It retains a share in the Oskarshamn power
station and holds a 65 per cent interest in Voxnans
Kraft AB. Voxnans produces and distributes
around 5,000 GWh per annum of electricity.


GULLSPÅNGS KRAFTAKTIEBOLAG
*Address:* Stubbengatan 2, Box 472, S-70106
   Örebro
   Telephone (019) 13 07 00  Telex 73308
*Gross Revenue:* Kr 365.5 million (1979)
*Total Assets:* Kr 685.3 million
*Energy Sector:* Electricity

Gullspångs Kraft AB is a producer and distributor of electricity in south central Sweden in the area between Örebro and Lake Vänern. Total transmission is around 3,000 GWh per annum. The company operates several power stations in its distribution area but it has interests in many more hydro-electric stations in the northern part of the country. Hydro-electric sources contribute some 45 per cent of the company's own availability of electricity.

Gullspångs Kraft has important interests in several thermal power stations in the southern part of the country. These include some fossil fuelled stations. The company has a 6.25 per cent direct share in the Oskarshamn nuclear power station and a similar share in the Forsmark station through Mellansvensk Kraftgrupp AB.

## KRÅNGEDE AB

*Address:* Birger Jarlsgatan 41A, Box 7593,
   S-10393 Stockholm
   Telephone (08) 23 30 25  Telex 10116
*Gross Revenue:* Kr 306.9 million (1978)
*Total Assets:* Kr 684.6 million
*Energy Sector:* Electricity

Krångede AB is the third largest supplier of electricity in Sweden, after the state-owned Vattenfallsverket and Sydkraft, representing a consortium of municipal authorites in southern Sweden. Electricity supplied by Krångede in 1979 totalled 6,800 GWh. Approximately two-thirds of Krångede's availability comes from its hydro-electric plants in northern Sweden. In that part of the country it also operates a thermal power station at Karskär and has an interest in Aroskraft.

Krångede has interests in two of Sweden's nuclear power stations. It has a 7.5 per cent share in the Oskarshamn power station and through participation in Mellansvensk Kraftgrupp AB it has a small interest in the Forsmark plant, north of Stockholm.

## MOBIL OIL AB SWEDEN

*Address:* Fack, S-18210, Danderyd 1
   Telephone (08) 755 25 20  Telex 1576
*Gross Revenue:* Kr 841.5 million (1979)
*Total Assets:* Kr 450.0 million
*Energy Sector:* Oil

Mobil Oil AB is a wholly owned subsidiary company of Mobil Corporation of New York. It is engaged in the distribution and marketing of petroleum products in Sweden, with sales of around one million cubic metres per annum of all products. It holds a 50 per cent interest in the fuel distributor AB Kol & Koks. In common with the approach taken by Mobil Corporation, Mobil Oil AB has extended its motor gasoline retailing operation into connected areas of motels and catering.

Mobil Oil AB has no refining capacity in Sweden and is reliant on product imported from other group refineries, particularly in the UK, Netherlands and West Germany. Alternative supply sources are Scandinavian refiners which may process crude oil for Mobil or supply finished products under international exchange arrangements.

## NYNÄS PETROLEUM AB

*Address:* Nybrogatan 11, Box 5842, S-10248
   Stockholm
   Telephone (08) 24 35 80  Telex 19042
*Gross Revenue:* Kr 1,955.1 million (1978)
*Total Assets:* Kr 1,177.5 million
*Energy Sector:* Oil

Nynäs Petroleum is part of the A Johnson group. It is involved in refining, distribution and marketing of oil products. The main Nynas refinery is on the east coast, south of Stockholm and has a capacity of two million tonnes per annum. There are also two small refineries, at Gothenburg and Malmö geared to the production of bitumen.

Oil products are consigned to other distribution companies in the Johnson group or to independent companies, and Nynäs also markets products itself, notably motor fuels.

## OLJEKONSUMENTERNAS FÖRBUND

*Address:* Sveavägen 153-155, S-11387 Stockholm
   Telephone (08) 736 00 00  Telex 17610
*Gross Revenue:* Kr 6,009.1 million (1979)
*Total Assets:* Kr 3,779.1 million
*Energy Sector:* Oil

OK is part of the national consumer co-operative organisation Kooperativa Förbundet, concerned with the major sector of oil product supply. Sales of oil products are around 5.7 million cubic metres per annum, making OK the largest single marketer in Sweden with some 15 per cent of total sales.

From being a product purchasing and retailing organisation OK has progressively moved into other aspects of oil supply. It is the majority shareholder in the Scanraff refinery at Lysekil on the west coast of Sweden. This is the country's largest refinery, with a throughput capacity of over eight million tonnes of crude oil per annum. OK also has a shareholding in Petroswede, which is involved in securing supplies of oil from abroad, either through exploration or through direct supply contracts.

## OLJEPROSPEKTERING AB

*Address:* Linnégatan 5, S-11447 Stockholm
   Telephone (08) 14 04 80  Telex 17648
*Energy Sector:* Oil

Oljeprospektering AB (OPAB) is a state-owned exploration company. Its direct parent companies are Statens Vattenfallsverk, the electricity supply undertaking, and LKAB, the mining company which is a subsidiary of the state holding company Statsföretag.

Since its establishment in 1969 OPAB has carried out a drilling programme continuously on the Swedish mainland and on Gotland, where the private sector has shown little interest. OPAB is able to exploit deposits, but up to the present time no significant quantities of either oil or gas have been identified.

## PETROSWEDE AB

*Address:* Linnégatan 5, S-11447 Stockholm
     Telephone (08) 14 04 80  Telex 17648
*Energy Sector:* Oil

Petroswede was set up in 1973 in order to carry out exploration and development of oil and gas outside Swedish territory. The organisation of Petroswede is more broadly based than that of Oljeprospektering AB, which is concerned with the search for oil and gas in Sweden. The partners in OPAB, the industrial concern LKAB, and the state electricity authority Statens Vattenfallsverk, each holds 25 per cent. The balance is held by a group of private industrial and financial companies and includes the co-operative union Kooperativa Förbundet.

## AB SKANDINAVSKA ELVERK

*Address:* Kammakargatan 7, Box 3118, S-10362
     Stockholm
     Telephone (08) 23 33 50  Telex 10448
*Gross Revenue:* Kr 740.7 million (1979)
*Total Assets:* Kr 844.0 million
*Energy Sector:* Electricity

Skandinavska Elverk (SEV) is a producer and distributor of electricity in western Sweden. Total deliveries of electricity in 1979 amounted to 3,900 GWh. Distribution is carried out by several subsidiary companies. SEV has electricity production capacity of 340 MW of which the majority is hydro-electric plant. But an appreciable amount of electricity is now being obtained from the nuclear power station at Oskarshamn, where the associated company Voxnans Kraft AB holds a 15 per cent interest through its participation in the consortium Mellansvensk Kraftgrupp.

## STATENS VATTENFALLSVERK

*Address:* Jämtlandsgatan 99, S-16287 Vällingby
     Telephone (08) 87 00 00  Telex 19086
*Gross Revenue (Power Division):* Kr 4,863.0
     million (1979)
*Total Assets (Power Division):* Kr 25,534.9 million
*Energy Sectors:* Electricity, oil, gas

Vattenfall is the state-owned undertaking engaged in the production, distribution and sale of electricity. It has a general responsibility for the planning, co-ordination and operation of the national electricity supply system, under the overall supervision of the Ministry of Industry. Vattenfall also provides finance towards investment by other undertakings in new generating and transmission equipment.

Vattenfall produces 45 per cent of all electricity in Sweden. Historically this has been based largely on water power and today it still supplies over half of total hydro-electric power, and its operations include the largest hydro-electric station, at Harsprånget on the Lule river. However, Vattenfall has a prominent role in the development of nuclear power. It is sole owner of the Ringhals station, near Gothenburg, and has a 75 per cent interest in the Forsmark project. The last of the four units at Ringhals is expected to be completed in 1982 giving a total capacity of 3,400 MW. Two 900 MW units at Forsmark have been built but have not been in operation pending government permission to fuel them.

The extent of electricity supply at the retail level undertaken by Vattenfall is relatively limited, but it has interests in a number of regional and municipal supply companies. Outside the electricity sector Vattenfall now has interests in the development of oil and gas. It has a 50 per cent shareholding in both Svenska Petroleum and Swedegas.

## STATSFÖRETAG AB

*Address:* Hamngatan 6, Box 7827, S-10397
     Stockholm
     Telephone (08) 24 29 00  Telex 11454
*Gross Revenue:* Kr 10,104.5 million (1978)
*Total Assets:* Kr 17,571.7 million
*Energy Sectors:* Oil, gas

Statsföretag is the state holding company, with interests in many industries throughout Sweden. It has a major involvement in mining in the north of the country, through its ownership of Luossavaara-Kiirunavaara AB (LKAB) and in the forestry sector.

The scale of Statsföretag's operations in the energy sector is relatively limited at present but as the government takes an increasing interest and direct involvement in energy matters, so its investment is likely to increase. Statsföretag holds interests of 50 per cent in Oljeprospektering and Svenska Petroleum, 25 per cent in Petroswede and 51 per cent in Swedegas. In addition it has a subsidiary company, Statsraff, which is the vehicle for a projected oil refinery on the west coast. Statsföretag already has an interest in petrochemicals manufacture in that area through its shareholding in Berol Kemi.

## STOCKHOLMS ENERGIVERK

*Address:* Tulegatan 7-13, Fack, S-10432
  Stockholm
  Telephone (08) 736 70 00  Telex 10119
*Gross Revenue:* Kr 1,203.0 million
*Enegy Sectors:* Electricity, gas, heat

Stockholm's Energiverk is a municipally owned undertaking supplying electricity, gas and district heating in Stockholm. Its principal concern is electricity, and its subsidiary company Svarthalsforsen AB operates several power stations in and around the capital, some of which are also used to provide district heating. The electricity needs of Stockholm are such, however, that capacity in other power stations has to be earmarked for supplying the area.

## STORA KOPPARBERGS BERGSLAGS AB

*Address:* Åsgatan 22, S-79180 Falun
  Telephone (023) 800 00  Telex 84010
*Gross Revenue:* Kr 3,720.0 million (1978)
*Total Assets:* Kr 5,312.2 million
*Energy Sector:* Electricity

Stora Kopparberg is a major forestry company, operating over an area of two million acres in central Sweden. It is also the sixth largest producer of electricity in the country. Total electricity turnover is some 5,000 GWh per annum, of which over 70 per cent is used in the course of company operations. But Stora Kopparberg produces a net surplus of electricity of 1,000 GWh for the public supply system in its area.

The electricity generated by Stora Kopparberg is derived mainly from hydro-electric resources within the area of its forestry operations. Plants on the Ljusnan and Dalälven rivers produce 3,300 GWh of electricity in a year. The balance of the company's electricity availability derives from interests in oil-fired power stations at Vasterås and Karlshamn and from the 10 per cent shareholding in the Oskarshamn nuclear power station.

## SVENSKA BP AB

*Address:* Vartaveien 67, Box 27088, S-10251
  Stockholm
  Telephone (08) 22 30 40  Telex 19388
*Gross Revenue:* Kr 3,066.0 million (1978)
*Enegy Sector:* Oil

Svenska BP is the Swedish affiliate of British Petroleum Co. It is the second largest marketer of oil products in Sweden with a sales volume of around four million cubic metres per annum of all main products, equivalent to over 13 per cent of the market. Marketing is carried out directly through company owned distribution and sales outlets or through independent bulk distributors.

BP's marketing operations in Sweden are backed up by the group's oil refinery near Gothenburg.

This refinery has a capacity of five million tonnes per annum and is able to produce all the mainline products required for the Swedish market.

## SVENSKA PETROLEUM AB

*Address:* Regeringsgatan 30-37, Box 16101,
  S-10323 Stockholm
  Telephone (08) 24 98 60  Telex 19917
*Energy Sector:* Oil

The Swedish Petroleum Company was set up as a state oil company, to look after the public's commercial interests in oil supply. Its primary objectives are to increase the security of Sweden's oil supplies and to diversify the sources of supply. The state's ownership is exercised through Statens Vattenfallsverk and Statsföretag AB, the state holding company, which each hold 50 per cent of Svenska Petroleum's shares.

Initially the activities of Svenska Petroleum concentrated on making supply arrangements for crude oil and petroleum products directly with producer-country governments and on the international market. It has subsequently moved into direct marketing of products and has built up a significant share in the market particularly for heating and fuel oils. In 1979 it was announced that Svenska Petroleum would become a partner in the Scanraff refinery at Lysekil on the west coast of Sweden, taking up the capacity made available in a further expansion of the country's largest refinery.

## SVENSKA SHELL AB

*Address:* Armegatan 38, S-17179 Solna
  Telephone (08) 730 80 00  Telex 19360
*Gross Revenue:* Kr 2,492.9 million (1978)
*Energy Sector:* Oil

Svenska Shell is an affiliate of the Royal Dutch/Shell group, involved in all aspects of the oil industry in Sweden. It is one of the leading marketers of oil products, supplying some 3.5 million cubic metres per annum of all products representing a 12 per cent market share. The company is strongly represented itself at the retail level but also supplies products to independent distributors.

A subsidiary company of Svenska Shell operates a refinery near Gothenburg. The refinery has a capacity of five million tonnes per annum of crude oil, which is sufficient to meet much of the company's marketing requirement. Additional products can also quite readily be imported from the refinery owned by the Danish affiliate of Royal Dutch/Shell at Fredericia.

## SWEDEGAS AB

*Address:* Norrtullsgatan 6, Box 6405,
  S-11382 Stockholm
  Telephone (08) 34 09 85  Telex 13593
*Energy Sector:* Gas

Swedegas was set up to examine the possibilities for introducing natural gas into Sweden. The majority holding is in the hands of the state, through the agency of Statens Vattenfallsverk, with 51 per cent. The balance is held by Svenska Gasföreningens Service AB, representing a cross-section of the membership of the Swedish Gas Association, which includes companies with interests in natural gas, towns gas and oil.

## SYDKRAFT AB

*Address:* Carl Gustafs Veien 1, Fack, S-20070
   Malmö
   Telephone (040) 24 50 00  Telex 32810
*Gross Revenue:* Kr 1,985.0 million (1978)
*Total Assets:* Kr 4,041.00 million
*Energy Sector:* Electricity

Sydkraft is the second largest electricity supply undertaking in Sweden. It represents a consortium of municipal authorities and the consumers union Kooperativa Förbundet, although there are also a number of private shareholders. It is responsible for the supply of electricity to the southernmost part of Sweden. In 1979 total transmission amounted to nearly 14,000 GWh.

Sydkraft relies upon nuclear power for most of its supplies. Around two-thirds of its requirements are met from the Barsebäck station near Malmö and the Oskarshamn station. Sydkraft is sole owner of the Barsebäck plant which has a capacity of 1,140 MW and a 36 per cent interest in Oskarshamn, which is of a similar size. It is also majority shareholder in Karlshamnsverket, which is the largest non-nuclear station in Sweden.

## PROFESSIONAL INSTITUTIONS AND TRADE ASSOCIATIONS

### CENTRALA DRIFTLEDNINGEN

*Address:* Brahegatan 47, Fack, S-10240
   Stockholm
   Telephone (09) 63 54 60  Telex 13108
*Energy Sector:* Electricity

Centrala Driftledningen is the organisation representing the principal electricity producers. Apart from Statens Vattenfallsverk, it includes 13 private and public enterprises and provides information and advice on behalf of the producers to official commissions, technical bodies and the public.

### SVENSKA ELVERKSFÖRENINGEN

*Address:* Norrtullsgatan 6, Box 6405,
   S-11382 Stockholm
   Telephone (08) 22 58 90  Telex 13593
*Energy Sector:* Electricity

The Swedish Association of Electricity Supply Undertakings has over 300 members representing distributors of electricity to 95 per cent of all consumers. This number also includes the main electricity producers, since they are all involved to some extent in distribution and sales of electricity. Member undertakings account for over 90 per cent of total electricity production, the only significant non-members being auto-producers in industry whose capacity is geared solely to their own requirements.

The Association is the industry's representative body on many issues. It is concerned with the technical, administrative and commercial aspects of distribution, and with consumer issues such as tariff levels and safety of equipment. Within the industry the Association's primary objective is to organise co-operation with a view to maintenance of a rational and efficient supply system.

### SVENSKA GASFÖRENINGEN

*Address:* Norrtullsgatan 6, Box 6405, S-11382
   Stockholm
   Telephone (08) 34 09 85  Telex 13593
*Energy Sector:* Gas

The Swedish Gas Association is the principal representative organisation in the Swedish gas industry. Its membership comprises undertakings with interests in natural gas and includes producers of towns gas as well as the oil companies.

### SVENSKA KRAFTVERKSFÖRENINGEN

*Address:* Birger Jarlsgatan 41A, Box 1704,
   S-11187 Stockholm 1
   Telephone (08) 24 23 90
*Energy Sector:* Electricity

The Swedish Power Producers Association is a grouping of the larger electricity producers in order to represent to the public and to government the interests of operators of large-scale electrical plant. It includes both industrial producers and local authorities.

### SVENSKA PETROLEUM INSTITUTET

*Address:* Sveavägen 21, S-1134 Stockholm
   Telephone (08) 23 58 00  Telex 10324
*Energy Sector:* Oil

The Swedish Petroleum Institute is the representative organisation for oil companies operating in Sweden. The Institute deals with a wide range of topics on behalf of the industry as a whole. These include technical specifications, environmental pollution, safety and commercial operations. It provides advice and information on the industry and is often involved in the work of specialist enquiries and committees.

## SVENSKA VÄRMEVERKSFÖRENINGEN
*Address:* Kammakargatan 62, S-11124 Stockholm
   Telephone (08) 14 24 75
*Energy Sector:* Heat

The Swedish District Heating Association is a specialist association of heat producing companies. These are for the most part municipal authorities. The Association actively supports research and development work related to district heating and carries out its own programme of work on development and standards.

## SVERIGES GROSSISTFÖRBUND
*Address:* Grevgatan 34, Box 5512, S-11485
   Stockholm
   Telephone (08) 63 52 80  Telex 19673
*Energy Sectors:* Oil, coal

The Swedish Wholesalers' Federation is a representative trade association. It includes sections specifically for members who are involved in oil and coal trades.

## SWEDISH ATOMIC FORUM
*Address:* Storgatan 19, Box 5506, S-11485
   Stockholm
   Telephone (08) 63 50 20
*Energy Sector:* Nuclear power

The Swedish Atomic Forum provides the framework for all parties interested in the development of nuclear power to represent their views. It includes companies and other organisations involved in research work, reactor and other technological construction and electricity production. The Forum operates under the general auspices of Sveriges Mekanforbund.

# Continental Europe

## Austria

### GOVERNMENT DEPARTMENTS AND OFFICIAL AGENCIES

BUNDESMINISTERIUM FÜR GESUNDHEIT UND UMWELTSCHUTZ
*Address:* Stubenring 1, A-1010 Wien
    Telephone (0222) 75 00

The Ministry for Health and Environmental Protection is responsible for the whole range of environmental questions. It deals with measures to control pollution of the environment and has under it various technical establishments engaged in monitoring and investigation. The Ministry is also involved in international programmes aimed at environmental improvement.

BUNDESMINISTERIUM FÜR HANDEL, GEWERBE UND INDUSTRIE
*Address:* Schwarzenbergplatz 1, A-1010 Wien 1
    Telephone (0222) 73 35 11  Telex 131373

The Ministry for Trade, Commerce and Industry has responsibilities for wide areas of the economy. Within the ministry is a section specifically concerned with energy. It handles matters of policy, the administration of federal measures on energy and questions of energy supply and distribution.

The Ministry is also involved in the energy sector through its responsibility for the major state-owned holding companies and the supervision of pricing controls through the Paritätische Kommission.

BUNDESMINISTERIUM FÜR WISSENSCHAFT UND FORSCHUNG
*Address:* Minoritenplatz 5, A-1014 Wien
    Telephone (0222) 66 21  Telex 75532

The Ministry for Science and Research has particular responsibilities for research and development work in the field of energy. It co-ordinates the activity of academic institutions and the industrial sector, and works with the European Commission and the International Energy Agency on programmes of common interest.

### ENTERPRISES (PUBLIC AND PRIVATE SECTOR COMPANIES)

ENNSKRAFTWERKE AG
*Address:* Resthofstrasse 2, A-4403 Steyr
    Telephone (07252) 63341  Telex 28107
*Energy Sector:* Electricity

Ennskraftwerke AG operates 12 hydro-electric power stations along the Rivers Enns in north central Austria. The state electricity supply undertaking, the Verbundkonzern, holds 50 per cent of the shares of Ennskraftwerke. Output from Ennskraftwerke amounts to around 1,700 GWh per annum, approximately two-thirds of which is supplied to the Verbundkonzern, the balance to Oberösterreichische Kraftwerke AG.

GRAZ-KÖFLACHER EISENBAHN- UND BERGBAUGESELLSCHAFT
*Address:* Grazbachgasse 39, A-8010 Graz
    Telephone (0316) 76691  Telex 31318
*Gross Revenue:* S915.0 million (1978)
*Total Assets:* S819.0 million
*Energy Sector:* Coal

The Graz-Köflacher Railway and Mining Company is one of the two principal coal producing companies in Austria. It is owned by the state holding company ÖIAG. Production is of lignite from the Graz area of Styria province, totalling some two million tonnes per annum. Output is expected to increase in 1980 with the bringing into production of a new open-cast mine at Oberdorf, dedicated to the supply of Österreichische Draukraftwerke's new power station at Voitsberg.

## MOBIL OIL AUSTRIA AG

*Address:* Schwarzenbergplatz 16, A-1015 Wien 1
  Telephone (0222) 65 86 11  Telex 131822
*Energy Sectors:* Oil, gas

Mobil Oil Austria is a wholly owned subsidiary of Mobil Corporation of New York. It is engaged in exploration, processing, distribution and marketing of oil products.

Mobil, in partnership with Shell Austria, carries out exploration activity in eastern Styria and parts of Upper Austria and Salzburg provinces. This activity is undertaken through a jointly owned company Rohöl-Gewinnungs-AG. (RAG). RAG currently produces some oil and gas from fields in Lower and Upper Austria.

Mobil Oil, in common with other marketing companies in Austria, obtains petroleum products from crude oil refined at the Schwechat refinery of the state oil supply company ÖMV. Mobil does however operate a small refinery at Kagran in north-east Austria, which produces lubricating oil from locally produced heavy crude oil.

## NIEDERÖSTERREICHISCHE ELEKTRIZITÄTSWERKE AG

*Address:* Johann Steinbock Strasse 1, A-2344
  Maria Enzersdorf
  Telephone (02236) 83 61 10  Telex 79140
*Gross Revenue:* S2,440.0 million (1978)
*Total Assets:* S13,592.0 million
*Energy Sectors:* Electricity, gas

NEWAG is a publicly owned electricity producer in Lower Austria. Its own capacity is 750 MW of thermal plant. But NEWAG has an interest in Österreichische Donaukraftwerke AG and other joint-venture power stations. These include a 320 MW unit in the Korneuburg power station and the power station based on Polish coal which is being substituted for the formerly projected Tullnerfeld nuclear power station. NEWAG is also participating through the Korneuburg operating company in the project to build a 600 MW power station using Hungarian coal.

NEWAG is a major distributor of natural gas through NIOGAS AG, which obtains supplies of Soviet natural gas through the state oil and gas supply company ÖMV.

## ÖMV AG

*Address:* Otto-Wagnerplatz 5, Postfach 15,
  A-1090 Wien 9
  Telephone (0222) 42 36 21  Telex 074801
*Gross Revenue:* S32,953.2 million (1978)
*Total Assets:* S25,776.0 million
*Energy Sectors:* Oil, gas, petrochemicals

ÖMV, formerly the Österreichische Mineralöl-verwaltung AG, is a state-owned company with extensive responsibilities for the supply of oil and gas to the Austrian economy. ÖMV produces 81 per cent of Austria's indigenous crude oil and 62 per cent of the natural gas. As far as imported hydrocarbons are concerned ÖMV is solely responsible for arranging imports and developing the necessary trunk pipelines for import and distribution. Crude oil is imported by individual marketing companies but has to be processed in ÖMV's refinery at Schwechat. Supply is effected via the Adria-Wien Pipeline in which ÖMV has a 51 per cent share and other marketers participate pro rata to market requirements.

The Schwechat refinery provides the basis for ÖMV's own distribution and marketing operations. It is a major marketer through its 'Martha' and 'Elan' subsidiaries. The refinery also produces basic petrochemicals for the nearby works of Danubia Olefinwerke.

## ÖSTERREICHISCHE DONAUKRAFTWERKE AG

*Address:* Hochhaus Gartenbau, Parkring 12,
  A-1011 Wien
  Telephone (0222) 526671  Telex 111366
*Gross Revenue:* S1,667.1 million (1978)
*Total Assets:* S20,822.8 million
*Energy Sector:* Electricity

Österreichische Donaukraftwerke is the largest producer of electricity in Austria. Its hydro-electric stations on the river Danube contribute nearly 8,000 GWh per annum, approaching 25 per cent of the country's electricity demand. The state electricity undertaking holds 93.1 per cent of Österreichische Donaukraftwerke's capital. DoKW is continuing to exploit the potential of the Danube, having commissioned three new stations since 1973, with work in progress on additional projects.

## ÖSTERREICHISCHE DRAUKRAFTWERKE AG

*Address:* Kohldorfer Strasse 98, A-9020 Klagenfurt
  Telephone (04222) 21 5 51-0  Telex 42451
*Energy Sector:* Electricity

Österreichische Draukraftwerke is an important electricity producer, operating power stations in southern Austria. These include hydro-electric plant, which ÖDK is continuing to build and new coal-fired plant. ÖDK is bringing into service in 1980 a 330 MW station at Voitsberg (Styria) based on locally mined lignite. Total output of electricity by ÖDK is currently around 4,000 GWh per annum, with 80 per cent generated by hydro-electric plant on the River Drau.

Österreichische Draukraftwerke is controlled by the state electricity supply undertaking, the Verbundkonzern, which holds 51 per cent of ÖDK's shares.

## ÖSTERREICHISCHE ELEKTRIZITÄTS-WIRTSCHAFTS-AG

*Address:* Am Hof 6A, A-1010 Wien
Telephone (0222) 6613-0  Telex 07-4234
*Gross Revenue:* S7,507.1 million (1979)
*Total Assets:* S18,209.6 million
*Energy Sector:* Electricity

Österreichische Elektrizitätswirtschafts-AG, also known as Verbundkonzern, is a state undertaking responsible for the supply of electricity in the Austrian economy. It is engaged in the production of electricity and operates the national high-voltage grid system.

Principal subsidiary company producing electricity is Österreichische Donaukraftwerke, which operates several hydro-electric stations on the river Danube. Verbundkonzern holds major interests in electricity producers in other provinces of Austria, including Tauernkraftwerke AG (Salzburg), Österreichische Draukraftwerke (Carinthia), Ennskraftwerke (Styria) and Vorarlberger Illwerke (Vorarlberg). It is also 50 per cent shareholder in the Zwentendorf nuclear power station.

## SHELL AUSTRIA AG

*Address:* Rennweg 12, A-1030 Wien 3
Telephone (0222) 75 09-0  Telex 3241
*Energy Sectors:* Oil, gas

Shell Austria is a wholly-owned company of the international Royal Dutch/Shell group. It is the largest marketer of oil products in Austria, aside from ÖMV, the state oil supply company. Products are obtained from ÖMV's refinery at Schwechat. The refinery processes crude oil for Shell Austria, imported via the Adria-Wien Pipeline, in which the company has a 14.5 per cent interest.

Shell is a partner with Mobil Oil Austria in Rohöl-Gewinnungs-AG (RAG) which is engaged in exploration and production of oil and gas in Austria.

## TAUERNKRAFTWERKE AG

*Address:* Rainerstrasse 29, Postfach 161,
A-5021 Salzburg
Telephone (06222) 72 5 01-0  Telex 633973
*Gross Revenue:* S941.0 million (1978)
*Total Assets:* S12,003.0 million
*Energy Sector:* Electricity

Tauernkraftwerke AG is an electricity production company with output derived from the hydro-electric potential of the Tauern area of the Tirol, which includes the mountainous areas of the Gross Glockner. Tauernkraftwerke, which is 91.5 per cent owned by the state electricity undertaking, produces some 2,600 GWh per annum, which is supplied to the national grid.

## VORARLBERGER ILLWERE AG

*Address:* Josef Huter-Strasse 35, A-6901, Bregenz
Telephone (05574) 24 5 91-0  Telex 57723
*Gross Revenue:* S1,562.0 million (1979)
*Total Assets:* S9,631.0 million
*Energy Sector:* Electricity

Vorarlberger Illwerke is the principal electricity production company in the western Tirol area. The state electricity supply undertaking, Verbundkonzern, holds 69 per cent of the shares.

VIW utilises the considerable hydro-electric potential of the area, but as consumption is relatively low in that part of the country a high proportion of output is exported to southern Germany or fed into the national grid. Total capacity is 1,600 MW producing currently 1,300 GWh per annum, approximately 1,100 GWh of which is sold to West German electricity supply companies.

## WIENER STADTWERKE

*Address:* Schottenring 30, Wien 1
Telephone (0222) 63 66 06
*Gross Revenue:* S12,391.0 million (1978)
*Total Assets:* S29,676.0 million
*Energy Sectors:* Electricity, gas, heat

The municipality of Vienna is a major producer and distributor of energy in the capital. Its total sales of electricity amount to around 6,000 GWh per annum of which 3,600 GWh are produced in its own power stations, principally the 1050 MW Simmering plant. The Simmering and Donaustadt power stations are also used to supply district heat to parts of the city area.

Gas sales are running at over 600 million cubic metres per annum of natural gas equivalent. Part of this is produced as towns gas but the process of converting some three-quarters of a million consumers to natural gas supply has been effected during the 1970s.

## WOLFSEGG-TRAUNTHALER KOHLENWERK-AG

*Address:* Walterstrasse 22, A-4010 Linz
Telephone (0732) 70 5 01  Telex 21278
*Gross Revenue:* S195.0 million (1978)
*Total Assets:* S121.0 million
*Energy Sector:* Coal

The Wolfsegg-Traunthaler Coal-mining Company is an important domestic producer of coal. It produces lignite from mines in Upper Austria, almost all of which is used as fuel in power stations. The company is wholly owned by the state holding company ÖIAG.

## PROFESSIONAL INSTITUTIONS AND TRADE ASSOCIATIONS

### FACHVERBAND DER ERDÖLINDUSTRIE ÖSTERREICHS

*Address:* Erdbergstrasse 72, A-1031 Wien 3
  Telephone (0222) 73 23 48
*Energy Sectors:* Oil, gas

The Federation of Austrian Petroleum Industries is an organisation representing producers and distributors of oil and gas. It provides the main forum for presenting industry views to government and a central source of information on the oil and gas industries.

### FACHVERBAND DER GAS UND WÄRMEVERSORGUNGSUNTERNEHMUNGEN

*Address:* Gusshausstrasse 30, A-1041 Wien
  Telephone (0222) 65 17 57
*Energy Sectors:* Gas, heat

The Association of Gas and Heat Supply Undertakings is a representative organisation for companies producing towns gas and particularly those with integrated district heating plant.

### ÖSTERREICHISCHE VEREINIGUNG FÜR DAS GAS-UND WASSERFACH

*Address:* Gusshausstrasse 30, A-1041 Wien
  Telephone (0222) 65 17 57
*Energy Sector:* Gas

The Austrian Institute for Gas and Water is the main professional organisation for technical and technico-economic aspects of the gas supply industry. It is a member body of the International Gas Union.

### ÖSTERREICHISCHER VERBAND FÜR FLÜSSIGGAS

*Address:* Karlweisgasse 23, A-1180 Wien
  Telephone (0222) 47 23 89
*Energy Sector:* Gas

The Austrian Society for Liquid Gas is an association representing the liquefied petroleum gas industry, including producers and distributors and companies involved in the manufacture of equipment and appliances. The association deals with standards and technical aspects and more general subjects affecting the industry.

### VERBAND DER ELEKTRIZITÄTSWERKE ÖSTERREICHS

*Address:* Brahmsplatz 3, A-1040 Wien
  Telephone (0222) 65 17 27 0  Telex 131100
*Energy Sector:* Electricity

The Association of Austrian Electricity Producers brings together the state-owned, municipal and private sector producers of electricity. It provides the channel for exchange of information between companies and with foreign associations on questions of large-scale power generation and transmission.

# Belgium

## GOVERNMENT DEPARTMENTS AND OFFICIAL AGENCIES

### ADMINISTRATION DE L'ENERGIE

*Address:* 30 Rue de Mot, B-1040 Bruxelles
  Telephone (02) 233 61 11  Telex 23509

The Administration de l'Energie is a specialised division within the Ministry of Economic Affairs. It is concerned with the coordination of energy policy and has specific responsibility for the coal sector and the electricity and gas supply industries.

### ADMINISTRATION DE L'INDUSTRIE

*Address:* 23 Square de Meeûs, B-1040 Bruxelles
  Telephone (02) 512 66 90  Telex 21062

The Administration de l'Industrie forms part of the Ministry of Economic Affairs. It deals with matters of industrial policy and specifically with the coke-manufacturing and chemicals industries. It is also responsible for the promotion of technological developments relevant to industry, including research and development in energy-conserving processes.

### ADMINISTRATION DES MINES

*Address:* 30 Rue de Mot, B-1040 Bruxelles
  Telephone (02) 233 61 11 7

The Administration des Mines is a specialised division within the Ministry of Economic Affairs, dealing with the whole range of economic and social policies related to the Belgian coal-mining industry.

### COMITE DE CONTROLE DE L'ELECTRICITE ET DU GAZ

*Address:* 8 Boulevard du Régent, B-1000 Bruxelles
  Telephone (02) 511 81 63

The Control Committee for Electricity and Gas is a consultative body representing the employers and trade union organisations. It is concerned with tariffs, pricing, investment programmes and profitability in the electricity and gas industries, providing recommendations to the Ministry of

Economic Affairs, which is represented on the committee and has the right of initiative and veto. The committee has full access to data on electricity and gas supply undertakings and its own panel of expert advisers.

## ENTERPRISES (PUBLIC AND PRIVATE SECTOR COMPANIES)

### BP BELGIUM NV
*Address:* Jan van Rijswijcklaan 162,
   B-2020 Antwerpen
   Telephone (031) 38 78 30  Telex 31290
*Gross Revenue:* BF17,847.7 million (1978)
*Total Assets:* BF6,013.6 million
*Energy Sector:* Oil

BP Belgium is a wholly owned subsidiary of the international oil company British Petroleum. It is one of the leading distributors and marketers of petroleum products in Belgium. Supply of products is based on the group's 50 per cent shareholding in the important Antwerp refinery operated by SIBP. This refinery has a throughput capacity of 17 million tonnes per annum.

### SA CHEVRON OIL BELGIUM NV
*Address:* Avenue Louise 166, B-1050 Bruxelles
   Telephone (02) 648 80 08  Telex 21338
*Gross Revenue:* BF30,376.4 million (1979)
*Total Assets:* BF13,742.9 million
*Energy Sector:* Oil

Chevron Oil Belgium is a subsidiary company of the major international oil company Standard Oil Company of California. It is a leading supplier of petroleum products in the Belgian market, selling over five million tonnes per annum.

Distribution operations are backed up by the company's refinery at Feluy, south of Brussels, which is supplied with crude oil by pipeline from Antwerp. The refinery has a capacity of seven million tonnes per annum.

### COMITE DE GESTION DES ENTREPRISES D'ELECTRICITE
*Address:* Boîte 10, 3 Galerie Ravenstein,
   B-1000 Bruxelles
   Telephone (02) 511 19 70
*Energy Sector:* Electricity

The Supply Committee of Electricity Companies is the organisation which coordinates the investment proposals, tariffs and pricing policies of private electricity generating companies. Individual companies concede to the committee a considerable degree of independence in determining policies which are conducive to optimal efficiency in power supply.

### CPTE-SOCIETE POUR LA COORDINATION DE LA PRODUCTION ET DU TRANSPORT DE L'ENERGIE ELECTRIQUE
*Address:* 31 Rue Belliard, B-1040 Bruxelles
   Telephone (02) 358 59 69
*Energy Sector:* Electricity

CPTE acts as the coordinating group for day-to-day operations in electricity distribution. Its shareholders are the three key production and distribution companies in the public supply system. INTERCOM holds 50.6 per cent of the shares, UNERG 28.9 per cent and EBES 20.5 per cent. The objective of CPTE is to operate the public supply system as a single system for maximum efficiency.

### CTD-GAZ
*Address:* 4 Avenue Palmerston, B-1040 Bruxelles
   Telephone (02) 230 43 85
*Energy Sector:* Gas

CTD-GAZ is an organisation within the Fédération de l'Industrie de Gaz concerned with the coordination of gas transmission and distribution. It occupies a central role in formulating proposals on investment and pricing for consideration by the Ministry of Economic Affairs and coordinates operational relationships between the private sector gas undertakings.

### DISTRIGAZ SA
*Address:* Avenue des Arts 31, B-1040 Bruxelles
   Telephone (02) 230 50 20  Telex 63738
*Gross Revenue:* BF34,719,922 million (1979)
*Total Assets:* BF15,043,062 million
*Energy Sector:* Gas

Distrigaz is the main bulk supplier of gas to industrial consumers and utilities in Belgium. It is responsible for procuring imports of natural gas and has a 3,200 kilometre long high-pressure pipeline grid within the country for distribution. The state holds a substantial interest in Distrigaz and gas distributors also participate.

The Distrigaz network is linked to natural gas systems in neighbouring countries, bringing in gas from the Netherlands (mostly Dutch but also Ekofisk gas). The system is also used to transport some Dutch gas into France. Distrigaz has negotiated a contract for supply of liquefied natural gas from Algeria to supplement existing supplies and is building an import terminal at Zeebrugge.

### EBES
*Address:* Mechelsesteenweg 172,
   B-2000 Antwerpen
   Telephone (031) 30 78 00  Telex 33475
*Gross Revenue:* BF31,539.0 million (1979)
*Total Assets:* BF87,554.9 million
*Energy Sectors:* Electricity, gas, heat

EBES, Sociétés Réunies du Bassin de l'Escaut SA, is one of the major distributors of electricity in Belgium. Total sales in 1969 by EBES direct to bulk customers, and to retail consumers through the intercommunal groups which EBES manages, totalled 16,300 GWh. A significant proportion of the power was provided by the three nuclear power stations in which EBES has a shareholding. EBES is also participating in the development by Electricité de France of the nuclear power station at Tricastin.

In addition to sales of electricity EBES distributes gas obtained from Distrigaz and supplies heat from its power stations.

## ELECTROBEL
*Address:* 1 Place du Trône, B-1000 Bruxelles
    Telephone (02) 511 72 40  Telex 21852
*Gross Revenue:* BF4,616.1 million (1979)
*Total Assets:* BF21,570.2 million
*Energy Sectors:* Electricity, gas, nuclear power

Electrobel is a major diversified energy company involved in many aspects of energy supply both in Belgium and abroad. Electrobel is primarily an electrical engineering with interests in the production and distribution of electricity and gas. It has shareholdings in EBES and INTERCOM, the two leading electricity supply groups, of 14 and 22 per cent respectively and 31 per cent of Distrigaz. It is also the principal shareholder in Synatom, the service company responsible for handling nuclear fuel for Belgian nuclear power stations.

## ESSO NV
*Address:* Frankrijklei 101, B-2000 Antwerpen
    Telephone (031) 31 96 00
*Gross Revenue:* $1,231.0 million (1978)
*Total Assets:* $430.0 million
*Energy Sector:* Oil

Esso NV is a wholly owned subsidiary company of Exxon Corporation of New York. It is a leading oil company in Belgium, supplying approximately 14 per cent of all products. Distribution and marketing is centred on the important refinery which Esso operates at Antwerp. The refinery has a crude oil throughput capacity of 12 million tonnes per annum, supplied via the industry pipeline from Rotterdam.

## FINA SA
*Address:* Rue de la Science 37, B-1040 Bruxelles
    Telephone (02) 512 24 20  Telex 21544
*Gross Revenue:* BF22,950.6 million (1978)
*Energy Sector:* Oil

Fina SA is the principal Belgian owned distributor and marketer of products, being a wholly owned subsidiary of the international oil company Petrofina SA. Fina is one of the leading marketers.

Products are made available from the SIBP refinery at Antwerp, in which the Petrofina group has a 50 per cent interest.

## INTERCOM
*Address:* Place du Trône 1, B-1000 Bruxelles
    Telephone (02) 512 67 00  Telex 21852
*Gross Revenue:* BF71,526.0 million (1978)
*Total Assets:* BF118,738.0 million
*Energy Sectors:* Electricity, gas

INTERCOM (Société Intercommunale Belge de Gaz et d'Electricité) is one of the key distributors of electricity and gas in Belgium. It is responsible for supplying a number of communal groupings with electricity and gas for retail sale. These groups hold an interest in INTERCOM, and Electrobel, the major energy engineering company holds a 22 per cent interest.

INTERCOM supplies around 17,000 GWh of electricity. Over 25 per cent of this is generated from nuclear capacity in which the company participates. Electricity generating capacity available to INTERCOM is 2,600 MW. The company also handles very large quantities of gas, and its network distributes over 76,000 terajoules of gas, supplied to the company by Distrigaz.

## KEMPENSE STEENKOLENMIJNEN
*Address:* Bisschoffsheimlaan 22, B-1000 Bruxelles
    Telephone (02) 217 99 66  Telex 39109
*Gross Revenue:* BF10,170.1 million (1979)
*Total Assets:* BF10,151.7 million
*Energy Sector:* Coal

Kempense Steenkolenmijnen operates hard coal mines in the Limburg province of Belgium. Production is at a level of about five and a half million tonnes per annum, representing a high proportion of Belgian output. Approximately 70 per cent of production is used in coke-making plants and much of the balance in thermal power stations.

## SOCIETE DE TRACTION & D'ELECTRICITE
*Address:* Rue de la Science 31, B-1040 Bruxelles
    Telephone (02) 513 78 90  Telex 21514
*Gross Revenue:* BF4,138.4 million (1978)
*Total Assets:* BF17,845.6 million
*Energy Sectors:* Electricity, gas, oil, nuclear power

Tractionel is a major Belgian industrial and financial enterprise, particularly involved in the energy industries. It has substantial shareholdings in several important producers and distributors of energy. Directly or indirectly these holdings include EBES, UNERG, INTERCOM, Distrigaz and Petrofina.

## SYNATOM
*Address:* 1 Place du Trône, B-1000 Bruxelles
   Telephone (02) 511 72 40
*Energy Sector:* Nuclear power

Synatom is a specialist company set up by the energy undertakings involved in the construction and operation of nuclear power stations in Belgium. Major participant is Electrobel, with a 49 per cent shareholding. The electricity production and supply companies EBES and UNERG have 36 per cent and 15 per cent interests respectively. Synatom deals with all aspects of the nuclear fuel cycle, and is responsible for procuring nuclear fuel and handling spent fuel for reprocessing.

## UNERG
*Address:* Chaussée d'Ixelles 133, Ixelles,
   B-1050 Bruxelles
   Telephone (02) 512 58 40
*Gross Revenue:* BF17,933.0 million (1979)
*Total Assets:* BF38,374.8 million
*Energy Sectors:* Electricity, gas

UNERG is one of the three principal producers and distributors of electricity in Belgium. Total sales in 1979 amounted to 10,900 GWh of which 5,600 GWh was sold direct to industry and 4,100 GWh to the inter-communal associations which UNERG is contracted to supply. UNERG's supply area is in the southern part of the country.

UNERG operates five thermal power stations and has interests in a number of others, including the nuclear power stations at Doel, Tihange and Chooz. Total capacity available to UNERG is 1,800 MW.

UNERG also supplies gas in southern Belgium to the communes for retail sale. In 1979 supplies totalled 30.7 terajoules. Gas is obtained from Distrigaz via the national natural gas trunk pipeline network.

## PROFESSIONAL INSTITUTIONS AND TRADE ASSOCIATIONS

## ASSOCIATION BELGO-LUXEMBOURGEOISE DES GAZ DE PETROLE LIQUEFIES
*Address:* 4 Rue de la Science, B-1040 Bruxelles
   Telephone (02) 513 37 34
*Energy Sector:* Gas

The Association of Liquefied Petroleum Gas represents the interests of LPG industry, including producers and distributors and companies involved in the manufacture of equipment and appliances. The association deals with standards and technical matters as well as more general subjects affecting the industry.

## ASSOCIATION ROYALE DES GAZIERS BELGES
*Address:* 4 Avenue Palmerston, B-1040 Bruxelles
   Telephone (02) 230 43 85
*Energy Sector:* Gas

The Association Royale is a professional institution for the gas industry concerned with technical standards and specifications for gas and gas equipment.

## FEDERATION DE L'INDUSTRIE DU GAZ
*Address:* 4 Avenue Palmerston, B-1040 Bruxelles
   Telephone (02) 230 43 85
*Energy Sector:* Gas

FIGAZ is the industry association for gas producers and distributors. Members in the section 'production-transport' comprise essentially Distrigaz, the natural gas importing company, and four coke manufacturers. The section for 'distribution' includes 30 inter-communal associations and the main companies supplying them. FIGAZ is the main representative body for the gas industry and forms part of the structure of control supervised by the Ministry of Economic Affairs.

## FEDERATION PETROLIERE BELGE
*Address:* 4 Rue de la Science, B-1040 Bruxelles
   Telephone (02) 512 30 03  Telex 26930
*Energy Sector:* Oil

The Belgian Petroleum Federation is the principal organisation of the oil industry in Belgium. It provides the means to present a common view on matters affecting the industry, particularly questions of pricing and supplies in which the Ministry of Economic Affairs is concerned.

## FEDERATION PROFESSIONNELLE DES PRODUCTEURS ET DISTRIBUTEURS D'ELECTRICITE DE BELGIQUE
*Address:* 34 Avenue de Tervueren, Boîte 38,
   B-1040 Bruxelles
   Telephone (02) 733 96 07
*Energy Sector:* Electricity

The FPE is the representative organisation of the electricity supply industry. It is concerned with economic and technical aspects of the industry, and provides a coordinated view on specifications, standards, operations and tariffs.

## UNION DES EXPLOITATIONS ELECTRIQUES EN BELGIQUE
*Address:* 4 Galerie Ravenstein, Boîte 6,
   B-1000 Bruxelles
   Telephone (02) 511 19 70  Telex 62409
*Energy Sector:* Electricity

The UEEB is an industry association for undertakings involved in the production of electricity. It includes the main public supply companies, industrial auto-producers and other small communal operations.

# France

## GOVERNMENT DEPARTMENTS AND OFFICIAL AGENCIES

### AGENCE POUR LES ECONOMIES D'ENERGIE
*Address:* 30 Rue Cambronne, F-75737 Paris
Cedex 15
Telephone (1) 578 61 94

The Energy Conservation Agency was set up in 1974 following a government initiative to promote energy conservation. Under the general supervision of the Minister for Industry, the Agency is charged with providing the necessary information to formulate energy conservation policy and to carry out studies which will promote the development of new sources of energy.

### COMMISSARIAT A L'ENERGIE ATOMIQUE
*Address:* 29-33 Rue de la Fédération, BP 510,
F-75752 Paris Cedex 15
Telephone (1) 273 60 00 Telex 200671

The Atomic Energy Commission is a body established under the Ministry of Industry to ensure that the appropriate work is undertaken and information available for the development of policy on nuclear power. The Commission is responsible for various committees and advisory councils dealing with scientific, technological and safety aspects.

### COMMISSARIAT A L'ENERGIE SOLAIRE
*Address:* 208 Rue Raymond-Losserand,
F-75014 Paris
Telephone (1) 545 67 60 Telex 203712

The Solar Energy Commission was established in 1978 as a scientific and technical agency under the Minister for Industry. Its main character is of an industrial and commercial nature. It is responsible for coordinating policy, research work and studies relating to solar energy.

### DIRECTION DE LA PREVENTION DES POLLUTIONS
*Address:* 14 Boulevard du Général Leclerc,
F-92521 Neuilly-sur-Seine
Telephone (1) 758 12 12 Telex 620602

The Directorate for Pollution Prevention forms part of the Ministry of the Environment. It is responsible for safeguarding the environment and administering regulations on emissions and effluents.

### DIRECTION DES HYDROCARBURES
*Address:* 3-5 Rue Barbet-de-Jouy, F-75700 Paris
Telephone (1) 555 93 00

The Directorate for Hydrocarbons of the Ministry for Industry, deals with the administration of policy towards the oil and gas industries including exploration and development, licencing, refining and marketing allocations and relations with international organisations.

### DIRECTION DES MINES
*Address:* 99 Rue de Grenelle, F-75700 Paris 7
Telephone (1) 555 93 00 Telex 270257

The Mines Directorate is responsible for the supervision of mines and mining activity, including the search for uranium. Included in its responsibilities is the safety of nuclear installations. Two principal establishments of the Direction des Mines are the Bureau de Recherche Géologique et Minière and the Service Central de Sûrete des Installations Nucléaires. The Directorate falls under the Ministry of Industry.

### DIRECTION DU GAZ, DE L'ELECTRICITE ET DU CHARBON
*Address:* 3-5 Rue Barbet-de-Jouy, F-75700 Paris
Telephone (1) 555 93 00

The Directorate for Gas, Electricity and Coal is part of the Ministry for Industry. Its various divisions are responsible for monitoring developments and implementing policies on production, imports, distribution and tariffs. The Directorate has specific responsibilities for Electricité de France, Gaz de France, Compagnie National du Rhône, Charbonnages de France and the Houillères de Bassin.

### DIRECTION GENERALE DE L'INDUSTRIE
*Address:* 68 Rue de Bellechasse,
F-75700 Paris 7
Telephone (1) 555 93 00 Telex 200818

The Directorate-General for Industry of the Ministry for Industry deals with the application of policy towards industry in general, although included in its remit is responsibility for the state of the chemicals sector. The Directorate-General is involved in questions of energy conservation in industry and the development of new technologies in industry.

## ENTERPRISES (PUBLIC AND PRIVATE SECTOR COMPANIES)

### CHARBONNAGES DE FRANCE
*Address:* 9 Avenue Percier, BP 39608,
    F-75360 Paris 8
    Telephone (1) 563 11 20  Telex 650203
*Gross Revenue:* F14,526.2 (1978)
*Total Assets:* F20,783.2
*Energy Sectors:* Coal, electricity

Charbonnages de France is a state-owned company producing the larger part of national coal output. CdF is responsible for the exploitation of coal in three regions of France, in each of which there is a self-contained production company. These companies are the Houillères de Bassin du Centre et du Midi, Houillères du Bassin de Lorraine and Houillères du Bassin du Nord et du Pas de Calais. These companies employ 80,000 miners, producing over 20 million tonnes of coal per annum.

CdF uses part of its coal output in its own power stations. There are 23 of these in the coal-producing regions, contributing seven per cent of national electricity supplies. Much of this electricity is fed into the national grid.

### COMPAGNIE FRAÑCAISE DE RAFFINAGE
*Address:* 22 Rue Boileau, F-75781 Paris 16
    Telephone (1) 524 46 46  Telex 611961
*Gross Revenue:* F23,511.0 million (1978 -
    excl. taxes)
*Energy Sector:* Oil

CFR is the largest oil refining company in France supplying the domestic distribution and marketing operations of Compagnie Française des Pétroles, which has a controlling 63 per cent interest. It also sells substantial quantities of products direct to major bulk consumers.

CFR's principal refinery is at Gonfreville (Basse Seine), which has a capacity of 22 million tonnes per annum. The company also operates a refinery of 10.5 million tonnes per annum at La Mède on the Mediterranean. Throughput at these and other wholly or part-owned refineries exceeds 33 million tonnes per annum.

### COMPAGNIE NATIONALE DU RHONE
*Address:* 2 Rue André Bonin, F-69316
    Lyon Cedex 1
    Telephone (78) 29 04 31  Telex 330453
*Gross Revenue:* F601.2 million (1978)
*Total Assets:* F13,288.2 million
*Energy Sector:* Electricity

Compagnie Nationale du Rhône is a state-owned undertaking responsible for the development and regulation of use of the river Rhône. Its remit is to balance exploitation of hydro-electric power potential with the additional requirement for irrigation and the use of the river as an artery of navigation.

CNR has progressively increased the amount of electricity generated from the Rhône, such that the various generating stations can provide 16,500 GWh per annum to the national grid. At present, production amounts to 20 per cent of all hydro-electric output in France.

### ELECTRICITE DE FRANCE
*Address:* 2 Rue Louis Murat, F-75384 Paris 8
    Telephone (1) 764 22 22  Telex 640017
*Gross Revenue:* F49,797.0 million (1978)
*Total Assets:* F124,482.8 million
*Energy Sector:* Electricity

Electricité de France is a nationalised undertaking responsible for the production and distribution of electricity throughout France. Of the total consumption of 236,000 GWh per annum EdF supplies 219,000 GWh. The balance is derived from power stations associated with coal-producing and steel-making enterprises.

EdF uses hydro-electric and nuclear power as well as conventional thermal power stations. Currently nuclear capacity is around 30,000 MW and EdF is undertaking a major programme of nuclear power station development.

### ENTREPRISE DE RECHERCHES ET D'ACTIVITES PETROLIERES
*Address:* 7 Rue Nelaton, F-75739 Paris 15
    Telephone (1) 578 61 00  Telex 25968
*Energy Sectors:* Oil, gas

ERAP is a state-owned company which has consolidated a strong position in all aspects of the French oil industry. It is also concerned in the production of natural gas from the Lacq basin. The main vehicle for its activity in France is Société Nationale Elf Aquitaine, in which it holds 70 per cent. But there are also operating subsidiaries engaged in exploration, production, refining and marketing in many other countries.

## ESSO SAF

*Address:* 6 Avenue André Prothin, F-92080
  Courbevoie, Paris
  Telephone (1) 788 50 00  Telex 620031
*Gross Revenue:* F14,880.0 million (1979 excl
  taxes)
*Energy Sector:* Oil

ESSO SAF is a leading oil refining, distribution
and marketing company in France, in which the
international oil company Exxon Corporation of
New York has a 63 per cent interest.

Total sales of products by ESSO SAF exceed 17
million tonnes per annum. Distribution and
marketing activities are backed up by substantial
refining capacity at strategic locations in the
country. There are wholly owned refineries at Fos,
on the Mediterranean, Bordeaux, on the west
coast, and at Port Jérôme, in Basse Seine. The
company also participates in other industry
refineries.

## GAZ DE FRANCE

*Address:* 23 Rue Philibert-Delorme, F-75840
  Paris, Cedex 17
  Telephone (1) 766 52 62  Telex 650483
*Gross Revenue:* F14,935.9 million (1979)
*Total Assets:* F24,802.2 million
*Energy Sector:* Gas

Gaz de France was established in 1946 through
nationalisation of the existing gas industries. It
is therefore responsible for the production or
supply of almost all gas in France.

GdF has almost completed its programme of conversion to the use of natural gas. Over 90 per cent
of consumers now use natural gas. Part of this gas
is obtained from indigenous resources in south-
west France. But the larger part of GdF's supplies
are imported. Gas is imported by pipeline through
Belgium, supplied directly or indirectly from
Dutch, Norwegian and Soviet sources. Liquefied
natural gas is imported in substantial quantities
from Algeria via terminals at Le Havre, Saint
Nazaire and Fos.

## MOBIL OIL FRANCAISE

*Address:* Tour Septentrion, 20 Avenue André-
  Prothin, F-92400 Courbevoie, Paris 9
  Telephone (1) 776 42 41  Telex 610412
*Gross Revenue:* F12,484.4 million (1979)
*Total Assets:* F4,428.8 million
*Energy Sector:* Oil

Mobil Française is a subsidiary of the major international oil company Mobil Corporation. It is
engaged in oil refining, distribution and marketing
in France. The company's operations are based on
refining capacity at Gravenchon, in the Paris
region, Frontignan, in the south and Reichstett in
the east. The refineries at Gravenchon and
Frontignan are wholly owned and have a combined
capacity of over nine million tonnes per annum. At
Reichstett Mobil is a participant jointly with Shell
and Elf.

## SHELL FRANCAISE

*Address:* 29 Rue de Berri, F-75397 Paris 8
  Telephone (1) 561 82 82  Telex 280125
*Gross Revenue:* F26,365.0 million (1978 excl
  taxes)
*Total Assets:* F10,603.0
*Energy Sectors:* Oil, petrochemicals

Shell Française is a wholly owned company of the
Royal Dutch/Shell group. It is one of the leading
marketers of oil products. Products supply is based
on two large refining complexes at Petit Couronne,
in Basse Seine, and at Berre, on the Mediterranean
coast. The company also operates a smaller
refinery at Pauillac, in the Bordeaux area. The
capacities of the Petit Couronne and Berre
refineries are 18.8 and 13.5 million tonnes per
annum respectively. The Berre refinery also
provides feedstock for the associate company Shell
Chimie.

## SOCIETE FRANCAISE DES PETROLES BP

*Address:* 10 Quai Paul Doumer, F-92462
  Courbevoie
  Telephone (1) 334 40 00  Telex 620392
*Gross Revenue:* F17,353.7 million (1978)
*Total Assets:* F6,896.6 million
*Energy Sectors:* Oil, petrochemicals

SFBP is an affiliate of the international oil company British Petroleum, which holds 80 per cent of
the shares. The balance is held by the French
government. SFBP is one of the principal
marketers of petroleum products in France.

SFBP operates three refineries in France. The
largest, with a throughput capacity of 8.5 million
tonnes per annum, is at Lavéra, on the Mediterranean coast. The other refineries are at Dunkirk
on the north-east coast and at Vernon, in the Seine
valley, and is fed by pipeline from Le Havre.
SFBP also holds an interest in the Strasbourg
refinery. The Lavéra refinery is linked to the petrochemical complex of Naphtachimie, in which
SFBP has a 43 per cent interest.

## SOCIETE NATIONALE ELF AQUITAINE

*Address:* 7 Rue Nelaton, F-75739 Paris 15
  Telephone (1) 571 72 73  Telex 203607
*Gross Revenue:* F42,534.0 million (1978)
*Total Assets:* F52,503.0 million
*Energy Sectors:* Oil, gas

SNEA is a state-supported company engaged in
exploration, production, refining and marketing
in France and abroad. The state hydrocarbons
agency ERAP holds 70 per cent of SNEA's shares.

Total sales of petroleum products on the French market are around 20 million tonnes per annum, sold under the brand names of Elf or Antar, a company with strong refining interests which was taken over by ERAP. The group operates refineries at Grandpuits and Gargenville in the Ile de France, Donges and Vern-sur-Seiche in Brittany, and Feyzin, near Lyon. It also participates in several other refineries.

SNEA is the principal producer of natural gas from the Lacq area of south-west France. Output is just under 8,000 million cubic metres per annum.

## TOTAL COMPAGNIE FRANCAISE DE DISTRIBUTION
*Address:* 84 Rue de Villiers F-92538 Levallois-Perret
Telephone (1) 758 12 11 Telex 630871
*Gross Revenue:* F19,348.0 million (1978)
*Energy Sector:* Oil

TOTAL is the marketing subsidiary of Compagnie Française des Pétroles. It handles around 35 per cent of the output of products from the refineries of CFR. CFR holds almost 90 per cent of the shares in TOTAL so that CFP has indirect controlling interest. TOTAL is one of the leading brand names in petroleum products, especially in the higher value ones, including motor gasoline.

## TOTALGAZ
*Address:* 84 Rue de Villiers, F-95539 Levallois-Perret
Telephone (1) 758 12 11 Telex 620047
*Gross Revenue:* F654.0 million (1978 excl taxes)
*Energy Sector:* Gas

TOTALGAZ is engaged in the distribution and marketing of liquefied petroleum gases. It operates as part of the Compagnie Française des Pétroles group, as CFP holds indirectly an 84 per cent interest.

TOTALGAZ is a leading marketer of LPG, with sales of around half a million tonnes per annum, equivalent to one-fifth of the total market.

## PROFESSIONAL INSTITUTIONS AND TRADE ASSOCIATIONS

### BRANCHE NATIONAL DES NEGOCIANTS EN PRODUITS PETROLIERS
*Address:* 6 Rue Leonardo da Vinci, F-75116 Paris
Telephone (1) 553 63 74
*Energy Sector:* Oil

The BNNPP is a trade assocation for firms trading in petroleum products. These include independent importers, wholesalers and distributors. The association is concerned to safeguard the distributor/dealer sector and provides an information service on developments in product markets.

## COMITE PROFESSIONNEL DU BUTANE ET DU PROPANE
*Address:* 4 Avenue Hoche, F-75008 Paris
Telephone (1) 227 48 12
*Energy Sector:* Gas

The CPBP is a professional grouping of firms involved in production and trade in liquefied petroleum gas. It is concerned with economic as well as technical aspects, such as specifications for products and equipment and standards of safety and operating procedures.

## COMITE PROFESSIONNEL DU PETROLE
*Address:* 51 Boulevard de Courcelles, F-75008 Paris
Telephone (1) 924 98 94 Telex 650436
*Energy Sector:* Oil

The Comité Professionnel du Pétrole is an organisation within the French oil industry providing information about the industry to outside bodies, including official ones, and servicing companies in all stages of the oil industry with information relevant to their activities, particularly concerning developments in supply, organisation, pricing and taxation.

## L'INSTITUT FRANCAIS DE L'ENERGIE
*Address:* 3 Rue Henri-Heine, F-75016 Paris
Telephone (1) 524 46 14
*Energy Sector:* Energy

The IFE is an institution bringing together producers of energy, consumer organisations and other bodies interested in energy issues. Its objectives are to increase communication of expertise and knowledge about all aspects of energy and to develop the state of understanding of energy sciences.

## INSTITUT FRANCAIS DU PETROLE
*Address:* 1 et 4 Avenue de Bois-Préau, BP 311, F-92506 Rueil Malmaison
Telephone (1) 749 02 14 Telex 203050
*Energy Sectors:* Oil, gas, petrochemicals

The IFP is a professional institution forming the central core of technical expertise in matters concerned with the development and use of oil and gas. Its principal objectives are: to promote and carry out research and development work; to train technicians and engineers; to provide a centre of information on the technological capability of the French oil and gas industries.

The work of the IFP is carried out under its own auspices or by groups in institutes and in industry working within a general programme of development of knowledge and technology. A major part of the IFP's finance is derived from a levy on certain petroleum products.

## UNION DES CHAMBRES SYNDICALES DE L'INDUSTRIE DU PETROLE

*Address:* 16 Avenue Kléber, F-75116 Paris
    Telephone (1) 502 11 20
*Energy Sectors:* Oil, gas

UCSIP is a federation of associations representing firms in specific sectors of the oil industry. There are separate 'Chambres Syndicales' for: exploration and production of oil and natural gas; refining; products distribution; petroleum transportation; bitumen.

# Greece

## GOVERNMENT DEPARTMENTS AND OFFICIAL AGENCIES

### GENERAL DIRECTORATE OF MINES

*Address:* 13 Xenofontos Street, Athens
    Telephone 779 37 11

The General Directorate of Mines falls within the general administration of the Ministry of Industry and Energy. It is concerned with the administration of policies towards mining and with ensuring that exploitation and mining operations are carried out under the proper conditions.

### MINISTRY OF INDUSTRY AND ENERGY

*Address:* 80 Michalacopoualou Street, Athens
    Telephone 770 86 15  Telex 215811

The Ministry of Industry and Energy has wide responsibilities for the development of basic industries, including oil refining and power supply. It is concerned with the development of energy policy and has direct responsibility for the activities of the public energy undertakings.

## ENTERPRISES (PUBLIC AND PRIVATE SECTOR COMPANIES)

### ESSO PAPPAS INDUSTRIAL CO SA

*Address:* Vas Sophias & Messoghion Avenue,
    Athens
    Telephone 770 54 01  Telex 216322
*Gross Revenue:* $460.0 million (1978)
*Total Assets:* $53.0 million
*Energy Sector:* Oil

Esso Pappas is a wholly owned subsidiary of Exxon Corporation of New York. It is a leading marketer of petroleum products on the domestic market, and the only foreign-based company to have refining capacity in Greece. Esso Pappas supplies about 11 per cent of the total market for products. These are obtained from the associate company Thessaloniki Refining Company, which operates a refinery at Salonika, and from the state-owned refinery at Aspropyrgos.

### FINA SA

*Address:* 236 Sygrou Avenue, Callithea, Athens
    Telephone 959 34 11  Telex 216863
*Gross Revenue:* Drs 553.0 million (1978)
*Total Assets:* Drs 1,576.1 million
*Energy Sectors:* Oil, gas

Fina SA is a subsidiary company of the Belgian international oil company Petrofina. Fina SA is one of the principal distributors and marketers of petroleum products to the Greek domestic market. Products are obtained in accordance with the state-designated supply programme, from the Salonika and Aspropyrgos refineries.

Fina has a particularly strong interest in the important market for liquefied petroleum gas, with a substantial shareholding in the specialist distributor Petrogaz.

### HELLENIC ASPROPYRGOS REFINERY SA

*Address:* 18 Ermou, Athens
    Telephone 323 66 01  Telex 215443
*Gross Revenue:* Drs 1,331.1 million (1978)
*Total Assets:* Drs 6,241.5 million
*Energy Sector:* Oil

The Aspropyrgos refinery is owned by the state. The Aspropyrgos Refinery Company operates under the general control of the Ministry of Industry and Energy.

The refinery has a throughput capacity of five million tonnes per annum and is the principal source of petroleum products for all marketing companies.

### MOBIL OIL HELLAS SA

*Address:* 194 Sygrou Avenue, Callithea, Athens
    Telephone 951 31 11
*Gross Revenue:* Drs 872.9 million (1978)
*Total Assets:* Drs 1,786.3 million
*Energy Sector:* Oil

Mobil Oil Hellas is a wholly owned subsidiary company of Mobil Corporation, the New York based international oil company. It is one of the leading foreign-based companies engaged in marketing and distribution of all main petroleum products in the Greek internal market.

## MOTOR OIL (HELLAS) CORINTH REFINERIES SA

*Address:* 2 Karageorgi Servias, Athens
    Telephone 324 63 11  Telex 215741
*Gross Revenue:* Drs 799.1 million (1978)
*Total Assets:* Drs 8,177.4 million
*Energy Sector:* Oil

The Corinth refinery is owned by private Greek interests. It is of a relatively simple type producing a few major petroleum products. The refinery has a capacity of seven million tonnes per annum, and runs state-owned crude oil, partly for supply to the domestic market, but largely for export.

## PETROGAZ SA

*Address:* 57 Academias Street, Athens
    Telephone 361 20 76
*Gross Revenue:* Drs 455.5 million (1978)
*Total Assets:* Drs 721.4 million
*Energy Sector:* Gas

Petrogaz SA is the leading distributor of liquefied petroleum gas in the Greek market. The company operates nine installations for handling LPG in bulk and bottling it for retail sale throughout the country. Petrogaz also has a related trade in appliances for using LPG.

Petrogaz obtains LPG from the various refineries located in Greece. The company has substantial foreign shareholdings. Principal foreign shareholder is the Belgian international oil company Petrofina.

## PETROLA (HELLAS) SA

*Address:* 8 Othonos, Athens
    Telephone 323 01 81  Telex 214511
*Gross Revenue:* Drs 981.8 million (1978)
*Total Assets:* Drs 4,631.4 million
*Energy Sector:* Oil

Petrola SA is a Greek-owned company operating a refinery at Elefsis, near Athens. The refinery, which has a capacity of over five million tonnes per annum, processes crude oil almost entirely for export markets.

## PUBLIC PETROLEUM CORPORATION

*Address:* 54 Academias Street, Athens
    Telephone 644 41 11
*Gross Revenue:* Drs 34.1 million (1978)
*Total Assets:* Drs 1,938.2 million
*Energy Sectors:* Oil, gas

The Public Petroleum Corporation was set up to increase the state's direct involvement in the oil and gas sector. The Corporation falls within the general area of responsibility of the Ministry of Industry and Energy.

The principal objective of the Corporation is to increase the level of exploration activity in Greek offshore waters and to participate in the exploitation of any oil and gas resources discovered.

## PUBLIC POWER CORPORATION

*Address:* 30 Chalcocondylis Street, Athens 102
    Telephone
*Gross Revenue:* Drs20,881.6 million (1977)
*Total Assets:* Drs100,355.1 million
*Energy Sectors:* Electricity, coal

The Public Power Corporation is a state undertaking responsible for the production and distribution of electricity throughout Greece. Power is generated from thermal and hydro-electric stations. Small turbine generators provide self-contained electricity supply systems on the numerous smaller islands in the Aegean.

The Power Corporation utilises hydro-electric potential at eight stations on the mainland and the Peloponnese. But a substantial amount of electricity is provided by plant fired with lignite. The Corporation owns the principal coal mines in Greece, at Ptolemais, in the north and Megalopolis, in the west. Production at these mines is dedicated to electricity generating plant.

## TEXACO GREEK PETROLEUM COMPANY

*Address:* 75 Catechaki-Kifissias Avenue, Athens
    Telephone 324 11 11
*Gross Revenue:* Drs 524.7 million (1978)
*Total Assets:* Drs 970.4 million
*Energy Sector:* Oil

Texaco Greek Petroleum Company is a wholly owned subsidiary of the major international oil company Texaco Inc of the United States. It has distribution and marketing operations, based on four main installations, supplying the principal petroleum products.

## PROFESSIONAL INSTITUTIONS AND TRADE ASSOCIATIONS

## COMITE PROFESSIONNEL DES DISTRIBUTEURS DE LPG EN GRECE

*Address:* 4 Aiginitou Street, Athens 611
    Telephone 73 09 76
*Energy Sector:* Gas

The Comite Professionnel des Distributeurs de LPG is an organisation representing the technical and economic aspects of the LPG supply industry. It is a professional association in that it is concerned with  technical aspects of  gas and gas-using equipment, including matters of fuel efficiency and safety. But the Comite also provides a forum for concerted views on more general matters affecting the industry.

# Italy

## GOVERNMENT DEPARTMENTS AND OFFICIAL AGENCIES

### COMITATO INTERMINISTERIALE DEI PREZZI
*Address:* Via San Basilio 9, Roma
   Telephone (06) 46 57 27

The CIP is the inter-departmental committee on prices, reporting to the Council of Ministers. It is concerned with monitoring cost and price developments over a wide range of basic commodities which are subject to regulation. These include most of the main oil products and electricity and gas prices. The CIP is responsible for appraising claims for price increases and establishing the scope for reductions.

### CONSIGLIO NAZIONALE DELLE RICERCHE
*Address:* Piazzale delle Scienze 7, 00100 Roma
   Telephone (06) 49 93

The National Council for Research is responsible for promoting scientific and technical progress. It has a number of specialist advisory councils and is responsible for research institutions. The Council's programme of research includes energy conservation, new technologies, development of the use of methanol and other means of traction.

### DIREZIONE GENERALE DELLE FONTI DI ENERGIA E DELLE INDUSTRIE DI BASE
*Address:* Via Vittorio Veneto 33, 00100 Roma
   Telephone (06) 49 85

The Directorate General for Energy Sources and Basic Materials forms part of the Ministry of Industry, Trade and Commerce. It is responsible for the licensing of exploration and development activity, for energy transformation industries, including electricity generation and oil refining. It has particular responsibilities for the state electricity undertaking ENEL and the operation of nuclear installations.

### DIREZIONE GENERALE DELLE MINIERE
*Address:* Via Vittorio Veneto 33, 00100 Roma
   Telephone (06) 49 85

The Directorate General for Mines is responsible for the licensing of mining exploration and development and supervision of mining operations. It has specialist advisory committees on mining, technology and geology.

## ENTERPRISES (PUBLIC AND PRIVATE SECTOR COMPANIES)

### AGIP SPA
*Address:* San Donato Milanese, 20097 Milan
   Telephone (02) 53 53 60 74  Telex 310246
*Gross Revenue:* L3,176,136.4 million (1978)
*Total Assets:* L3,311,310.3 million
*Energy Sectors:* Oil, gas, uranium

AGIP is one of the principal operating companies of the state hydrocarbons agency ENI. It is engaged in exploration, production, processing and distribution in Italy and abroad. It has extensive exploration activity in Italy, for oil, gas and uranium. It produces indigenous crude oil and substantial amounts of natural gas. Crude oil is refined either in its own refineries or in those of its associate company Industria Italiana Petroli.

AGIP handles 12,000 million cubic metres of natural gas per annum and around 20 million tonnes of petroleum products; representing around 25 per cent of total consumption in Italy.

### AGIP NUCLEARE
*Address:* Corso di Porta Romana 68, 20122 Milano
   Telephone (02) 53 531  Telex 320192
*Energy Sector:* Nuclear power

AGIP NUCLEARE is a specialised company within the state-owned ENI group. It is concerned with all stages of the nuclear fuel cycle downstream from the basic mining and milling of uranium, which fall within the area of activity of the group's principal exploration and development company AGIP SpA.

### AZIENDA ELETTRICA MUNICIPALE MILANO
*Address:* Corso di Porta Vittoria 4, Milano
   Telephone (02) 77 20  Telex 26170
*Gross Revenue:* L62,060.9 million (1978)
*Total Assets:* L368,402.5 million
*Energy Sector:* Electricity

Azienda Elettrica Municipale Milano is the municipally owned electricity production and distribution authority. Total amount of electricity handled is some 3,000 GWh per annum. This is produced almost entirely from the authority's hydro-electric power stations around Milan, which have a capacity of 550 MW.

## ENTE NAZIONALE PER L'ENERGIA ELETTRICA

*Address:* Via GB Martini 3, 00198 Roma
   Telephone (06) 85 09
*Gross Revenue:* L3,046,209.5 million (1978)
*Total Assets:* L614,605.3 million
*Energy Sector:* Electricity

ENEL is a state-owned undertaking responsible for the supply of electricity throughout Italy. It produces a high proportion of total electricity requirements from its own power stations and handles exchanges with neighbouring countries. ENEL is also the main distributor to consumers although local and regional undertakings also take supplies from ENEL for retail sale.

ENEL has hydro-electric plant capable of producing a quarter of the undertaking's electricity requirement, but for the most part ENEL is reliant on thermal power plant based on fuel oil. Of the total of 35,000 MW capacity of ENEL, almost two-thirds is thermal plant. Included in this figure is nuclear capacity of only 1,400 MW and the small amount of geothermal energy produced in southern Italy.

## ESSO ITALIANA SPA

*Address:* Piazzale dell'Industria 46, 00144 Roma
   Telephone (06) 59 951  Telex 610580
*Gross Revenue:* $3,008.0 million (1978)
*Total Assets:* $419.0 million
*Energy Sector:* Oil

Esso Italiana is almost wholly owned by the international oil company Exxon Corporation of New York. It is one of the leading foreign-based marketers of petroleum products in Italy, holding a market share of around ten per cent.

Esso Italiana is one of the most important private sector oil refining companies. It operates a refinery of ten million tonnes per annum capacity at Augusta in Sicily, and a 64 per cent interest in the 14 million tonnes per annum refinery at Trecate, near Milan. It is also a joint partner with the state-owned company ANIC SpA in a five million tonne per annum refinery at Livorno.

## INDUSTRIA ITALIANA PETROLI SPA

*Address:* Piazzale della Vittoria 1, 16121 Genova
   Telephone (010) 59941  Telex 270107
*Gross Revenue:* L2,146,138.0 million (1978)
*Total Assets:* L917,907.3 million
*Energy Sector:* Oil

IIP is an integral part of the state-owned ENI group. It was formed to take over and operate the former Shell refineries at Taranto, La Spezia and Rho. These refineries have a combined total capacity of 15 million tonnes per annum of crude oil. Throughput is around ten million tonnes per annum and IIP handles refinery output directly to consumers, to other group marketing companies or independent distributors.

## ITALGAS SPA

*Address:* Via XX Settembre 41, 10121 Torino
   Telephone (011) 239 51
*Gross Revenue:* L238,097.7 million (1979)
*Total Assets:* L429,627.6 million
*Energy Sector:* Gas

Italgas, the Societa Italiana per il Gas, is a distributor of gas in the major centres of north-west Italy. It handles gas supplied by the state-owned gas production and transportation companies.

The sales area of Italgas includes Milan, Venice, Turin and Florence. It also distributes gas at the retail level in Rome. In 1979 the company's 1.6 million customers took 1,400 million cubic metres of gas. Of this total 1,050 million cubic metres was natural gas. The balance consisted of towns gas produced in the company's own plant.

## SNAM SPA

*Address:* Piazza Vanoni 2, San Donato Milanese
   Telephone (02) 5 35 31  Telex 310246
*Energy Sector:* Gas

SNAM is one of the key companies within the state-owned ENI group. It is responsible for the supply and transportation of gas for the Italian market. This involves construction and maintenance of the national trunk pipeline network and the international pipelines for imports from the Netherlands, the Soviet Union and Algeria. SNAM is also concerned in the transportation by pipeline of crude oil and petroleum products.

## TOTAL SPA

*Address:* Viale Francesco Restelli 1, 20124 Milano
   Telephone (02) 69 86  Telex 330404
*Gross Revenue:* L646,500.0 million (1978)
*Energy Sector:* Oil

TOTAL SpA is a subsidiary company of the major international oil company Compagnie Française des Pétroles. It is involved in the refining of crude oil and distribution and marketing of finished products. Distribution of products is based on the Aquila refinery, near Trieste, which has a capacity of five million tonnes per annum. TOTAL also has an interest in Raffineria di Roma, which operates a refinery near Rome.

## PROFESSIONAL INSTITUTIONS AND TRADE ASSOCIATIONS

## ASSOCIAZIONE NAZIONALE DELL' INDUSTRIA CHIMICA

*Address:* Via Fatebenefratelli 10, 20121 Milano
   Telephone (02) 63 25 32  Telex 39488
*Energy Sector:* Gas

ASCHIMICI is an industry association within the chemicals sector. It is the principal organisation concerned with liquefied petroleum gas. It represents the industry's interest in the LPG market and deals with technical aspects of products and LPG equipment.

## FIGISC

*Address:* Piazza GG Belli 2, 00153 Roma
Telephone (06) 58 87 83
*Energy Sector:* Oil

FIGISC, the Federazione Italiana Gestori Impianti Stradali Carburanti, is a trade association for retailers of motor fuels. It is active in presenting a common view to the oil supply companies and to government departments and agencies.

## UNAPACE

*Address:* Via Paraguay 2, 00198 Roma
Telephone (06) 86 46 02
*Energy Sector:* Electricity

UNAPACE, the Unione Nazionale Aziende Produttrici Auto-Consumatrici di Energie Elettrica, is a representative organisation of companies with significant internal production and use of electricity.

## UNIONE PETROLIFERA

*Address:* Viale della Civilta del Lavoro 38, 00144 Roma
Telephone (06) 591 58 69  Telex 62455
*Energy Sector:* Oil

The Unione Petrolifera is the professional and trade association for the oil industry. It includes all the leading private sector companies, but the state oil company ENI is not a member. The Unione provides co-ordination of information concerning its members' activities, in particular measures emanating from official agencies. It also plays an active part in presenting the industry's views on the state of the Italian oil market, oil supply and pricing.

# Luxembourg

## GOVERNMENT DEPARTMENTS AND OFFICIAL AGENCIES

MINISTERE DE L'ENERGIE
*Address:* 19 Boulevard Royal, Luxembourg
Telephone 2 19 21

The Ministry of Energy has general responsibilities for the overall energy policy of the Grand Duchy, including questions of energy conservation. It is supported by advisory councils on electricity and gas, and acts as centre for information relating to nuclear energy.

SERVICE DE L'ENERGIE DE L'ETAT
*Address:* 19 Boulevard Royal, Luxembourg
Telephone 2 68 80

The State Energy Service falls under the general responsibility of the Ministry of Energy, but has specific operational responsibilities in respect of electricity production at the hydro-electric power stations at Esch-sur-Sure and Rosport, which are state-owned, and for the supervision of electricity and gas distribution. The Service formulates and administers regulations, advises on electricity installations and is responsible for exploitation of hydro-electric resources.

## ENTERPRISES (PUBLIC AND PRIVATE SECTOR COMPANIES)

ARBED SA
*Address:* 29 Avenue de la Liberté, BP 1802 Luxembourg
Telephone 4 79 21  Telex 2777
*Gross Revenue:* LF 45,413.4 million (1979)
*Total Assets:* LF 79,046.6 million
*Energy Sectors:* Electricity, coal, gas

ARBED is essentially a steel-producing company but is also an important producer of energy. It uses all forms of energy to generate electricity in its own power plants and the production of coke gives rise to substantial amounts of gas, which is again largely used within the industry.

ARBED has a 96.5 per cent shareholding in Eschweiler Bergwerks-Verein which operates coal mines at Herzogenrath in north-west Germany. Production of coal exceeds six million tonnes per annum.

CEGEDEL SA
*Address:* 29 Avenue de la Porte-Neuve
Telephone 4 28 21  Telex 2375
*Energy Sector:* Electricity

The Compagnie Grande-Ducale d'Electricité du Luxembourg holds the concession from the state for operating the main electricity transmission system in Luxembourg. CEGEDEL integrates the output from the state-owned hydro-electric plants with supplementary supplies for public distribution obtained from the Société Electrique de l'Our and the West German producer Rheinisch-Westfälisches Elektrizitätswerk.

## COMPAGNIE GENERAL POUR LE GAZ
*Address:* 135 Rue de Luxembourg, Esch/Alzette
	Telephone 55 36 55
*Energy Sector:* Gas

The Compagnie Générale pour le Gaz is a publicly owned company engaged in the distribution of gas in the Esch/Alzette area.

## SHELL LUXEMBOURGEOISE SA
*Address:* 7 Rue de l'Industrie, Bertrange
	Telephone 31 11 41-1  Telex 3435
*Energy Sector:* Oil

Shell Luxembourgeoise is a wholly owned company of the Royal Dutch/Shell and one of the leading marketers of petroleum products in the Grand Duchy. All products are imported, for the most part from Belgium and supply operations are integrated with those of main group affiliates in Belgium and the Netherlands.

## SOCIETE DE TRANSPORT D'ENERGIE ELECTRIQUE
*Address:* Rue de Belvaux, Esch/Alzette
	Telephone 5 29 31
*Energy Sector:* Electricity

SOTEL is a company operating under statutory provisions concerned with transmission of electricity for bulk industrial consumers, notably the steel-making industry. SOTEL's primary role is to import the large amounts of electricity required by these industries and its system is largely independent of the public network operated by CEGEDEL.

## SOCIETE DE TRANSPORT DE GAZ
*Address:* Esch/Alzette
	Telephone 50 27 93
*Energy Sector:* Gas

SOTEG is a company established to procure and transport supplies of natural gas. SOTEG operates under statutory controls and is engaged in discussions to increase the quantities of gas under contracts from Distrigaz and Saarferngas. Gas is supplied to local authority distributors and bulk consumers.

## SOCIETE ELECTRIQUE DE L'OUR SA
*Address:* 2 Rue Pierre d'Aspelt, Luxembourg
	Telephone 2 19 69  Telex 2235
*Energy Sector:* Electricity

SEO is a producer of electricity from hydroelectric plant on the Our and Moselle rivers. The main generating station, at Vianden, produces around 250 GWh per annum. Output from the two stations at Grevenmacher and Palzem, on the Moselle, amounts to some 45 GWh, part of which is fed into the West German grid.

## PROFESSIONAL INSTITUTIONS AND TRADE ASSOCIATIONS

## ASSOCIATION BELGO-LUXEMBOURGEOISE DES GAZ DE PETROLE LIQUEFIES
*Address:* 4 Rue de la Science, B-1040 Bruxelles, Belgium
	Telephone (02) 513 37 34
*Energy Sector:* Gas

The Belgium-Luxembourg LPG association is a professional and trade association of firms engaged in distribution of liquefied petroleum gas. It presents the industry view of economic and technical questions, and is concerned with specifications and safety of products and LPG-using equipment.

# Netherlands

## GOVERNMENT DEPARTMENTS AND OFFICIAL AGENCIES

## DIRECTORAAT-GENERAAL VOOR ENERGIE
*Address:* Bezuidenhoutseweg 30, PB 20101, 2500 EC Den Haag
	Telephone (070) 81 40 11  Telex 31099

The Directorate-General for Energy forms part of the Ministry of Economic Affairs. It carries the responsibilities for most aspects of the energy sector, including gas supply, electricity supply and nuclear power.

## ELEKTRICITEITSRAAD
*Address:* Bezuidenhoutseweg 6, 2594 AV Den Haag
	Telephone (070) 81 40 11

The Electricity Council is attached to the Ministry of Economic Affairs, with responsibility for advice to the Directorate-General for Energy on all aspects of electricity.

## ENERGIEONDERZOEK CENTRUM NEDERLAND
*Address:* Scheveningseweg 112, PO Box 80404, 2508 GK Den Haag
	Telephone (070) 51 45 81  Telex 31459

The Energy Research Centre is a public research foundation, mainly financed by the state, carrying out research and development work in all areas of energy supply. The ECN is particularly involved in the development of nuclear power with an experimental plant at Dodewaard.

## INDUSTRIELE RAAD VOOR DE KERNENERGIE

*Address:* Bezuidenhoutseweg 95, Den Haag
 Telephone (070) 81 40 11

The Nuclear Power Council is a specialist advisory group attached to the Ministry of Economic Affairs. It includes representation from interests in nuclear power development and was to provide information and advice for the Directorate-General for Energy.

## ENTERPRISES (PUBLIC AND PRIVATE SECTOR COMPANIES)

### NV DSM

*Address:* Van Der Maesenstraat 2, PB 65,
 6400 AB Heerlen
 Telephone (045) 78 81 11  Telex 11618
*Gross Revenue:* Fl 12,750.0 million (1979)
*Total Assets:* Fl 9,293.0 million
*Energy Sectors:* Petrochemicals, Gas

DSM, Dutch State Mines, is a state-owned company mainly engaged in petrochemicals manufacture. It does however have important interests in natural gas. It holds 40 per cent of the company distributing and selling gas from the Groningen field and a similar level of holding in various onshore and offshore licences. DSM is also directly involved in exploration work in the Netherlands, Ireland and the UK.

DSM has a 40 per cent holding in Nederlandse Gasunie, which is responsible for transporting and marketing natural gas within the Netherlands.

### ESSO NEDERLAND BV

*Address:* PB 110 Den Haag
 Telephone (070) 73 99 11
*Gross Revenue:* $1,380.0 million (1978)
*Total Assets:* $796.0 million
*Energy Sector:* Oil

Esso Nederland is a wholly owned subsidiary of Exxon Corporation of New York. It is a leading distributor and marketer of petroleum products in the Netherlands with sales of over five million tonnes per annum. The company operates a major refinery at Rotterdam, with a throughput capacity of over nine million tonnes per annum. The refinery supplies the requirements of the Dutch market and exports products to other companies o of the Exxon group in northern Europe.

### MOBIL OIL BV

*Address:* PB 1131, 3000 BC Rotterdam
 Telephone (010) 14 70 11  Telex 22317
*Energy Sector:* Oil

Mobil Oil is a subsidiary company of Mobil Corporation of New York. It is engaged in oil refining and marketing in the Netherlands, and associate companies of the group are involved in exploration for oil and gas and production of petrochemicals.

Mobil Oil operates a modern refinery at Amsterdam, with a capacity of 6.5 million tonnes per annum. The refinery, which is fed through a crude oil pipeline from Rotterdam, produces a wide range of products for the Dutch market and for export to other Mobil companies in northern Europe.

### NEDERLANDSE AARDOLIE MAATSCHAPPIJ

*Address:* Schepersmaat 2, PB 28, 9400 AA Assen
 Telephone (05920) 2 71 11  Telex 53347
*Energy Sector:* Gas

NAM is a joint-venture company in which the Royal Dutch/Shell and Exxon groups are equal partners. NAM is involved in extensive exploration and production activity in the Netherlands. Principal activity is exploitation of the giant Groningen natural gas field, which is undertaken in conjunction with the state-controlled companies DSM and Nederlandse Gasunie.

### NV NEDERLANDSE GASUNIE

*Address:* Laan Corpus den Hoorn 102, PB 19,
 9700 MA Groningen
 Telephone (050) 21 91 11  Telex 53448
*Gross Revenue:* Fl 12,702.5 million (1978)
*Total Assets:* Fl 6,552.5 million
*Energy Sector:* Gas

Gasunie is responsible for the purchase, transport and marketing of natural gas in the Netherlands. The state holds a 50 per cent interest, ten per cent directly, the rest through DSM. The other participants are the Royal Dutch/Shell and Exxon groups which are engaged in the production of most of the natural gas in the Netherlands.

Gasunie operates a trunk pipeline system within the Netherlands, and distributes the gas to local and regional undertakings or direct to bulk industrial consumers. The Gasunie system also carries large quantities of gas under export contracts.

### PROVINCIAL ELECTRICITEITSBEDRIJF IN FRIESLAND

*Address:* Emmakade 59, PB 413, 8901 BE
 Leeuwarden
 Telephone (05100) 94 91 1  Telex 46495
*Gross Revenue:* Fl 339.6 million (1978)
*Total Assets:* Fl 1,069.8 million
*Energy Sector:* Electricity

PEB is a publicly owned undertaking responsible for the generation and distribution of electricity in Friesland province. The company's supply position is based on operation of a 640 MW power station at Bergum.


## NV PROVINCIALE LIMBURGSE ELEKTRICITEITS MIJ

*Address:* Prins Bisschopsingel 22, Maastricht
   Telephone
*Gross Revenue:* Fl 527.2 million (1978)
*Total Assets:* Fl 1,690.8 million
*Energy Sector:* Electricity

PLEM is a public electricity supply undertaking for the Limburg province of southern Netherlands. It is a generator and distributor of electricity with a system closely integrated with other undertakings both in Netherlands and in West Germany. PLEM operates two power stations on the Maas with a total capacity of 2,000 MW.


## PROVINCIALE ZEEUWSE ENERGIE-MAATSCHAPPIJ

*Address:* Poelendaelesingel 10, PB 48,
   4330 AA Middelburg
   Telephone (01180) 25 35-1  Telex 55275
*Gross Revenue:* Fl 361.5 million (1978)
*Total Assets:* Fl 1,071.6 million
*Energy Sector:* Electricity

PZEM is a public electricity supply undertaking operating in the south-western part of the Netherlands. It distributes over 5,000 GWh of electricity per annum. This is largely generated in its own plant, including the nuclear generating station at Borssele, which has a capacity of 470MW.


## SHELL NEDERLAND BV

*Address:* Shellgebouw, Hofplein 20, PB 1222,
   3000 BE Rotterdam
   Telephone (010) 69 69 11  Telex 21049
*Energy Sectors:* Oil, gas, petrochemicals

Shell Nederland operates or manages the principal interests of the Royal Dutch/Shell group in the Netherlands. These include operation of the major refining complex at Pernis, associated petrochemical plant, and petroleum products marketing. Shell Nederland is also involved in management of Shell interests in NAM and Gasunie.

Shell is the largest single marketer of oil products in the Netherlands, accounting for over 25 per cent of all sales. Products are supplied from the Pernis refinery (Rotterdam) which has a capacity of 25 million tonnes per annum, producing the whole range of products. Approximately half of the output from Pernis is exported.


## SHV HOLDINGS NV

*Address:* Rijnkade 1, PB 2065, 3500 GB Utrecht
   Telephone (030) 33 88 33  Telex 47285
*Gross Revenue:* £2,393.4 million (1979)
*Total Assets:* £429.0 million
*Energy Sectors:* Coal, oil

SHV Holdings is a broadly based company with interests in shipping and trade in raw materials as well as general wholesaling and retailing of consumer products. Approximately 30 per cent of turnover is derived from trade in energy products. This includes trading in coal and oil and bunkering of vessels.


# PROFESSIONAL INSTITUTIONS AND TRADE ASSOCIATIONS


## KONINKLIJKE VERENIGING VAN GASFABRIKANTEN IN NEDERLAND

*Address:* Wilmersdorf 50, PB 137,
   7300 AC Apeldoorn
   Telephone (055) 23 08 08  Telex 49456
*Energy Sector:* Gas

The KVGN is a professional institution for engineers in gas industry concerned with technical and technico-economic aspects of the industry. It is a constituent member of the International Gas Union, contributing to the Union's three-yearly congress.


## VERENIGING TECHNISCHE COMMISSIE VLOEIBAAR GAS

*Address:* Zuid-Hollandlaan 7, PB 110,
   2501 AL Den Haag
   Telephone (070) 73 99 11  Telex 28756
*Energy Sector:* Gas

The Technical Committee on Liquid Gas is the main association representing distributors of liquefied petroleum gas. Its primary concern is with the technical aspects of LPG and gas-using equipment.


## VERENIGING VAN EXPLOITANTEN VAN GASBEDRIJVEN

*Address:* Wilmersdorf 50, PB 137,
   7300 AC Apeldoorn
   Telephone (055) 23 08 08  Telex 49456
*Energy Sector:* Gas

The Association of Gas Undertakings is a representative association for the gas distribution companies. Its main objective is to coordinate discussions with Gasunie over supplies and tariffs. The Association is also involved in questions of consumer interest such as safety and general information about the industry.

# Portugal

## GOVERNMENT DEPARTMENTS AND OFFICIAL AGENCIES

### DIRECÇÃO-GERAL DA ENERGIA
*Address:* Benef. 241, Lisboa 4
  Telephone 77 10 13

The Directorate-General for Energy is responsible for administration of the public interest in energy planning and supply. It is concerned with all fuels, the development of renewable energy resources and energy conservation measures. The Directorate forms part of the Ministry for Industry and Energy.

### DIRECÇÃO-GERAL DA GEOLOGIA E MINAS
*Address:* Rua Antonio Enes 7-5°, Lisboa 1
  Telephone 54 91 08

The Directorate-General for Geology and Mining is a specialised division within the Ministry of Industry and Energy, concerned with the technical aspects of exploration and development policy for hydrocarbons and minerals.

### MINISTERIO DA INDUSTRIA E ENERGIA
*Address:* Rua Horta Seca 15, Lisboa 2
  Telephone 32 73 91

The Ministry for Industry and Energy has general responsibilities for the development of industry, including the energy industries and the availability of energy to industrial consumers. These responsibilities include general considerations of the structure of industrial development, energy conservation and performance of the energy supply industries.

## ENTERPRISES (PUBLIC AND PRIVATE SECTOR COMPANIES)

### ELECTRICIDADE DE PORTUGAL
*Address:* Avenida Infante Santo 15,
  Apartado 3096, Lisboa 3
  Telephone 60 80 11  Telex 12816
*Gross Revenue:* Esc15,549,934.1 million (1978)
*Total Assets:* Esc76,637,908.8 million
*Energy Sectors:* Electricity, gas

Electricidade de Portugal was established in 1976 as a result of the nationalisation of electricity generating companies. EDP is now responsible for generation, transmission and distribution throughout Portugal. At the retail level EDP sells around 40 per cent of all low-voltage electricity.

EDP generates a high proportion of its electricity from hydro-electric plant. It has 2,250 MW of hydro-electric capacity out of a total of 3,390 MW. But with the high rate of utilisation of hydro-electric plant, this source provides nearly 80 per cent of power output.

EDP is investigating the use of coal as power station fuel, and is examining the use of both indigenous and imported coal. It is also carrying out site investigations and design work for a possible nuclear power station project.

With the take-over of the company supplying electricity in the Lisbon area, EDP acquired a towns gas system, which sends out 150 million cubic metres per annum of gas.

### PETROLEOS DE PORTUGAL
*Address:* Rua das Flores 7, 1200 Lisboa
  Telephone 32 80 35  Telex 12521
*Gross Revenue:* Esc36,817,823.1 million (1978)
*Total Assets:* Esc76,305,453.6 million
*Energy Sector:* Oil

Petrogal was set up in 1976 as a state undertaking with responsibility for the supply of oil products to the Portuguese market. It took over the existing refineries at Lisbon and Oporto as well as the new refinery then under construction at Sines to the south of Lisbon.

Total refining capacity is nominally 19.5 million tonnes per annum, which is well in excess of the requirements of the domestic economy. Refining is to be concentrated at the Sines refinery, which has a capacity of ten million tonnes per annum and is linked to a petrochemical plant, and at Oporto, where there is a refinery of 7.5 million tonnes per annum capacity.

Petrogal supplies the whole range of petroleum products and has established itself as a major marketer, including a leading role in the LPG market. The balance of output is sold in bulk to other marketers, mainly affiliates of the international oil companies.

## PROFESSIONAL INSTITUTIONS AND TRADE ASSOCIATIONS

### ASSOSIACAO PORTUGUESA DE GASES DE PETROLEO LIQUEFEITOS
*Address:* Apartado 2403, Lisboa 2
  Telephone 38 47 71  Telex 12837
*Energy Sector:* Gas

The Portuguese Association for Liquefied Petroleum Gas represents the general interests of LPG distributors. It is concerned with technical as well as commercial aspects of the industry, including specifications for LPG gases and appliances and questions of safety.

GREMIO NACIONAL DOS INDUSTRIAIS DE
ELECTRICIDADE
*Address:* Av Republica 44-5º, Lisboa 1
   Telephone 76 77 47

The National Council of Industrial Electricity
Companies is an association of electricity producers
in the industrial sector, where there are a number
of significant auto-producers.

# Spain

## GOVERNMENT DEPARTMENTS AND OFFICIAL AGENCIES

MINISTERIO DE HACIENDA
*Address:* Alcala 5, Madrid 14
   Telephone (1) 243 17 00

The Ministry of the Interior includes within its
responsibilities some aspects of the energy industries. Principal amongst these is administration of
the state monopoly in petroleum and the operation
of CAMPSA. The Ministry is also involved in some
aspects of energy conservation.

MINISTERIO DE INDUSTRIA Y ENERGIA
*Address:* Serrano 35, Madrid 1
   Telephone (1) 225 01 89

The Ministry of Industry and Energy is responsible
for many aspects of the energy sector, including
energy planning, mineral resources, fuel supplies
and the use of energy by industry.

## ENTERPRISES (PUBLIC AND PRIVATE SECTOR COMPANIES)

BUTANO SA
*Address:* Arcipreste de Hita 10, Madrid 15
   Telephone (1) 449 26 00  Telex 27358
*Gross Revenue:* Ptas41,402.0 million (1978)
*Total Assets:* Ptas58,007.8 million
*Energy Sector:* Gas

Butano SA is the principal company involved in
the distribution and marketing of liquefied
petroleum gas in Spain. Butano is a state-owned
company, shares being held equally by CAMPSA,
which holds the state monopoly for petroleum
products supply, and INI, the industrial holding
company. Sales by Butano are around 2.3 million
tonnes per annum, almost the entire retail market
requirement for LPG.

CAMPSA
*Address:* Capitan Haya 41, Madrid 20
   Telephone (1) 456 16 00
*Energy Sectors:* Oil, gas

CAMPSA, the Compania Arrendataria del
Monopolio de Petroleos, is a state-controlled
company with the delegated monopoly of supply
of petroleum products to the Spanish domestic
market. Other marketing companies, including
affiliates of the international oil companies, are
subject to control by CAMPSA.

CAMPSA holds a 33 per cent interest in the eight
million tonnes per annum capacity refinery at
Bilbao, and 50 per cent in Butano, the principal
distributor of liquefied petroleum gas.

CATALANA DE GAS Y ELECTRICIDAD SA
*Address:* Avenida Puerta del Angel 20,
   Barcelona 2
   Telephone (3) 318 00 00
*Energy Sector:* Gas

Catalana de Gas y Electricidad is one of the largest
gas distribution undertakings in Spain, selling gas
to over half a million consumers in the Barcelona
region. Catalana de Gas has total sales of the
equivalent of 300 million cubic metres per annum
of natural gas, of which part consists of towns gas
manufactured from naphtha, and the balance
natural gas supplied by ENAGAS from its import
terminal in Barcelona.

COMPANIA ESPAÑOLA DE PETROLEOS SA
*Address:* Apartado 671, Avenida de America 32,
   Madrid 2
   Telephone (1) 256 53 00  Telex 27722
*Energy Sectors:* Oil, petrochemicals

Compania Española de Petroleos SA (CEPSA) is
one of the largest privately owned companies in
Spain, operating a refinery at Algeciras, in southern
Spain, and at Tenerife in the Canary Islands. Each
refinery has a throughput capacity of eight million
tonnes per annum. Capacity is partly oriented
towards export and bunkering markets. The
Algeciras refinery also provides feedstock for
petrochemical operations, in which CEPSA has
an interest.

COMPANIA IBERICA REFINADORA DE
PETROLEOS SA
*Address:* Avenida Jose Antonio  20, Madrid
   Telephone (1) 448 00 39  Telex 22572
*Gross Revenue:* Ptas 33,973.6 million (1978)
*Total Assets:* Ptas14,691.2 million
*Energy Sector:* Oil

Compania Iberica Refinadora de Petroleos (PETROLIBER) operates an oil refinery at Corunna. The United States oil company Marathon holds a 28 per cent share, but the majority is held by the Spanish state and private Spanish groups.

The refinery has a capacity of five million tonnes per annum and supplies petroleum products in the north-western part of the country.

## EMPRESA NACIONAL CARBONIFERA DEL SUR SA

*Address:* Monte Esquinza 24, Madrid
   Telephone (1) 419 14 94
*Gross Revenue:* Ptas 2,438.1 million (1978)
*Total Assets:* Ptas 3,666.5 million
*Energy Sector:* Coal

Empresa Nacional Carbonifera del Sur is a state-owned mining company producing coal in central Spain. INI, the state holding company has a 71 per cent interest. Two mines are in operation, at Penarroya and Puertollano, each producing half a million tonnes per annum. The latter has been in production only since 1977 and is expanding. Both mines supply primarily electricity generating stations.

## EMPRESA NACIONAL DE ELECTRICIDAD SA

*Address:* Velazquez 132, Madrid
   Telephone (1) 261 41 76
*Gross Revenue:* Ptas17,845.6 million (1978)
*Total Assets:* Ptas259,273.7 million
*Energy Sectors:* Electricity, coal

Empresa Nacional de Electricidad SA (ENDESA), which is owned 96 per cent by the state holding company INI is a major producer of electricity in northern Spain. Total power generation is some 8,700 GWh per annum. Of this figure 1,000 GWh is produced by hydro-electric plant, but the larger part of output is based on thermal generating stations based on coal or nuclear power.

ENDESA has developed a substantial base of power supply using indigenous lignite deposits. Production of lignite is approaching six million tonnes per annum.

## EMPRESA NACIONAL DEL GAS SA

*Address:* Avenida de America 38, Madrid 2
   Telephone (1) 246 34 00  Telex 44448
*Gross Revenue:* Ptas8,952.0 million (1978)
*Total Assets:* Ptas89,610.6 million
*Energy Sector:* Gas

Empresa Nacional del Gas SA (ENAGAS) is a state-owned company with responsibility for the supply of gas in Spain, in particular the development of natural gas as a major fuel.

ENAGAS' operations are centred on Barcelona, where the company has a receiving terminal for liquefied natural gas imported from Algeria and Libya. The LNG is regasified and transmitted to local distribution companies, in four of which ENAGAS itself has substantial interest. Principal distributor is Catalana de Gas y Electricidad.

## EMPRESA NACIONAL DEL PETROLEOS SA

*Address:* General Sanjurjo 41, Madrid
   Telephone (1) 442 41 00  Telex 27325
*Gross Revenue:* Ptas177,100.5 million (1978)
*Total Assets:* Ptas194,026.9 million
*Energy Sectors:* Oil, petrochemicals

The Empresa Nacional del Petroleos SA (ENPETROL) was formed in 1974 from three existing oil refining companies. ENPETROL is controlled by the state holding company INI, which holds 72 per cent of the shares, but much of the balance is held equally by Spanish affiliates of the international oil companies Texaco Inc and Standard Oil Company of California, with 11 per cent each.

ENPETROL has modern refineries at Cartagena, Puertollano and Tarragona, with a total capacity of 26 million tonnes per annum. Total quantity of products placed on the domestic and export markets is some 18 million tonnes per annum.

## EMPRESA NACIONAL DEL URANIO SA

*Address:* Santiago Rusiñol 12, Madrid
   Telephone (1) 233 98 16  Telex 43042
*Gross Revenue:* Ptas1,049.0 million (1978)
*Total Assets:* Ptas25,600.5 million
*Energy Sector:* Uranium

The Empresa Nacional del Uranio is involved in exploiting uranium reserves in Spain, producing uranium concentrate at Ciudad Rodrigo of 130 tonnes per annum. The company is exploring in Spain and abroad.

Empresa Nacional del Uranio is owned 60 per cent by INI, the state holding company. The remaining shares are held by seven electricity producing companies.

## EMPRESA NACIONAL HIDROELECTRICA DEL RIBAGORZANA SA

*Address:* Paseo de Gracia 132, Barcelona 8
   Telephone (3) 217 70 00  Telex 52802
*Gross Revenue:* Ptas17,425.5 million (1979)
*Total Assets:* Ptas280,465.3 million
*Energy Sector:* Electricity

Empresa Nacional Hidroelectrica del Ribagorzana SA (ENHER), of which the state holding company INI has 79 per cent of the shares, is a producer of electricity in north-eastern Spain. It produces 4,000 GWh per annum from hydro-electric sources, supplemented by 700 GWh from its share in the Vandellos nuclear power station, and some conventional thermal power. Total electricity handled by ENHER's system is over 7,600 GWh per annum, necessitating additional purchases of power from other producers.

## EMPRESA NACIONAL HULLERAS DEL NORTE SA
*Address:* Joaquin Garcia Morato 31-7º, Madrid
   Telephone (1) 448 56 50
*Gross Revenue:* Ptas14,661.0 million (1978)
*Total Assets:* Ptas43,606.0 million
*Energy Sector:* Coal

Empresa Nacional Hulleras del Norte SA (HUNOSA) is wholly owned by the state holding company INI. It is engaged primarily in mining coal in the Oviedo area, producing 3.5 million tonnes per annum. About half of this output is used by the steel industry and HUNOSA participates with the state steel company ENSIDER in Parque de Carbones de Abono, which utilises the coal for coke-manufacture.

## ENIEPSA
*Address:* Pez Volador 2, Madrid
   Telephone (1) 274 72 00
*Gross Revenue:* Ptas1,273.2 million (1978)
*Total Assets:* Ptas18,732.7 million
*Energy Sectors:* Oil, gas

ENIEPSA, the Empresa Nacional de Investigacion y Explotacion de Petroleo SA, is a state owned company established to explore for and develop oil and gas deposits in Spain. ENIEPSA has substantial interests in the Amposta, Casablanca and Dorado oil fields, and the Castillo gas field.

## FUERZAS ELECTRICAS DE CATALUÑA SA
*Address:* Plaza de Cataluña 2, Barcelona 2
   Telephone (3) 318 08 08  Telex 54673
*Gross Revenue:* Ptas 36,199.0 million (1978)
*Total Assets:* Ptas212,507.0 million
*Energy Sector:* Electricity

Fuerzas Electricas de Cataluña SA (FECSA) is an important producer of electricity in north-eastern Spain including supply to the city of Barcelona. FECSA supplies 1.8 million customers in this area. The company has 3,000 MW of generating capacity, with a high proportion of oil-fired plant.

Annual output of electricity is around 12,000 GWh, of which 45 per cent has been derived from oil-fired power stations. Less than a quarter comes from hydro-electric plant. FECSA uses a significant amount of coal in power generation and also has a share in the Vandellos nuclear power station.

## GAS MADRID SA
*Address:* Ronda de Toledo 10, Madrid 5
   Telephone (1) 265 12 08
*Energy Sector:* Gas

Gas Madrid is a public gas supply company distributing gas in Madrid and Valladolid to a total of 330,000 customers. The company supplies towns gas equivalent to 135 million cubic metres per annum of natural gas.

## HIDROELECTRICA ESPAÑOLA SA
*Address:* Hermosilla 3, Madrid 1
   Telephone (1) 402 40 36
*Gross Revenue:* Ptas46,123.0 million (1978)
*Total Assets:* Ptas345,516.0 million
*Energy Sector:* Electricity

Hidroelectrica Espanola is a leading producer of electricity in Spain, generating over 14,000 GWh per annum, mainly for distribution in central Spain and exchange with other electricity undertakings. Hidroelectrica itself supplies over three million customers.

Hidroelectrica Espanola derives a considerable proportion of its electricity from hydraulic capacity, but also has a share in the nuclear power station at Almaraz.

## HISPANOIL
*Address:* Pez Volador 2, Madrid
   Telephone (1) 274 72 00
*Gross Revenue:* Ptas35,197.0 million (1978)
*Total Assets:* Ptas22,009.7 million
*Energy Sector:* Oil

Hispanoil is a state-owned company, set up to search for and exploit oil and gas deposits outside Spanish territory. It has interests in exploration and production in many parts of the world, both onshore and offshore. Production of crude oil attributable to Hispanoil's interests is around five million tonnes per annum which represents a degree of additional security in Spanish crude oil supplies.

In addition to the production of oil Hispanoil also acts as the trading concern for handling ten million tonnes per annum of other crude oil for Spanish refineries.

## IBERDUERO SA
*Address:* Serrano 26, Madrid
   Telephone (1) 276 66 00  Telex 33793
*Gross Revenue:* Ptas55,903.0 million (1978)
*Total Assets:* Ptas419,787.0 million
*Energy Sector:* Electricity

Iberduero SA is one of the principal electricity producing companies in Spain. It has a generating capacity of 5,300 MW. The major element in this capacity is hydro-electric plant but Iberduero also has significant production from conventional thermal and nuclear generating plant. Total annual output by Iberduero is around 20,000 GWh. High utilisation of hydro-electric capacity enables 75 per cent to be met from this source. Nuclear power availability is 1,600 GWh, but this is increasing as capacity is developed at the Lemoniz and Santa Maria de Garona (Burgos) stations, in which Iberduero has an interest.

Iberduero's main supply areas are in the north and central western areas of Spain, and the company supplies 2.6 million customers itself. Marginal output is exchanged with other transmission companies.

## INSTITUTO NACIONAL DE INDUSTRIA

*Address:* Plaza de Salamanca 8, Madrid 6
   Telephone (1) 402 33 99
*Energy Sectors:* Electricity, coal, gas, oil, uranium

The Instituto Nacional de Industria (INI) is a state holding company with interest in many energy production and distribution companies. Production of coal and electricity attributable to INI's interests is equivalent to 60 per cent and 16 per cent of total national output respectively. INI also has a significant share in production of oil and gas, although quantities are small. INI is major shareholder in Empresa Nacional del Uranio, which produces uranium in Salamanca province.

## UNIDAD ELECTRICA SA

*Address:* Francisco Gervas 3, Madrid 20
   Telephone (1) 270 44 00  Telex 27626
*Energy Sector:* Electricity

Unidad Electrica SA (UNESA) is a specially established co-ordinating group within the Spanish electricity supply industry. All the principal producers of electricity are involved, totalling 23 in all, and including those responsible for supply in the Balearic and Canary Islands. UNESA co-ordinates the operations of utilities so that maximum efficiency is achieved, and controls thereby the production and transmission of over 96 per cent of total Spanish electricity supply.

## UNION ELECTRICA SA

*Address:* Capitan Haya 53, Madrid
   Telephone (1) 279 25 00
*Gross Revenue:* Ptas25,612.3 million (1979)
*Total Assets:* Ptas210,726.8 million
*Energy Sector:* Electricity

Union Electrica is a producer and distributor of electricity in eastern and central Spain. The company has a diversified pattern of fuel generation in which hydraulic, nuclear, coal- and oil-fired plant are all significant.

Output from Union Electrica's own power stations in 1979 totalled 6,500 GWh, of which 2,300 GWh was generated by hydro-electric plant. Thermal fuel plants contributed 3,200 GWh. The Narcea station is one of the main coal-fired plants in Spain (using anthracite) and at La Robla there is an important power station based on hard coal.

Union Electrica has a wholly owned nuclear power station at Jose Cabrera (Guadalajara) which contributed 1,000 GWh in 1979. The company also has a share in the nuclear power station under construction at Almaraz.

## PROFESSIONAL INSTITUTIONS AND TRADE ASSOCIATIONS

## CLUB ESPAÑOL DEL PETROLEO

*Address:* Serrano 57, Madrid 6/E
*Energy Sectors:* Oil, gas

The Club Español del Petroleo (CEPE) is a professional institution for the oil industry. It has been established to represent the industry's views on oil industry matters and to provide advice on technical and economic questions. It also acts as a central source of information for the industry.

## FORUM ATOMICO ESPAÑOL

*Address:* Claudio Coello 20, Madrid 1
   Telephone (1) 276 56 71
*Energy Sector:* Nuclear power

The Forum Atomico Español is an association formed to promote investigation, discussion and dissemination of information in the field of nuclear power. It has been active in examining the role of nuclear power in Spain in the context of the development of the government's energy policy.

## SEDIGAS

*Address:* Balmes 357, Barcelona 6
   Telephone (3) 247 28 04
*Energy Sector:* Gas

Sedigas is an association of gas producers and distributors. Its objectives are: to provide a comprehensive source of information on production, transportation, distribution and use of gas; to examine and develop new techniques to improve supply and services provided by the industry; to establish standards for plant and equipment; and to carry out commercial studies.

# Switzerland

## GOVERNMENT DEPARTMENTS AND OFFICIAL AGENCIES

### EIDGENÖSSISCHES AMT FÜR ENERGIEWIRTSCHAFT

*Address:* Kapellenstrasse 14, Postfach,
   CH-3001 Bern
   Telephone (031) 61 56 11

The Federal Office of Energy Economy is concerned with the general development of energy supply in Switzerland. It formulates federal policy on supply and guidelines for the development and operation of installations.

### EIDGENÖSSISCHES AMT FÜR UMWELTSCHUTZ (AfU)

*Address:* CH-3003 Bern
   Telephone (031) 61 93 11

The Federal Office for Environmental Protection is responsible for monitoring, and administering regulations on pollution of air and water. This includes questions of power station emissions and storage of nuclear waste.

### EIDGENÖSSISCHES INSTITUT FÜR REAKTOR-FORSCHUNG (EIR)

*Address:* CH-5303 Würenlingen
   Telephone (056) 98 17 41  Telex 53714

The Swiss Federal Institute for Reactor Research is a state establishment concerned with research and development work and operational aspects of nuclear power. It provides services and training for specialists. The EIR is also involved in the work of the Commission for Safety in Nuclear Installations.

### EIDGENÖSSISCHES POLITISCHES DEPARTEMENT (EPD)

*Address:* Bundeshaus West, CH-3003 Bern
   Telephone (031) 61 21 11

The Federal Political Department handles energy and environmental questions at the international level. This includes participation in nuclear non-proliferation agreements and co-operation in energy conservation and research and development.

## ENTERPRISES (PUBLIC AND PRIVATE SECTOR COMPANIES)

### AARE-TESSIN AG FÜR ELEKTRIZITÄT (ATEL)

*Address:* Bahnhofquai 12, CH-4600 Olten
   Telephone (062) 21 61 51  Telex 68168
*Gross Revenue:* SF399.6 million (1979)
*Total Assets:* SF775.6 million
*Energy Sector:* Electricity

ATEL is a producer and distributor of electricity with a turnover of 6,200 GWh per annum. Electricity is transmitted in bulk either to industrial consumers or to local distribution companies. ATEL operates hydro-electric power stations which supply the larger part of its output and has some thermal capacity. ATEL is a participant in both of the nuclear power plants which are under construction, at Gösgen-Däniken and Leibstadt, and in the two planned for Kaiseraugst and Graben.

### BERNISCHE KRAFTWERKE AG

*Address:* Viktoriaplatz 2, Postfach,
   CH-3000 Bern 25
   Telephone (031) 40 51 11  Telex 32196
*Energy Sector:* Electricity

Bernische Kraftwerke is a municipally owned undertaking responsible for the supply and distribution of electricity to the Bern area. It is owner of the nuclear power station at Mühleberg, which has a capacity of 650 MW, supplying the canton and surrounding areas.

### CENTRALSCHWEIZERISCHE KRAFTWERKE (CKW)

*Address:* Hirschengraben 3, CH-6003 Luzern
   Telephone (041) 26 51 11  Telex 78642
*Energy Sector:* Electricity

CKW is an electricity production and distribution company supplying electricity to the Lucerne region. It has become an important participant in nuclear power projects in order to meet its area's electricity requirements. CKW holds interests in the two nuclear power stations under construction at Gösgen-Däniken and Leibstadt, 12.5 and 10.0 per cent respectively. It will also have an interest in both of the planned stations at Kaiseraugst and Graben and has proposed construction of its own power station at Inwil.

CKW also holds a 15 per cent share in the consortium of companies involved in developing capacity at Electricité de France's nuclear power station at Bugey.

## ESSO (SCHWEIZ)

*Address:* Uraniastrasse 40, CH-8021 Zürich
Telephone (01) 214 41 11
*Gross Revenue:* $626.0 million (1978)
*Total Assets:* $154.0 million
*Energy Sector:* Oil

Esso (Schweiz) is a wholly owned subsidiary of Exxon Corporation of New York. It is one of the leading distributors and marketers of oil products in Switzerland, with sales of over two million tonnes per annum. Part of the company's product requirements are met from the refinery at Aigle, operated by Raffinerie du Sud-Ouest SA, in which the Exxon group has a 34 per cent interest. The balance of products sold by Esso is imported from neighbouring countries, especially south Germany, or from Benelux sources via the Rhine.

## MIGROS GENOSSENSCHAFTS-BUND

*Address:* Limmatstrasse 152, Postfach 266, CH-8031 Zürich
Telephone (01) 44 44 11
*Gross Revenue:* SF7,710.0 million (1979)
*Energy Sector:* Oil

Migros is an organisation of co-operative societies dealing in the whole range of consumer goods. Its 12 regional member societies have over 500 outlets and a total membership of 1.1 million. The Migros group includes in its retailing operations high-throughput outlets for motor fuels. Migros is also active in purchasing bulk supplies from Swiss companies and abroad to maintain its competitive position.

## NORDOSTSCHWEIZERISCHE KRAFTWERKE AG (NOK)

*Address:* Kernkraftwerk Beznau, CH-5321 Doettingen
Telephone (056) 45 20 84  Telex 58027
*Energy Sector:* Electricity

Nordostschweizerische Kraftwerke is the operating company of the first nuclear power station to be built in Switzerland, at Beznau in the Aargau Canton. Capacity of the power station is in excess of 700 MW. A substantial amount of the electricity produced by NOK is transmitted to the Zürich area for distribution by the cantonal and city authorities, which hold a 37 per cent share in NOK.

NOK is itself involved in several other nuclear power station projects. It holds 25 per cent in the Gösgen-Däniken plant and eight per cent in Leibstadt, both of which are under construction, and ten per cent of the capacity in the projected Kaiseraugst power station.

## SERVICES INDUSTRIELS DE GENEVE

*Address:* Pont de la Machine, CP 272, CH-1211 Genève 11
Telephone (022) 20 88 11
*Gross Revenue:* SF274.0 million (1978)
*Total Assets:* SF558.2 million
*Energy Sectors:* Electricity, gas, heat

Services Industriels de Genève is the publicly owned utility company supplying Geneva with electricity, gas and water. The company supplies 1,500 GWh of electricity per annum of which 35 per cent is generated from its own hydroelectric plant. But 50 per cent of the power supply is bought in from L'Energie de l'Ouest Suisse, which includes a substantial contribution generated by the experimental nuclear research station (CERN).

Geneva is supplied with natural gas under contract from the Netherlands. Annual supply of gas is 50 million cubic meters, part of which is used in district heating plant.

## SHELL (SWITZERLAND)

*Address:* Bederstrasse 66, CH-8002 Zürich
Telephone (01) 206 21 11
*Energy Sector:* Oil

Shell (Switzerland) is a wholly owned subsidiary company of the Royal Dutch/Shell group, distributing and marketing petroleum products in Switzerland. Products are for the most part obtained from the refinery near Neuchâtel, operated by Raffinerie de Cressier SA, in which the Shell group has a 75 per cent interest.

# PROFESSIONAL INSTITUTIONS AND TRADE ASSOCIATIONS

## ERDÖL-VEREINIGUNG

*Address:* Zentralstrasse 70, CH-8003 Zürich
Telephone (01) 66 14 30
*Energy Sector:* Oil

The Erdöl-Vereinigung is the professional institution and trade association for the oil industry. Its membership of 38 includes most of the principal firms engaged in exploration, refining, importing, distribution and marketing. The EV represents the industry on many federal and cantonal committees, concerned with technical, commercial and environmental questions.

SCHWEIZERISCHE VEREINIGUNG FÜR
ATOMENERGIE
*Address:* Bärenplatz 2, Postfach 2613, CH-3001
   Bern
   Telephone (031) 22 58 82  Telex 33528
*Energy Sector:* Nuclear power

The Swiss Association for Atomic Energy is a
non-profit making organisation with the objective
of promoting the peaceful uses of atomic energy
in Switzerland. Membership is over 800, including
corporate and individual members, representing
electric utilities, industry, construction, finance,
engineering, consulting, research and education.

SCHWEIZERISCHER VEREIN DES GAS- UND
WASSERFACHES
*Address:* Grütlistrasse 44, Postfach 658
   CH-8002 Zurich
   Telephone (01) 201 56 36
*Energy Sector:* Gas

The SVGW is a professional institution for the gas
and water supply industries. Its primary concerns
are the technical aspects of operations, product
quality, distribution and utilisation. The SVGW is
a consitutuent member of the International Gas
Union. The institution also deals with more general
and economic aspects of the industry.

VERBAND SCHWEIZERISCHER
ELEKTRIZITÄTSWERKE
*Address:* Bahnhofplatz 3, Postfach 3295,
   CH-8023 Zürich
   Telephone (01) 211 51 91
*Energy Sector:* Electricity

The Union of Swiss Electricity Producers is an
association of power companies. Its general objectives are: the collation and dissemination of
information as a service within the industry and
outside; the study of issues affecting the industry;
training and education within the industry. The
association also represents the views of the
industry to government departments and official
bodies.

VEREINIGUNG EXPORTIERENDER
ELEKTRIZITÄTSUNTERNEHMUNGEN
*Address:* Parkstrasse 23, Postfach NOK,
   CH-5401 Baden
   Telephone (056) 20 31 11
*Energy Sector:* Electricity

The VEE is an association of electricity exporting
companies. Membership includes 11 principal
electricity producers, in some of which foreign
companies are participants. The purpose of the
Association is to encourage the economic exploitation of electricity and represent the common
interests of electricity exporters.

# West Germany

## GOVERNMENT DEPARTMENTS AND OFFICIAL AGENCIES

BUNDESMINISTERIUM FÜR FORSCHUNG
UND TECHNOLOGIE
*Address:* Stresemannstrasse 2, D-5300 Bonn-Bad
   Godesberg
   Telephone (02221) 59-1

The Federal Ministry of Research and Technology
is responsible for the extensive programme of
research and development work in the field of
energy. The programme covers: nuclear power
development; radioactive waste; exploitation of oil
and gas; technologies of energy in use; new sources
of energy; energy conservation.

BUNDESMINISTERIUM FÜR WIRTSCHAFT
*Address:* Villemombler Strasse 76, D-5300
   Bonn-Duisdorf
   Telephone (02221) 76-1  Telex 886747

The Federal Ministry of Economics is generally
responsible for the development of energy supply
industries, including security and adequacy of
foreign sources of energy, import agreements,
pricing and market competition.

## ENTERPRISES (PUBLIC AND PRIVATE SECTOR COMPANIES)

ARAL AG
*Address:* Wittener Strasse 45, D-4630 Bochum 1
   Telephone (0234) 31 51
*Gross Revenue:* DM10,505.0 million (1978)
*Energy Sector:* Oil

ARAL is the leading marketer of motor fuels in
West Germany, and sales of all products are well
over ten million tonnes per annum.

Following the take-over by Veba of Gelsenberg
AG the reconstituted Veba Oel group now holds
56 per cent of the shares in ARAL. Other shareholdings are Mobil Oil AG (28 per cent) and
Wintershall AG (15 per cent).

BADENWERK AG
*Address:* Postfach 1680, D-7500 Karlsruhe 1
   Telephone (0721) 69 21  Telex 7825803
*Gross Revenue:* DM1,450.0 million (1979)
*Energy Sector:* Electricity

Badenwerk is the distribution undertaking for the province of Baden. Total quantity of electricity distributed in 1979 was 13,100 GWh. Of this total 10,700 GWh was generated from the company's own electricity plant. Badenwerk is a partner with Energie-Versorgung Schwaben in a nuclear power station at Philippsburg on the Rhine. This power station has a capacity of 900 MW, with expansion to 2,160 MW planned for 1981. The two undertakings are also constructing a second nuclear power station at Wyhl.

## BAYERNWERK AG

*Address:* Blutenburgstrasse 6, Postfach 200340,
   D-8000 München 2
   Telephone (089) 1 25 41  Telex 523172
*Gross Revenue:* DM2,112.6 million (1978)
*Total Assets:* DM8,534.0 million
*Energy Sectors:* Electricity, coal

Bayernwerk is the main electricity supply undertaking for Bavaria. In 1979 total electricity supplied to the retail distribution networks, which include the municipal authorities of Munich and Nuremberg, was 16,400 GWh. Of this total 75 per cent was produced in Bayernwerk's own power stations and much of the rest in other Bavarian stations.

At present, the main sources of Bayernwerk's electricity are the 700 MW plant at Schwandorf fuelled by brown coal mined by the subsidiary company Bayerische Braunkohlen-Industrie AG, and a 500 MW plant using hard coal from the Ruhr and Saarland.

Bayernwerk operates a 1,300 MW nuclear power station at Grafenrheinfeld am Main and is a participant in other nuclear power stations at Isar and Gundremmingen. Capacity at Isar is 900 MW and at Gundremmingen 250 MW, but with expansion to 2,800 MW planned.

## BERLINER KRAFT- UND LICHT AG

*Address:* Stauffenbergstrasse 26, D-1000
   Berlin 30
   Telephone (030) 267 24 13
*Gross Revenue:* DM1,398.9 million (1979 excl
   taxes)
*Total Assets:* DM5,202.1 million
*Energy Sectors:* Electricity, heat

Berliner Kraft- und Licht AG (BEWAG) is the electricity supply company for the city of Berlin. BEWAG has eight power stations in the city with capacities between 75 and 450 MW. Total capacity is 2,250 MW. Annual output of electricity is 8,300 GWh. Most of the stations are designed to produce district heat as well.

BEWAG's capacity is largely based on coal as boiler fuel, using over two million tonnes per annum. The rest is based on oil, of which BEWAG uses one million tonnes per annum.

## BRAUNSCHWEIGISCHE KOHLEN-BERGWERKE

*Address:* Schöninger Strasse 2, D-3330 Helmstedt
   Telephone (05351) 181  Telex 095526
*Energy Sectors:* Coal, electricity

Braunschweigische Kohlen-Bergwerke is a coal-mining and electricity production company. Preussische Elektrizitäts-AG and Electrowerke AG each have a 49 per cent shareholding.

Annual output of coal is some four million tonnes from the Alversdorf mine. This is used to feed a power station at Offleben, producing 4,400 GWh per annum.

## DEMINEX AG

*Address:* Dorotheenstrasse 1, Postfach 100944,
   D-4300 Essen
   Telephone (0201) 72 61  Telex 8571141
*Energy Sector:* Oil

DEMINEX was set up in 1969 by German-based companies in the oil sector with the objective of obtaining a secure position in crude oil resources, so as to at least maintain the share of the total oil market which the companies had and to diversify the country's crude oil sources. The shareholders in DEMINEX are Veba Oel (54 per cent), Union Rheinische Braunkohlen Kraftstoff and Wintershall (18.5 per cent each) and Saarbergwerke (9 per cent).

DEMINEX is involved in exploration and production in several parts of the world, including United Kingdom and Irish offshore waters. DEMINEX has interests in the Thistle and Beatrice fields.

## DEUTSCHE BP AG

*Address:* Überseering 2, D-2000 Hamburg 60
   Telephone (040) 63 51
*Gross Revenue:* DM10,571.2 million (1978)
*Total Assets:* DM3,123.0 million
*Energy Sectors:* Oil, gas

Deutsche BP is a wholly owned subsidiary of the major international oil company British Petroleum. It is one of the leading marketers of oil products in West Germany and has substantial oil refining capacity.

Total refining capacity of Deutsche BP is close to 20 million tonnes per annum. Largest refinery is at Dinslaken (Ruhr), at ten million tonnes per annum. Smaller refineries are located at Hamburg and Vohburg (Bavaria), which is fed by pipeline from the Mediterranean.

Deutsche BP is not involved in production of oil or gas in West Germany, but it has become a major shareholder in the leading gas supply company Ruhrgas, with a 25 per cent holding.

## DEUTSCHE SHELL AG

*Address:* Überseering 35, Postfach 602809,
    D-2000 Hamburg 60
    Telephone (040) 63 41
*Gross Revenue:* DM11,304.8 million 1978
*Total Assets:* DM3,974.4 million
*Energy Sectors:* Oil, gas

Deutsche Shell is a wholly owned subsidiary of
the Royal Dutch/Shell group of companies. It
is engaged in exploration, production, refining
and marketing. It is one of the leading distributors
and marketers of petroleum products.

Production of oil and gas is carried out by the
companies Gewerkschaft Brigitta and Gewerkschaft
Elwerath which produce a combined total of
12,000 million cubic metres of natural gas and 1.5
million tonnes of crude oil per annum. Shell has a
50 per cent interest in both companies.

Shell has extensive refining capacity in West
Germany, totalling 18 million tonnes per annum.
Principal refineries are at Godorf, on the Rhine,
and Hamburg.

## DEUTSCHE TEXACO AG

*Address:* Überseering 40, Postfach 600449,
    D-2000 Hamburg 60
    Telephone (040) 63 75 1
*Gross Revenue:* DM8,159.2 million (1979)
*Total Assets:* DM2,634.9 million
*Energy Sectors:* Oil, gas

Deutsche Texaco is a wholly owned subsidiary of
the international oil company Texaco Inc. It is
engaged in production of oil and gas, oil refining
and marketing of finished products. Texaco's
production interests give rise to output of 0.9
million tonnes of crude oil and 450 million cubic
metres of natural gas per annum.

Deutsche Texaco is a marketer of all main oil
products. Supply is based on the company's
refinery at Heide (Schleswig-Holstein) and shares in
the Caltex refinery at Speyer and the Karlsruhe
refinery of Oberrheinische Mineralölwerke, giving a
total capacity of some ten million tonnes per
annum.

## ENERGIE-VERSORGUNG SCHWABEN AG

*Address:* Kriegsbergstrasse 32, D-7000 Stuttgart 1
    Telephone (0711) 2 08 31  Telex 723715
*Gross Revenue:* DM1,500.0 million (1979)
*Energy Sector:* Electricity

Energie-Versorgung Schwaben (EVS) is the main
electricity supply undertaking in south-central
Germany, including the major urban centre of
Stuttgart. Total sales of electricity by EVS, either
direct to bulk consumers or to local distributors,
were 12,750 GWh in 1979. EVS is a participant
in the Philippsburg nuclear power station on the

Rhine. This station has a capacity of 900 MW,
with expansion to 2,160 MW planned. EVS also
has a share in the nuclear power station being
constructed at Wyhl, on the Rhine.

## ESCHWEILER BERGWERKS VEREIN AG

*Address:* Roermonder Strasse 63, D-5120
    Herzogenrath
    Telephone (02407) 51-1  Telex 08329513
*Energy Sectors:* Coal, electricity

Eschweiler Bergwerks Verein is a coal-mining
company in north-west Germany. It is however
owned 95.83 per cent by the Luxembourg steel-
making company ARBED. The company produces
over six million tonnes per annum of hard coal
and is also geared to producing coke. Most of the
balance of coal output is used to fuel a power
station operated by Eschweiler Bergwerks Verein,
producing 1,700 GWh per annum. Off-gas from the
coke operation amounts to 1,200 million cubic
metres per annum.

## ESSO AG

*Address:* Kapstadtring 2, Postfach 600620,
    D-2000 Hamburg 60
    Telephone (040) 63 31
*Gross Revenue:* $6,228.0 million (1978)
*Total Assets:* $879.0 million
*Energy Sectors:* Oil, gas

ESSO AG is a wholly owned subsidiary of Exxon
Corporation of New York. It is engaged in production of oil and gas, oil refining and distribution
and marketing of petroleum products. It is one of
the leading marketers selling around 18.5 million
tonnes per annum.

Production of oil and gas is from Gewerkschaft
Brigitta and Gewerkschaft Elwerath, in both of
which Esso has a 50 per cent interest. Combined
output of these companies is 12,000 million cubic
metres of natural gas and 1.5 million tonnes of
crude oil per annum.

Esso AG's finished products are supplied from four
refineries strategically located at Hamburg,
Cologne, Karlsruhe and Ingolstadt. Total capacity
of these refineries is around 25 million tonnes per
annum.

## GEWERKSCHAFT BRIGITTA

*Address:* Riethorst 12, D-3000 Hannover 51
    Telephone (0511) 61 61
*Energy Sectors:* Gas, oil

Gewerkschaft Brigitta is an oil and gas production
company operating fields in north-west Germany.
Main output is of natural gas, with a total of 9,400
million cubic metres per annum. Output of crude
oil totals 140,000 tonnes per annum.

Arising from this production of natural gas Gewerkschaft Brigitta has a 25 per cent shareholding in Ruhrgas, the principal natural gas distributor in West Germany. Gewerkschaft Brigitta is itself owned by Deutsche Shell and Esso AG.

## GEWERKSCHAFT ELWERATH
*Address:* Riethorst 12, D-3000 Hannover 51
Telephone (0511) 61 61
*Energy Sectors:* Oil, gas

Gewerkschaft Elwerath is a producer of oil and gas in both northern and southern parts of the country. Output of crude oil is over one million tonnes per annum and of gas 2,600 million cubic metres per annum. Deutsche Shell and Esso AG are equal partners in the company.

## HAMBURGISCHE ELECTRICITÄTS-WERKE-AG
*Address:* Überseering 12, Postfach 600960,
D-2000 Hamburg 60
Telephone (040) 63 61  Telex 217421
*Gross Revenue:* DM1,628.0 million (1978)
*Total Assets:* DM5,721.9 million
*Energy Sectors:* Electricity, heat

Hamburgische Electricitäts-Werke (HEW) is a public company responsible for the supply of electricity in the Hamburg region. Total supplies of electricity are 12,000 GWh per annum. In addition, HEW supplies heat to the equivalent of 5,000 GWh per annum.

HEW operates several power stations itself, largest of which are at Moorburg (1,000 MW) and Wedel (700 MW). Total capacity is 2,800 MW. In addition, HEW participates in three nuclear power stations in north Germany, which provide a further 700 MW of capacity. Nuclear plant provides nearly 30 per cent of HEW's electricity. HEW's wholly owned plant is based mainly on coal and natural gas.

## MOBIL OIL AG
*Address:* Steinstrasse 5, D-2000 Hamburg 1
Telephone (040) 30 41
*Gross Revenue:* DM6,800.0 million (1979)
*Energy Sectors:* Oil, gas

Mobil Oil AG is a subsidiary company of Mobil Corporation of New York. It is involved in oil and gas production, oil refining and distribution and marketing of finished products. Total sales in the West German market amount to nearly nine million tonnes per annum. Motor fuels are marketed primarily through ARAL AG, in which Mobil Oil has a 28 per cent interest.

Mobil Oil produces 4,500 million cubic metres of natural gas and 700,000 tonnes of crude oil per annum from indigenous resources. It has two modern refineries, at Wilhelmshaven and Wörth,

and is a 50 per cent shareholder in a refinery at Neustadt. Total capacity available to Mobil is 15 million tonnes per annum.

## PREUSSAG AG
*Address:* Leibnizufer 9, PO Box 4827,
D-3000 Hannover 1
Telephone (0511) 19 32-1  Telex 0922828
*Gross Revenue:* DM3,179.0 million (1979)
*Total Assets:* DM2,412.0 million
*Energy Sectors:* Coal, gas, oil, electricity

Preussag is a diversified company with interests in minerals, energy, engineering, construction, petrochemicals and transportation. Energy activities in West Germany include production of coal, gas and oil and generation of electricity.

Preussag produces oil and gas in both northern and southern fields, with output of 500,000 tonnes of crude oil and 900 million cubic metres of gas per annum. Coal is mined at Ibbenbüren in north Germany for sale to electricity utilities, industry and households. Output is over two million tonnes per annum, used partly for Preussag's electricity generating plant which produces 1,200 GWh per annum. Coal output will be at least maintained following agreement with Rheinisch-Westfälisches Elektrizitätswerk to build a coal-fired power station in the area.

## RHEINISCHE BRAUNKOHLENWERKE AG
*Address:* Stüttgenweg 2, D-5000 Köln 41
Telephone (0221) 4 80-1  Telex 8883011
*Gross Revenue:* DM1,936.2 million (1979)
*Total Assets:* DM3,752.1 million
*Energy Sector:* Coal

Rheinische Braunkohlenwerke is the largest coal producer in Germany. Annual output is 110 million tonnes of lignite, mainly for use in the power stations of RWE, which holds almost all of the shares of the company.

Production takes place in three areas of the Rhineland. The northern area (Westphalia) yields nearly three-quarters of total output. Other areas centre on Cologne and Hambach.

## RHEINISCH-WESTFÄLISCHES ELEKTRIZITÄTSWERK AG
*Address:* Kruppstrasse 5, Postfach 27,
D-4300 Essen
Telephone (0201) 18 51  Telex 857851
*Gross Revenue:* DM15,669.1 million (1979)
*Total Assets:* DM21,303.1 million
*Energy Sectors:* Electricity, coal

Rheinisch-Westfälisches Elektrizitätswerke (RWE) is the largest electricity supply company in West Germany. Supply areas of the company include the provinces of Rhineland-Palatinate and North-

Rhine-Westphalia and part of southern Germany. Provincial and local authorites hold a majority of RWE's shares.

RWE's system accounts for around 40 per cent of total electricity supply in West Germany, including as it does large industrial centres. RWE's electricity is based on coal and nuclear power. Rheinische Braunkohlenwerke AG is a subsidiary company producing almost all the country's brown coal, which is used for power station fuel. RWE has also been involved in the development of nuclear power stations from the outset. Today it operates the 2,500 MW Biblis (Hesse) and 1,300 MW Mülheim power stations, and is a partner in the Gundremmingen (Bavaria) station, which may be expanded to nearly 3,000 MW. RWE plans to double the size of Biblis and has plans for additional nuclear plant on the Rhine.

## RUHRGAS AG
*Address:* Huttropstrasse 60, Postfach 103252,
    D-4300 Essen 1
    Telephone (0201) 1 84-1  Telex 0857818
*Gross Revenue:* DM6,244.5 million (1979)
*Total Assets:* DM4,620.9 million
*Energy Sector:* Gas

Ruhrgas is the dominant undertaking involved in bulk supply of natural gas in West Germany. The company handles two-thirds of all the gas used in the country. In 1979, Ruhrgas' supply of gas totalled more than 400,000 GWh, of which 95 per cent was natural gas.

Ruhrgas obtains only a quarter of its supplies from indigenous sources. It has become involved in major importing projects with gas from the Netherlands, the Soviet Union and the North Sea. These involve trunk pipelines for importation and for distribution within Germany, and Ruhrgas is a partner in the main gas transporting companies.

To supplement existing sources of natural gas, Ruhrgas is planning to import liquefied natural gas from Algeria. LNG may also be brought in from Nigeria.

## RUHRKOHLE AG
*Address:* Rellinghause Strasse 1, Postfach 5,
    D-4300 Essen 1
    Telephone (0201) 1 77-1  Telex 857651
*Gross Revenue:* DM16,221.9 million (1979)
*Total Assets:* DM12,366.2 million
*Energy Sectors:* Coal, electricity

Ruhrkohle is a major producer of coal in West Germany, accounting for virtually all of the output of hard coal in the Ruhr/Rhine area. Total production exceeds 60 million tonnes per annum. The company also produces some 14 million tonnes per annum of coke. Ruhrkohle is one of the economy's leading companies, employing 129,000 people. It is owned by a group of leading industrial companies. Veba holds 27 per cent and six other companies hold 5-11 per cent each.

Coal production takes place through three district operators; Bergbau AG Niederrhein, Bergbau AG Lippe and Bergbau AG Westfalen. These operating companies each produce between 18 and 22 million tonnes of coal per annum.

The major part of Ruhrkohle's production is used in electricity generation. The company is 69 per cent shareholder in STEAG AG which operates 16 coal fired power stations with a total capacity of 3,140 MW. These contribute some 14,000 GWh per annum to the national electricity supply, principally through the system of Rheinisch-Westfälisches Elektrizitätswerke, which is also a shareholder in STEAG.

## SAARBERGWERKE AG
*Address:* Trierer Strasse 1, Postfach 1030,
    D-6600 Saarbrücken
    Telephone (0681) 405-1  Telex 4421240
*Gross Revenue:* DM3,821.2 million (1978)
*Total Assets:* DM3,112.5 million
*Energy Sectors:* Coal, electricity, oil

Saarbergwerke is a publicly owned company operating coal mines in the province of Saarland. The federal government holds 74 per cent of the shares and Saarland the rest.

Saarbergwerke produces nine million tonnes of coal per annum. Of this total more than six million tonnes is used as fuel for power generation. Saarbergwerke itself operates three power stations, which consume nearly three million tonnes. Output of these stations is over 6,000 GWh per annum. The company produces 1.4 million tonnes of coke too. Saarbergwerke is a participant in Deminex, the oil exploration consortium and in the Saarland refinery at Klarenthal.

## UNION RHEINISCHE BRAUNKOHLEN KRAFTSTOFF AG
*Address:* Postfach 8, D-5047 Wesseling
    Telephone (022) 36 791  Telex 8886947
*Energy Sectors:* Oil, petrochemicals

Union Rheinische Braunkohlen Kraftstoff (URBK) is an oil refining company with a refinery at Wesseling, near Cologne, having a throughput capacity of six million tonnes per annum. The refinery is orientated to providing feedstock for petrochemicals manufacture.

URBK has extended its interests into related areas of transportation and exploration. It is a partner in DEMINEX, the exploration consortium of German oil companies, and also has other interests in licences in the United Kingdom sector of the North Sea.

## VEBA OEL AG

*Address:* Pawikerstrasse 30, Postfach 45,
   D-4660 Gelsenkirchen-Buer
   Telephone (0209) 3 66-1 Telex 824881
*Gross Revenue:* DM14,463.0 million (1979 — excl
   taxes)
*Energy Sector:* Oil

Veba Oel is part of the general German oil and petrochemicals concern Veba AG. Veba Oel is the principal subsidiary involved in exploration, production, processing and marketing of oil. It operates a refinery at Gelsenkirchen and is a participant in refineries at Neustadt and Karlsruhe. Motor fuels are handled by the leading West German marketer ARAL AG, in which Veba Oel has a 56 per cent interest. Heating oils are distributed mainly by the subsidiary company Raab Karcher.

Veba Oel is the major participant in the German oil exploration consortium DEMINEX. The company thus has interests in exploration and production in several areas abroad, including the United Kingdom sector of the North Sea.

## VEREINIGTE ELEKTRIZITÄTSWERKE WESTFALEN AG

*Address:* Rheinlanddamm 24, Postfach 941,
   D-4600 Dortmund 1
   Telephone (0231) 54 41 Telex 822121
*Gross Revenue:* DM3,450.0 million (1979)
*Total Assets:* DM9,113.0 million
*Energy Sector:* Electricity

Vereinigte Elektrizitätswerke Westfalen AG (VEW) is the second largest electricity supply company in West Germany serving an important area of the Rhineland. The company's electricity output is based mainly on conventional thermal power stations, particularly using coal produced in the Rhine/Ruhr area. VEW operates only one small nuclear power station, of 250 MW at Lingen (Lower Saxony).

## WINTERSHALL AG

*Address:* Friedrich-Ebert-Strasse 60,
   Postfach 104020, D-3500 Kassel
   Telephone (0561) 30 11
*Energy Sectors:* Oil, gas, petrochemicals

Wintershall is engaged in exploration, production and processing of oil and distribution of oil products. Over 95 per cent of the shares of Wintershall are held by the major chemicals company BASF.

Wintershall operates a refinery at Salzbergen, in north-west Germany, which processes locally produced crude, and has a 60 per cent interest in a refinery at Mannheim, which is linked to BASF's chemical complex at Ludwigshafen.

Wintershall produces oil and gas from indigenous sources totalling 800,000 tonnes and 1,600 million cubic metres per annum respectively. It is 18.5 per cent shareholder in the exploration consortium DEMINEX and is involved in other exploration groups.

# PROFESSIONAL INSTITUTIONS AND TRADE ASSOCIATIONS

## BERGBAU-ELEKTRIZITÄTS-VERBUNDGEMEINSCHAFT

*Address:* Bismarckstrasse 54, D-4300 Essen 1
   Telephone (0201) 79 94 1
*Energy Sectors:* Coal, electricity

The Bergbau-Elektrizitäts-Verbundgemeinschaft is an association representing those companies with combined interests in coal mining and electricity production.

## BUNDESVERBAND DER DEUTSCHEN GAS-UND WASSERWIRTSCHAFT eV (BGW)

*Address:* Postfach 140152, D-5300 Bonn 1
   Telephone (0228) 61 10 01
*Energy Sector:* Gas

The BGW is an industry institution for gas and water supply. It is a representative body for these industries on a wide range of technical, commercial and economic issues; dealing with official bodies and international gas industry groupings.

## DEUTSCHE VERBUNDGESELLSCHAFT

*Address:* Ziegelhäuser Landstrasse 5, D-6900
   Heidelberg 1
   Telephone (06221) 4 50 17
*Energy Sector:* Electricity

The Deutsche Verbundgesellschaft is an association of nine principal electricity supply companies, which handle a very high proportion of total West German requirements. It therefore represents those companies most concerned with development of the national power supply system.

## DEUTSCHER BRAUNKOHLEN-INDUSTRIE-VEREIN eV

*Address:* Apostelnkloster 21-25, Postfach 100446,
   D-5000 Köln 1
   Telephone (0221) 23 56 82
*Energy Sector:* Coal

The Deutscher Braunkohlen-Industrie-Verein is an association for companies concerned with mining and exploitation of brown coal in West Germany. It represents the common interest of these companies in development of the country's brown coal deposits.

DEUTSCHES ATOMFORUM eV
*Address:* Heussallée 10, D-5300 Bonn 1
   Telephone (02221) 50 71 16  Telex 8869444
*Energy Sector:* Nuclear power

The Deutsches Atomforum was set up in 1959 by a group of organisations and institutions involved in the development of nuclear power. Its objectives are to foster the exchange of information between scientists and technologists, disseminate information and promote discussion about nuclear issues, and provide opinions and advice to official bodies.

GESAMTVERBAND DES DEUTSCHEN
STEINKOHLENBERGBAUS
*Address:* Friedrichstrasse 1, Postfach 1708,
   D-4300 Essen
   Telephone (0201) 10 51
*Energy Sector:* Coal

The Gesamtverband des Deutschen Steinkohlenbergbaus is a trade association representing companies engaged in mining hard coal. It provides a central service of information for the industry and publicises issues affecting the West German coal industry.

MINERALÖLWIRTSCHAFTSVERBAND eV
*Address:* Steindamm 71, D-2000 Hamburg 1
   Telephone (040) 2 80 11 41
*Energy Sectors:* Oil, gas

The Mineralölwirtschaftsverband (MWV) is the principal association of oil industry companies, including the main refiners and marketers of petroleum products. It is a central focus of information about the industry and represents the views of the oil industry to government departments and other official bodies.

STEINKOHLENBERGBAUVEREIN
*Address:* Franz Fischer Weg 61, D-4300
   Essen-Kray
   Telephone (0201) 10 51
*Energy Sector:* Coal

The Steinkohlenbergbauverein is an association of the six main hard coal mining companies of West Germany, established to promote the group's special interests.

VERBAND FÜR FLÜSSIGGAS eV
*Address:* Lindenstrasse 15, D-6000
   Frankfurt/Main 17
   Telephone (0611) 74 60 41  Telex 0413113
*Energy Sector:* Gas

The Verband für Flüssiggas is a trade association for companies involved in the distribution of liquefied petroleum gas. It is concerned with both commercial and technical aspects of the industry, including specifications of products and LPG— using equipment and questions of safety.

VEREIN DEUTSCHER KOHLEN-
IMPORTEURE eV
*Address:* Bergstrasse 7, D-2000 Hamburg 1
   Telephone (040) 32 74 84
*Energy Sector:* Coal

The Verein Deutscher Kohlenimporteure is a trade association for companies involved in coal trading, and in particular those importing coal into West Germany. The Association monitors developments in international coal trade and issues in the West German economy affecting coal consumption.

VEREINIGUNG DEUTSCHER ELEKTRIZITATS-
WERKE eV (VDEW)
*Address:* Stresemannallée 23, D-6000
   Frankfurt/Main
   Telephone (0611) 63 04-1
*Energy Sector:* Electricity

The VDEW is an association representing companies involved in public electricity supply. Its general objectives are the further development of an efficient electricity supply industry. The VDEW deals with questions of energy supply and demand, energy policy, electro-technology, efficient electricity use, heat and power, legislative background, administration and information. Total membership is over 730 undertakings.

WIRTSCHAFTSVERBAND ERDÖL- UND
ERDGASGEWINNUNG eV (WEG)
*Address:* Bruhlstrasse 9, D-3000 Hannover 1
   Telephone (0511) 32 60 16
*Energy Sectors:* Oil, gas

The WEG is an association representing companies engaged in exploration and production of oil and gas in West Germany. It includes firms whose areas of activity are in mining, engineering and drilling. Total membership is 27, including some parent companies of production subsidiaries.

# Index to Organisations

# Part Four:
# Energy Publications

# International

**001  AGIP—ANNUAL REPORT**
AGIP SpA, Rome

English annual 90pp

Contains a review of the international energy situation and information about operations in markets of concern to the AGIP group.

**002  ALTERNATIVE ENERGY STRATEGIES**
Holt-Saunders Ltd, Eastbourne

English 1976 204pp £14.00

Studies alternative energy programmes to meet the needs of the principal consuming nations, and analyses policy options in terms of technological, economic, political and environmental considerations.

**003  AMCOAL—ANNUAL REPORT**
AMCOAL, Johannesburg

English annual 42pp

Gives background information on the South African coal industry and the developing export trade.

**004  ANALYTICAL TABLES OF FOREIGN TRADE
B 25-27 MINERAL PRODUCTS**
Eurostat, Luxembourg

Multi-language annual $14.00

External trade statistics of the European Economic Community, using the NIMEXE nomenclature, identifying types of energy product by country of origin/destination.

**005  ANALYTICAL TABLES OF FOREIGN TRADE
VOLUME 1**
Eurostat, Luxembourg

Multi-language annual c390pp $80.50

External trade statistics of the European Community and member states, analysed by commodity for each country.

**006  ANALYTICAL TABLES OF FOREIGN TRADE
VOLUME 2**
Eurostat, Luxembourg

Multi-language annual c390pp $80.50

Tables of foreign trade statistics of the European Community and member countries, including imports and exports of fuel products.

**007  ANEP 19—: EUROPEAN PETROLEUM
YEARBOOK**
Otto Vieth Verlag, Hamburg

English/French/German annual c400pp

Directory of oil industry companies by country. Also includes survey sections and statistics on production, consumption and trade, discoveries and pipelines.

**008  ANNUAL BULLETIN OF COAL STATISTICS FOR
EUROPE**
UN Economic Commission for Europe, Geneva

English/French/Russian annual 98pp $8.00

Detailed coal statistics for Western Europe including production, consumption and trade. Data by type of solid fuel and by country.

**009  ANNUAL BULLETIN OF ELECTRIC ENERGY
STATISTICS FOR EUROPE**
UN Economic Commission for Europe, Geneva

English/French/Russian annual 98pp $8.00

Detailed information on: electricity production and consumption; power station capacity; fuel used. Analyses by country.

**010  ANNUAL BULLETIN OF GAS STATISTICS FOR
EUROPE**
UN Economic Commission for Europe, Geneva

English/French/Russian annual 94pp $8.50

Information by country on: the supply of natural gas; towns gas production; consumption; gas supply facilities. Data cover a period of several years.

**011   ANNUAL BULLETIN OF GENERAL ENERGY STATISTICS FOR EUROPE**
UN Economic Commission for Europe, Geneva

English/French  annual  160pp  $12.00

Detailed energy statistics including production, consumption and trade information for different types of fuel, presented by country.

**012   ANNUAL BULLETIN OF TRADE IN CHEMICAL PRODUCTS**
UN Economic Commission for Europe, Geneva

English/French/Russian  annual  285pp  $16.00

Annual statistics for the import and export of chemical products in Europe.

**013   ARAB OIL AND GAS**
The Arab Petroleum Research Center, Paris

English/French/Arabic  fortnightly  34pp
$390.00 p.a.

Commentary on developments in oil and gas industries, particularly in the Middle East, news and OPEC and OAPEC statistics.

**014   ARAB OIL AND GAS DIRECTORY 1977-78**
The Arab Petroleum Research Center, Paris

English  1978  400pp  $135.00

Survey of oil and gas activities in individual Arab countries, including statistics on production and exports, revenues and developments in the energy sector.

**015   AVAILABILITY OF WORLD ENERGY RESOURCES**
Graham & Trotman Ltd, London

English  1975  234pp  £9.00

Survey by D C Ion of resources of hydrocarbons, solid fuels, coal, uranium and thorium. Estimates of total energy content, proved reserves. Reserves, production and consumption figures in key countries. Energy forecasts.

**016   AVAILABILITY OF WORLD ENERGY RESOURCES—FIRST SUPPLEMENT**
Graham & Trotman Ltd, London

English  1976  104pp

Additional analysis of energy supply and demand and prospects for natural gas, coal and uranium.

**017   AVAILABILITY OF WORLD ENERGY RESOURCES—SECOND SUPPLEMENT**
Graham & Trotman Ltd, London

English  1978  108pp

Review and analysis of suggestions and issues raised in energy studies published in 1977, with sections on demand, supply and the energy balance.

**018   THE BALANCE OF SUPPLY AND DEMAND 1978-1990**
The Uranium Institute/Mining Journal Books Ltd

English  1979  60pp  £8.50

Report analysing demand on the basis of installed nuclear capacity and enrichment capacity and review of supply capabilities and constraints. Includes a number of key tables on capacity of nuclear plant, enrichment capacity and uranium production.

**019   BASIC STATISTICS OF THE COMMUNITY**
Eurostat, Luxembourg

Multi-language  annual  198pp  $5.00

Contains a special section dealing with energy, giving production and consumption data for each fuel. Includes some comparative statistics for non-Community countries.

**020   BILANS GLOBAUX DE L'ENERGIE 1970-77**
OCED, Paris

French  1979  70pp  $10.00

Energy balance figures for OECD member countries expressed in terms of tonnes of oil equivalent.

**021   THE BRITISH PETROLEUM COMPANY LIMITED —ANNUAL REPORT**
British Petroleum Co Ltd, London

English  annual  c50pp

Contains a review of company activities in Europe and data on crude oil sources, prices, development work, refinery throughputs and sales.

**022   BULLETIN DE L'INDUSTRIE PETROLIERE**
SOCIDOC, Paris

French  daily  10-20pp

Bulletin of news on developments in all phases of the oil and gas industries, including statistical and survey supplements.

**023   CAPITAL INVESTMENT IN THE WORLD OIL INDUSTRY**
Chase Manhattan Bank, New York

English  annual  c40pp

Analysis of the pattern of investment of international oil companies, broken down into main types of activity with figures for main regions of the world, including Western Europe.

**024 CHEMFACTS SCANDINAVIA**
IPC Industrial Press Ltd, London

English 1977 130pp £35.00

Analysis of market trends, plant capacity and investment; trade in individual chemicals and profiles of the leading companies in Norway, Sweden, Denmark and Finland.

**025 CHEMICAL COMPANY PROFILES: WESTERN EUROPE**
IPC Industrial Press Ltd, London

English 1979 390pp £40.00

Directory of chemical companies in Western Europe, including background information and notes on activities and finance.

**026 CHEMICALS INFORMATION HANDBOOK 1979-80**
Shell International Chemical Co Ltd, London

English 1979 96pp

Handbook of information on chemicals, with particular reference to the activities of the Royal Dutch/ Shell group of companies. Sections deal with: general background to the chemicals industry, demand, supply, trade and investment; petro-chemical feedstocks and products; details of Shell plant and products.

**027 CLEAN FUEL SUPPLY**
OECD, Paris

English 1978 104pp $6.25

Analyses the technological and economic factors affecting the availability of low sulphur fuels and the introduction of fuel desulphurisation technologies in the OECD region up to the mid 1980s.

**028 COAL: 1985 AND BEYOND**
Pergamon Press, Oxford

English 1978 116pp £8.00

Edited by the United Nations Economic Commission for Europe, contains a survey of the coal industry in individual countries of Europe, with an analysis of resource potential, requirements of capital and labour, and questions of competitiveness.

**029 COAL AND ENERGY**
Ernest Benn Ltd, London

English 1978 182pp £5.95

Review by Sir Derek Ezra of the energy situation pre- and post- 1973 and the role which coal may be expected to play in meeting energy demand. Deals with the issues of energy and the environment and government attitudes.

**030 COAL AND ENERGY QUARTERLY**
National Coal Board, London

English quarterly c40pp

Articles on coal industry issues and matters of interest to the coal industry.

**031 COAL—BRIDGE TO THE FUTURE**
Harper and Row, New York

English 1980 300pp £7.95

Report of the World Coal Study (WOCOL) project teams under Professor Carroll Wilson of Massachusetts Institute of Technology. Examines in detail the availability of energy resources, particularly coal, and the need to expand rapidly the international exploitation of, and trade in, coal.

**032 COAL—ENERGY FOR THE FUTURE**
Shell International Petroleum Co Ltd, London

English 1980 12pp free

Summary of the report 'Coal—Bridge to the Future' produced by the World Coal Study project at Massachusetts Institute of Technology. Published in the series 'Shell Briefing Service.'

**033 COAL EXPORT REVIEW**
National Coal Association, Washington

English monthly 20pp

Statistics with commentary on the international coal trade.

**034 COAL INTERNATIONAL**
Zinder-Neris Inc, Washington

English monthly 48pp $170.00 p.a.

Journal including both economic and statistical information about the coal industry and coal trade.

**035 COAL: ITS FUTURE ROLE IN TOMORROW'S TECHNOLOGY**
Pergamon Press, Oxford

English 1978 326pp £35.00

Surveys reserves and general energy balances of individual countries. Identification of import needs for coal. Examines work being done on coal conversion techniques, exploration, development and treatment.

**036   COAL—MONTHLY BULLETIN**
Eurostat, Luxembourg

Multi-language   11 issues p.a.   c16pp   $9.70 p.a.

Contains regular statistical series on coal supplies, demand, stocks and trade within the EEC member countries.

**037   THE COAL SITUATION IN THE ECE REGION IN 19— AND ITS PROSPECTS**
UN Economic Commission for Europe, Geneva

English annual 85pp

Review of developments in the coal sector of each country in Europe, with statistics on production, consumption and import/export trade.

**038   COAL STATISTICS**
Eurostat, Luxembourg

English/French annual 80pp $4.90

Detailed statistics of production, consumption and trade of coal in the member countries of the European Community. Data cover hard coal, brown coal and coke; mining operations; price indicators.

**039   COMMUNITY ENERGY POLICY**
Commission of the European Communities, Brussels

Multi-language 1976 258pp $6.00

Compilation of secondary legislation concerning energy, comprising regulations, resolutions, directives and decisions affecting the coal, gas and electricity industries.

**040   COMMUNITY ENERGY POLICY—SUPPLEMENT NUMBER 1**
Commission of the European Communities, Brussels

Multi-language 1979 172pp

Up-dates to end 1978 the basic document published in 1976, giving secondary legislation affecting the energy industries.

**041   COMPAGNIE FRANCAISE DES PETROLES— ANNUAL REPORT**
Compagnie Française des Pétroles, Paris

English annual c60pp

English version of the CFP group annual report, with information on the activities of TOTAL affiliate companies throughout Western Europe.

**042   DEMAND FOR WORLD COAL THROUGH 1995**
US Department of Energy, Washington

English 1979 36pp

Collates the results of several models of coal demand in the long term.

**043   THE DEVELOPMENT OF CATALYTIC SNG PROCESSES**
The Institution of Gas Engineers, London

English 1975 20pp £1.00

Paper reviewing the state of methanation processes to produce synthetic natural gas, including comparative data on seven such processes.

**044   DIRECTORY OF SHIPOWNERS, SHIPBUILDERS AND MARINE ENGINEERS**
IPC Industrial Press Ltd, London

English annual 1,500pp £15.00

Shipping company data with sections on each main type of vessel; shipbuilders/repairers and their dock facilities; engine builders and their licensees; classification societies and their offices worldwide; consultants, government departments, associations and experiment tanks.

**045   ECONOMIC BULLETIN FOR EUROPE**
UN Economic Commission for Europe, Geneva

English annual c130pp $10.00

Two-part study dealing with (a) recent changes in Europe's trade and (b) development of east-west trade and payments in the previous decade. Includes comment on the impact of energy issues on the economies of European countries.

**046   ECONOMIC SURVEY OF EUROPE IN 19—: PART ONE**
UN Economic Commission for Europe, Geneva

English annual 170pp £10.00

Annual survey including statistical data on energy and other industrial and economic aspects of European economies.

**047   ECSC—FINANCIAL REPORT**
Commission of the European Communities, Brussels

English annual 50pp $10.40

Report of the activities of the European Coal and Steel Community, including information on loans made to member countries relating to the coal industry.

**048   ELECTRICAL ENERGY—MONTHLY BULLETIN**
Eurostat, Luxembourg

Multi-language   11 issues p.a.   c16pp   $9.70 p.a.

Contains regular statistical series on short-term movements in the demand for, and supply of, electrical energy including output by type of plant and imports/exports of electricity.

### 049 ELECTRICAL ENERGY STATISTICS
Eurostat, Luxembourg

English/French annual c108pp $6.50

Contains statistics on electricity production and consumption and power station capacity and development.

### 050 THE ELECTRICITY SUPPLY INDUSTRY
OECD, Paris

English/French 1978 82pp $7.50

Results and analysis of the 24th, 25th and 26th annual enquiries into electricity supply industries in OECD countries. Statistical data on plant, operations, investments, production and programmes.

### 051 THE ELECTRICITY SUPPLY INDUSTRY IN OECD COUNTRIES 1974-76 AND PROSPECTS TO 1980/1985/1990
OECD, Paris

English/French 1978 190pp $9.00

Review of electricity supply in individual OECD member countries, covering: capacity, production, consumption, investment, fuel used in generation, and analysis of power consumption in transport and industry.

### 052 EMISSIONS AND EFFLUENTS FROM EUROPEAN REFINERIES
CONCAWE, The Hague

English 1977 23pp

Survey of the growth of refinery operations in Western Europe and consequent wastes and emissions. Quantifies pollution and reductions which have been made. Indicative costs associated with reducing pollution.

### 053 EMPLOYMENT AND UNEMPLOYMENT 1972-78
Eurostat, Luxembourg

Multi-language 1979 248pp $17.00

Includes statistics of employment in the main energy sectors of the member countries of the European Economic Community.

### 054 ENERGY
Pergamon Press, Oxford

English monthly 100-200pp $182.00 p.a.

Journal carrying substantial articles on issues and developments in the energy sector of a economic, technical and political nature.

### 055 ENERGY AND HYDROCARBONS
Ente Nazionale Idrocarburi, Rome

English/Italian annual 238pp

Basic statistics on: energy consumption and production; reserves, production, trade and consumption of oil; refineries; nuclear power; uranium reserves and production.

### 056 ENERGY AND THE INVESTMENT CHALLENGE
Shell International Petroleum Co Ltd, London

English 1979 8pp free

Review of the changing energy situation and the financial implications of developing new and higher cost resources of energy. Includes indicative figures for investment costs of different forms of energy and total investments by the world petroleum industry. Published in the series 'Shell Briefing Service.'

### 057 ENERGY BALANCES OF OECD COUNTRIES 1960-74
OECD, Paris

English/French 1976 512pp $25.00

Long-run statistics for primary and secondary energy sources on a common basis. Details of consumption of fuels by main sectors of the economy. Figures for individual countries and regional groupings. Tables of economic growth rates and energy:GNP coefficients.

### 058 ENERGY BALANCES OF OECD COUNTRIES 1973-75
OECD, Paris

English/French 1977 132pp $10.00

Primary and secondary energy supply on a common basis. Details of consumption of fuels in the main sectors of the economy. Figures for individual countries and regional groupings.

### 059 ENERGY BALANCES OF OECD COUNTRIES 1974-76
OECD, Paris

English/French 1978 130pp $9.00

Basic data on primary energy supply and demand by fuel in OECD member countries. Data given in common units. Pattern of fuels and energy sources used in electricity production.

### 060 ENERGY BALANCE OF OECD COUNTRIES 1975/77
OECD, Paris

English/French 1979 106pp $9.00

Statistics for the three-year period 1975-77 for individual OECD countries and regional groupings, covering: primary and secondary energy sources; consumption of fuels by sectors; pattern of electriciy production.

**061    ENERGY CONSERVATION: A STUDY OF ENERGY CONSUMPTION IN BUILDINGS AND POSSIBLE MEANS OF SAVING ENERGY IN HOUSING**
Building Research Establishment, Watford

English 1975 64pp

Discusses the pattern of fuel consumption and utilisation, based on United Kingdom data. Reviews the scope for energy conservation for each use and the cost-effectiveness of energy conservation measures in housing.

**062    ENERGY CONSERVATION IN INDUSTRY**
OECD, Paris

English 1979 76pp

Analysis of member countries' policies towards energy conservation in industry under the following headings: financial and fiscal incentives; target setting, reporting and auditing; information and advice; combined heat and power production; utilisation of waste heat and waste fuels. Also reviews price developments and the relationship of energy consumption to industrial production.

**063    ENERGY CONSERVATION IN THE IEA**
OECD, Paris

English 1976 58pp $6.00

Survey by the International Energy Agency of measures taken in individual member countries to encourage energy conservation.

**064    ENERGY CONSERVATION IN THE IEA— 1978 REVIEW**
OECD, Paris

English 1979

Review of progress in OECD member countries towards achieving energy conservation objectives. Analyses of measures in effect and proposed.

**065    THE ENERGY CRISIS AND THE ENVIRONMENT**
Holt-Saunders Ltd, Eastbourne

English 1977 264pp £16.25

Assesses the impact of relative scarcity or abundance of fuel supplies on environmental policies in industrial and developing nations.

**066    ENERGY DEVELOPMENTS**
Organization of Arab Petroleum Exporting Countries, Kuwait

English 1978 90pp

Surveys world developments in energy consumption in the period 1973-77, energy policies in the main industrialised countries and developments of energy resources. Statistical appendix includes figures for exploration and production activity, reserves, consumption and international trade.

**067    ENERGY EFFICIENCY**
Shell International Petroleum Co Ltd, London

English 1979 82pp

Reviews the potential for improved energy efficiency and the available technologies for reducing energy consumption. Considers the economics of capital investment for energy conservation and other social and psychological factors which need to be taken into account when formulating policy towards energy conservation.

**068    ENERGY FOR EUROPE**
American Enterprise Institute for Public Policy Review, Washington

English 1977 120pp $3.25

Considers the energy needs of Europe within the world context, the use of resources and national policies in France, Norway, Netherlands, Sweden, West Germany and the United Kingdom.

**069    ENERGY FOR INDUSTRY AND COMMERCE**
Cambridge Information and Research Services Ltd, Cambridge

English annual c100pp £15.00

Review of energy supply and consumption, including developments in international markets and the outlook for supplies and prices, with particular reference to purchasers in industry and commerce.

**070    ENERGY FOR INDUSTRY AND COMMERCE QUARTERLY BULLETIN**
Cambridge Information and Research Services Ltd, Cambridge

English quarterly 16-24pp £25.00 p.a.

Quarterly briefing service for industrial and commercial managers, carrying a review of the general situation in the international oil market and an assessment of trends in prices of fuel supplies.

**071    ENERGY FROM BIOMASS**
Shell International Petroleum Co Ltd, London

English 1980 8pp free

Summary of the energy content of biomass in the world and possibilities for using it as an energy source. Sections on: sugar cane and ethanol; wood; aquatic resources; bio-gas from wastes. Published in the series 'Shell Briefing Service.'

072 ENERGY: FROM SURPLUS TO SCARCITY?
Applied Science Publishers, Barking

English 1974 242pp

Proceedings of a seminar of the Institute of Petroleum, covering the prospects for each energy form, including oil sands, shales and synthetics. Review of the situation in Western Europe and other principal regions.

073 ENERGY FROM THE BIOMASS
The Watt Committee on Energy Ltd, London

English 1979 75pp £10.50

Examination of the potential of biomass as a source of energy.

074 ENERGY—GLOBAL PROSPECTS 1985-2000
McGraw-Hill Publications, Washington

English 1977 292pp $14.95

General analysis of the energy situation under the project Workshops on Alternative Energy Strategies at the Massachusetts Institute of Technology. Examines each fuel, energy demand, conservation, geothermal and solar energy.

075 ENERGY INTERNATIONAL
Miller Freeman Publications, San Francisco

English monthly 32pp

Publication containing general energy news, and reports on technical and technological developments. Distributed free within the industry. Available on subscription at $25 p.a. outside the industry.

076 ENERGY IN THE WORLD ECONOMY
Resources for the Future Inc, Washington

English 1971 876pp £10.70

Statistical review of trends in output, trade and consumption. Figures for individual countries/areas and types of fuels. Most series from 1925.

077 ENERGY IN WESTERN EUROPE—VITAL ROLE OF COAL
CEPCEO, London

English 1977 42pp free

Analysis by Western Europe's coal producers of the energy situation in the EEC and Spain, and prospects for coal in the period to 1985.

078 ENERGY PERSPECTIVES AFTER OIL AND NATURAL GAS
The Institution of Gas Engineers, London

English 1979 24pp £1.50

Paper analysing the pattern of demands for energy in an industrial community and the development of new integrated energy systems.

079 ENERGY POLICIES AND PROGRAMMES OF IEA MEMBER COUNTRIES—1977 REVIEW
OECD, Paris

English 1978 336pp $24.00

First evaluation of the energy policies and programmes of member countries of the International Energy Agency. Reviews policies on energy supply and demand, research and development. Includes energy forecasts for 1985 and 1990.

080 ENERGY POLICIES AND PROGRAMMES OF IEA COUNTRIES: 1978 REVIEW
OECD, Paris

English 1979 298pp $25.00

Second annual evaluation of the energy policies and programmes of IEA member countries. Reviews national policies for improving the balance of energy supply and demand and research and development programmes. Provides energy forecasts for 1985 and 1990.

081 ENERGY POLICY
IPC Science and Technology Press, Guildford

English quarterly 80pp £40.00 p.a.

Journal with analytical articles and comment on questions of energy policy.

082 ENERGY PRODUCTION AND ENVIRONMENT
OECD, Paris

English 1977 108pp $5.50

Examines the questions of: siting major energy facilities; the environmental impact arising from development of offshore oil and gas; problems associated with coal exploitation; interdependence of energy policies and those concerned with sulphur pollution.

083 THE ENERGY PROGRAMME OF THE EUROPEAN COMMUNITIES
Commission of the European Communities, Brussels

English 1979 34pp

Reviews the short- and longer-term energy position of the European Community, considers Community resolutions of 1974-75 on energy use and objectives.

Surveys existing and proposed measures in the fields of: forecasting, analysis and objectives; prices and investment; energy saving; research and development; demonstration projects; electricity and nuclear power; coal; oil; gas; and international relations.

084 **ENERGY PROSPECTS TO 1985**
     OECD, Paris

English/French 1974 2 vols $11.25

Detailed analysis of energy resources and prospective demand. Studies the issues of energy conservation in electricity generation, industry and the transport, residential and commercial sectors. Vol 1 main report; vol 2 annexes and statistics.

085 **ENERGY R & D**
     OECD, Paris

English 1975 244pp $8.75

Analyses issues in energy research and development and the policies and programmes of OECD member countries.

086 **ENERGY REPORT**
     Microinfo Ltd, Alton

English monthly 16pp £35.00 p.a.

Regular news service on a wide range of energy matters of a general, political, economic and semi-technical nature.

087 **ENERGY RESEARCH AND DEVELOPMENT
     PROGRAMMES IN WESTERN EUROPE**
     Elsevier Scientific Publishing Co, Amsterdam

English 1978 324pp

Review of the energy situation in Western European countries. Summarises activities in research and development taking place in EEC member countries.

088 **THE ENERGY SITUATION IN THE COMMUNITY**
     Commission of the European Communities, Brussels

English annual 18pp $0.85

Summary for the previous year of main points for each energy sector. Includes a forecast for production, consumption and trade in the current year.

089 **ENERGY STATISTICS 1973-75**
     OECD, Paris

English/French 1977 244pp $10.00

Statistics for all OECD member countries of primary and secondary energy: analyses the sources of energy and pattern of consumption in individual sectors. Covers only the three-year period 1973-75.

090 **ENERGY STATISTICS 1975-77**
     OECD, Paris

English/French 1979 196pp $12.50

Detailed statistics for the three years 1975-77 of primary and secondary energy sources. With analysis of consumption by sector. Figures for individual OECD member countries and regions. Some price tables.

091 **ENERGY STATISTICS YEARBOOK 1970-75**
     Eurostat, Luxembourg

English/French 1976 294pp $20.00

Long-run series of statistics for EEC member countries, covering: production, consumption and trade; refining and electricity production capacity; price indicators.

092 **ENERGY STATISTICS YEARBOOK 1973-77**
     Eurostat, Luxembourg

Multi-language 1979 350pp $27.00

Basic statistics on supply, distribution and consumption of individual fuels. Statistics for member countries of the EEC, including: energy balance sheets, production and consumption by fuel and indicators of the general energy economy.

093 **ENI—ANNUAL REPORT**
     Ente Nazionale Idrocarburi, Rome

English annual

English version of the annual report of the Italian state oil and gas enterprise. Includes a general review of energy in Europe and statistics relating to supply and consumption in Europe.

094 **EUROPEAN CHEMICAL INDUSTRY HANDBOOK**
     Hedderwick, Stirling Grumbar & Co, London

English £100.00 p.a.

Up-dated loose-leaf file in three parts: general information on the chemical industry internationally and in individual countries; product data; company reviews and analysis.

095 **EUROPEAN CHEMICAL NEWS**
     IPC Industrial Press Ltd, London

Engish weekly c40pp £30.00

Weekly journal carrying news and articles about petrochemical developments and the gas-based chemicals industry.

096 **EUROPEAN COAL 2000**
     CEPCEO, London

English 1977 8pp free

Review of coal markets and reserves in the EEC. Basic statistics for energy production and demand. Projections/forecasts for the period up to the year 2000.

## 097 THE EUROPEAN COMMUNITY AND THE ENERGY PROBLEM
Commission of the European Communities, Brussels

English 1978 24pp free

Summary of the energy situation in the Community, measures that have been taken or proposed and outline of the stance of the European Commission.

## 098 THE EUROPEAN COMMUNITY'S ENVIRON-MENTAL POLICY
Commission of the European Communities, Brussels

English 1977 32pp $1.50

General information summarising Community action on pollution control, the development of environment policy and the new action programme.

## 099 EUROPEAN ECONOMY
Commission of the European Communities, Brussels

English 3 issues p.a. c125pp $35.60 p.a.

Includes sections with basic statistics of the energy sector in Community countries: energy balance sheets; pattern of fuels; price indicators. Also contains an assessment of policy and future outlook.

## 100 EUROPEAN ENERGY OUTLOOK TO 1985
Graham and Trotman Ltd, London

English 1978 123pp £63.00

Contains forecasts of requirements, production and supply of the various fuels up to 1985 in all West European countries. Also includes global estimates of energy supply/demand.

## 101 EUROPEAN ENERGY REPORT
The Financial Times Ltd, London

English fortnightly 16pp £140.00 p.a.

Regular bulletin of news on energy supply and consumption in Western Europe.

## 102 THE EUROPEAN OIL INDUSTRY AND THE ENVIRONMENT
CONCAWE, The Hague

English 1978 24pp

Deals with measures taken and approach of the oil industry, in exploration, production, transportation, refining and distribution. Cost indications for improving standards in product qualities and emissions.

## 103 EUROP-OIL PRICES
Europ-Oil Prices, London

English twice weekly c8pp £200.00 p.a.

News bulletin covering international markets in petroleum products: contracts, supplies and prices.

## 104 EVALUATION OF ENERGY USE
The Watt Committee on Energy Ltd, London

English 1979 112pp £4.50

Series of papers dealing with: energy accounting; energy content of some significant materials; capital goods; applications of energy evaluation.

## 105 EXXON CORPORATION—ANNUAL REPORT
Exxon Corporation, New York

English annual c50pp

Includes a general review of developments in the oil industry, notes on Exxon activity throughout the world and operating data for Western Europe and other main regions.

## 106 FINANCIAL AND OPERATIONAL INFORMATION 1970-79
Royal Dutch/Shell Group, London/The Hague

English 1979 24pp free

Supplement to the 1979 annual reports of the Royal Dutch Petroleum Co and Shell Transport and Trading Co Ltd, containing long-run data on the group's income, assets, liabilities, capital expenditure, oil production, tanker and dry cargo fleet and geographical extent of group exploration and production, natural gas processing, coal, nuclear energy, chemicals, metals and research activity.

## 107 THE FUTURE ROLE OF GASIFICATION PROCESSES
The Institution of Gas Engineers, London

English 1979 32pp £1.50

Paper outlining the scope for applying gasification processes: to upgrade heavy oil; for advanced power cycles; for the ironmaking industry; as substitute natural gas.

## 108 THE GAS INDUSTRY AND THE ENVIRONMENT
UN Economic Commission for Europe, Geneva

English 1978 280pp £17.00

Proceedings of a symposium on gas, dealing with the use of gas in industry, commerce and domestic sectors and the impact on the environment.

**109  GAS PRICES 1970-76**
Eurostat, Luxembourg

English 1977 59pp $24.00

Survey of prices in member countries of the European Community. Data for various classes of consumers at numerous locations within the EEC.

**110  GAS PRICES 1976-78**
Eurostat, Luxembourg

English/French/German/Italian 1979 134pp $17.70

Up-dates the study of gas prices 1970-76 with commentary and analysis, description of new tariff arrangements and details of fiscal changes. Includes an international comparison of prices based on purchasing power parities. Gas prices in 30 towns or conurbations in the nine Community countries, covering industrial and residential use.

**111  GAS STATISTICS**
Eurostat, Luxembourg

English/French annual c60pp $3.40

Basic statisitcs on supply and disposal of natural gas, coke oven gas, blast furnace and works gas. Also contains data on gas-manufacturing plant.

**112  GAS SUPPLIES INTO CONTINENTAL EUROPE IN THE 80s**
The Institution of Gas Engineers, London

English 1978 16pp £1.50

Paper by Dr Ing C Brecht of Ruhrgas AG. Survey of natural gas supply arrangements and the role of natural gas; the European natural gas pipeline grid; future likely projects.

**113  GASTECH 78**
Gastech Ltd, Rickmansworth

English 1979 346pp

Report of proceedings at the 1978 international LNG/LPG conference. Covers: resources, country reviews, trade, transportation, markets, pricing and safety aspects.

**114  GAS WORLD**
Benn Publications Ltd, London

English monthly 40pp £20.00 p.a.

Journal containing news and articles on the gas industry.

**115  GENERAL REVIEW OF THE WORLD COAL INDUSTRY**
Muir Coal Industry Information Service, Hazlemere

English half-yearly 86pp

Commentary on economic and technologic developments in the coal industry and international coal trade.

**116  GLÜCKAUF**
Verlag Glückauf GmbH, Essen

German/English DM162.00 p.a.

Journal carrying economic and technical articles on mining, current statistics and news. An additional English translation series is available at a total cost of DM396.00 p.a.

**117  GOVERNMENT FINANCING OF RESEARCH AND DEVELOPMENT 1970-78**
Eurostat, Luxembourg

Multi-language 1978 164pp $17.00

Statistics and commentary on research and development programmes relating to energy. Programmes itemised by country.

**118  HALF-YEARLY BULLETIN OF ELECTRIC ENERGY STATISTICS FOR EUROPE**
UN Economic Commission for Europe, Geneva

English/French/Russian half-yearly 26pp $2.00

Statistics for each European country: electricity production by fuel type; consumption by main sectors of the economy. Figures on a monthly basis.

**119  HEAT PRODUCTION AND DISTRIBUTION: THE SCOPE FOR REDUCING THERMAL AND AIR POLLUTION**
OECD, Paris

English 1978 46pp $3.00

Examines the options for heat production and distribution including use of waste heat which combat air pollution and thermal pollution from power generation. Deals with obstacles to increasing the production of combined heat and power in industries and municipalities.

**120  HYDROCARBON PRODUCTION FROM SEA BED INSTALLATIONS IN DEEP WATER**
The Institution of Gas Engineers, London

English 1980 26pp £2.50

Paper on the development of production systems for producing oil and gas in deep water, particularly based on North Sea experience.

**121  HYDROCARBONS—MONTHLY BULLETIN**
Eurostat, Luxembourg

Multi-language 11 issues p.a. 20pp $19.40 p.a.

Contains the principal statistics by month on the petroleum and gas industries in the European Community countries. Includes indicative prices for motor gasoline and automotive diesel.

122 THE HYDROGEN ENERGY ECONOMY
Holt-Saunders Ltd, Eastbourne

English 1977 332pp £16.25

Discusses the economic feasibility and costs of a hydrogen-based economy, dealing with technical obstacles, safety issues, public attitudes and the interest of oil and gas industries.

123 HYDROGEN ENERGY SYSTEM
Pergamon Press, Oxford

English 1979 5 vols £150.00

Proceedings of the 2nd World Hydrogen Energy Conference, covering: methods of hydrogen production; transmission, distribution and storage; uses of hydrogen in technical processes and the energy sector; special applications of hydrogen; overall systems economics and environmental aspects.

124 HYDROGEN R & D IN THE COMMUNITY
Commission of the European Communities, Brussels

English 1978 4pp free

Summary of research and development work on hydrogen. Prepared as R & D information note no 15/78.

125 THE IMPACT OF NORTH SEA GAS ON THE DEVELOPMENT OF THE EUROPEAN LPG MARKET
International Gas Union, Paris

English 1979 18pp

Reviews the use of LPG in European markets, the availability of LPG from the North Sea and potential market development. Paper given at the IGU's 1979 conference.

126 THE IMPACT OF NORTH SEA HYDROCARBONS
Pergamon Press, Oxford

English 1978 63pp £10.00

Contains chapters on: potential for natural gas from the North Sea in relation to Western Europe's market for gas by the mid-1980s; the utilisation of North Sea hydrocarbons as raw material for petrochemical manufacture; oil-related developments in North Scotland; patterns of recruitment to the oil industry in Norway.

127 THE IMPACT OF SULPHUR LIMITATIONS ON REFINERY FACILITIES
CONCAWE, The Hague

English 1976 24pp

Indicates costs for different types of European refinery for equipment needed to produce low-sulphur fuel oils.

128 IMPROVED ENERGY EFFICIENCY
Shell International Petroleum Co Ltd, London

English 1979 10pp free

Identifies the principal areas in which energy conservation would be significant in industry, domestic and transport sectors. Published in the series 'Shell Briefing Service.'

129 INDUSTRIAL SHORT-TERM TRENDS
Eurostat, Luxembourg

Multi-language monthly 48pp $16.25 p.a.

Includes indicators of output for energy, petroleum and natural gas production, mining, oil refining.

130 INFORMATION HANDBOOK 1979-80
Shell International Petroleum Co Ltd, London

English 1979 128pp

Pocket handbook of information about oil and natural gas, coal, nuclear as well as petrochemicals and metals industries, with particular reference to activities of the Royal Dutch/Shell group of companies. Chapters deal with: exploration and production, marine transportation, refining, demand and supply, natural gas, coal, and nuclear energy. Contains statistics on many key aspects of energy supply.

131 INPUT-OUTPUT TABLES 1970
Eurostat, Luxembourg

Multi-language 9 vols $71.60

Tables on a standard basis for EEC member countries indicating the resources used in each sector of the economy. Includes data on use of resources by the energy industries and use of energy in other sectors.

132 INTERNATIONAL ATOMIC ENERGY AGENCY— ANNUAL REPORT
International Atomic Energy Agency, Vienna

English annual c60pp

Includes a survey of developments in nuclear engineering and nuclear power generation, reports on international nuclear programmes and statistics of nuclear installations in individual countries.

133 INTERNATIONAL GAS TECHNOLOGY HIGHLIGHTS
International Gas Technology, Chicago

English fortnightly 4pp $35.00 p.a.

Current information service covering gas plant, contracts, supply situation and general energy developments.

**134  INTERNATIONAL PETROLEUM ANNUAL**
Energy Information Administration, Washington

English annual 34pp

Contains data on production, consumption, oil refining and reserves throughout the world, with tables of indicative prices for principal oil products.

**135  INTERNATIONAL PETROLEUM TIMES**
IPC Industrial Press Ltd, London

English fortnightly c45pp £22.00 p.a.

Journal of news and articles of an economic and semi-technical nature dealing with oil and gas developments. Includes information on oil prices in Europe.

**136  INTERNATIONAL POWER GENERATION**
Fuel & Metallurgical Journals Ltd, Redhill

English monthly c70pp $55.00 p.a.

Periodical with articles on technological developments in electricity production. Includes reports on electricity and the general energy situation in individual countries and news of new projects.

**137  INTERNATIONAL SYMPOSIUM ON URANIUM
SUPPLY AND DEMAND**
Mining Journal Books Ltd, Edenbridge

English 1979 370pp £10.00

Compendium of papers submitted at the 1978 symposium organised by the Uranium Institute.

**138  INVESTMENT OF THE COALMINING AND IRON
AND STEEL INDUSTRIES**
Commission of the European Communities, Brussels

Multi-language 1979 119pp $13.80

Results of the 1979 survey of investments in the Community coal and steel industries, covering actual and forecast expenditure and production potential of enterprises. Separate chapters deal with coal-mining, coking plants and briquetting plants.

**139  LLOYD'S REGISTER OF SHIPPING—ANNUAL
REPORT**
Lloyd's, London

English annual c50pp

Includes a brief review of developments in the shipping sector, including bulk carriers and tankers.

**140  LLOYD'S REGISTER OF SHIPPING—
STATISTICAL TABLES**
Lloyd's, London

English annual c80pp

Contains details of the world's merchant fleets, new-buildings, ships lost, broken-up and laid up. Fleet analysed by type, size, age and tonnage.

**141  LNG REVIEW 1977**
Energy Economics Research Ltd, Wokingham

English 1977 136pp

Review of the technical, economic, market and financial aspects of liquefied natural gas. Analysis of LNG projects, plant, trade and transportation.

**142  MARITIME TRANSPORT**
OECD, Paris

English annual c170pp £4.30

Annual report of the Maritime Transport Committee of OECD. Review of developments and longer-term trends in shipping; policies towards shipping; demand for shipping services; shipping availability; the freight markets. Annex carries statistics on: trade; flag, size and structure of fleets; indices of freight market rates.

**143  MIDDLE EAST ECONOMIC SURVEY**
Middle East Petroleum & Economic Publications, Nicosia

English weekly c24pp $600.00 p.a.

Regular news and commentary on events in the Middle East and North Africa, including oil and gas projects, supplies and production/export statistics.

**144  MINING ANNUAL REVIEW**
Mining Journal Ltd, Edenbridge

English annual c500pp £15.00

Survey of activities and developments in the mining industry during the past year. General articles, reviews of individual countries. Information on companies and mines.

**145  MINING JOURNAL**
Mining Journal Ltd, Edenbridge

English weekly 26pp

Contains news of mining companies, economic and technological developments in mining, and information about contracts and markets. Available only on a combined subscription including Mining Magazine and Mining Annual Review at a cost of £45.00 p.a.

**146  MINING MAGAZINE**
Mining Journal Ltd, Edenbridge

English monthly c100pp £8.00 p.a.

Carries articles on mining and specific mining development or projects. A large part is devoted to coal industry matters.

147 MOBIL CORPORATION—ANNUAL REPORT
Mobil Corporation, New York

English annual c50pp

Includes notes on Mobil activities in Europe and general comment on developments in the international oil industry.

148 MONTHLY BULLETIN OF STATISTICS
United Nations, Geneva

English/French monthly c250pp $84.00 p.a.

Includes statistics of mining, electricity and gas production in individual countries of Western Europe.

149 MONTHLY EXTERNAL TRADE BULLETIN
Eurostat, Luxembourg

Multi-language monthly c130pp $48.50 p.a.

Foreign trade statistics by country and product with coverage of trends in the EEC countries and the main non-members.

150 NATURAL GAS
Scientific Press Ltd, Beaconsfield

English 1979 368pp

Third edition of the general survey of natural gas by E N Tiratsoo. Deals with: geology; technical background; pipelines and transmission systems for liquefied natural gas; potential sources of gas, both conventional and non-conventional.

151 NEW ISSUES AFFECTING THE ENERGY ECONOMY OF THE EEC REGION IN THE MEDIUM AND LONG TERM
UN Economic Commission for Europe, Geneva

English 1978 30pp $3.00

Summary of the energy situation in Europe and assessment of basic factors affecting the area in the longer term.

152 NEW TECHNOLOGIES FOR EXPLORATION AND EXPLOITATION OF OIL AND GAS RESOURCES
Graham & Trotman Ltd, London

English 1979 2 vols £45.00

Proceedings of a 1979 symposium organised by the Commission of the European Communities. Papers by experts from leading EEC oil technology companies. Subjects covered: geophysics; drilling; platforms; production operations; pipelines; enhanced recovery; natural gas; submersibles/diving; storage; safety.

153 NOROIL
Noroil Publishing House, Stavanger

English monthly 90pp Kr162.00 p.a.

Monthly periodical containing news on all aspects of offshore development, especially in the North Sea.

154 NORTH SEA AND EUROPE OFFSHORE YEARBOOK AND BUYER'S GUIDE
The Financial Times Ltd, London

English annual c400pp £19.50

Information on companies engaged in offshore exploration and production and in related supply and service industries. Review of development activities. Buyer's guide to products and services.

155 THE NORTH SEA AND ITS IMPORTANCE TO THE GAS INDUSTRY
International Gas Union, Paris

English 1979 84pp

Symposium at the IGU's 1979 Conference, dealing with the importance of North Sea gas for Belgium, France, Netherlands, West Germany and the UK. Looks at gas supplies in West European countries with production of, or contracts for, North Sea gas, and includes information on exploration and production.

156 NORTH SEA LETTER
The Financial Times Ltd, London

English weekly 14pp £195.00 p.a.

Regular monitor of developments on the North West Continental Shelf covering exploration, onshore activities, offshore supplies, production, people, finance and politics.

157 NORTH SEA OBSERVER
North Sea Observer, Oslo

English weekly 28pp Kr30.00 p.a.

Newspaper carrying information on developments in Norwegian, United Kingdom and other sectors of the North Sea.

158 THE NORTH SEA OIL PROVINCE
Kogan Page Ltd, London

English 1975 74pp £20.00

Assessment by P Odell and K Rosing of ultimate recoverable reserves in the North Sea, using computer simulation techniques.

159 NORTH SEA SERVICE
Wood, Mackenzie and Co

English £500.00 p.a.

Consists of a basic reference file of detailed geological and economic information on the North Sea, up-dated by a monthly report which also contains commentary on political and economic developments, a review of activity in exploration and production, and reappraisal analyses of the profitability of individual fields.

**160   NUCLEAR ENERGY AGENCY—ACTIVITY
REPORT**
OECD, Paris

English/French  annual  116pp

Annual review of the activities of the nuclear energy agency attached to the OECD.

**161   NUCLEAR ENGINEERING INTERNATIONAL**
International Publishing Corporation Ltd, London

English  monthly  70pp  £40.00 p.a.

Journal containing articles and news of developments in nuclear industries; profiles of individual power plants.

**162   THE NUCLEAR FUEL BANK ISSUE AS SEEN
BY URANIUM PRODUCERS AND CONSUMERS**
Uranium Institute, London

English  1979  12pp  free

Considers the practicability of an internationally regulated bank for nuclear fuel and outlines several alternative lines of approach designed to minimise disruption to the international trade in uranium and nuclear fuel.

**163   NUCLEAR POWER AND THE ENERGY CRISIS:
POLITICS AND THE ATOMIC INDUSTRY**
Trade Policy Research Centre, London

English  1978  367pp  £12.00

Analysis of decision-making in Western Europe and the United States in the field of nuclear power policy.

**164   NUCLEAR POWER: THE FUTURE**
Graham & Trotman Ltd, London

English  1979  220pp  £16.00

Analyses trends in world energy demand and supply. Discusses environmental and safety aspects of nuclear power generation.

**165   OAPEC BULLETIN**
Organisation of Arab Petroleum Exporting Countries, Kuwait

English  monthly  32pp  $16.00 p.a.

News and analysis of energy issues affecting OAPEC member countires, information on projects, statistics.

**166   OECD ECONOMIC OUTLOOK**
OECD, Paris

English  half-yearly  c150pp  $17.50 p.a.

Review of the economic situation in OECD member countries and the international situation facing their economies, an important aspect of which is the cost and uncertain availability of imported energy.

**167   OECD OBSERVER**
OECD, Paris

English/French  bi-monthly  c35pp  $7.50 p.a.

General periodical carrying news of OECD activities and publications. Includes articles on energy in OECD and summaries of major reports on energy.

**168   OFFSHORE CONTRACTORS AND EQUIPMENT**
Petroleum Publishing Co, Tulsa

English  1978  408pp  $35.00

Includes information about European companies engaged in: equipment contracting; geophysical surveying; diving; supply transportation.

**169   OFFSHORE DEVELOPMENT**
The Financial Times Ltd, London

English  1979  3 vols  £80.00

Comprises papers from five conferences on offshore development organised by the Financial Times. Vol 1: Engineering and supply—progress in technology and construction. Vol 2: Engineering and supply—development of exploration and production activity in the Celtic Sea. Vol 3: Finance, taxation and government—financial and political issues relevant to oil and gas companies.

**170   OFFSHORE INSPECTION AND MAINTENANCE**
The Financial Times Ltd, London

English  1978  130pp  £50.00

Review of inspection and maintenance aspects of offshore development on the basis of experience in the Gulf of Mexico, Alaska, Venezuela and the North Sea. Examines the requirements and buying practices of operating companies.

**171   OFFSHORE OIL AND GAS NORTH-WEST
EUROPE**
Shell International Petroleum Co Ltd, London

English  1976  12pp

Notes on offshore developments covering: reserves; discovery and development; natural gas and gas liquids; technology; costs; policies. Includes details of oil and gas discoveries to date. Published in the series 'Shell Briefing Service.'

172 OFFSHORE OIL AND GAS YEARBOOK
Kogan Page Ltd, London

English 1978 376pp £25.00

Annual guide and directory to offshore oil and gas exploration in all sectors of the European continental shelf.

173 OIL AND GAS IN COMECON
Kogan Page Ltd, London

English 1979 300pp £15.00

Analysis of the development of oil and natural gas in the Comecon countries between 1945 and 1975, and assessment of the role of hydrocarbon fuels in the energy balance up to 1985. Impact on the pattern of Soviet trade and relations with other oil and gas producers.

174 OIL AND GAS INTERNATIONAL YEARBOOK
The Financial Times Ltd, London

English annual 779pp £16.00

Provides information on the major oil and gas companies including directors and registered offices, exploration news, subsidiaries and affiliates, production figures and financial data.

175 OIL AND GAS JOURNAL
Petroleum Publishing Co, Tulsa

English weekly c250pp $65.00 p.a.

Periodical carrying worldwide news of the oil and gas industries, covering offshore activity, petrochemicals, technological developments, general political and economic news. Annual review supplements, with statistics on main aspects of the oil and gas industries. Subscription within the industries is $24.00 p.a.

176 OIL CRISIS . . . . . . . AGAIN?
British Petroleum Co Ltd, London

English 1979 20pp

Study of the oil supply situation in the non-communist world, dealing with: oil production and reserves; the influence of the United States and OPEC; the impact of the 1973 crisis; the potential of oil, nuclear power and coal in the period 1980-85.

177 OIL DATA SHEET
The Institute of Petroleum, London

English

Series of information sheets on all aspects of the United Kingdom and international oil industry.

178 OIL ECONOMISTS' HANDBOOK
Applied Science Publishers, Barking

English 1977 192pp

Contains a large statistical section with some long-run data, covering main aspects of oil industry operations. Some price information.

179 OIL, ENERGY AND GROWTH: THE NEXT TWENTY YEARS
EuroEconomics, Paris

English/French 1978 61pp FF1,200

Study of the long-term energy supply and demand balance. Sections on: petroleum potential, conventional and non-conventional; other energy sources; prospective growth in demand; analysis of price trends.

180 OIL FIELDS OF THE WORLD
Scientific Press Ltd, Beaconsfield

English 1976 400pp $32.00

Survey of the background to development of oilfields in individual countries of the world. Statistics of reserves and production.

181 OIL GAS
Urban-Verlag, Hamburg/Vienna

English monthly 55pp

International edition of 'Erdoel Erdgas Zeitschrift', covering general news and developments in geology, production, engineering, processing, refining and marketing.

182 OIL IN THE MIDDLE EAST
Economist Intelligence Unit, London

English quarterly 36pp £30.00 p.a.

Review of exploration, production, refining, consumption and export trade of Middle East countries. Annual supplement provides a summary of statistics and developments.

183 OIL IN WESTERN EUROPE
Economist Intelligence Unit, London

English quarterly 36pp £30.00 p.a.

Each issue reviews exploration, production, refining, distribution and relevant political issues. Annual supplement provides a brief summary of statistics and developments.

184 OIL STATISTICS
OECD, Paris

English/French annual c280pp $20.00

Contains data for all OECD countries on supply and disposal of crude oil, feedstocks, natural gas liquids, natural gas and 17 different petroleum products; exports and imports identified by 58 different origins and destinations; shows refinery input and output. Consumption of main petroleum products is broken down into 28 different end-use sectors.

185   THE OILMAN
      Maclean-Hunter Ltd, London

      English weekly 8pp £36.00 p.a.

      News bulletin on oil and gas developments in the North Sea, including details of rig activity and other exploration work.

186   OPEC
      Deutsche Bank AG, Frankfurt/Main

      English/German 1978 68pp

      Analyses the financial and economic impact of higher oil prices since 1973. Includes figures for oil reserves of exporting countries and balance of payments flows attributable to oil exports.

187   OPEC—ANNUAL REPORT
      Organization of Petroleum Exporting Countries, Vienna

      English annual 106pp

      Includes a review of the general economic situation in the industrialised and developing economies; developments in the petroleum industry; worldwide exploration, production and reserves; the world tanker fleet; the oil industry in OPEC member countries. Statistical section gives figures for production, reserves, refinery operations, consumption and exports of OPEC countries.

188   OPEC BULLETIN
      Organization of Petroleum Exporting Countries, Vienna

      English monthly

      News digest of matters relevant to OPEC member countries, commentary and analysis. Most issues include a supplement on operations of OPEC or topical issues.

189   OPEC OIL REPORT
      Petroleum Press Bureau Ltd, London

      English 1979 302pp £42.00

      Compendium of data on OPEC member countries with sections on: revenues, prices; world energy consumption; international trade; natural gas and LNG availability and trade; refining and petrochemicals developments.

190   OPERATING EXPERIENCE WITH NUCLEAR POWER STATIONS IN MEMBER STATES IN 19—
      International Atomic Energy Agency, Vienna

      English annual 324pp $24.00

      Contains operating information on over 160 units in countries subject to IAEA supervision.

191   OPERATING EXPERIENCE WITH NUCLEAR POWER STATIONS IN MEMBER STATES— PERFORMANCE ANALYSIS REPORT 19—
      International Atomic Energy Agency, Vienna

      English annual 27pp $4.00

      Analytical report based on operating experience in IAEA countries. Covers: construction time span; performance factors. unavailability of plant; comparisons with conventional thermal power plant.

192   OPERATION OF NUCLEAR POWER STATIONS IN 19—
      Eurostat, Luxembourg

      English/French annual 130pp $13.60

      Contains the main operating statistics for the past year and gives an outline of the nuclear plant situation, including units in operation and under construction. Operating data given on a monthly basis for each nuclear power station in the Community, including load diagrams and reasons for unavailability.

193   OPTIMAL DEVELOPMENT OF THE NORTH SEA'S OIL FIELDS
      Kogan Page Ltd, London

      English 1976 190pp £30.00

      Study by P Odell and K Rosing of the choice of production systems for North Sea oil fields and the consequences for recoverable reserves.

194   ORGANIZATIONS OF ARAB PETROLEUM EXPORTING COUNTRIES—ANNUAL REPORT
      Organization of Arab Petroleum Exporting Countries, Kuwait

      English annual c104pp

      Reviews: trends in energy consumption in the principal economies; export destinations of Arab crude oil; exploration, production and reserves situation. Reports on developments in the Arab world affecting the international oil situation, with statistics on most aspects.

195   OUR INDUSTRY—PETROLEUM
      British Petroleum Co Ltd, London

      English 1977 600pp

Handbook on oil industry operations, with special reference to BP. Includes a statistical section with basic figures for production, reserves and consumption in the main countries and regions of the world.

**196 OUTLOOK FOR THE LONG-TERM COAL SUPPLY AND DEMAND TREND IN THE COMMUNITY**
Commission of the European Communities, Brussels

English 1980 26pp

Reviews the outlook for coal supply and demand in the period 1980-2000. Considers the relationship of economic growth to primary energy consumption; analyses consumption by energy source and makes estimates of coal demand and coal supply.

**197 OVERALL ENERGY BALANCE SHEETS 1963-75**
Eurostat, Luxembourg

English/French 1977

Balance sheets of the availability and disposal of energy, presented in common units, for the EEC and individual member countries.

**198 OVERALL ENERGY BALANCE SHEETS 1970-77**
Eurostat, Luxembourg

French 1979 68pp $10.00

Balances of availability and disposal of energy in common units for individual countries and the Community as a whole. Balances for each fuel with tables of growth rates.

**199 THE PETROCHEMICAL INDUSTRY: TRENDS IN PRODUCTION AND INVESTMENT TO 1985**
OECD, Paris

English 1979 76pp $8.00

Covers trends in demand, availability of feedstock and investment in the petrochemical industry in OECD countries to 1985. Brief analysis of likely developments in non-member countries over the same period.

**200 PETROLEUM DIRECTORY—EASTERN HEMISPHERE 1978**
Petroleum Publishing Co, Tulsa

English 1978 550pp $50.00

Directory of companies engaged in exploration, production, drilling, pipelines, processing, engineering, construction and services. Indexed by country and type of activity.

**201 PETROLEUM ECONOMIST**
Petroleum Press Bureau Ltd, London

English/French/Japanese monthly c40pp £29.00 p.a.

Periodical with news of the oil and gas industries and articles on specific energy topics. Includes reports on the international petroleum products and freight markets.

**202 PETROLEUM INTELLIGENCE WEEKLY**
Petroleum Intelligence Weekly Inc, New York

English weekly c12pp $950.00 p.a.

New service worldwide for oil and gas developments. Regularly includes information on crude oil and product prices at export terminals and in the principal bulk markets.

**203 PETROLEUM RESERVES**
The Institute of Petroleum, London

English 1978 5pp free

Summary of reserves of crude oil in the main areas of the world, with comment on the situation in individual countries and areas.

**204 PETROLEUM STATISTICAL BULLETIN**
Ministry of Petroleum and Mineral Resources, Riyadh

English/Arabic annual 46pp

Detailed information and statistics for Saudi Arabia covering: concession areas; producing fields, reserves; production of crude oil and petroleum products; tanker loadings; refineries; prices and revenues.

**205 PETROLEUM STATISTICS**
Eurostat, Luxembourg

English/French annual 64pp $4.90

Harmonised data for the petroleum industry for the past year. Updates series in the Energy Statistics Yearbook. Covers individual main petroleum products.

**206 PHILLIPS PETROLEUM COMPANY—ANNUAL REPORT**
Phillips Petroleum Co, Bartlesville

English annual c55pp

Includes information about Phillips' involvement in North Sea development: production, discoveries, investment and average crude oil revenues.

**207 PIPELINES AND CONTRACTORS 1978 WORLD-WIDE DIRECTORY**
Petroleum Publishing Co, Tulsa

English 1978 212pp $25.00

Includes information on pipelines in Europe: operating companies, pipeline data, contractors and services relating to pipelines.

208  PLATTS OILGRAM NEWS SERVICE
McGraw-Hill Publications, Washington

English  daily  4-8pp  $707.00 p.a.

Daily news intelligence service covering political and
economic developments worldwide in or affecting the
oil industry.


209  PLATTS OILGRAM PRICE SERVICE
McGraw-Hill Publications, Washington

English  daily  4-8pp  $707.00 p.a.

Daily news intelligence service carrying information
on prices of crude oil and products in international
and domestic markets throughout the world.


210  PORTS OF THE WORLD
Benn Publications Ltd, Tunbridge Wells

English  annual  1,092pp  £25.00

Details of over 2,000 ports giving: latitude and long-
itude; authority; documents; approach; accom-
modation (depths), wharves, storage, equipment,
provisions, water; container and ro/ro facilities;
ore and bulk cargo facilities; tanker and liquefied gas
terminals; bunkers; offshore facilities. development;
ship repairs; charges; towage; pilotage; traffic figures;
medical facilities; airport; working hours; local
holidays; cargo handled in a working day; officials
(Harbour Master, Lloyd's Agents etc).


211  POWER REACTORS IN MEMBER STATES
International Atomic Energy Agency, Vienna

English  1978  125pp  $9.00

Fourth issue of the IAEA's computer-based listing
of civilian nuclear reactors as at May 1978, including
plant in operation, under construction, planned or
shut down.


212  PRICES OF BUNKER OILS 1965-73
Eurostat, Luxembourg

Multi-language  1975

Analysis of consumption of bunker diesel and fuel
oil in the nine EEC member countries. Contains
price series for each country and the Rotterdam
international market.


213  PROCEEDINGS OF THE 10TH WORLD
PETROLEUM CONGRESS
Heyden & Son Ltd, London

English  1980  6 vols  £230.00

Proceedings of the congress in the following volumes:
Vol 1 General; Vol 2 Exploration Supply and
Demand; Vol 3 Production; Vol 4 Storage, Transport
and Processing; Vol 5 Conservation, Environment,
Safety and Training; Vol 6 Index. Volumes are
available individually.


214  PROCEEDINGS OF THE 10TH WORLD
PETROLEUM CONGRESS VOL 2 EXPLORATION,
SUPPLY AND DEMAND
Heyden & Son Ltd, London

English  1980  464pp  £55.00

Includes papers on: exploration in new areas; drilling
in hostile environments; world reserves of oil and gas;
world supply and demand for oil and gas.


215  PROCEEDINGS OF THE 10TH WORLD
PETROLEUM CONGRESS VOL 3 PRODUCTION
Heyden & Son Ltd, London

English  1980  424pp  £67.50

Papers deal with: technical and economic evaluation
of enhanced recovery of crude oil; economics of
synthetic hydrocarbons; production from oil sands,
oil shale and coal.


216  PROCEEDINGS OF THE 10TH WORLD
PETROLEUM CONGRESS VOL 4 STORAGE,
TRANSPORT AND PROCESSING
Heyden & Son Ltd, London

English  1980  486pp  £65.00

Includes papers on the following subjects: technical and economic aspects of the storage and
transport of oil and gas; developments in natural gas
liquefaction, handling and transport; technology of
processing heavy crude oils and residuals.


217  PROCEEDINGS OF THE 10TH WORLD PETRO-
LEUM CONGRESS VOL 5 CONSERVATION,
ENVIRONMENT, SAFETY AND TRAINING
Heyden & Son Ltd, London

English  1980  372pp  £55.00

Includes papers dealing with: environmental standards of the petroleum and petrochemical plants in
the 1980s and their cost implications; energy conservation in refining and its cost benefits.


218  PRODUCT DIVERSIFICATION OF OIL
COMPANIES
EuroEconomics, Paris

English/French  1978  55pp  FF2,000

Study of the changing pattern of investment by oil
companies, including diversification into the development of coal, nuclear power and alternative energy
sources.


219  PUBLISHED PLANS AND PROJECTIONS OF
COAL PRODUCTION, TRADE AND CON-
SUMPTION
IEA Coal Research, London

English  1977  100pp

Brings together plans and forecasts relevant to the principal consuming countries, with an outline of the coal situation in those countries.

220  PUBLISHED REGULATORY GUIDELINES OF CONCERN TO THE OIL INDUSTRY IN WESTERN EUROPE
CONCAWE, The Hague

English 1979 62pp

Summarises standard product specifications and legal limits on motor gasoline quality, sulphur content of fuel oils, emissions and other environmental standards.

221  QUARTERLY BULLETIN OF COAL STATISTICS FOR EUROPE
UN Economic Commission for Europe, Geneva

English/French/Russian 44pp $4.00

Basic statistics on production and disposal of solid fuels in Europe and the USA.

222  QUARTERLY BULLETIN OF INDUSTRIAL PRODUCTION
Eurostat, Luxembourg

Multi-language quarterly 118pp $25.00 p.a.

Quarterly data on output of coal, coke, lignite, crude oil, natural gas, oil products and electricity.

223  QUARTERLY OIL STATISTICS
OECD, Paris

English/French c300pp $30.00 p.a.

Regular statistics on oil production, consumption, stocks and trade flows for OECD member countries.

224  THE RATIONAL USE OF ENERGY
The Watt Committee on Energy Ltd, London

English 1978 71pp £8.50

Examines: the use of energy in the homes and in hospitals; the applications of heat pumps; the relationship of people to systems with regard to the use of energy.

225  THE RATIONAL UTILISATION OF FUELS IN PRIVATE TRANSPORT
CONCAWE, The Hague

English 1978 32pp

Study carried out as part of an EEC review of motor vehicle technology and standards, assessing costs to the refinery sector of reducing the level of lead alkyl in motor gasoline to the suggested standards of the European Commission.

226  REFINING AND GAS PROCESSING 1979-80 WORLDWIDE DIRECTORY
Petroleum Publishing Co, Tulsa

English 1979 380pp $50.00

Includes information for West European countries and companies: information on capacity and personnel, some data at plant level.

227  REPORT ON THE COMMUNITY PROGRAMME FOR THE RATIONAL USE OF ENERGY
Commission of the European Communities, Brussels

English 1977 132pp

Reviews progress in energy conservation in the EEC, indicating priorities for future measures. Includes comparisons of the performance of member states and reports on particular subjects, including thermal insulation, road transport, industrial processes and power.

228  RESEARCH ON THE PRODUCTION OF HYDROGEN
International Gas Union, Paris

French 1979 22pp

Reviews existing processes for hydrogen production, concentrating on the hydrolysis of water. Gives indicative figures for investment and operating costs; discusses storage and transport questions. Paper given at the IGU's 1979 international conference.

229  REVIEW OF MARITIME TRANSPORT
United Nations, New York

English annual 95pp $7.00

Annual survey of maritime fleets and principal freight markets, including bulk carriers and tankers.

230  A REVIEW OF THE POTENTIAL FOR THE USE OF NUCLEAR REACTORS FOR HYDROGEN PRODUCTION
Royal Society of Arts, London

English 1977 22pp

Paper by N G Worley of Babcock & Wilcox, reviewing the technology for producing hydrogen, with indications of costs of fuel requirements of the processes.

231  REVIEW OF THE WORLD COAL INDUSTRY TO 1990
Miller Freeman Publications, SanFrancisco

English 1975 134pp

General survey of the coal industry by W L G Muir. Part I survey of the main consuming countries. Part II the major export sources.

232  REVUE DE L'ENERGIE
Les Editions Techniques et Economiques, Paris

French monthly 55pp FF317.00 p.a.

Journal containing articles on energy subjects of an economic or technical nature.

233  THE ROTTERDAM OIL MARKET
Petroleum Press Bureau Ltd, London

English 1979 20pp

Analysis by J Roeber of the Rotterdam market, the extent of trade in the bulk market and the relationship of bulk market prices to domestic price levels in European countries.

234  THE SEABORNE TRANSPORTATION OF
LIQUEFIED NATURAL GAS 1977-85
H P Drewry, London

English 1977 116pp $140.00

Analysis of the likely costs and revenues of vessels engaged in moving liquefied natural gas, and review of trading patterns in the period to 1985.

235  SHELL BRIEFING SERVICE
Shell International Petroleum Co Ltd, London

English

Series of publications on key aspects of energy supply and markets. Produced for internal information purposes, Shell Briefing Service publications can be obtained on request.

236  SHELL TRANSPORT AND TRADING COMPANY
LIMITED—ANNUAL REPORT
Shell International Petroleum Co Ltd, London

English annual c65pp

Contains a review of group operations in Europe and data on oil supplies, refining, oil, natural gas and chemical sales.

237  SHIPPING STATISTICS AND ECONOMICS
H P Drewry, London

English monthly 60pp £240.00 p.a.

Continuously up-dated statistics on tanker tonnage, new buildings, orders, scrappage, sales, tankers laid-up, fixings and market freight rates. Figures analysed by type or size of vessel.

238  SITING OF MAJOR ENERGY FACILITIES
OECD, Paris

English 1979 126pp $7.50

Describes the technical environmental and socio-economic effects of major energy facilities. Identifies the causes of public opposition, describes the development of regulatory procedures and policies on siting.

239  SNG FROM RESIDUAL OIL
International Gas Union, Paris

English 1979 16pp

Reviews the state of processes for producing synthetic natural gas from heavy distillates. Paper given at the IGU's 1979 international conference.

240  SOLAR ENERGY
Shell International Petroleum Co Ltd, London

English 1978 8pp free

Identifies the distribution of solar energy throughout the main regions of the world and the means of producing heat and electricity from solar radiation. Published in the series 'Shell Briefing Service.'

241  THE SOVIET ENERGY BALANCE
Holt-Saunders Ltd, Eastbourne

English 1974 288pp £13.25

Traces the development of the oil, gas, coal, peat and oil shale industries to date. Discusses nuclear energy and hydro-electric power and projects possible developments in solar, geothermal, wind, tide and magnetohydrodynamic energy sources. Provides a basis for assessing the USSR's position in a world context up to the year 2000.

242  STANDARD OIL COMPANY OF CALIFORNIA—
ANNUAL REPORT
Standard Oil Co of California, San Francisco

English annual c50pp

Contains a review of Standard Oil Co activities in Europe and general oil and energy developments.

243  STATISTICAL REVIEW OF THE WORLD OIL
INDUSTRY
British Petroleum Co Ltd, London

English annual 32pp free

Annual statistics on world oil production, reserves, refining, transportation, trade and consumption. Also gives data on total primary energy, natural gas, coal and hydro/nuclear power consumption.

244  STATISTICAL YEARBOOK: TRANSPORT,
COMMUNICATIONS, TOURISM
Eurostat, Luxembourg

Multi-language annual 154pp

Contains a section dealing with pipelines, including data on movements of crude oil and petroleum products in the European Community.

245  STATISTICS OF FOREIGN TRADE—MONTHLY
BULLETIN
OECD, Paris

English/French monthly c116pp $45.00 p.a.

Quarterly figures for value of foreign trade by country for each OECD member country. Trade indices. Total trade of EEC, OECD and rest of world. Analysis of trade by broad tariff heading.

246  STATISTICS OF FOREIGN TRADE—TABLES
BY COMMODITIES
OECD, Paris

English/French annual 2 vols $30.00

Details for each member country of foreign trade by country of origin/destination under main SITC tariff headings. Vol 1: Imports. Vol 2: Exports.

247  STATISTICS OF FOREIGN TRADE—TABLES
BY REPORTING COUNTRY
OECD, Paris

English/French annual 4 vols $30.00

Foreign trade statistics of member countries by main SITC tariff heading and by country of origin/destination.

248  STEAM COAL AND EUROPEAN ENERGY NEEDS
TO 1985
Economist Intelligence Unit, London

English 1978 £25.00

An EIU special report (number 52) setting out the likely demand for steam coal to 1985 in 11 West European countries. Reviews electricity production prospects and the competition likely from nuclear power and fuel oil.

249  STEAM COAL PROSPECTS TO 2000
OECD, Paris

English 1978 160pp $12.00

Projections of steam coal demand and trade to the year 2000 in an overall energy context. Analyses constraints on the expansion of coal use and trade and identifies policies to encourage the substitution of steam coal for oil.

250  SUN: MANKIND'S FUTURE SOURCE OF
ENERGY
Pergamon Press, Oxford

English 1978 3 vols £125.00

Proceedings of the International Solar Energy Congress of 1978, covering: international and national plans and programmes; economic and policy aspects; technology of harnessing solar energy; ocean thermal gradients; wind power; agricultural and industrial applications.

251  SURVEY OF ENERGY RESOURCES 1978
World Energy Conference, London

English/French 1978 84pp

Up-date of information presented at the 1974 World Energy Conference covering: solid fossil fuel; crude oil and natural gas liquids; oil shale and bituminous sands; natural gas; hydraulic resources; uranium and thorium; renewable energy resources.

252  TANKERS FOR THE 1980s
H P Drewry, London

English 1980 100pp $295.00

Analysis of the supply and demand situation in the tanker market with an assessment of the market for its investment potential.

253  TEXACO INC—ANNUAL REPORT
Texaco Inc, White Plains

English annual c60pp

Includes notes on Texaco activities in Europe and data on refinery runs in principal areas of operation.

254  TOWARDS A EUROPEAN ENERGY POLICY
Commission of the European Communities, Brussels

English 1979 8pp free

Summary of the position of the European Community on energy issues and notes of actions taken or proposed in this field.

255  TWENTY-FIVE YEARS OF THE COMMON
MARKET IN COAL 1953-78
Commission of the European Communities, Brussels

English 1978 186pp $8.00

Survey of the coal industry in the European Community since 1953. Includes a statistical section covering production, trade, consumption, collieries, capital expenditure and operating costs.

256  ULCC TRADING OPPORTUNITIES
H P Drewry, London

English 1977 70pp $150.00

An assessment of the market for tankers of over 300,000 deadweight tonnes.

257  URANIUM AND NUCLEAR ENERGY
Mining Journal Books Ltd, Edenbridge

English  1979  326pp  £16.00

Proceedings of the fourth international symposium
held by the Uranium Institute. Papers in Part I deal
with: the energy outlook; uranium supply and
demand; uranium from sea water; use of thorium;
fast breeder reactors. Part II is concerned with
nuclear issues.

258  URANIUM ORE PROCESSING
International Atomic Energy Agency, Vienna

English  1976  238pp  $19.00

Proceedings of an IAEA advisory group examining
the capacity to meet an expanding demand for
uranium and processes available to new milling
plants. Also deals with in-situ treatment and uranium
from sea water.

259  URANIUM RESOURCES, PRODUCTION AND
DEMAND
OECD, Paris

English  1978  138pp  $9.00

Joint report by the Nuclear Energy Agency and the
International Atomic Energy Agency on the situation
and prospects for uranium development.

260  URBAN DISTRICT HEATING USING NUCLEAR
HEAT
International Atomic Energy Agency, Vienna

English/French/Russian  1977  207pp  $15.00

Proceedings of an IAEA advisory group covering
technological, economic and environmental aspects
of the utilisation of waste heat from nuclear power
stations for district heating purposes.

261  VEREIN DEUTSCHER KOHLENIMPORTEURE-
JAHRESBERICHT
Verein Deutscher Kohlenimporteure, Hamburg

German  annual  140pp

Annual report of the association of German coalimporters. Reviews the international trade in hard
coal and developments in individual European and
other coal-exporting countries. Statistical section
gives figures for production imports and exports in
principal countries.

262  WATER AND BIOMASS AS ENERGY RESOURCES
International Gas Union, Paris

English  1979  14pp

Comparative economic analysis of costs of producing
energy from different types of biomass. Paper given
at the IGU's 1979 conference.

263  WESTERN ENERGY POLICY
Macmillan Press Ltd, London

English  1978  198pp  £10.00

Part I looks at past policies in a comparative assessment and energy trends in the European Community.
Part II examines specifically policies in the United
Kingdom, West Germany and the United States;
prospects for global energy 1985-2000.

264  WESTFIELD—THE DEVELOPMENT OF
PROCESSES FOR THE PRODUCTION OF SNG
FROM COAL
The Institution of Gas Engineers, London

English  1976  24pp  £1.25

Paper dealing with work done at the Westfield processing plant to produce synthetic natural gas from
coal, particularly of grades imported from the United
States.

265  WINDOW ON OIL
The Financial Times Ltd, London

English  1978  188pp  £50.00

Study by B F Grossling of the prospects for oil
production outside the Middle East, including
possible resources in offshore areas of Europe.

266  WORKSHOPS ON ENERGY SUPPLY AND
DEMAND
OECD, Paris

English  1979  502pp  $30.00

Set of 20 papers presented in workshops held in 1976
and 1977, dealing with aspects of present and future
world energy supply and demand.

267  WORLD COAL
Miller Freeman Publications Inc, San Francisco

English  monthly  50pp

Journal containing news and reports on coal developments. Distributed free within the industry. Subscription outside the industry $25.00 p.a.

268  WORLD COAL INDUSTRY REPORT AND
DIRECTORY 1979-80
Miller Freeman Publications Inc, San Francisco

English  1979  328pp

Survey of the coal industry in principal countries
throughout the world, dealing with: reserves, development, operations and trade. Describes individual
mines. Section on the international coal trade, with
buyers guide.

269 WORLD ENERGY BOOK
Kogan Page Ltd, London

English 1978 264pp £12.00

An atlas and statistical source book on energy. Includes a 40 page section covering world consumption and production of the principal fuels.

270 WORLD ENERGY OUTLOOK
Exxon Corporation, New York

English 1979 32pp free

Assesses the general situation of the world economy and energy demand, prospective energy supply, the outlook for electricity, nuclear power, coal, gas, oil and synthetic fuels. Reviews the energy situation in the United States, Europe and Japan.

271 WORLD ENERGY OUTLOOK
OECD, Paris

English/French 1977 106pp $12.00

Review of energy supply and demand prospects for OECD countries up to 1985 and in the period beyond 1990. Examines the potential for energy conservation in industry, transport, commerce and the residential sectors. Annexes include energy balance sheets.

272 WORLD ENERGY RESOURCES 1985-2000
IPC Science & Technology Press Ltd, Guildford

English 1978 260pp

Executive summaries of papers presented at the World Energy Conference, covering reserves, demand and conservation.

273 WORLD ENERGY SUPPLIES 1950-74
United Nations, New York

English 1976 826pp $38.00

Long-run data on production, consumption and trade in solid fuels, crude petroleum, petroleum products, gaseous fuels, electrical energy and uranium, for individual countries throughout the world. Includes figures for electricity generation plant by type in public and industrial sectors.

274 WORLD ENERGY SUPPLIES 1973-78
United Nations, New York

English 1979 234pp $20.00

Up-dated statistics for the period 1973-78 covering: production, consumption and trade of solid fuels, crude petroleum, petroleum products, gaseous fuels, electrical energy and uranium. Includes data on capacity in oil refining and electricity generation.

275 WORLD GAS REPORT
Noroil Publishing House, Stavanger

English weekly 10pp £15.00 p.a.

Journal containing news items and comment on discoveries, project developments, supply and pricing in international gas trade.

276 WORLD MINERAL STATISTICS 1972-76
Institute of Geological Sciences/HMSO

English 1979 216pp £8.50

Includes data on coal and uranium. Production, imports and exports of coal, by main type. Production of uranium in nine key countries.

277 WORLD MINING
Miller Freeman Publications Ltd, San Francisco

English monthly 90pp

Journal containing general news on the mining industry and economic technical articles. Distributed free within the industry and at a subscription of $30-40.00 p.a. to other interested parties.

278 WORLD OIL
Gulf Publishing Co, Tulsa

English monthly c140pp

Journal with news on oil and gas industries and articles of an economic or technical nature. Distributed free within the industry and on subscription of $8-12.00 p.a. to interested parties outside the industry.

279 WORLD OIL STATISTICS
Institute of Petroleum, London

English 1978 8pp free

Statistics for crude oil reserves, petroleum production, oil refining, consumption, the world oil trade and tanker fleet.

280 WORLD PETROCHEMICALS
The Financial Times Ltd, London

English 1978 127pp £50.00

Collection of papers on the petrochemical industry since 1973. Subjects discussed include the role of producer states and the impact of rising feedstock costs.

281 WORLD STATISTICS
The Institute of Petroleum, London

English 1978 8pp free

Figures for crude oil reserves and production, refinery capacity, consumption of petroleum products, tanker tonnage and international oil trade, analysed by countries or main areas of the world.

282  WORLD TANKER FLEET REVIEW
John I Jacobs and Co Ltd, London

English  half-yearly  £25.00 p.a.

Statistical analysis of world tanker fleet with commentary on the previous six-months events relating to tankers, port and shipyard development, technical aspects, LPG and LNG carriers, combined carriers, sale and purchase, market highlights and future outlook.

283  WORLD URANIUM POTENTIAL: AN INTERNATIONAL EVALUATION
OECD, Paris

English  1979  176pp  $16.00

Describes the areas of the world containing significant uranium deposits and identifies other areas believed to be favourable for the discovery of uranium resources. Describes efforts currently being undertaken in uranium exploration.

284  WORLDWIDE OPERATING EXPERIENCE WITH COMMERCIAL PLANTS PRODUCING SNG FROM LIGHT PETROLEUM
International Gas Union, Paris

English  1979  20pp

Review of technologies and operating results of plants in Italy, France, the United Kingdom, Japan and the United States. Paper given at the IGU's 1979 international conference.

285  WORLDWIDE PETROCHEMICAL DIRECTORY 1979
Petroleum Publishing Co, Tulsa

English  1979  286pp  $40.00

Includes information on companies producing petrochemicals in Europe. Data on companies and individual plants.

286  WORLDWIDE SURVEY OF MOTOR GASOLINE QUALITY
Associated Octel Ltd, London

English  annual  c100pp

Contains data on average octane ratings and lead alkyl content of gasoline in countries throughout the world, with figures for total gasoline market in each country.

287  YEARBOOK OF INTERNATIONAL TRADE STATISTICS
UN Economic Commission for Europe, Geneva

English  annual  2 vols  $60.00

Detailed tables of international trade in two volumes not sold separately. Vol 1: Trade by country (c1,000 pp). Vol 2: Trade by commodity (c1,200 pp).

288  YEARBOOK OF NORDIC STATISTICS
Nordic Council, Stockholm

English/Swedish  annual  c365pp

Compendium of statistics on political, social, economic and cultural matters in Denmark, Finland, Iceland, Norway and Sweden. Includes a special energy section, covering: gross energy supply; consumption of individual energy sources; energy balance sheets; the electricity network; generating capacity by type; oil refinery capacity.

# Great Britain and Ireland

## United Kingdom

**350 ACCOUNTABILITY '77**
Central Electricity Generating Board

English 1977 90pp £3.50

Handbook of the Central Electricity Generating Board, with information on its structure, organisation, responsibilities and operations.

**351 ADVISORY COUNCIL ON ENERGY CONSERVATION INDUSTRY GROUP REPORT 1975-76**
Department of Energy/HMSO

English 1976 39pp £1.20

Report containing 35 recommendations towards increasing energy conservation in industry. Published as Energy Paper No 15.

**352 ADVISORY COUNCIL ON ENERGY CONSERVATION: REPORT OF THE WORKING GROUP ON BUILDINGS**
Department of Energy/HMSO

English 1978 32pp £1.50

Analysis of the use of energy in domestic and commercial buildings. Contains estimates of energy consumption and costs attached to energy conservation measures under UK conditions. Published as Energy Paper No 25.

**353 ADVISORY COUNCIL ON ENERGY CONSERVATION: REPORT TO THE SECRETARY OF STATE**
Department of Energy/HMSO

English 1979 £3.25

Annual report of the ACEC on its activities in the United Kingdom. Published as Energy Paper No 40.

**354 ADVISORY COUNCIL ON ENERGY CONSERVATION: REPORT TO THE SECRETARY OF STATE FOR ENERGY**
Department of Energy/HMSO

English 1978 28pp £1.75

Report recommends that a saving of 20 per cent of final energy consumption should be achieved by the year 2000. Identifies the need for greater awareness, increased financial incentives and improved technology. Brings together the more significant findings of ACEC working groups. Published as Energy Paper No 31.

**355 ATOM**
United Kingdom Atomic Energy Authority

English monthly 26pp free

Monthly bulletin of the UKAEA including: articles on nuclear power; news of developments in the nuclear field; coverage of relevant topics raised in Parliament.

**356 BENEATH THE NORTH SEA**
Mobil North Sea Ltd

English 1979 9pp free

Information booklet giving the background to exploration and development in the North Sea, with particular reference to the Beryl field, of which Mobil is the operator.

**357 BNOC**
The British National Oil Corporation

English 1979 12pp free

Background information about the state oil corporation. Sections deal with: powers and duties; licence interests; exploration and appraisal; development; financial basis of the corporation; organisation and manpower.

358  BRITAIN'S OIL
Hamish Hamilton Ltd

English 1978 388pp £8.95

History of the development of oil in the United
Kingdom with commentary on technical, economic,
financial and political aspects.

359  BRITISH COMBUSTION
Chichester Design Associates Ltd

English 18pp

Journal of the British Combustion Equipment
Manufacturers' Association, containing news on
combustion equipment and efficient fuel use.

360  BRITISH GAS CORPORATION—ANNUAL
REPORT
British Gas Corporation/HMSO

English annual 80pp

Contains: review of the gas industry and general
energy situation in the United Kingdom; detailed
financial and sales information, broken down by
regions; other operational data concerning exploration, distribution, employment, customers and
plant.

361  THE BRITISH GAS DIRECTORY OF ENERGY-
SAVING EQUIPMENT
Cambridge Information and Research Services Ltd

English 1980 160pp £7.50

Directory of energy-saving equipment available to
industrial and commercial firms in the United
Kingdom. Each item is described and a statement
made of its energy-saving potential.

362  BRITISH GAS: FACTS AND FIGURES
British Gas Corporation

English annual 10pp free

Booklet summarising the activities of British Gas
Corporation. Includes data on output, consumption,
sales, prices and balance sheet results.

363  THE BRITISH NATIONAL OIL CORPORATION—
ANNUAL REPORT
The British National Oil Corporation/HMSO

English annual c54pp £2.00

Contains a review of oil and gas activities in the
United Kingdom, in which BNOC is involved.

364  BRITISH NUCLEAR ACHIEVEMENTS
The Electricity Council

English 1979 24pp free

Text of a paper given by the chairman of the Electricity Council. Reviews the development of nuclear
power in the United Kingdom.

365  BUSINESS MONITORS ANNUAL CENSUS OF
PRODUCTION REPORTS
Business Statistics Office/HMSO

English annual c12pp £0.60 each

Series of individual industry reports which tabulate
results of the latest annual census of production,
including data on: sales, costs, net output, investment, establishments, employment. Business
Monitors in this series relating to the energy sector
are: PA 101 Coal-mining; PA 104 Petroleum and
natural gas; PA 602 Electricity; PA 603 Gas; PA
339.1 Mining machinery. For details of quarterly
Business Monitors see individual titles.

366  CEGB DIGEST
Central Electricity Generating Board

English monthly 24pp

Abstracts of papers and reports on matters of interest
to the electricity supply industry. Available on subscription to outside organisations.

367  CEGB STATISTICAL YEARBOOK
Central Electricity Generating Board

English annual 20pp free

Compendium of statistics on the electricity supply
industry in England and Wales. Details of generating
plant, fuels used, costs of generation and plant construction programme. Many data given for individual
locations or regions.

368  CENTRAL ELECTRICITY GENERATING BOARD
—ANNUAL REPORT
Central Electricity Generating Board

English annual c60pp £2.00

Contains a review of the electricity supply industry
in England and Wales; a report on developments in
production, transmission and sales; data on generating
plant; construction programme and economic
outlook.

369  THE CHALLENGES OF NORTH SEA OIL
Mobil North Sea Ltd

English 1979 12pp free

Series of explanatory notes on the exploitation of
North Sea oil and gas resources, with a particular
emphasis on the technology of exploration and
production.

**370 CHEMFACTS UK**
IPC Industrial Press Ltd

English 1977 £35.00

Analysis of market trends; plant capacity and investment; trade in individual chemicals and profiles of leading companies.

**371 CIVIL AVIATION**
Department of Energy/HMSO

English 1979 26pp £2.25

Report by the Advisory Council on Energy Conservation. Considers present and future patterns of fuel consumption of UK airlines in the light of rising oil prices, technological advances and forecasts of traffic trends to the end of the century. Published as Energy Paper No 36.

**372 COAL AND NUCLEAR POWER STATION COSTS**
Department of Energy

English 1978 14pp

Note prepared by the Department of Energy for the Energy Commission on the assumed use of nuclear power station capacity in the United Kingdom with indications of cost. Includes comparative figures for steam-generating heavy water, advanced gas-cooled, and pressurised water reactors in relation to coal-fired plant. Published as Energy Commission Paper No 6.

**373 COAL FOR THE FUTURE**
Department of Energy

English 1978 24pp

Review of progress with 'Plan for Coal', with assessment of prospects for the coal industry up to the year 2000. Reaffirmed the general approach towards expansion of the industry.

**374 COAL IN . . . . . . .**
National Coal Board

English 1978-80

Series of 12 brochures giving detailed background information on mining regions of Great Britain. Data for individual collieries include depth, output, employment, new investment. Detailed maps included.

**375 COAL IN THE UK**
Department of Energy

English 1977 18pp

Contains background information on the coal industry in the United Kingdom: organisation and responsibilities of the industry; government policies affecting coal; basic data on coal resources and production.

**376 COAL INDUSTRY EXAMINATION**
Department of Energy

English 1974 36pp

Review of the position of the coal industry in the United Kingdom and the contribution which coal might make towards national energy requirements, particularly in the period up to 1985, including investment needs of the industry.

**377 COAL MINING**
Business Statistics Office/HMSO

English quarterly 4pp £4.00 p.a.

Business Monitor No PQ 101, containing regular statistics on coal output, in terms of volume and value, manpower in mining and productivity.

**378 COLLIERY GUARDIAN**
Fuel & Metallurgical Journals Ltd

English monthly c20pp £23.00

Journal carrying news of developments in the United Kingdom mining industry. Subscription includes the quarterly issue of Coal International.

**379 COMBINED HEAT AND ELECTRICAL POWER GENERATION IN THE UK**
Department of Energy/HMSO

English 1979 171pp £3.75

Discusses the future of combined heat and power schemes in the UK and the factors which have inhibited its development so far. Advocates the identification of some key cities and towns in which to implement lead schemes. Published as Energy Paper No 35.

**380 CONSUMPTION AND REFINERY PRODUCTION**
Institute of Petroleum

English annual 10pp

Detailed statistics of refinery output and consumption of individual refinery products by sectors of the economy. Compiled from oil industry sources in advance of official statistics.

**381 DEPLOYMENT OF NATIONAL RESOURCES IN THE PROVISION OF ENERGY IN THE UNITED KINGDOM 1975-2025**
The Watt Committee on Energy Ltd

English 1977 60pp £10.50

Depicts seven possible scenarios for the United Kingdom's future energy situation and evaluates them in terms of capital investment, manpower and materials, with emphasis on financial aspects.

**382  THE DEVELOPMENT OF COAL LIQUEFACTION PROCESSES IN THE UNITED KINGDOM**
Institution of Gas Engineers

English 1979 20pp £1.50

Paper reviewing the state of liquefaction technology, in particular processes of liquid solvent extraction and supercritical gas extraction.

**383  DEVELOPMENT OF THE OIL AND GAS RESOURCES OF THE UNITED KINGDOM**
Department of Energy/HMSO

English annual 60pp

The 'Brown Book'. Official review of activity in exploration and development of oil and gas in the United Kingdom and its offshore waters. Field by field details of production, reserves and participating companies. Summary of exploration activity includes statistics on drilling, exploration and employment. Includes an analysis of orders for equipment placed in the UK and abroad.

**384  DIGEST OF ENERGY STATISTICS**
Department of Energy/HMSO

English annual 140pp £7.50

Statistics of the availability and disposal of energy in total and by fuel type. Details of: indigenous production, imports and exports; pattern of consumption by sector and by industry; operations of production and transformation undertakings; oil and gas reserves; principal financial data for the nationalised undertakings. Some figures for fuel prices and consumers' expenditure on fuels.

**385  DIGEST OF WELSH STATISTICS**
Welsh Office/HMSO

English annual c200pp £6.75

Includes a section on energy supply and consumption in Wales, with details of the operations of each energy industry and details of consumption.

**386  DISTRICT HEATING COMBINED WITH ELECTRICITY GENERATION IN THE UNITED KINGDOM**
Department of Energy/HMSO

English 1977 120pp £3.75

Examines the medium- and long-term possibilities of district heating schemes in the United Kingdom in the light of the complex economic considerations involved.

**387  DOMESTIC GAS IN AN ENERGY CONSCIOUS FUTURE**
Institution of Gas Engineers

English 1977 28pp £1.25

Paper on the changing role of gas in the United Kingdom energy balance, the importance of energy conservation and the value of using gas for its most appropriate markets. Reviews developments in energy conservation in the domestic sector.

**388  DOMESTIC MARKETING—THE CHANGING SCENE**
Institution of Gas Engineers

English 1978 34pp £1.50

Analyses the domestic gas market in the United Kingdom, ownership of appliances and possible trends, the impact of energy conservation and the state of the appliance manufacturing sector.

**389  THE ECONOMIC IMPACT OF NORTH SEA OIL ON SCOTLAND**
Scottish Economic Planning Dept/HMSO

English 1978 101pp £5.00

Final report by the Department of Political Economy at Aberdeen University of a programme of economic analysis commissioned by the Scottish office. Examines the economic, financial, industrial and social aspects of North Sea oil and gas developments.

**390  THE ECONOMICS AND POLITICS OF NORTH SEA OIL**
Croom Helm Ltd

English 1979 224pp £9.95

Comparative study of the impact of North Sea oil on the United Kingdom and Norway. Particular attention is paid to government policy on taxation, state participation and depletion.

**391  ECONOMIES OF SCALE IN ELECTRICITY GENERATION AND TRANSMISSION SINCE 1945**
Mechanical Engineering Publications Ltd

English 1978 10pp £1.00

Text of a lecture given by the chairman of the Electricity Council. Includes data on prices, fuel utilisation, energy efficiency and other economic aspects of power stations in the United Kingdom.

**392  THE EFFICIENT USE OF NATURAL GAS IN INDUSTRY**
International Gas Union

English 1979 14pp

Recounts the activities and approach of British Gas Corporation and reviews factors relevant to fuel efficiency and management. Paper given at the 1979 congress.

393 ELECTRICAL REVIEW
IPC Electrical-Electronic Press Ltd

English weekly 66pp £0.30 per issue

Periodical dealing with news and technical developments relating to electricity utilisation and equipment for producers and consumers of electricity.

394 ELECTRICAL TIMES
IPC Electrical-Electronic Press Ltd

English weekly 16pp £10.00 p.a.

Weekly newspaper carrying news of general developments in the electrical engineering industry and electricity consumption.

395 ELECTRICITY
Business Statistics Office/HMSO

English quarterly 6pp £4.00 p.a.

Business Monitor No PQ 602, containing indicators of sales of electricity, in terms of quantity and value in each of the main sectors of consumption. Also includes data on: sales of appliances; pattern of electricity generation; fuels used in generation.

396 THE ELECTRICITY COUNCIL—ANNUAL REPORT
HMSO

English annual £1.80

Includes detailed statistics on electricity sales in England and Wales and operations of the various area boards. An abridged version, including the main figures and an outline of developments in the sector, is available free of charge from the Electricity Council.

397 ELECTRICITY—NEW POSSIBILITIES FOR GENERATION AND USE
The Electricity Council

English 1978 14pp free

Text of a lecture given to the Royal Society of Arts by the chairman of the Electricity Council. Survey of usable energy resources and related technologies.

398 ELECTRICITY SUPPLY AND THE ENVIRONMENT
Central Electricity Generating Board

English 1979 64pp

Covers the issues of siting, pollution and distribution arising from electricity plant and looks at the location of new plant in relation to fuel supply sources.

399 ELECTRICITY SUPPLY HANDBOOK
Electrical Times

English annual 300pp £6.00

Contains details of the organisation of the electricity supply industry and directory of the industry and of government departments, associations and societies related to the electricity industry.

400 ELECTRICITY SUPPLY IN THE UNITED KINGDOM
The Electricity Council

English 1978 60pp

Background to the electricity supply industry throughout the United Kingdom, dealing with the organisation of the undertakings, their operations and finances. Basic statistics cover plant, grid systems, distribution, customers, sales, prices, employment and finance of the Central Electricity Generating Board, the Electricity Council, the South of Scotland Electricity Board, North of Scotland Hydro-Electric Board and the Northern Ireland Electricity Service.

401 ENERGY
HMSO

English 1979 32pp £1.25

Reference book produced by the Central Office of Information on energy industries in the United Kingdom. Information deals with: historical development; structure; scale of operations; policies; environmental issues.

402 ENERGY CONSERVATION IN THE UK
National Economic Development Office

English 1975 106pp £3.40

Analysis of the scope for saving energy in industry, commerce and at home.

403 ENERGY CONSERVATION RESEARCH DEVELOPMENT AND DEMONSTRATION
Department of Energy/HMSO

English 1978 51pp £2.25

Report outlining principal ways in which energy conservation in industry should be advanced, identifying the need to modify an existing bias towards investment in energy supply, the scope for greater efficiency in use and priorities for technological development, including waste-heat recovery. Published as Energy Paper No 32.

404 ENERGY CONSERVATION: SCOPE FOR NEW MEASURES AND LONG TERM STRATEGY
Department of Energy/HMSO

English 1978 £2.00

Review by the Department of Energy of progress in energy conservation, suggesting additional measures which might be taken and the long-term contribution of energy conservation to the overall energy picture.

**405  ENERGY DEVELOPMENT AND LAND IN THE UNITED KINGDOM**
The Watt Committee on Energy Ltd

English 1979 59pp £20.50

Review of the use of land in the United Kingdom with maps illustrating potential land needs as coal, oil, gas, nuclear and alternative energy sources are developed. Extensive tables and diagrams. Includes 9 full colour maps.

**406  ENERGY DIGEST**
Energy Digest

English c50pp £28.50 p.a.

Journal of news comment and analysis of energy subjects, including research and development projects, energy conservation, combined heat and power, waste heat utilisation and non-conventional forms of energy.

**407  ENERGY FOR INDUSTRY AND COMMERCE**
Cambridge Information and Research Services Ltd

English annual c100pp £15.00

Annual review of the energy situation in the United Kingdom: developments in supply and demand of individual fuels; government policies; prices and availability.

**408  ENERGY FOR INDUSTRY AND COMMERCE QUARTERLY BULLETIN**
Cambridge Information and Research Services Ltd

English quarterly c24pp £25.00 p.a.

Regular bulletin on developments affecting prices and availability of fuels for industrial and commercial consumers. Sections deal with the international context, individual fuels and energy conservation.

**409  ENERGY FOR TRANSPORT**
Department of Energy/HMSO

English 1978 20pp £1.25

Report by the Advisory Council on Energy Conservation, urging the development of non-oil fuel sources for transport, in particular battery power for vehicles. Published as Energy Paper No 26.

**410  ENERGY IN THE FUTURE**
Institution of Gas Engineers

English 1979 36pp £1.50

Review of: world energy demand and the supply potential of oil, coal, gas, nuclear power and renewable energy sources; the extent of energy conservation in industry, transport and the domestic sectors; government policy and the nationalised energy industries.

**411  ENERGY MANAGEMENT**
Department of Energy

English monthly 8pp

Information and news bulletin concerned with energy conservation. Carries: reports on activity in the public sector and private companies; news of policies and programmes; case studies and projects; and advice on energy conservation.

**412  THE ENERGY MARKETS TO 1990**
Cambridge Information and Research Services Ltd

English 1977 78pp £16.95

Contains forecasts of UK energy demand in the industrial, commercial and domestic sectors matching these to supply prospects and concluding with the implications for management action.

**413  ENERGY POLICY: A CONSULTATIVE DOCUMENT**
HMSO

English 1978 128pp £2.15

Official 'green paper' setting out the state of development of energy supply in the United Kingdom, with background on legislation, organisation and government policies. Includes a general projection of energy demand and possible patterns of supply.

**414  ENERGY POLICY REVIEW**
Department of Energy/HMSO

English 1977 50pp £1.75

Review of the general energy situation of the UK. Contains data on trends and patterns of energy consumption in the UK, with projections of supply and demand through to the year 2000. Summarises the situation in each of the energy industries. Published as Energy Paper No 22.

**415  ENERGY RESEARCH AND DEVELOPMENT IN THE UK**
Institution of Gas Engineers

English 1977 28pp £1.25

Paper by the energy research director of the Atomic Energy Research Establishment reviewing the R & D programme in the United Kingdom, the state of alternative energy technologies and developments in energy conservation.

**416  ENERGY RESEARCH AND DEVELOPMENT IN THE UNITED KINGDOM**
Department of Energy/HMSO

English 1976 £2.65

Review of the extent of research and development work taking place in the field of energy. Published as Energy Paper No 11.

**417 ENERGY TECHNOLOGIES FOR THE UNITED KINGDOM: AN APPRAISAL OF R, D & D PLANNING**
Department of Energy/HMSO

English 1979 2 vols £3.00

Review of approaches and objectives in the planning of research and development and demonstration projects. Published as Energy Paper No 39.

**418 ENERGY THE FACTS OF LIFE**
Woodhead-Faulkner

English 1979 128pp £0.95

An assessment of the energy situation of the United Kingdom and its international context, prospects of future energy supplies and means of conserving energy.

**419 ENERGY: THE KEY RESOURCE**
Department of Energy/HMSO

English 1975 £0.43

Summary of the significance which energy supply has in the general economy. Published as Energy Paper No 4.

**420 ENERGY TRENDS**
Department of Energy/COI

English monthly 8pp

Bulletin giving statistics for supply and disposal of total energy and individual fuels. Also figures for stocks of oil and coal and employment in mining. Series cover several years including most recent quarters or months.

**421 ENERGY WORLD**
Institute of Energy

English monthly 24pp

Bulletin of the Institute of Energy. Includes articles on issues in the energy sector and a digest of political, economic and commercial topics relevant to energy.

**422 THE ENGINEERING OF THE FRIGG PROJECT**
Institution of Gas Engineers

Background to the development of the Frigg gas field and the equipment installed both onshore and offshore. Contains technical data on production installations, the St Fergus terminal and onshore gas trunklines.

**423 ESSO PETROLEUM COMPANY—ANNUAL REPORT**
Esso Petroleum Company Ltd

English annual 44pp

Contains a review of the United Kingdom oil market and information on the operations of the company, which is one of the leading oil refiners and marketers of oil products. Includes annual accounts, which cover a ten-year period.

**424 EXPLORATION AND DEVELOPMENT OF UK CONTINENTAL SHELF OIL**
Department of Energy

English 1978 60pp free

Comments on the offshore exploration and development situation by the Offshore Operators Association, emphasizing the inter-dependence of government policies and industry activity. Includes information on the state of development of individual fields and comment on the commercial viability of discoveries. Published as Energy Commission Paper No 17.

**425 THE FINANCING OF NORTH SEA OIL**
HMSO

English 1978 64pp £1.50

Research Report No 2 of the committee reviewing the functioning of UK financial institutions (Wilson Committee). Detailed survey of the sources of finance, methods of financing and total investment in offshore oil and gas development projects.

**426 THE FLOW OF NORTH SEA ENERGY WEALTH**
The Financial Times Ltd

English 1979 £75.00

Economic and financial analysis by C Johnson of oil and gas exploitation and the impact which this has on the general economy in terms of the flow of funds and national accounts. Reviews policy options for applying the benefits within the economy.

**427 FORTIES: THE STORY OF BRITAIN'S FIRST MAJOR OILFIELD**
British Petroleum Co Ltd

English 1976 37pp free

Booklet covering the historical development of the Forties field, with technical and economic data and notes on production facilities.

**428 FREIGHT TRANSPORT**
Department of Energy/HMSO

English 1977 22pp £1.50

Report by the Advisory Council on Energy Conservation. Analyses energy consumption in terms of the various modes of transport available and their characteristic traffic flows. Concludes that significant energy savings could be achieved through greater use of diesel engines, electric road vehicles and intensified use of an electrified rail system. Published as Energy Paper No 24.

**429   FRIGG—GAS FROM THE NORTH SEA**
British Gas Corporation

English  1977  64pp

Information brochure giving data about this major North Sea gas field and its position in the overall gas supply situation. Contains a history of development of the field and main operational characteristics.

**430   FUEL PURCHASING HANDBOOK 1980-81**
Cambridge Information and Research Services Ltd

English  1980  160pp  £13.50

Contains contributions by practising managers in industry, commerce and local government and specialist analyses of the United Kingdom and international fuel markets.

**431   FUEL PURCHASING IN INDUSTRY AND COMMERCE**
Cambridge Information and Research Services Ltd

English  1977  104pp  £6.50

Guide to fuel purchasing policy and practice, with information about contract arrangements, available tariff levels and prospects for supplies and prices.

**432   FUEL SAVING: THE FUEL INDUSTRIES AND SOME LARGE FIRMS**
Department of Energy/HMSO

English  1975  64pp  £1.85

Examines case studies of energy conservation in BP, Esso, Shell, ICI, British Gas Corporation, British Steel Corporation, the coal industry and electricity supply. Summarises the approach taken, measures, programme of action and savings. Published as Energy Paper No 5.

**433   THE FUTURE OF THE UNITED KINGDOM POWER PLANT MANUFACTURING INDUSTRY**
HMSO

English  1976  102pp  £2.50

Report by the Central Policy Review Staff on the state of the power plant manufacturing industry. Analyses the industry and reviews the available power generation technologies. Addresses the issues of lead-times and the industry's role in world markets.

**434   FUTURE TRENDS IN DOMESTIC HEATING BY GAS**
Institution of Gas Engineers

English  1979  30pp  £1.50

Paper covering recent developments in the gas heating market, noting a shift from installation of new systems to increased scope for replacement and modernisation, the need for new equipment to take into account the impact of energy conservation measures and the potential of more sophisticated systems.

**435   GAS**
Business Statistics Office/HMSO

English  quarterly  4pp  £4.00 p.a.

Business Monitor No PQ 601, containing indicators of sales in main consuming sectors by volume and value, and series for sales of appliances.

**436   GAS 2029**
Institution of Gas Engineers

English  1979  20pp  £1.50

Examines the current state of energy supply and demand in the United Kingdom and reviews possible long-term trends and the implications of them for the gas industry.

**437   GAS DIRECTORY AND WHO'S WHO**
Benn Publications Ltd

English  annual  c200pp

Directory of the United Kingdom gas industry including institutions, associations and suppliers of goods and services. Contains a review of the year and buyer's guide of gas equipment and appliances.

**438   GAS FROM THE UK CONTINENTAL SHELF**
Department of Energy

English  1976  8pp  free

Basic information about the development and use of offshore gas. Background on organisation, policies, the gas industry, reserves, production and distribution.

**439   GAS GATHERING PIPELINE SYSTEMS IN THE NORTH SEA**
Department of Energy/HMSO

English  1978  65pp  £2.50

Report on the proposals for a pipeline system to utilize gas resources in a number of small and marginally economic fields in the North Sea. Published as Energy Paper No 30.

**440   GAS GATHERING PIPELINE SYSTEMS IN THE NORTH SEA**
Department of Energy

English  1976  8pp  free

Note by the Department of Energy giving a summary and initial comment on the major study of the scope for a gas-gathering pipeline system commissioned by the Department from consultants Williams-Merz.

**441   A GEOGRAPHY OF ENERGY IN THE UNITED KINGDOM**
Longman

English  1980  154pp  £5.50

Contains much historical and current background information on energy and related industries in the United Kingdom. Details of installations and locations, and some economic and cost information.

442 GEOTHERMAL ENERGY: THE CASE FOR RESEARCH IN THE UNITED KINGDOM
Department of Energy/HMSO

English 1976 £1.85

Survey of the state of geothermal energy development and the potential for tapping this source in the United Kingdom. Published as Energy Paper No 9.

443 GUIDE TO THE COALFIELDS
Fuel & Metallurgical Journals Ltd, Redhill

English annual 580pp £9.00

Details of the National Coal Board's structure and area administration. Directory of the industry, including a buyer's guide listing of suppliers to the industry.

444 HANDBOOK OF ELECTRICITY SUPPLY STATISTICS
The Electricity Council

English 1979 142pp

Detailed operational and financial statistics, covering: power stations, the grid system, distribution; electricity output; costs of generation; consumption by sector and industry; tariffs, prices and revenues; appliance sales. International section contains data on other EEC member countries.

445 HEAT LOADS IN BRITISH CITIES
Department of Energy/HMSO

English 1979 £2.75

Examines the proposals for introducing heat and power schemes in existing urban centres, analysing the pattern of heat consumption in various UK towns and cities. Published as Energy Paper No 34.

446 THE HISTORY OF NATURAL GAS CONVERSION IN GREAT BRITAIN
Cambridge Information and Research Services Ltd/British Gas Corporation

English 1980 118pp £12.50

Written by C Elliott, formerly chief press officer of British Gas Corporation. Chronicles the major exercise undertaken by the Corporation between 1967 and 1977 to convert its system and customers' equipment to the use of natural gas. Covers the technical, planning, managerial and other aspects of the project.

447 THE IMPACT OF ENERGY CONSERVATION ON THE DESIGN OF BUILDINGS AND HEATING SYSTEMS
International Gas Union

English 1979 22pp

Contains a review of regulations in the United Kingdom and France concerning energy conservation, and experience in implementation. Paper given at the IGU's 1979 congress.

448 THE INCREASED COST OF ENERGY— IMPLICATIONS FOR UK INDUSTRY
National Economic Development Office

English 1974 118pp £3.40

Analyses the energy situation and its effect on the UK economy and manufacturing industry in particular.

449 INDUSTRIAL COMBINED HEAT AND POWER: A CASE HISTORY
Ove Arup & Partners

English 1978 32pp

Paper presented at the National Energy Managers Conference discussing the scope for combined heat and power systems and the practical economic and technical questions involved in installing them.

450 INPUT-OUTPUT TABLES—UK 1970
Eurostat

English/French 1979 121pp S10.10

Standardised tables showing the expenditure on fuels in individual sectors of the economy and their relative cost significance.

451 KELLY'S MANUFACTURERS AND MERCHANTS DIRECTORY
Kelly's Directories Ltd

English (headings in French/German/Italian/Spanish) annual c2,100pp £20.00

Directory of manufacturing and service firms, including those in energy and energy-related industries. Classification by companies and by product/service. Includes information on products and basic company data.

452 KOMPASS UK
Kompass Publishers Ltd

English (headings in French/German/Italian/Spanish) annual 2 vols £45.00

Directory of British firms, including those engaged in the production and supply of energy and related goods and services. Vol 1 gives information on goods and services. Vol 2 gives basic company information.

**453 LAW AND OFFSHORE OIL DEVELOPMENT: THE NORTH SEA EXPERIENCE**
Holt-Saunders Ltd

English 1979 150pp £12.00

Examines the economic and political evolution of North Sea law, international law, legislation and regulations of the United Kingdom and Norway. Deals with law on licensing, taxation, safety, land planning and environmental protection.

**454 A LOW ENERGY STRATEGY FOR THE UNITED KINGDOM**
Science Reviews Ltd

English 1979 260pp

Study by the International Institute for Environment and Development. Analyses the use of energy in the United Kingdom and the technologies, processes and systems available with their specific energy requirements. Contains a statistical appendix on energy consumption.

**455 THE MARKETING OF FRIGG GAS**
Institution of Gas Engineers

English 1976 24pp £1.25

Paper by the marketing director of British Gas Corporation outlining the strategy for introducing into the existing system and market the substantial new quantities contracted for from the Anglo-Norwegian Frigg gas field.

**456 METHANE DERIVED ALCOHOLS: THEIR USE AS BLENDING COMPONENTS OF PETROL**
Department of Energy/HMSO

English 1975 £0.80

Review of the technical and economic aspects of the use of alcohol based on natural gas as substitute for a proportion of oil-based fuel. Published as Energy Paper No 2.

**457 MINING MACHINERY**
Business Statistics Office/HMSO

English quarterly 6pp £4.00 p.a.

Business Monitor No PQ 339.1, containing statistical series for the value of sales, exports and imports of various types of mining machinery.

**458 MOBIL IN THE UK**
Mobil Oil Co Ltd

English 1978 16pp free

Booklet giving background information on Mobil Oil Company and the Mobil group, covering exploration and production, transportation, refining, distribution, marketing and research.

**459 MONTHLY DIGEST OF STATISTICS**
Central Statistical Office/HMSO

English monthly 178pp £25.20 p.a.

Regular bulletin of official statistics including series for production, trade and consumption of oil, coal, gas and electricity.

**460 NATIONAL COAL BOARD—REPORT AND ACCOUNTS**
National Coal Board

English annual 92pp £1.50

Includes details of the coal industry's operations: output, employment and productivity, for individual mining areas; open-cast and deep-mined coal; main markets to which coal disposed; average earnings and costs. An abridged version of the annual report and accounts is available free of charge.

**461 NATIONAL ENERGY CONFERENCE JUNE 1976: PAPERS SUBMITTED**
Department of Energy/HMSO

English 1976 £3.35

Compendium of papers submitted to the 1976 conference by parties interested in questions of energy policy. Published as Energy Paper No 13, Volume 2.

**462 NATIONAL ENERGY CONFERENCE JUNE 1976: REPORT OF PROCEEDINGS**
Department of Energy/HMSO

English 1976 86pp £2.30

Statements and reviews of the energy situation, made at the 1976 energy conference by the fuel industries, industry, trade unions, professional associations and other bodies involved in energy policy. Published as Energy Paper No 13, Volume 1.

**463 NATIONAL ENERGY POLICY**
Department of Energy/HMSO

English 1979 8pp £1.50

Text of a speech by Sir Jack Rampton of the Department of Energy, setting out the official view of the energy situation of the United Kingdom, the objectives of policy and measures taken. Published as Energy Paper No 41.

**464 NATIONALISED INDUSTRIES AND THE EXPLOITATION OF NORTH SEA OIL AND GAS**
HMSO

English 1975

Proceedings of the Select Committee on nationalised industries examining the role and activities of the state undertakings in exploration and development of offshore resources. Published as House of Commons Paper No 345.

ENERGY PUBLICATIONS—GREAT BRITAIN AND IRELAND

**465  NATURAL GAS**
Benn Publications Ltd

English bi-monthly 36pp

Journal covering developments in the availability of natural gas in the United Kingdom and news of economic and technical developments affecting markets for natural gas.

**466  NATURAL GAS IN THE UK ENERGY MARKETS**
Cambridge Information and Research Services Ltd

English 1979 47pp £4.50

Analyses the pattern of energy supplies in the United Kingdom, past development of gas sales and the future role of gas. Discusses energy policies and price trends. Includes a section on gas in the European energy picture.

**467  NATURAL GAS PURCHASING**
Institution of Gas Engineers

English 1978 24pp £1.50

Sets out the approach by the British Gas Corporation to contracts made with producers of natural gas. Examines the structure and terms of contracts for purchase of associated and non-associated gas.

**468  NORTHERN IRELAND ELECTRICITY SERVICE—ANNUAL REPORT**
Northern Ireland Electricity Service

English annual c50pp

Contains basic information and statistics on the production, distribution and consumption of electricity in Northern Ireland: generation plant, fuels, costs, operating performance, sales by sector, number of customers.

**469  NORTHERN NORTH SEA OIL AND GAS DEVELOPMENTS: PIPELINES, PIPELAYING AND PIPECOATING**
The Institute of Petroleum

English 1978 5pp free

Listing of pipelines, with details of operator, length, diameter and development status; notes pipeline developments and contractors; map of the national gas transmission system. Issued by the Institute as an 'Oil Data Sheet.'

**470  NORTH OF SCOTLAND HYDRO-ELECTRIC BOARD—ANNUAL REPORT**
North of Scotland Hydro-Electric Board

English annual 58pp

Contains information on all aspects of the Board's activities, details of plant and production, and an analysis of consumption of electricity by the principal sectors.

**471  NORTH SEA COSTS ESCALATION STUDY**
Department of Energy/HMSO

English 1975 126pp £4.00

Report commissioned by the Department of Energy from independent accountants and consultants to investigate the factors behind escalation of costs in offshore oil and gas development. Published as Energy Paper No 7.

**472  THE NORTH SEA IN PERSPECTIVE**
Wood Mackenzie & Co

English 1979 83pp

Review of exploration and production projects in the North Sea. Analysis of development costs. Statistics on exploration and production. Considers the political context and legislative framework and the role of the British National Oil Corporation.

**473  NORTH SEA OIL**
Pergamon Press

English 1979

Sub-titled 'Resource requirements for UK development'. Analysis by J Klitz of the International Institute for Applied Systems Analysis. Considers technological and material requirements of production facilities.

**474  NORTH SEA OIL AND GAS**
David & Charles Ltd

English 1976 240pp £5.95

A geographical perspective of offshore oil and gas development. Records the growth of oil and gas production and looks at the economic impact of it.

**475  NORTH SEA OIL AND GAS 1975**
Sterling Professional Publications Ltd, London

English 1975 432pp

Information about North Sea oil and gas development with directory of firms involved in related manufacturing and service activities. Indexed by product/service.

**476  NORTH SEA OIL AND SCOTLAND'S ECONOMIC PROSPECTS**
Croom Helm Ltd

English 1979 160pp £7.95

Considers the particular impact of the development of offshore oil and gas on employment, industry and infrastructure in Scotland.

**477  NORTH SEA OIL AND THE UK ECONOMY**
The Institute of Petroleum

English 1978 10pp free

Review of the significance of oil and gas exploitation in the United Kingdom offshore sector, including the impact on the balance of payments and direct employment. Issued by the Institute as an 'Oil Data Sheet.'

**478    NORTH SEA OIL INFORMATION SHEET**
Scottish Economic Planning Department

English  quarterly

Summarises official actions and decisions affecting North Sea activities and their impact on oil and gas-related industries, particularly in Scotland. Includes data on rig activity, discoveries and licence awards.

**479    NORTH SEA OIL IN THE FUTURE: ECONOMIC ANALYSIS AND GOVERNMENT POLICY**
Trade Policy Research Centre

English  1978  233pp  £10.00

Detailed analysis by C Robinson and J Morgan of the economics of North Sea oil. Contains a critical analysis of the depletion and taxation policies of the United Kingdom and Norwegian governments. Discusses North Sea oil in an international context.

**480    NORTH SEA PROGRESS**
Shell International Petroleum Co Ltd

English  1979  10pp

Includes a review of the current situation in the UK sector in terms of development, finance and tax revenues and possible future developments. Includes map of oil and gas fields. Produced in the series 'Shell Briefing Service.'

**481    THE OFFSHORE ENERGY TECHNOLOGY BOARD: STRATEGY FOR RESEARCH AND DEVELOPMENT**
Department of Energy/HMSO

English  1975  15pp  £0.90

Report of the advisory board on offshore development, identifying the main areas in which research and development should be most valuable. Published as Energy Paper No 8.

**482    OFFSHORE OIL DIRECTORY**
North East Scotland Development Agency

English  half-yearly

Regularly up-dated directory of firms and organisations in Aberdeen and the north-east region of Scotland engaged in supplying the offshore oil and gas industry, including details of products and services supplied.

**483    OFFSHORE OIL POLICY**
Department of Energy

English  1978  11pp  free

Summary of the various aspects of policy relating to offshore development, including: licensing, royalties, taxation, depletion, environmental protection, disposal and pricing.

**484    OFFSHORE RESEARCH FOCUS**
Department of Energy/CIRIA

English  bi-monthly  8pp  free

Bulletin on technological problems and developments relating to offshore oil and gas exploitation. Distributed only in the United Kingdom.

**485    THE OFFSHORE SUPPLY MARKET**
Department of Industry (Leeds)

English  1976  292pp

Survey of offshore developments and the prospective demand for equipment and services. Produced by the Leeds office of the Department of Industry and containing a directory of firms in Yorkshire and Humberside capable of supplying the offshore industry.

**486    OIL FROM THE UK CONTINENTAL SHELF**
Department of Energy

English  1976  12pp  free

Background information on legislation and policies affecting offshore development, the extent and value of oil and gas reserves and the costs of exploitation.

**487    OSO INFORMATION OFFSHORE**
Offshore Supplies Office

English  1980  69pp

File of basic information on the market for offshore supplies. Sets out the role of the Offshore Supplies Office and other government departments and agencies, other organisations with an interest in offshore development, and offshore operating companies.

**488    OVERSEAS TRADE STATISTICS**
Department of Trade/HMSO

English  monthly  c550pp  £7.00 per issue

Includes imports and exports of fuel products according to the SITC commodity classification presented by country of origin and destination. Figures for volume and value.

**489    PASSENGER TRANSPORT: SHORT AND MEDIUM TERM CONSIDERATIONS**
Department of Energy/HMSO

English  1976  16pp  £0.90

Report by the Advisory Council on Energy Conservation identifying the principal means of saving energy in passenger transport. Published as Energy Paper No 10.

**490 PETROLEUM AND NATURAL GAS**
Business Statistics Office/HMSO

English quarterly 4pp £4.00 p.a.

Business Monitor PQ 104, containing statistics of output of crude oil, natural gas and natural gas liquids, by volume and value.

**491 PETROLEUM REVIEW**
Institute of Petroleum, London

English monthly 64pp

Journal of the Institute of Petroleum dealing with developments in the United Kingdom oil industry. Also includes articles of general interest and some statistical information. Available at £11.00 p.a. to non-members.

**492 PFA UTILIZATION**
Central Electricity Generation Board

English 1972 108pp £3.00

Comprehensive reference volume on the state of technology in utilisation of pulverised fuel ash.

**493 PLAN FOR COAL**
National Coal Board

English 1973 20pp free

Booklet setting out the objectives for the coal industry as proposed by the National Coal Board, and as basically accepted by the Coal Industry Examination of 1974. The 1973 plan envisaged investment of £1,400 million in the period 1975-85 in order to provide new capacity totalling 42 million tonnes per annum.

**494 THE POLITICAL ECONOMY OF NORTH SEA OIL**
Martin Robertson & Co Ltd

English 1975 208pp £3.25

Essay by D I Mackay and G A Mackay of Aberdeen University on the political and economic issues raised by the development of offshore oil and gas in the North Sea.

**495 THE POTENTIAL OF NATURAL ENERGY RESOURCES**
Central Electricity Generating Board

English 1975 13pp free

Brief survey of non-conventional energy resources and their potential for energy supply in the United Kingdom. Sections on solar, wind, wave, tidal and geothermal sources.

**496 THE PROSPECTS FOR THE GENERATION OF ELECTRICITY FROM WIND IN THE UK**
Department of Energy/HMSO

English 1977 66pp £2.25

Review of the resource potential, technology and possible locations for facilities to generate electricity from wind power. Analyses costs, availability, load factor and problems of connection to the main supply system. Also looks at the scope for small aerogenerators. Published as Energy Paper No 21.

**497 QUARTERLY BULLETIN OF PORT STATISTICS**
National Ports Council/HMSO

English quarterly £20.00 p.a.

Information from 30 port authorities covering over 90 per cent of total traffic. Figures by port for foodstuffs, basic materials, manufactured goods and fuels, numbers of container units and roll-on/roll-off traffic.

**498 REGIONAL STATISTICS**
HMSO

English 1979 224pp £7.50

Includes a section on energy, giving a breakdown for the standard planning regions of production, consumption by sector, sales value and employment for each fuel.

**499 RENEWABLE SOURCES OF ENERGY: THE PROSPECTS FOR ELECTRICITY**
Central Electricity Generating Board

English 1979 12pp free

Booklet containing a statement by the chairman of the CEGB on the Board's interest and involvement in assessing the potential value of solar, wind, tidal wave and geothermal energy sources in the UK energy balance.

**500 REPORT OF THE WORKING GROUP ON ENERGY ELASTICITIES**
Department of Energy/HMSO

English 1977 £2.00

Analysis of available statistical material relevant to assessing the response of energy consumption to price. Published as Energy Paper No 17.

**501 ROAD VEHICLE ENGINE DESIGN**
Department of Energy/HMSO

English 1977 38pp £1.75

Report by the Advisory Council on Energy Conservation. Considers alterations to fuel specifications, improvements to transmission and gearbox efficiency and questions of design. Published as Energy Paper No 18.

**502   THE ROLE OF LNG IN AN INTEGRATED GAS SUPPLY SYSTEM**
International Gas Union

English 1979 18pp

Deals with the planning and operation of LNG plants within the overall supply system of British Gas Corporation.

**503   SCOTTISH ABSTRACT OF STATISTICS**
Scottish Office/HMSO

English annual c132pp £6.25

General compendium of statistics relating to Scotland. Includes data on oil refining in Scotland, throughput of indigenous crude oil and details of onshore employment and industrial and service activity related to offshore oil and gas development.

**504   SCOTTISH ECONOMIC BULLETIN**
Scottish Economic Planning Dept/HMSO

English 3 issues p.a. 40pp £1.75 per issue

Articles on economic development in Scotland, including the results of studies and surveys of industrial activity and employment associated with offshore oil and gas development. Large statistical section includes data on oil and gas production, consumption and tanker shipments.

**505   SHELL UK—ANNUAL REPORT**
Shell UK Ltd

English annual c50pp

Contains a general review of the United Kingdom oil industry and supply situation and detailed information about activities in exploration, production, refining, distribution and research and development.

**506   SOLAR ENERGY: ITS POTENTIAL CONTRIBUTION WITHIN THE UNITED KINGDOM**
Department of Energy/HMSO

English 1976 £3.00

Review of the state of solar energy technology and the scope for utilising this resource in the United Kingdom. Published as Energy Paper No 16.

**507   SOUTH OF SCOTLAND ELECTRICITY BOARD— ANNUAL REPORT**
South of Scotland Electricity Board

English annual c62pp

Contains a review of electricity supply and consumption in the south and central part of Scotland. Statistical section includes: technical details of power stations; data on fuels and costs; customers; sales; distribution system.

**508   A STATISTICAL SURVEY OF INDUSTRIAL FUEL AND ENERGY USE**
Confederation of British Industry

English 1975 36pp £2.00

Results of a special survey carried out by the Confederation of British Industry for the Department of Energy into the use of fuel in individual industries. Results analysed according to size of establishment, purpose and type of fuel. Also notes decisions on changes in fuel used.

**509   STATISTICAL TABLES**
National Coal Board

English annual 12pp

Long-run series for: output, imports, exports, consumption and stock levels; manpower and productivity. Details of output, employment and earnings in the Board's 12 divisions.

**510   STRATEGIC PLANNING IN THE GAS INDUSTRY**
Institution of Gas Engineers

English 1976 24pp £1.25

Statement of the general planning objectives of British Gas Corporation and the planning system, including the role of the Area Boards. Includes an indicated energy supply pattern for the period up to the year 2000.

**511   STRATHCLYDE OIL REGISTER**
Strathclyde Regional Council

English annual

Directory, produced by the Council's Industrial Development Unit, of companies in west central Scotland providing products and services relevant to oil and gas development. Classified according to product/service.

**512   A STUDY OF GAS GATHERING PIPELINE SYSTEMS IN THE NORTH SEA**
Department of Energy

English 1976 £10.00

Study commissioned from engineering consultants Williams-Merz by the Department of Energy into the feasibility of pipeline systems to utilise associated gas and facilitate the development of marginal oil and gas fields in the North Sea.

**513 STUDY OF POTENTIAL BENEFITS TO BRITISH INDUSTRY FROM OFFSHORE OIL AND GAS DEVELOPMENTS**
Department of Trade and Industry/HMSO

English 1972 136pp £5.00

Report by the International Management and Engineering Group to the Department of Trade on the detailed requirements for products and services to be expected in exploiting offshore oil and gas resources. Includes a review of company policies and practices in offshore development projects.

**514 TEXACO IN THE UNITED KINGDOM**
Texaco Ltd

English 20pp free

Brochure containing basic information on the activities of Texaco. Includes data on exploration, refining, transportation and inland distribution system.

**515 THISTLE**
DEMINEX

English 1980 14pp

Information booklet on the Thistle field in the United Kingdom North Sea sector in which DEMINEX is a major participant. Background to development of the field and details of field potential, production facilities and participants.

**516 THE THISTLE FIELD**
The British National Oil Corporation

English 1979 16pp free

Contains background to the development of the Thistle field, of which BNOC is the operator; data on the field and its production facilities.

**517 TIDAL POWER BARRAGES IN THE SEVERN ESTUARY**
Department of Energy/HMSO

English 1977 £1.50

Review of proposals for building a barrage across the Severn Estuary as a new source of electricity. Published as Energy Paper No 23.

**518 TOWARDS AN ENERGY POLICY FOR TRANSPORT**
The Watt Committee on Energy Ltd

English 1980 94pp £20.50

Treats energy issues for all modes of transport. Papers cover: fuel type and future availability; road vehicles of the future; energy conservation in the railways; energy saving in ships; air transport energy requirements to 2025; telecommunications; transport and the consumer.

**519 TRADE AND INDUSTRY**
Department of Trade/HMSO

English weekly c75pp £0.40 per issue

Weekly journal containing reports and special articles on matters affecting industry and commerce. Includes news of government measures in licencing, taxation and finance in the energy sector.

**520 TRANSPORT STATISTICS**
HMSO

English annual 200pp

General transport statistics for the last ten years, giving movements of broad commodity groups by mode of transport. Includes pipeline movements, consumption of energy by each transport sector and price data on fuels used in transportation.

**521 UK NORTH SEA OIL AND GAS TERMINALS**
The Institute of Petroleum

English 1978 3pp free

Listing of oil and gas terminals, with details of operator, fields served, capacity and facilities. Issued by the Institute as an 'Oil Data Sheet.'

**522 UK OIL AND GAS: INSPECTION, MAINTENANCE AND REPAIR OPPORTUNITIES**
Scottish Council

English 1978 35pp £2.25

Summary of North Sea oil and gas developments and assessment of the consequential business in inspection, maintenance and repair activities.

**523 UK TRANSPORT STATISTICS**
The Institute of Petroleum

English 1978 2pp free

Statistics of movement of petroleum products by rail, road, coastal shipping, inland waterways and pipelines, giving quantity and average journey. Also gives consumption of oil products by transport industries.

**524 UNITED KINGDOM ATOMIC ENERGY AUTHORITY—ANNUAL REPORT**
HMSO

English annual 80pp £2.00

Contains information about: activities in atomic energy establishments in the United Kingdom; details of nuclear projects, and their purpose and commercial applications; general review of developments in nuclear power.

**525 UNITED KINGDOM MINERAL STATISTICS**
Institute of Geological Sciences/HMSO

English annual

Includes basic statistics for output of natural gas and petroleum from individual fields, supply and consumption of natural gas and production of coal.

**526  UNITED KINGDOM OIL SHALES: PAST AND POSSIBLE FUTURE EXPLOITATION**
Department of Energy/HMSO

English  1975  20pp  £1.15

Review of oil shale technology and assessment of the likelihood of resuming shale oil exploitation in the United Kingdom. Published as Energy Paper No 1.

**527  THE UNITED KINGDOM REFINING INDUSTRY**
The Institute of Petroleum

English  1978  14pp  free

Summary of the historical development of the United Kingdom oil refining industry. Long-run data on refinery capacity. Notes on individual refineries.

**528  WHAT'S WHAT IN ENERGY CONSERVATION**
RIBA Publications Ltd

English  1978  28pp

Directory of organisations involved in energy conservation, including: government departments, other official bodies, professional associations, independent interest groups.

**529  WORKING DOCUMENT ON ENERGY POLICY**
Department of Energy

English  1977  90pp

Compilation of background material for the Energy Commission, containing: review of the international energy situation; energy supply and demand in the United Kingdom; outline of the energy industries; research and development activity; analysis of consumption; illustrative forecast of consumption up to the year 2000. Published as Energy Commission Paper No 1.

# Republic of Ireland

**550  ELECTRICITY SUPPLY BOARD—ANNUAL REPORT**
Electricity Supply Board

English  annual  48pp

Contains a general review of the Irish energy situation and detailed information and statistics on electricity generation, transmission and sales. Details of plant, new projects, the transmission network, generation costs, customers and consumption by sector.

**551  ENERGY—IRELAND**
Stationery Office

English  1978  90pp  IR£0.90

Discussion document on energy issues and policy options, prepared by the then Department of Industry, Commerce and Energy. Reviews the situation in Irish energy supply and the international context. Discusses past and possible future development of all forms of energy.

**552  FIFTY YEARS OF POWER FOR PROGRESS**
Electricity Supply Board

English  1979  10pp  free

Brochure giving an outline of the development of the Electricity Supply Board and expansion of electricity consumption in the Republic of Ireland since 1927. Notes on the major projects undertaken and statistics of sales and numbers of customers.

**553  FOLDER OF IRISH ECONOMIC STATISTICS**
Central Bank of Ireland

English  annual  180pp

Contains long-run monthly or quarterly series for electricity output and consumption of electricity by industry.

**554  IRISH GAS BOARD—ANNUAL REPORT**
Irish Gas Board

English  annual

Report by the Board on the state of development of supply and distribution of natural gas and details of the Board's activity.

**555  IRISH OFFSHORE AND MINING DIRECTORY**
Offshore Intelligence Ltd

English  1979  288pp  IR£9.00

Handbook of organisations, agencies and companies involved in mining and offshore development. Contains background information on mining, exploration licences and port facilities.

**556  IRISH OFFSHORE REVIEW**
Offshore Intelligence Ltd

English  quarterly  22pp

Journal of news and articles relevant to Irish offshore development: notes on licence holders; operations of oil and gas companies; technology; government policies and measures.

557  IRISH STATISTICAL BULLETIN
Central Statistics Office

English quarterly c80pp IR£0.75 per issue

Results of census of production and other surveys of industries, including mining and oil refining. Statistical series for generation and distribution of electricity on a monthly basis.

558  REPORT ON POLLUTION CONTROL
Stationery Office

English 1978 81pp IR£1.20

Comprehensive review of environmental pollution controls, the existing provisions and programmes and responsibilities for monitoring and enforcement. Includes information about limitations on fuel emissions and product qualities.

559  THE ROLE OF THE ELECTRICITY SUPPLY BOARD
Electricity Supply Board

English 1973 46pp

Historical and general background to the development of the Electricity Supply Board. Sections deal with: tariff policy; rural electrification; the turf programme; major development projects; commercial, manpower and financial policies.

560  STATISTICAL ABSTRACT OF IRELAND
Central Statistics Office

English annual c400pp

Annual abstract of statistics. Includes information on the supply and consumption of energy and trade flows of energy products.

561  SUPPLIERS TO THE OFFSHORE INDUSTRY
Institute for Industrial Research and Standards

English 1975 140pp

Directory of Irish firms engaged in the provision of goods and services for offshore oil and gas development. Classified section lists companies by product/service. Directory section lists companies, with basic information on goods/services provided.

562  THOM'S COMMERCIAL DIRECTORY
Thom's Directories Ltd

English annual c920pp

Contains listings of organisations and companies supplying fuel products and related goods and services. Companies classified by product and service. Directory section gives basic company information.

563  TRADE STATISTICS OF IRELAND
Central Statistics Office

English monthly

Includes figures for imports and exports of energy, analysed by country of origin and destination according to the standard commodities classification. Figures given for the month and cumulatively for the year.

# Scandinavia

## Denmark

### 600 BENZIN & OLIE BLADET
Central Foreningen af Benzinforhandlere

Danish 11 issues p.a. $10.00 p.a.

Bulletin of the trade association of motor fuel dealers, containing information about the gasoline market and supply situation in Denmark.

### 601 DANMARKS SKIBE OG SKIBSFART
Danmarks Statistik

Danish (English notes) annual 120pp Kr14.75

Statistics of Danish shipping and movements through Danish ports. Includes data on liquid and solid fuels at individual ports. Published in the general statistical series 'Statistiske Meddelelser.'

### 602 DANMARKS VAREINDFØRSEL OG -UDFØRSEL
Danmarks Statistik

Danish (English notes) annual 3 vols

Foreign trade statistics. Vol 1: value of imports/exports under SITC classification by country or commodity; transit trade; commodities in volume and value. Vol 2: value of imports/exports under CCCN classification; analysis of commodities by volume and value. Vol 3: imports/exports by commodity and by country of origin/destination.

### 603 DANSK ELFORSYNING
Danske Elvaerkers Forening

Danish (English headings and summary) annual 40pp

Annual statistics of the Danish Electricity Supply Association. Review of developments and projects in electricity supply; statistics of production, consumption, investment; prices; plant. Details of individual power stations and supply networks.

### 604 DANSK ESSO—ÅRSBERETNING
Dansk Esso A/S

Danish annual 24pp

Annual report of one of Denmark's leading refining and marketing companies. Contains commentary on developments in the oil sector during the previous year as well as data on Dansk Esso operations.

### 605 DANSK OLIE & NATURGAS—ANNUAL REPORT
Dansk Olie & Naturgas A/S

English annual

Report of the state-owned oil and gas company. Includes a general review of the energy situation and information about the projected development of a natural gas system in Denmark.

### 606 DENMARK'S 2000 LARGEST COMPANIES
Teknisk Forlag A/S

English/Danish annual c190pp

Includes the principal producers and distributors of coal, oil, gas and electricity. Data cover turnover, output, employment, assets and profits.

### 607 ELKRAFT—ANNUAL REPORT
Elkraft

English/Danish annual

Report of the activities of Elkraft, the co-ordinating body for electricity supply east of the Great Belt. Includes statistics of electricity generation, distribution, sales, plant and exchanges with Sweden.

### 608 ELSAM—ANNUAL REPORT
Elsam

English annual 40pp

English version of the annual report of the co-ordinating group for electricity supply in Jutland and Funen. Review of activities in the industry: projects, investment, relations with neighbouring grids. Statistics on capacity, production, consumption, fuels used, power exchanges, district heating.

**609  ENERGY AUDITING**
Dansk Kedelforening

English 1979 16pp

Paper presented at the International Energy Management Conference in 1979 dealing with energy auditing in the context of subsidy schemes for energy-saving investment. Contains a survey of energy consumption in Denmark and details of Danish energy-saving schemes.

**610  GAS TEKNIK**
Dansk Gasteknisk Forening

Danish bi-monthly 20pp Kr60.00 p.a.

Contains articles on the gas supply industry in Denmark and news of developments in Denmark and the North Sea in general.

**611  GREENS—HANDBOGEN OM DANSK ERHVERSLIV**
Forlaget Børsen A/S

Danish annual 2 vols

Directory of Danish enterprises including producers and distributors of gas, electricity and oil products. Information covers company, financial and operational aspects, with balance sheet data for several years.

**612  INDUSTRISTATISTIK**
Danmarks Statistik

Danish (English notes) annual Kr20.95

Statistics on industrial production, employment, establishments investment profit and loss accounts; indices of output volume and value. Includes sections dealing with energy production and supply.

**613  KOMPASS DANMARK**
A/S Forlaget Kompas-Danmark

Multi-language annual 2 vols

Directory of Danish firms and their principal fields of activity. Includes a number of concerns engaged in the supply of energy and related goods and services. Vol 1 gives information on goods and services. Vol 2 gives basic company information.

**614  KORT NYT**
Danatom

Danish bi-monthly c10pp

Bulletin of the nuclear energy group of the Academy of Technical Sciences. News of developments and policies affecting nuclear power. A number of special supplements on key issues are published during the year.

**615  KVARTALSSTATISTIK FOR INDUSTRIEN: VARESTATISTIK**
Danmarks Statistik

Danish quarterly 140pp Kr27.95 per issue

Contains figures for sales, by volume and by value, for individual industry and major product groupings, including energy products. Figures for the latest quarter and cumulatively for the year.

**616  KVARTALSSTATISTIK OVER UDENRIGSHANDELEN**
Danmarks Statistik

Danish quarterly Kr142.65 p.a.

Foreign trade statistics according to the CCCN classification. Imports and exports listed by country of origin. Cumulative figures for the year.

**617  MÅNEDSSTATISTIK OVER UDENRIGSHANDELEN**
Danmarks Statistik

Danish (English notes) monthly Kr152.85 p.a.

Monthly bulletin of foreign trade with cumulative figures, arranged by CCCN and SITC headings. Imports and exports by country of origin.

**618  NORDEL—ANNUAL REPORT**
Nordel

Danish (English summary) annual 56pp free

Annual review of electricity production, distribution and consumption in Denmark and other Scandinavian countries. Review of the energy and electricity sectors, with statistics on: electricity output by type of plant; capacity of plant; international exchanges; distribution networks; patterns of consumption and future outlook. Deals with developments in distribution and production programmes and relations between the Nordic countries.

**619  NORTH SEA PROGRESS**
Shell International Petroleum Co Ltd

English 1979 10pp free

Includes notes on the current situation in oil and gas development in the Danish sector of the North Sea, possible future projects and map of North Sea fields. Published in the series 'Shell Briefing Service.'

**620 STATISTISK ÅRBOG**
Danmarks Statistik

Danish annual c600pp Kr50.95

Statistical yearbook, including data on output of oil products; production and consumption of gas and electricity; employment in energy industries; retail and wholesale fuel price indices.

# Finland

**625 BENSIINI UUTISET**
Suomen Bensiinikauppiaitten Liitto Ry

Finnish monthly free

Monthly bulletin of the Finnish association of motor fuel dealers, containing news and articles relating to distribution and marketing and current figures on prices and sales.

**626 DISTRICT HEATING IN HELSINKI**
Helsingin Kaupungin Energialaitos

English 1979 20pp

Booklet describing the development of district heating in Helsinki since 1952, giving information about the generation plant and distribution system, equipment, costs and charges.

**627 ENNAKKOTIETOJA SUOMEN TEOLLISUUDESTA VUONNA 19—**
Tilastokeskus

Finnish/Swedish (English headings) annual c100pp

Preliminary results of the annual survey of industry. Statistics on: employment; output; wages; value of output; value added; costs of materials. Data given for individual industries, including the energy sector, and analysed by province.

**628 FINLAND'S TWO THOUSAND LARGEST COMPANIES**
AB Yritystieto Oy

English/Finnish/Swedish annual c140pp

Includes the principal producers and distributors of coal, oil, gas and electricity. Data cover turnover, output, employment, assets and profits.

**629 FINNISH PETROLEUM FEDERATION—ANNUAL REPORT**
Finnish Petroleum Federation

English annual c20pp

Review of the general oil market situation, government energy policies, prices and taxation of oil products.

**630 HELSINGIN KAUPUNGIN ENERGIALAITOS—ANNUAL REPORT**
Helsingin Kaupungin Energialaitos

Finnish (Swedish/English headings) annual 44pp

Annual report of the energy supply authority for the Helsinki area covering: arrangements for supplies of electricity, gas and district heating; development of the distribution system; details of plant; statistics on consumption, sales, customers and power sources.

**631 IMATRAN VOIMA OY—ANNUAL REPORT**
Imatran Voima Oy

English annual 36pp

English version of the annual report of the state-owned power company. Report on activities and developments, prices, research and development and environmental protection. Includes statistics of plant capacity, production and consumption; map of the national grid and Imatran Voima's distribution network. Notes on other provincial power undertakings in which Imatran Voima participates.

**632 KAUKOLÄMPÖTILASTO**
Lämpölaitosyhdistys Ry

Finnish (English summary) 1978 16pp

Statistical survey of district heating in Finland with details of individual schemes and plant. Figures cover a number of years showing the development of district heating.

**633 NESTE OY—ANNUAL REPORT**
Neste Oy

Finnish/Swedish/English annual c50pp

Report on the a ivities of the state oil and gas company. Reviews the general energy situation and supply and demand in the Finnish market. Detailed statistics on refining, supply and consumption of oil products.

**634 NORDEL—ANNUAL REPORT**
Nordel

Danish (English summary) annual 56pp free

Annual review of electricity production, distribution and consumption in Finland and other Scandinavian countries. Review of energy and electricity sectors, with statistics on: electricity output by type of plant; capacity of plant; international exchanges; distribution network; patterns of consumption and future outlook. Deals with developments in distribution and production programmes and relations between Nordic countries.

**635 SÄHKÖ—ELECTRICITY IN FINLAND**
Suomen Sähkölaitosyhdistys Ry

Finnish/English

Regular bulletin of the electricity producers' association, containing news of economic, technical and political developments and recent statistical information.

**636 OY SHELL AB—ANNUAL REPORT**
Oy Shell AB

Finnish annual 16pp

Annual report of the Finnish affilliate of the Royal Dutch/Shell group. Includes a review of the market for oil products and indicative data on prices and trends.

**637 STATE-OWNED COMPANIES IN FINLAND**
Valtion Yhtiöiden Toimisto

English annual 80pp

English edition of the annual review of operations and financial situation of state-owned enterprises, including the energy companies Neste, Imatran Voima and Kemijoki. Data cover: turnover, investment, capital structure, financial performance, directors, employees, subsidiary companies and activities.

**638 STYV—TOIMINTAKERTOMUS**
Sähköntuottajien Yhteistyövaltuuskunta

Finnish (English summary) annual 32pp

Annual report of the co-ordinating organisation for Finnish power producers, dealing with production, transmission and consumption, plant and investment programmes.

**639 SUOMEN SÄHKÖLAITOSYHDISTYS—
TOIMINTAKERTOMUS**
Suomen Sähkölaitosyhdistys Ry

Finnish/Swedish (English summary) annual 24pp

Annual report of the Finnish Association of Electricity Supply Undertakings. Contains a review of electricity consumption, pattern of electricity production and information about new developments.

**640 SUOMEN SÄHKÖLAITOSYHDISTYS 50 VUOTTA**
Suomen Sähkölaitosyhdistys Ry

Finnish (English/Swedish summaries) 1976 28pp

General review of the historical development, present day organisations and statistical data on the electricity supply industry in Finland.

**641 SUOMEN TILASTOLLINEN VUOSIKIRJA**
Tilastokeskus

Finnish/Swedish (English headings) annual c500pp

Statistical yearbook for Finland. Includes sections dealing with: the generation of electricity and consumption, analysed by industry; output in energy industries; employment; indices of consumer and industry prices for energy.

**642 TEOLLISUUSTILASTO**
Tilastokeskus

Finnish/Swedish (English headings) annual 3 vols

Detailed results of the annual census of industry. Vol 1 gives output, sales, employment, value added, capital investment and energy consumption by industry, with some analysis by region. Vol 2 gives details of consumption of raw materials. Vol 3 includes details of fuel consumption.

**643 TILASTOKATSAUKSIA**
Tilastokeskus

Finnish/Swedish/English monthly 60pp

Monthly bulletin of statistics, including series for production/output of oil, gas and electricity supply industries, and basic foreign trade figures.

**644 ULKOMAANKAUPPA KUUKAUSIJULKAISU**
Tullihallitus

Finnish/Swedish (English headings) monthly

Foreign trade monthly bulletin showing exports and imports by CCCN and SITC commodity classifications, identifying energy products. Figures for month and cumulative for the year. English section gives imports/exports by SITC heading.

**645 ULKOMAANKAUPPA VUOSIJULKAISU**
Tullihallitus

Finnish/Swedish (English headings) annual 2 vols

Foreign trade. Vol 1: detailed tables of imports and exports, including fuels, classified by CCCN tariff headings, subdivided by countries of origin and destination. Vol 2: annual report of the Customs Department with tables showing breakdown of imports and exports by SITC heading; English section giving trade by country under SITC headings.

**646 YDINENERGIA JA ENERGIAHUOLTO**
Suomen Atomiteknillinen Seura

Finnish/Swedish 1979 34pp

Nuclear power and energy supply, published by the Finnish Nuclear Society. Reviews the potential of nuclear power and alternative energy sources, with particular reference to Finland's energy supply and demand situation.

# Norway

**650 DnC OIL NOW**
Den norske Creditbank

English c26pp

Series of publications by the Petroleum Department
of Den norske Creditbank, analysing specific aspects
of oil and gas development affecting Norway, particularly in the fields of finance and taxation.

**651 THE ECONOMICS AND POLITICS OF NORTH SEA
OIL**
Croom Helm Ltd

English 1979 224pp £9.95

Comparative study of the impact of North Sea oil
in Norway and the United Kingdom. Particular
attention is paid to government policy on taxation,
state participation and depletion.

**652 EKOFISK, ENERGY FROM THE NORTH SEA**
Phillips Petroleum Co

English 1979 20pp

Information booklet on the Ekofisk field dealing
with the historical exploration and development
programme, the facilities of the complex and technical data concerning production.

**653 ELEKTRISITETSSTATISTIKK**
Statistisk Sentralbyrå

Norwegian/English annual 96pp Kr11.00

Annual review of the electricity industry in Norway.
Details of plant and equipment; production and consumption, by region; prices, revenues and taxes.

**654 ENERGISTATISTIKK**
Statistisk Sentralbyrå

Norwegian/English annual 84pp Kr13.00

Annual compendium of energy statistics: energy
balances; production trade and consumption of
energy products; average prices, enterprises, plant
and equipment.

**655 ESSO I NORGE**
A/S Norske Esso

Norwegian annual 22pp

Annual report of the Norwegian affiliate of Exxon
and one of the principal refining/marketing companies
in Norway. Contains a review of the general oil
supply and market situation, pattern of oil consumption and price information.

**656 THE FLOW OF NORTH SEA ENERGY WEALTH**
The Financial Times Ltd

English 1979 £75.00

Economic and financial analysis by C Johnson of
oil and gas exploitation and the impact which this
has on the general economy in terms of the flow of
funds and national accounts. Reviews policy options
for applying the benefits within the economy.

**657 FRIGG—GAS FROM THE NORTH SEA**
British Gas Corporation

English 1977 64pp

Information brochure giving basic data about the
Frigg gas field. Contains a history of development of
the field and main operational characteristics.

**658 INDUSTRISTATISTIKK**
Statistisk Sentralbyrå

Norwegian (English headings) annual 198pp
Kr15.00

Annual statistical survey of Norwegian industry.
Includes production/output series for coal mining,
oil refining and gas production, and data on other oil-
related industries.

**659 KOMPASS NORGE**
Kompass-Norge A/S

Multi-language annual 2 vols

Directory of Norwegian firms and their principal
fields of activity. Includes firms engaged in the
supply of energy and related goods and services.
Vol 1 gives information on goods and services. Vol 2
gives basic company information.

**660 LAW AND OFFSHORE DEVELOPMENT: THE
NORTH SEA EXPERIENCE**
Holt-Saunders Ltd

English 1979 150pp £12.00

Examines the evolution of law relevant to North Sea
exploration and development, and the legislation and
regulations of Norway and the United Kingdom.
Deals with: licensing, taxation, safety, land planning
and environmental protection.

**661 LYSSTIKKA**
Oslo Lysverker

Norwegian (English summary)

Bulletin of the Oslo Lysverker, which includes a
special issue of its annual report. Contains details of
the supply of electricity and district heat to the Oslo
area and information on new developments, investment and energy supply costs.

**662 NORDEL—ANNUAL REPORT**
Nordel

Danish (English summary) annual 56pp free

Annual review of electricity production, distribution and consumption in Norway and other Scandinavian countries. Review of energy and electricity sectors, with statistics on: electricity output by type of plant; capacity of plant; international exchanges; distribution network; patterns of consumption and future outlook. Covers developments in distribution and production programmes and relations between the Nordic countries.

**663 NOROIL**
Noroil Publishing House

English monthly 90pp Kr162.00 p.a.

Journal of news, articles and statistics concerning the oil and gas industries, covering technological, economic, political, financial and operational aspects. Particularly concerned with Norwegian offshore matters.

**664 NORSK HYDRO A/S—ANNUAL REPORT**
Norsk Hydro A/S

English annual c40pp

Annual report of Norway's largest company and major energy producer and consumer. Review of each area of interest, including petroleum, petrochemicals, nitrogenous fertiliser and electric power.

**665 THE NORTH SEA IN PERSPECTIVE**
Wood Mackenzie & Co

English 1979 83pp

Review of North Sea oil and gas projects, with an analysis of development costs. Considers the political context and legislative framework for development. Includes statistics on exploration and production.

**666 NORTH SEA OIL IN THE FUTURE: ECONOMIC ANALYSIS AND GOVERNMENT POLICY**
Trade Policy Research Centre

English 1978 233pp £10.00

Detailed analysis by C Robinson and J Morgan of the economics of North Sea oil. Contains a critical analysis of the depletion and taxation policies of the Norwegian and United Kingdom governments. Discusses North Sea oil in an international context.

**667 NORTH SEA PROGRESS**
Shell International Petroleum Co Ltd

English 1979 10pp free

Review of project developments and financial and taxation issues affecting the Norwegian sector of the North Sea. Includes a map of North Sea oil and gas fields. Published in the series 'Shell Briefing Service.'

**668 OLJEDIREKTORATET—ÅRSBERETNING**
Oljedirektoratet

Norwegian annual 110pp

Official annual report of activities under the responsibility of the Oljedirektoratet. Includes details of exploration and production and the state of development of individual fields. Information on government programmes and policies; official initiatives and legislation; basic statistics. Brief summary in English.

**669 OLJEVIRKSOMHETEN**
Statistisk Sentralbyrå

Norwegian/English annual 60pp Kr11.00

Survey and commentary on developments in the oil industry. Statistics on exploration activity; investment; production and sales of crude oil and natural gas; employment and earnings; financial aspects; taxes; oil and the national accounts.

**670 OSLO LYSVERKER**
Oslo Lysverker

English/Norwegian 1977 50pp

Information book about the Oslo municipal energy authority, describing its historical background, the development of plant to supply the capital region and technical and economic data on production, transmission, distribution and sales.

**671 SAMKJØRINGEN—ANNUAL REPORT**
Elforsyningens Informasjonstjeneste

Norwegian (English summary) annual c60pp

Annual report by the organisation of the Norwegian power pool, containing a review of electricity supply and consumption in Norway and detailed statistics of the operations of individual plants and undertakings and consumption by sector.

**672 STATISTISK ÅRBOK**
Statistisk Sentralbyrå

Norwegian/English annual c500pp Kr20.00

Statistical yearbook including details of production, supply and consumption of energy.

**673 STATISTISK MÅNEDSHEFTE**
Statistisk Sentralbyrå

Norwegian (English headings) monthly c110pp

Monthly bulletin of statistics, including production series for the oil, gas and electricity supply industries.

**674  STATOIL**
Den Norske Stats Oljeselskap A/S

English 3 issues p.a. 20pp

Periodical journal of information about the activities of the Norwegian state oil company and matters of interest to the Norwegian oil supply situation. Provides background information on exploration, construction, refining and marketing activities.

**675  STATOIL—ANNUAL REPORT**
Den Norske Stats Oljeselskap A/S

English annual 40pp

English version of the annual report of the state oil company. Includes a survey of all aspects of oil and gas activity in Norway and information about the development of government policy.

**676  THE THOUSAND LARGEST COMPANIES IN NORWAY**
A/S Økonomisk Literatur

English/Norwegian 1979 348pp

Includes the principal producers and distributors of coal, oil, gas and electricity. Data cover turnover, output, employment, assets and profits.

**677  UTENRIKSHANDEL**
Statistisk Sentralbyrå

Norwegian (English headings) annual 2 vols

Foreign trade statistics. Vol 1: imports/exports by commodity, identifying main fuel products, analysed by country of origin/destination. Vol 2: imports/ exports by country of origin/destination analysed by commodities.

# Sweden

**700  AB NYNÄS PETROLEUM—ANNUAL REPORT**
AB Nynäs Petroleum

English annual 24pp

English version of the annual report. Includes a detailed review of the Swedish market for oil products and notes of price and other developments. Details of operations of the company's Swedish refineries and distribution outlets.

**701  ALLMÄN MÅNADSSTATISTIK**
Statistiska Centralbyrån

Swedish/English monthly

Includes basic series of statistics on energy production and consumption, imports and exports.

**702  BERGSHANTERING**
Statistiska Centralbyrån

Swedish (English headings) annual 106pp

Annual survey of mining and metal industries in Sweden. Substantial statistical sections containing data on: output of coal, peat and works gas; fuels used in the sector; consumption of fuels and electricity in mining and basic metal production.

**703  ELECTRICAL ENERGY PRODUCTION AND TECHNICAL EQUIPMENT IN POWER STATIONS**
Statistiska Centralbyrån

English/Swedish annual 8pp

Annual data for electricity supply, including: fuels used to generate electricity; oil equivalent of fuels; costs of electricity generated; supply by type of plant and for each province; import/export trade. Published in series Iv of 'Statistiska Meddelanden.'

**704  ELECTRICAL ENERGY SUPPLY AND DISTRICT HEATING**
Statistiska Centralbyrån

Swedish (English contents) annual 52pp

Annual survey of district heating covering: types of organisation; equipment; steam and hot water supply; fuels used; total sales; electrical space heating; energy consumption in dwellings. Figures cover several years with analysis by province and scale of scheme. Published in series Iv of 'Statistiska Meddelanden.'

**705  ENERGI HÄLSO- MILJÖ- OCH SÄKERHETSRISKER**
LiberFörlag

Swedish 1978

Final report of the Energy Commission examining the health, environmental and security issues arising from energy production and consumption.

**706  ENERGI, STRUKTUROMVANDLING OCH SYSSELSÄTTNING**
Delegationen för Energiforskning

Swedish 1978

Report of working groups under the Energy R & D Commission examining energy systems and structural issues in the energy economy. DFE report No 9.

707 ENERGIFORSKNINGSPROGRAMMET 1975-78
Delegationen för Energiforskning

Swedish 1979 6 vols

Reports on the energy research and development programme of the three-year period 1975-78, published as DFE reports Nos 14-19. Individual volumes are: No 14 report of activities; No 15 project results; No 16 evaluation; No 17 assessment of the programme on use of energy in industrial processes; No 18 assessment of the project on wind energy; No 19 assessment of the study of total energy systems.

708 ENERGIFÖRSÖRJNINGSALTERNATIV FÖR
SVERIGE ÅR 2000
Delegationen for Energiforskning

Swedish 1978 2 vols

Report by the Energy R & D Commission on alternative energy supply sources potentially available to the Swedish economy by the year 2000, and aspects meriting research and development work. Vol 1 Main report. Vol 2 Annexes.

709 ENERGY AND ECONOMIC GROWTH IN SWEDEN
Statens Industriverk

English 1976 320pp

Detailed analysis of historical trends in economic development and energy consumption and assessment of the current situation with the implications of decisions on energy issues.

710 ENERGY AND ENERGY POLICY IN SWEDEN
The Swedish Institute

English 1980 2pp free

Summary of Sweden's energy balance in 1978 and forecast for 1990, production of electricity and other sources of energy, and outline of government policy. Published as one of the Institute's 'Fact Sheets on Sweden.'

711 ENERGY RESEARCH AND DEVELOPMENT IN
SWEDEN
Delegationen för Energiforskning

English 1978 40pp

Survey by the Energy R & D Commission on the background to, and details of, the government's research and development programme for the period 1978-81. DFE report No 13.

712 ENVIRONMENT PROTECTION IN SWEDEN
Statens Naturvårdsverk

English 40pp

Publication of the National Swedish Environment Protection Board. Details of legislation, administrative organisation, grants and research work in the field of environment protection in Sweden.

713 ERA
Svenska Elverksföreningen

Swedish 11 issues p.a.

Periodical of the Swedish Association of Electricity Supply Undertakings dealing with technical news and development information about plant, equipment and installations.

714 FORSKNING OCH UTVECKLING PÅ
ENERGIOMRÅDET 1978-81
Delegationen för Energiforskning

Swedish 1978 64pp

Details of the national energy research and development programme, dealing with energy production and consumption in all main sectors. DFE report No 10.

715 FORSKNING UTVECKLING OCH
DEMONSTRATION INOM ENERGIOMRÅDET
Delegationen för Energiforskning

Swedish 1978

General review of research development and demonstration projects in Sweden and abroad. DFE report No 12.

716 FUELS: DELIVERIES AND CONSUMPTION OF
FUELS AND LUBRICANTS
Statistiska Centralbyrån

English/Swedish quarterly 20pp

Statistics, quarterly and cumulatively for the year, of deliveries of fuels to the domestic market, analysed by sector and for individual industries. Import and export figures for individual oil products. Published in series Iv of 'Statistiska Meddelanden.'

717 GASNYTT
Svenska Gasföreningen

Swedish 3 issues p.a. 20pp Kr25.00 p.a.

Bulletin of the Swedish Gas Association reporting on developments in the gas industry in Sweden.

718 INDUSTRI: DEL 1
Statistiska Centralbyrån

Swedish (English headings) annual c360pp

Annual statistics for mining, quarrying and manufacturing industry, including electricity and gas supply. Data on: number of establishments; employment; output; costs of production; raw materials consumption.

719  INDUSTRI: DEL 2
Statistiska Centralbyrån

Swedish (English headings) annual c260pp

Results of the annual census of industry analysed by
commodity under the CCCN tariff nomenclature
identifying energy industries. Contains information
on value and volume of sales.

720  INDUSTRISTATISTIK: STRUKTURSTATISTIK
FÖR INDUSTRIN
Statistiska Centralbyrån

Swedish (English contents) annual c125pp

Statistics by economic activity, including oil, electricity and gas industries, with comparison against
previous year, covering: establishments and employment; size-structure; sales and employment by size
of establishment by industry; production per head
and per hour worked.

721  KOL I SVERIGE
Nämden för Energiproduktionsforskning

Swedish 1978 2 vols

Study of the scope for using coal on a significant
scale in Sweden. The main report, dealing with the
possibility of bulk coal imports and the issues involved in its use, was published as Vol 2. Vol 1
contains general background information on production, trade, transportation, handling, combustion
and conversion of coal and the related environmental
aspects.

722  KOMPASS SVERIGE
Kompass Sverige

Multi-language annual 2 vols

Directory of Swedish firms and their principal fields
of activity. Includes firms engaged in the supply of
energy and related goods and services. Vol 1 gives
information on goods and services. Vol 2 gives basic
company information.

723  KONSUMENTPRISER OCH INDEX-
BERÄKNINGAR
Statistiska Centralbyrån

Swedish (English contents) annual 56pp

Details of prices or price indexes of consumer
products. Data given for gas, electricity and oil for
the last two years and index numbers covering the
last 25 years.

724  KRÅNGEDE AB—VERKSAMHETEN
Krångede AB

Swedish annual 16pp

Annual report on activities by Krångede AB and
related power-producing undertakings, which form
the largest private electricity producing group in
Sweden. Details of electricity production and information about several other power projects in Sweden.

725  LAGER INOM VARUHANDELN
Statistiska Centralbyrån

Swedish (English summary) quarterly 8pp

Quarterly bulletin of value of stocks held at retail
and wholesale level. Includes figures for fuel products.
Published in the series H of 'Statistiska Meddelanden.'

726  NORDEL—ANNUAL REPORT
Nordel

Danish (English summary) annual 56pp free

Annual review of electricity production, distribution
and consumption in Sweden and other Scandinavian
countries. Review of the general energy situation and
electricty supply sector, with statistics on: electricity
output by type of plant; international exchanges;
distribution network; patterns of consumption
and future outlook. Deals with developments in
production and distribution programmes and
relations between Nordic countries.

727  OK—VERKSAMHETEN
Oljekonsumenternas Förbund

Swedish annual c40pp

Report of the oil consumers' co-operative. Includes
information about the Swedish oil market and
related sectors and details of the activities of the oil
consumers' co-operative. A shorter version is published in English.

728  PLANERINGSRAPPORTER
Nämnden för Energiproduktionsforskning

Swedish

Series of background reports by the Council for
Energy Production Research. Subjects dealt with so
far include: peat, wind, geothermal, wave, solar,
ocean energy; coal, temperature gradients in Sweden.

729  PRODUCENT- EXPORT- OCH IMPORTPRISINDEX
Statistiska Centralbyrån

Swedish (English summary) monthly 20pp

Bulletin of producer, export and import prices and
internal sales. Includes price indices for principal
petroleum products. Published in series P of
'Statistiska Meddelanden.'

730 PRODUCTION AND CONSUMPTION OF
ELECTRICAL ENERGY
Statistiska Centralbyrån

English/Swedish monthly 4pp

Bulletin of electricity statistics with commentary.
Data on production by type of plant and consumption by main sectors. Details of consumption in individual industries. Published in series Iv of 'Statistiska Meddelanden.'

731 SKANDINAVISKA ELVERK—ÅRSREDOVISNING
AB Skandinaviska Elverk

Swedish annual 34pp

Annual review and report on activities by one of the leading producers of electric power. Includes details of plant, output and distribution and development of new projects.

732 SOL ELLER URAN—ATT VÄLJA-
ENERGIFRAMTID
LiberFörlag

Swedish 1978-79

Final report of a project, sponsored by the council for future studies, studying the energy issues in Sweden. The main report 'Sun or Uranium' is supported by a number of subsidiary reports dealing with individual aspects of energy supply and consumption, energy and the economy and energy policies.

733 SOLAR SWEDEN
Secretariat for Future Studies

English 1978 109pp

Study of the scope for utilising renewable energy resources in Sweden, outlining a system based on these resources, especially the use of solar energy.

734 STATISTISK ÅRSBOK
Statistiska Centralbyrån

Swedish (English notes) annual c600pp

Statistical yearbook for Sweden. Includes information on many aspects of the energy sector: production, investment and sales of the energy industries; water resources and power by region; energy balances; details of electricity generation and consumption; environmental controls and programmes; consumer fuel price series.

735 STORA KOPPARBERGS BERGSLAGS AB—
ANNUAL REPORT
Stora Kopparberg

English annual c40pp

Annual report of one of Sweden's major mining and power producing companies, including details of power generation and distribution activities.

736 SVENSK INDUSTRI KALENDER
Sveriges Industriförbund

Swedish (English headings) annual c900pp

Directory of Swedish firms, including many involved in production of electricity. Gives information on company status, activities and finance.

737 SVENSKA PETROLEUM INSTITUTET—
ÅRSREDOGÖRELSE
Svenska Petroleum Institutet

Swedish annual 46pp

Annual report by the Swedish Petroleum Institute on its activities, with a detailed review of all main aspects of the oil market and supply in Sweden and statistics on consumption and trade. Analysis by product and by company.

738 SVERIGES ELFÖRSÖRJNING 1975-85
Centrala Driftledningen

Swedish 1975 16pp

Study by the electricity producers' association of electricity supply in Sweden, with information on plant in operation and planned, cost data and discussion of issues.

739 SVERIGES ENERGIANVÄNDNING UNDER
1980- OCH 1990-TALEN
Statens Industriverk

Swedish 1977

Analysis by the National Swedish Industrial Board of energy demand for the years 1985, 1990 and 1995.

740 SVERIGES HANDELSKALENDER
Bonniers Företagsinformation AB

Swedish annual 2 vols

Directory of Swedish firms: Vol 1 information on companies; Vol 2 information on products and services. Includes companies engaged in producing and distributing energy products as well as related industries. Data cover company status, outline of activities, numbers employed and balance sheet information.

741 SVERIGES 1,000 STÖRSTA FÖRETAG
Liberläromedel

Swedish annual c150pp

Includes the principal producers and distributors of coal, oil, gas and electricity. Data cover turnover, output, employment, assets and profits.

**742  THE SWEDISH ASSOCIATION OF ELECTRICITY
SUPPLY UNDERTAKINGS**
Svenska Elverksföreningen

English  1978  16pp

Provides information about the electricity supply
industry in Sweden and the role of Svenska Elverks-
forening. Includes some long-run statistical indicators.

**743  SWEDISH PROGRAMME PROPOSAL FOR
ENERGY RESEARCH, DEVELOPMENT AND
DEMONSTRATION**
Delegationen för Energiforskning

English  1977  10pp  free

Summary in English of the report of the Energy R &
D Commission defining the various programmes for
research and development work.

**744  UTRIKESHANDEL**
Statistiska Centralbyrån

Swedish (English notes)  annual  2 vols

Foreign trade statistics. Vol 1: detailed tables of
imports and exports classified by commodities
according to CCN tariff headings, identifying individual energy products, subdivided by countries of
origin and destination. Vol 2: analysis by countries
of origin and destination, subdivided by SITC tariff
heading, and customs district.

**745  UTRIKESHANDEL KVARTALSSTATISTIK**
Statistiska Centralbyrån

Swedish (English headings)  quarterly  c210pp

Quarterly foreign trade figures, with cumulative
figures for the year, published in two series: Inforsel
(Imports) and Utforsel (Exports). Contains quantity
and value of imports and exports by tariff heading,
identifying fuel imports/exports, listed by country
of origin/destination.

**746  UTRIKESHANDEL MÅNADSSTATISTIK**
Statistiska Centralbyrån

Swedish (English headings)  monthly  c70pp

Basic foreign trade statistics identifying energy
imports and exports under the SITC and CCCN
tariff headings. Figures on a monthly basis and
cumulatively for the year.

**747  UTRIKESHANDELN FÖRDELAD PÅ
TRANSPORT OMRÅDEN OCH EFTER
VARORNAS TRANSPORTSÄTT**
Statistiska Centralbyrån

Swedish (English summary)  annual

Analysis of the latest year's foreign trade movements by mode of transport, main commodity
groupings and country of origin/destination. Published in Series T of 'Statistiska Meddelanden.'

**748  VATTENFALL—ANNUAL REPORT**
Swedish State Power Board

English  annual  36pp  free

English version of the Swedish State Power Board's
annual report. Includes commentary on the Swedish
energy situation and review of the electricity supply
industry in Sweden. Five-year summary of financial
and operations data. Latest pattern of electricity
consumption. Structure of the electricity industry.
Data on the Power Board's plants.

# Continental Europe

## Austria

**800   DER AUSSENHANDEL ÖSTERREICHS SERIE 1A**
Österreichisches Statistisches Zentralamt

German quarterly c280pp S900 p.a.

Quarterly and cumulative figures for imports and exports: volume and value by product, volume and value by country; listing of countries by commodity, identifying main energy products.

**801   DER AUSSENHANDEL ÖSTERREICHS SERIE 1B**
Österreichisches Statistisches Zentralamt

German half-yearly c290pp S340 p.a.

Import and export statistics by volume and value listed by commodity, including energy products according to the Austrian customs classification, and by country of origin/destination.

**802   DER AUSSENHANDEL ÖSTERREICHS SERIE 2**
Österreichisches Statistisches Zentralamt

German half-yearly c130pp S270 p.a.

Analysis of foreign trade statistics including energy products according to the SITC classification; volume and value by country and by tariff heading; percentage breakdown by main countries; indexes for imports and exports.

**803   AUSTRIA OIL AND GAS**
Fachverband der Erdölundustrie Österreichs

English 1979 28pp

Background to the development of oil and gas in Austria. Details of fields and licence areas. Production and refinery throughput figures for the period 1968-78. Volume and pattern of consumption of oil products. General energy consumption pattern.

**804   BETRIEBSSTATISTIK DER ÖSTER-REICHISCHEN ELEKTRIZITÄTSWIRTSCHAFT**
Bundesministerium für Handel Gewerbe und Industrie

German annual 250pp

Detailed statistical information on the supply and consumption of electricity. Sections deal with total supply; public electricity supply; industrial electricity consumption; fuel used in heat stations.

**805   BRENNSTOFFSTATISTIK**
Bundesministerium für Handel Gewerbe und Industrie

German annual 280pp

Detailed fuel statistics. Part A gives relevant data for electricity producers: plant capacity, output and fuels used. Part B shows general energy balance, imports/exports, consumption by product. Figures on a monthly basis and analysed by province. Also contains information about the operations of main energy undertakings.

**806   ENERGIEWIRTSCHAFTLICHER BETRIEBSBERICHT**
Tauernkraftwerke AG

German annual 53pp

Annual report on the operations of the central Austrian electricity producer. Includes a review of the Austrian energy situation and information on plant capacity and output. Detailed statistics of distribution and sales.

**807   ERDOEL-DIENST**
Liess

German twice weekly 4-8pp

Journal of news on the oil and gas industries, and detailed information and statistics of these industries' operations in Austria.

808 ERDOEL ERDGAS ZEITSCHRIFT
Urban-Verlag

German monthly

Journal of the Deutsche Vereinigung der
Erdölgeologen und Erdölingenieure, the Fachverband
der Erdölindustrie and the Österreichische Gesellschaft für Erdölwissenschaften. Contains news and
articles of a technico-economic nature on the oil
and gas industries and information about general
developments, including statistics.

809 FACHVERBAND DER ERDÖLINDUSTRIE
ÖSTERREICHS—JAHRESBERICHT
Fachverband der Erdölindustrie Österreichs

German annual

Annual report of the oil industry association which
includes a detailed survey of the sector during the
past year and statistics on all main aspects of the
industry.

810 GAS VERWENDUNG
ZfGW-Verlag GmbH

German monthly c70pp DM53.00 p.a.

Journal dealing with aspects of distribution and
markets for gas, and including information about
environmental factors in marketing/consumption.

811 GAS WASSER WÄRME
Österreichische Vereinigung für das Gas- und
Wasserfach

German monthly 34pp S675 p.a.

Journal of the industry associations for gas water
and heating. Contains news and general articles about
the industry and main statistical data.

812 GEWERBESTATISTIK 19— TEIL 1
Österreichisches Statistisches Zentralamt

German annual

Statistics of Austrian trade and industry, published
in two parts. TEIL 1 deals with major industries,
giving volume and value of output by commodity,
employment and energy consumption, with data for
the previous year, and includes results of a quarterly
production survey amongst firms with 20 or more
employees.

813 GEWERBESTATISTIK 19— TEIL 2
Österreichisches Statistisches Zentralamt

German annual

Second volume of annual statistics on Austrian
businesses, giving statistics for establishments of less
than 20 employees, obtained by sample survey.

814 HANDELSREGISTER ÖSTERREICH
Jupiter Verlagsgesellschaft mbH

German annual c1950pp

Directory of Austrian businesses and public undertakings. Includes energy producers and distributors
and supplies of goods and services relevant to them.
Part 1 gives administrative information. Part 2
classifies businesses according to activity.

815 INDUSTRIE-COMPASS ÖSTERREICH
Compass-Verlagsgesellschaft mbH

German annual 2500pp

General directory of Austrian industrial concerns,
including sections on energy producers and distributors and related manufacturing and service
sectors. Includes basic company information and
some notes on operations.

816 INDUSTRIESTATISTIK 19—
Österreichisches Statistisches Zentralamt

German annual c470pp

Industry statistics, in two parts. Part 1 gives volume
and value of production by industry, employment,
hours of work, energy consumption, level of orders.
Part 2 gives gross and net output, labour costs,
occupational breakdown, investment, analysis by
scale of output and employment, stocks; much
information analysed by province.

817 ÖMV
ÖMV AG

German (English summary) annual 60pp

Annual report of the state oil and gas company.
Includes a review of the international oil market,
Austrian energy supply and the internal oil market.
Detailed statistics of production of oil products at
the Schwechat refinery. Information about explor-
ation and production in Austria.

818 ÖSTERREICHISCHE DONAUKRAFTWERE AG—
GESCHÄFTSBERICHT
Österreichische Donaukraftwerke AG

German annual c40pp

Review of activities in production of electricity from
power stations on the Danube. Details of individual
plant and new projects and statistics of monthly
production.

819 ÖSTERREICHISCHE ZEITSCHRIFT FÜR
ELEKTRIZITÄTSWIRTSCHAFT
Verband der Elektrizitätswerke Österreichs

German monthly 24pp

Journal of the electricity producers' association containing information and articles about electricity production and consumption in Austria.

**820 ÖSTERREICHISCHES MONTANHANDBUCH**
Bundesministerium für Handel Gewerbe und Industrie

German annual c270pp

Review of activities in mining and the energy sector, product supply, employment and regulations. Includes indexes and directory information and statistical tables.

**821 STATISTISCHE NACHRICHTEN**
Österreichisches Statistisches Zentralamt

German monthly c60pp

Statistical news, containing reports on the current work of the central statistical office. A regular supplement 'Statistische Ubersichten' contains production series for products of the mining and oil and gas industries.

**822 STATISTISCHES HANDBUCH FÜR DIE REPUBLIK ÖSTERREICH**
Österreichisches Statistisches Zentralamt

German annual c650pp

Annual statistical handbook for Austria. Includes sections on energy supply and consumption. Statistics cover: production of oil, coal, natural gas and towns gas; imports and exports of fuel products; electricity supply; consumption by sector; employment. Some consumer price series. Many series analysed by province.

**823 TASCHENBUCH FÜR ENERGIESTATISTIK**
Bundesministerium für Handel Gewerbe und Industrie

German annual 136pp

Annual pocket-book of energy statistics. Detailed statistics on reserves, production, consumption and foreign trade in energy products. Primary energy balances. Notes on developments in the energy sector. Some price information. Many series analysed by province.

**824 VERBUNDGESELLSCHAFT—GESCHÄFTSBERICHT**
Österreichische Elektrizitätswirtschafts-AG

German annual 55pp

Review and report of the public electricity supply authority. Includes a review of the general energy situation and electricity supply in Austria and statistics on: electricity supply by main groups of organisation; capacity; fuels used. Reports on provincial undertakings in which the Verbundgesellschaft has an interest.

**825 VERBUNDKONZERN—ZAHLEN DATEN FAKTEN**
Österreichische Elektrizitätswirtschafts AG

German annual 12pp free

Brochure containing summary data on all aspects of Austrian electricity supply. Figures covering a period of several years for: electricity supply; consumption; international exchanges; pattern of output; plant by type of fuels used; project plans; distribution network; interests of the Verbundkonzern.

**826 VERKEHR, NACHRICHTENUBERMITTLUNG 1976**
Österreichisches Statistisches Zentralamt

German 1979 412pp

Heft 509 in the series 'Beiträge zur Österreichischen Statistik'. Details of traffic by mode of transport and by province. Includes information about energy consumption in the various sectors of the transport industry.

**827 VORARLBERGER ILLWERKE—JAHRESBERICHT**
Vorarlberger Illwerke AG

German annual c50pp

Report by the principal electricity undertaking in western Austria, containing details of plant capacity and development, electricity exports to West Germany and local electricity consumption.

**828 WIENER STADTWERKE—JAHRESBERICHT**
Wiener Stadtwerke

German annual c50pp

Annual report of the municipal energy supply authority. Includes statistics on: production of electricity and heat in own installations; purchased energy; fuels used; costs; distribution; towns gas and natural gas consumption.

**829 WIRTSSCHAFTSSTATISTIK DER ELEKTRIZITÄTS-VERSORGUNGSUNTERNEHMEN**
Österreichisches Statistisches Zentralamt

German annual 42pp

Analysis of activities of electricity supply undertakings with data on electricity, sales, employment, stocks of fuels and balance sheet information. Data analysed by province.

# Belgium

### 850    ANNALES DES MINES DE BELGIQUE
Institut National des Industries Extractives

French/Dutch monthly c85pp

Monthly journal and bulletin. Contains articles on the Belgian mining industry, news of economic and political developments and current industry statistics. Produced jointly with the Administration des Mines.

### 851    ANNUAIRE STATISTIQUE
Fédération Professionnelle des Producteurs et Distributeurs d'Electricité

French annual 75pp

Comprehensive statistics of the Belgian electricity industry, covering: capacity; transmission network; production; fuels used; exchanges; consumption by sector; the public distribution system. Figures for several years, analysed by province, type of producer and plant.

### 852    ANNUAIRE STATISTIQUE DE LA BELGIQUE
Institut National de Statistique

French/Dutch annual c700pp

Annual abstract of general statistics covering all sections of the economy. Includes statistics of production, trade and consumption of oil, gas, coal, electricity. Price indices for coal and oil products. Transportation of oil.

### 853    ANNUAIRE STATISTIQUE DE L'INDUSTRIE DU GAZ
Fédération de l'Industrie du Gaz

French/Dutch annual 52pp

Statistical compendium, covering: equipment and investment; disposals and sales; revenues and average prices; employment. Many series on a monthly basis, analysed by province and covering several years.

### 854    BILANS ENERGETIQUES
Administration de l'Energie

French/Dutch quarterly 86pp

Statistics of the availability and disposal of coal, coke, petroleum products, towns gas, natural gas and electricity; total primary energy balance; imports/exports; stocks, price indicators for all fuels. Published as a supplement to 'Apercu de l'Evolution Economique.'

### 855    BULLETIN D'INFORMATION
Fedération Professionnelle des Producteurs et Distributeurs d'Electricité

French bi-monthly

Bulletin of statistics and other general information about the electricity industry from the producers' and distributors' organisation.

### 856    BULLETIN D'INFORMATION
Fédération de l'Industrie du Gaz

French/Dutch monthly 14pp

Bulletin of the gas industry association. Commentary on the energy and gas situation of Belgium, statistics, and news of general developments affecting the industry.

### 857    BULLETIN DU MINISTERE DES AFFAIRES ECONOMIQUES: ADMINISTRATION DES MINES
Administration des Mines

French monthly

Bulletin giving main statistics on production and trade for mines, quarries, fuels, steel and non-ferrous metals.

### 858    BULLETIN MENSUEL DE L'ENERGIE ELECTRIQUE
Administration de l'Energie

French/Dutch monthly 12pp

Official statistical bulletin of electricity supply. Production by category of organisation, imports/exports of electricity, pattern of fuels used in generation. Cumulative figures for the year and comparison with previous year.

### 859    BULLETIN MENSUEL DU COMMERCE EXTERIEUR DE L'UNION ECONOMIQUE BELGO-LUXEMBOURGEOISE
Institut National de Statistique

French/Dutch monthly

Monthly bulletin with cumulative figures of the foreign trade of the BLEU. Includes: imports and exports arranged by commodity classification, identifying main energy products, and subdivided by countries of origin and destination.

### 860    CHEMFACTS BELGIUM
IPC Industrial Press Ltd

English 1977 138pp £40.00

Analysis of market trends, plant capacity and investment; trade in individual chemicals and profiles of the leading companies.

861 COMITE DE CONTROLE DE L'ELECTRICITE
ET DU GAZ—RAPPORT ANNUEL
Comité de Contrôle de l'Electricité et du Gaz

French annual c70pp

Review of the electricity and gas industries, dealing
with policy, organisation, technical and commercial
aspects. Carries data on prices, revenues, investment,
costs and sales of electricity and gas.

862 LE COMMERCE EXTERIEUR DE L'UNION
BELGO-LUXEMBOURGEOISE
Office Belge du Commerce Extérieur

French annual

Analysis of foreign trade and detailed trade statistics
with each major region of the world, identifying
imports and exports of energy products.

863 CONSOMMATION D'ELECTRICITE PAR
PROVINCES ET PAR REGIONS
Fédération Professionnelle des Producteurs et
Distributeurs d'Electricité

French annual

Detailed breakdown of electricity consumption at
the provincial and regional level, analysed by sector
of consumption.

864 DISTRIGAZ
Distrigaz SA

English 1978 40pp

Information booklet about Distrigaz and the supply
of gas in Belgium. Deals with historical growth of gas
supply and outlines the use of natural gas in the
economy. Includes statistics on production and consumption.

865 EBES—RAPPORT ANNUEL
Sociétés Réunies d'Energie du Bassin de l'Escaut SA

French annual c35pp

Annual report of one of Belgium's principal distributors of electricity. Includes statistics of: deliveries
to consumers; sources of electricity drawn upon;
interests in production capacity; average revenues.

866 L'ECONOMIE BELGE FACE A LA CRISE
MONDIALE DE L'ENERGIE
Société de Traction et d'Electricité

French 1979 50pp

Presentation by M A Voue chief engineer of Société
de Traction et d'Electricité, analysing the Belgian
energy situation and possibilities of reducing the
degree of import-dependence.

867 ELECTRICITE
Union des Exploitations Electriques en Belgique

French half-yearly c50pp BF120 p.a.

Periodical review with technical and economic
articles about developments in the Belgian electricity supply industry. Also published in a Dutch
edition under the title 'Electriciteit.'

868 ELECTRONUCLEAIRE SA—RAPPORT
D'ACTIVITE
Electronucléaire SA

French/Dutch annual 20pp

Report by the nuclear engineering associate of the
principal electricity producers on the operation and
development of nuclear power stations in Belgium
and general economic and political events affecting
the nuclear industry.

869 FEDERATION PETROLIERE BELGE 50$^{eme}$
ANNIVERSAIRE
Fédération Pétrolière Belge

French 1976 56pp

Review of the historical development of the Belgian
oil industry association, setting out current regulations and policies affecting the industries and the
structure of the operating companies. Also includes
basic statistics of oil in the Belgian economy.

870 FIGAZ—EXERCICE SOCIAL
Fédération de l'Industrie du Gaz

French/Dutch annual 40pp

Annual review of the activities of the gas industry
association and review of the position of gas in the
economy for the past year. Commentary on new and
prospective developments, analysis of consumption
and details of investment in plant and distribution
equipment.

871 FPB—RAPPORT D'ACTIVITE
Fédération Pétrolière Belge

French annual 36pp

Review of developments in the oil industry during
the previous year, with analysis commentary and
statistics. Contains figures for production, imports,
exports and consumption of individual oil products,
refining and marketing facilities, employment and
price indicators.

872 FPE—RAPPORT ANNUEL
Fédération Professionnelle des Producteurs et
Distributeurs d'Electricité

French annual c85pp

Annual report of the electricity producers' and
distributors' association, including a detailed review
of electricity supply and consumption. Large statistical section covering: consumption; production;
cross-border exchanges; primary fuels used; investment by type of project; tariff elements.

873   INPUT-OUTPUT TABLES—BELGIË/BELGIQUE
      1970
      Eurostat

      Dutch/French 1978 120pp $10.10

Standardised tables showing the expenditure on
fuels in individual sectors of the economy and their
relative cost significance.

874   INTERCOM—RAPPORT ANNUEL
      INTERCOM

      French annual c40pp

Annual rreport on the activities of one of Belgium's
principal electricity distributors. Contains a review
of the electricity supply situation and statistics of
deliveries to principal consumption sectors, sources
of electricity and cost and price information.

875   KOMPASS BELGIUM LUXEMBOURG
      Kompass Belgium SA

      Multi-language annual 2 vols

Directory of firms in Belgium and Luxembourg and
their principal fields of activity. Includes firms
engaged in the supply of energy and related goods
and services. Vol 1 gives information on goods and
services. Vol 2 gives basic company information.

876   ORGANISATION DU SECTEUR DE L'ENERGIE
      ELECTRIQUE
      Administration de l'Energie

      French 1975 30pp

Summary of the legislative background of electricity
supply and distribution and the structure of organisations in the industry. Details of official bodies,
associations and undertakings.

877   PETROFINA—ANNUAL REPORT
      Petrofina SA

      English annual 48pp

English language edition of the annual report of
Belgium's major oil company. Includes a general
review of the oil industry, main features of the
company's operations and details of group companies in the energy sector.

878   REPERTOIRE DES CENTRALES ELECTRIQUES
      Fédération Professionnelle des Producteurs et
      Distributeurs d'Electricité

      French annual

Listing of all major power plant in Belgium giving
basic technico-economic information, fuel type,
output, operating organisation.

879   REVUE GENERALE DU GAZ
      Association Royale des Gaziers Belges

      French/Dutch quarterly 36pp BF800 p.a.

Review of the Belgian gas industry, containing
general information about developments and statistics of production, distribution and consumption.

880   SOCIETE GENERALE—ANNUAL REPORT
      Société Générale de Belgique

      English annual 130pp

Includes a general review of the Belgian economy and
energy developments. Review of activities of
affiliated companies involved in energy production
icluding Société de Traction et de l'Electricité,
Petrofina and Charbonnages de Minceau-Fontaine.

881   STATISTIQUES
      Union des Exploitations Electriques en Belgique

      French annual 24pp

Annual statistical survey of electricity supply in
Belgium. Notes and statistics on: electricity output;
plant by type; fuels used in generation; pattern of
electricity consumption; average prices.

882   STATISTIQUES 19—
      Administration des Mines

      French/Dutch annual 50pp

Official annual statistics on coal production and
deliveries, detailed by grade and by province. Other
data on stocks, employment and productivity.

883   STATISTIQUES DE BASE D L'INDUSTRIE
      CHARBONNIERE
      Comptoir Belges des Charbons

      French/Dutch annual 12pp

Summary statistics of the Belgian coal industry:
long-run data on production by region; number of
collieries; employment; production by grade; stocks;
deliveries to consumers.

884   STATISTIQUES ELECTRICITE
      Administration de l'Energie

      French annual 2 vols

Official annual statistics for electricity. Vol 1 presents
Belgian statistics in comparison with other leading
industrial countries and charts the development of
generating capacity and electricity output. Vol 2
analyses distribution and consumption in detail and
contains special studies of the sector.

**885 STATISTIQUES ELECTRICITE 1974-77 MOYENS DE PRODUCTION**
Administration de l'Energie

French 1979 24pp

Detailed breakdown of electricity generating capacity by type of undertaking; auto-producers analysed by industrial sector. Identifies new power stations commissioned in the period 1974-77 and programmed for 1978-83.

**886 STATISTIQUES HEBDOMADAIRES**
Fédération Professionnelle des Producteurs et Distributeurs d'Electricité

French weekly

Rapid information service giving current basic statistics of production and consumption of electricity.

**887 STATISTIQUES PROVISOIRES**
Fédération Professionnelle des Producteurs et Distributeurs d'Electricité

French annual 12pp

Preliminary review of the past year with main statistics of electricity supply and consumption and developments in production plant and transmission system.

**888 STATISTISCH MAANDBERICHT—HAVEN VAN ANTWERPEN**
Stad Antwerpen Havenbedrijf

Dutch monthly c10pp

Statistics of imports, exports and transit trade by product at Belgium's principal oil port. Monthly figures for the year to date: analysis by mode of transport and main countries of origin/destination.

**889 TE NEWS**
Société de Traction et de l'Electricité

English/French/Dutch half-yearly 20pp free

Information bulletin containing news and notes on developments in the Belgian energy sector and related technologies in which STE is involved.

**890 UNERG—RAPPORT ANNUEL**
UNERG SA

French annual 65pp

Details of activities in gas and electricity supply by one of Belgium's major distribution undertakings. Includes a general review of consumption, supply, new plant, research and development and prices. Some details of Distrigaz operations.

# France

**900 ACTIVITE DE L'INDUSTRIE PETROLIERE**
Direction des Hydrocarbures

French monthly c30pp

Bulletin of information and statistics relating to the French oil industry, including details of exploration and development activity and series for production and consumption.

**901 ANNALES DES MINES**
Bureau de Documentation Minière

French monthly

Bulletin of information about a range of aspects of the coal industry in France, including commercial, political, technical and environmental matters.

**902 ANNUAIRE DESFOSSES—TOME 2**
Cote Desfossés/DAFSA

French annual 2,100pp

Yearbook of stock, share and other financial information on French companies, including principal undertakings in the electricity, oil, coal and gas industries. Contains detailed administrative, financial and balance sheet information, and some data on operational activities.

**903 ANNUAIRE STATISTIQUE DE LA FRANCE**
INSEE

French annual c850pp

Contains sections on oil, gas, coal and electricity, with statistics of production, consumption, plant, imports/exports and some price indicators.

**904 BULLETIN DE L'INDUSTRIE PETROLIERE**
SOCIDOC

French daily 10-20pp

Bulletin of news on developments in all phases of the oil, gas and petrochemical industries, including statistics and special reports.

**905 BULLETIN MENSUEL DE STATISTIQUE INDUSTRIELLE**
Ministère de l'Industrie

French monthly 48pp F150.00 p.a.

Contains regular statistical series of output and trade for individual energy products. Monthly or quarterly data.

**906 CHARBONNAGES DE FRANCE—RAPPORT D'ACTIVITES**
Charbonnages de France

French annual 144pp

Annual report of the state coal mining company. Contains a review of the coal sector and description of the state of the French industry. Statistics of coal supply and deliveries.

**907 CHEMFACTS FRANCE**
IPC Industrial Press Ltd

English 1978 172pp £40.00

Analysis of market trends, plant capacity and investment; trade in individual chemicals and profiles of the leading companies.

**908 LES CHIFFRES CLES DE L'ENERGIE**
Ministère de l'Industrie

French annual 60pp

General review of the international and French energy situation, and main statistics for each energy industry.

**909 COMPAGNIE FRANCAISE DES PETROLES— ANNUAL REPORT**
Compagnie Française des Pétroles

French annual

Annual report of the leading French oil refining and marketing company. Includes a review of all aspects of oil industry activities in France and information about group operations.

**910 LA COMPAGNIE NATIONAL DU RHONE**
Compagnie Nationale du Rhône

French 1978 62pp

Information book about the state company responsible for electricity production on the Rhône. Deals with: organisation, plant and facilities; hydraulic features; production and distribution of electricity; exploitation programme.

**911 CPDP—BULLETIN MENSUEL**
Comité Professionnel du Pétrole

French monthly c50pp F310.00 p.a.

Monthly bulletin of news and statistics for the oil industry. Latest trade, consumption and refinery output figures. Analysis of consumption. Price information.

**912 LES DOSSIERS DE L'ENERGIE**
Ministère de l'Industrie

French

Series of reports and studies from a variety of sources on key issues in the energy sector, including: L'Avenir du Charbon; Les Economies d'Energie; Orientations de la Politique Energetique (Commission Gregory); La Production d'Electricité d'Origine Hydraulique.

**913 LES ECONOMIES D'ENERGIE DANS LES ENTREPRISES**
Agence pour les Economies d'Energie

French 1979 30pp

Proceedings of a colloquium organised by the Conseil National du Patronat and the Agence pour les Economies d'Energie, dealing with the scope for energy conservation in industry, case histories and investment requirements.

**914 EDF 19—**
Electricité de France

English annual 32pp

English summary of the main annual report of the French state electricity undertaking, containing statistics on all aspects of electricity supply and consumption.

**915 EDF—STRUCTURES ET ORGANISATION**
Electricité de France

French 1976

Folder of nine brochures giving details of the organisation, responsibilities and general activities of the state electricity undertaking. Brochures individually of 8-16 pages.

**916 ELECTRICITE DE FRANCE—RAPPORT D'ACTIVITES COMPTE DE GESTION**
Electricité de France

French annual 120pp

Annual report of the state electricity undertaking giving details of all aspects of its activities. Review of electricity production and use in France and of general energy situation.

**917 ENERGIE**
INSEE

French annual

Data on the energy sector obtained in the course of the annual census of industry. Includes data on: number of enterprises; turnover; employment; investment. Analysis by size of enterprise.

**918 L'ENERGIE SOLAIRE**
Commissariat à l'Energie Solaire

French 1979 60pp

Review of the scope for using solar energy, with particular reference to French conditions. Includes information about existing projects in France.

**919 ESSO—ANNUAL REPORT**
ESSO SAF

English annual c40pp

English language version of the annual report of the French refining and marketing affiliate of Exxon. Includes commentary on the French oil supply situation and its international context.

**920 ESSO INFORMATIONS**
ESSO SAF

French monthly 12-20pp

Information bulletin about the French oil industry and activities of Esso SAF. Includes details of changes in official prices, other regulations, statistics.

**921 GAZ D'AUJOURD'HUI**
Société du Journal des Usines à Gaz

French monthly 40pp F300.00 p.a.

Journal with news of the French gas industry, technical developments and more general articles.

**922 GAZ DE FRANCE INFORMATION**
Gaz de France

French monthly 30pp

Articles giving general background information on the French gas industry.

**923 GAZ DE FRANCE—STATISTIQUES**
Gaz de France

French annual 100pp

Detailed statistical information on operations and finances of Gaz de France. Material also analysed by district: number of customers, and consumption by sector; appliances and equipment.

**924 GAZ DE FRANCE—STATISTIQUES PROVISOIRES**
Gaz de France

French annual 16pp

Key statistics of the operations of Gaz de France during the past year: pattern of sales; revenues by region; sources of gas; heating installations.

**925 THE IMPACT OF ENERGY CONSERVATION ON THE DESIGN OF BUILDINGS AND HEATING SYSTEMS**
International Gas Union

English 1979 22pp

Contains a review of regulations in France and the United Kingdom concerning energy conservation, and experience in implementation. Paper given at the IGU's 1979 congress.

**926 IMPORTATIONS DE PRODUITS FINIS PETROLIERS PAR POINT D'ENTREE ET PAR MODE DE TRANSPORT**
Comité Professionnel du Pétrole

French annual 12pp

Summary data from customs statistics of imports of finished products analysed by point of entry, by mode of transport and by product.

**927 IMPORTATIONS ET EXPORTATIONS FRANCAISES DE PETROLE**
Comité Professionnel du Pétrole

French monthly 4pp

Bulletin of foreign trade statistics for crude oil and finished products by country of origin/destination.

**928 L'INDUSTRIE DU PETROLE**
Editions Olivier Lesourd

French/English monthly 110pp F551.20 p.a.

Periodical dealing with developments in oil, gas and petrochemicals both in France and abroad. Articles on economics of the industries and related technologies.

**929 L'INDUSTRIE FRANCAISE DU PETROLE**
UCSIP

French annual 72pp

General review of activity in all sectors of the French oil industry, with an international section. Includes many statistics covering: exploration; production; tankers and pipelines; refining; petrochemicals; natural gas; distribution/marketing; consumption.

**930 INPUT-OUTPUT TABLES—FRANCE**
Eurostat

French/English 1978 124pp $10.10

Standardised tables showing the expenditure on fuels in individual sectors of the economy and their relative cost significance.

**931 KOMPASS FRANCE**
SNEI

French/English/German/Italian annual 4 vols

Directory of French firms and their principal fields of activity. Includes leading suppliers of energy and related goods and services. Vols 1 and 2 give information on goods and services. Vols 3 and 4 give basic company information.

**932 LIVRAISONS DE PRODUITS BLANCS ET DE FUEL-OILS**
Comité Professionnel du Pétrole

French monthly 4pp

Regular bulletin of statistics for deliveries to consumers of main petroleum products during the previous month with cumulative figures for the year. Also includes data on stocks in the distribution sector.

**933 LUBRIFIANTS**
Centre Professionnel des Lubrifiants

French annual 98pp

Review of the lubricants market and long-run statistical series on availability and disposal. Consumption statistics in detail. Includes basic statistics on other main countries and areas.

**934 LE MARCHE PETROLIER FRANCAIS EN 19—**
Comité Professionnel du Pétrole

French annual 122pp

Summary statistics for the past year as available by February of the following year, covering consumption of oil products by region and departement. Figures for individual products on a monthly basis.

**935 PETROLE**
Comité Professionnel du Pétrole

French annual 396pp F300.00

Annual compendium of statistics of the French oil industry. Review of the French economy and energy situation. Detailed statistics of: the energy balance; production; refining; maritime transport; imports/exports; distribution; consumption; petrochemicals; prices.

**936 PETROLE INFORMATIONS**
SOCIDOC

French fortnightly c60pp F500.00 p.a.

Journal containing news and statistics of the French oil sector, notes on technical developments and articles on economics and technology. An English language edition is published under the title 'Pétrole Informations International'.

**937 LE PLAN NATIONAL D'ECONOMIES D'ENERGIE**
Agence pour les Economies d'Energie

French 1979 24pp

Details of the decisions of the Council of Ministers in respect of energy conservation. Includes a review of energy consumption in France and comments on new measures to be taken.

**938 PRODUCTION ET DISTRIBUTION DE L'ENERGIE ELECTRIQUE EN FRANCE**
Direction du Gaz, de l'Electricité et du Charbon

French annual 94pp

Detailed statistics on production and consumption of electricity in France, covering: thermal plant; hydro-electric plant; fuels used; consumption in detail; distribution network. Many data given by departement.

**939 RECHERCHES ET PRODUCTION D'HYDRO-CARBURES EN FRANCE**
Service de Conservation des Gisements d' Hydrocarbures

French annual 140pp

Annual official report on exploration activity in France. Contains data on licences, drilling, seismic activity and production.

**940 REPARTITION GEOGRAPHIQUE DES VENTES**
Comité Professionnel du Pétrole

French monthly 20pp

Up-to-date statistics for sales of oil products in individual departements and regions of France. Published in three series dealing with: motor fuels and kerosine; solvents and white spirit; heating and fuel oil.

**941 REVUE DE L'ENERGIE**
Editions Techniques et Economiques

French monthly c50pp

Journal containing analytical articles on energy questions dealing with economic and technical aspects.

**942 REVUE DE L'INSTITUT FRANCAIS DU PETROLE**
Editions Technip

French bi-monthly F360.00 p.a.

Regular journal of the Institut including the results of work on new technology and technical advances in oil production, processing and utilisation and economic studies on aspects of the industry.

**943 STATISTIQUE ANNUELLE**
Charbonnages de France

French annual

Annual statistics for the French coal industry produced by the state-owned mining company. Data on production, foreign trade and consumption by grade of fuel, and for individual sectors of consumption.

**944 STATISTIQUE DE L'INDUSTRIE MINERALE**
Ministère de l'Industrie

French annual 150pp F70.00

Annual statistics of mineral and energy industries. Includes: production of coal, oil. natural gas and towns gas; imports and exports; consumption. Figures for individual regions of France.

**945 STATISTIQUE MENSUELLE**
Charbonnages de France

French monthly

Current figures on the French coal industry including output from French mines, deliveries to the market, employment and foreign trade information.

**946 STATISTIQUE MENSUELLE DE L'ENERGIE**
Direction Générale de l'Industrie

French monthly

Monthly bulletin of statistics giving the most recent data for all forms of energy: production, consumption and trade.

**947 STATISTIQUES DE LA PRODUCTION ET DE LA CONSOMMATION**
EDF-Direction de la Production et du Transport

French annual 98pp

Annual statistical survey of electricity production and consumption in France. Statistical series cover the last ten years.

**948 STATISTIQUES DE L'INDUSTRIE GAZIERE**
Direction du Gaz, de l'Electricité et du Charbon

French annual 32pp

Statistical information on the gas industry. Part one contains details of availability and disposal, by sector and by region for the industry as a whole. Part 2 gives information on Gaz de France and other organisations involved in production and distribution.

**949 STATISTIQUES DU COMMERCE EXTERIEUR DE LA FRANCE—IMPORTATIONS-EXPORTATIONS**
Direction Générale des Douanes et Droits Indirects

French annual c1150pp

Detailed figures for imports and exports, including energy products, following the Nomenclature Generale des Produits. Tables of volume and value by country and main tariff headings.

**950 STATISTIQUES DU COMMERCE EXTERIEUR DE LA FRANCE—RESULTATS ANNUELS**
Direction Générale des Douanes et Droits Indirects

French annual c190pp

Imports/exports by product and by country, for the last three years. Imports and exports over three years grouped by product and grouped by country. Commentary on the main characteristics of the foreign trade figures.

**951 STATISTIQUES DU COMMERCE EXTERIEUR DE LA FRANCE: TABLEAU GENERAL DES TRANSPORTS**
Direction Générale des Douanes et Droits Indirects

French annual c900pp

Detailed import/export figures, identifying energy products. Part 1: analysis by commodity with countries of origin/destination, specifying mode of transport. Part 2: classification of commodity movements by country of origin/destination.

**952 STATISTIQUES MENSUELLES**
Gaz de France

French monthly

Bulletin of statistics on a monthly basis from the state gas undertaking. Includes data on production, exchanges and distribution of gas.

**953 TECHNICAL OPERATION RESULTS**
EDF-Direction de la Production et du Transport

English/French annual 32pp

Summary of the main features of the EdF operations. Includes long-run data on generating plant, output, consumption, fuels used, pattern of consumption by sector.

**954 TECHNIQUES DE L'ENERGIE**
SOCIDOC

French monthly F156.00 p.a.

Journal containing articles of a technico-economic nature in the field of energy and news of technological developments.

**955 TRAVAUX D'INVESTISSEMENT**
Electricité de France

French (summary in English/German/Spanish) annual c50pp

Details of investment in plant and facilities brought into service in the past year.

**956 UNION DES INDUSTRIES CHIMIQUES— EXERCICE**
Union des Industries Chimiques

French annual 50pp

Report on the activities of the UIC, containing a review of the chemicals industry in France and statistical section giving production and trade for individual products.

**957 USEFUL ENERGY BALANCE SHEETS**
Eurostat

English/French/German 1978 38pp

Explains the structure and composition of balance sheets of useful energy and gives a statistical analysis of the French and West German energy economies in 1975.

# Greece

**1000 BULLETIN DE STATISTIQUE DU COMMERCE EXTERIEUR**
National Statistical Service of Greece

French/Greek quarterly

Monthly figures of imports/exports identifying energy products under the Greek trade classification and the SITC, analysed by mode of transport and point of entry. Indices of import/export volumes. Commodities analysed by country only at aggregated levels.

**1001 BULLETIN ON THE MINING ACTIVITIES OF GREECE**
National Statistical Service of Greece

English/Greek annual c70pp

Contains a review of activities in the mining/quarrying sector; statistics on production; list of enterprises.

**1002 FINANCIAL DIRECTORY OF GREEK COMPANIES**
ICAP Hellas SA

English/Greek annual 4 vols $145.00

Includes information on directors, employment, balance sheet information for the latest years and notes on activities and operations. Vol 1 includes companies manufacturing chemicals, petroleum and coal products and mining companies. Vol 2 includes a section on petroleum distribution companies. Vol 3 includes public utilities. (Vol 4 is a directory of products and services.)

**1003 MONTHLY STATISTICAL BULLETIN**
National Statistical Service of Greece

English/Greek monthly c90pp

Bulletin of official statistics covering all aspects of the economy. Includes series for output of coal, oil products and electricity.

**1004 PUBLIC POWER CORPORATION—ACTIVITIES REPORT**
Public Power Corporation

English annual c90pp

Annual report of the state electricity monopoly. Comprehensive review of the electricity industry in Greece. Includes information on: primary energy consumption; electricity plant, fuels used, Greek coal-mines; electricity production, transmission and sales.

**1005 SHIPPING STATISTICS**
National Statistical Service of Greece

English/Greek annual c165pp

Details of the Greek merchant fleet and traffic at Greek ports. Data cover: size and age of the fleet; shipping mortgaged against loans; laid-up shipping; arrivals of shipping by type and flag; coastal traffic; building and repairing; foreign exchange earnings.

**1006 STATISTICAL YEARBOOK OF GREECE**
National Statistical Service of Greece

English/Greek annual c500pp

Statistics on all social and economic aspects of Greece, including: basic statistics of production and consumption of energy: coal mining; oil refining; foreign trade in energy; pattern of electricity supply.

# Italy

**1025 AEM—INFORMAZIONI**
Azienda Elettrica Municipale di Milano

Italian monthly c30pp

Monthly magazine of the Milan municipal electricity authority. Carries news of official actions affecting the electricity industry, commentary on developments in the field of energy and general articles on a range of topics in the electricity industry.

**1026 AGIP—ANNUAL REPORT**
AGIP SpA

English annual 90pp

English version of the annual report of the leading Italian oil marketer. Includes a detailed review of the Italian oil industry and statistics of the companies operations.

1027 ANNUARIO DI STATISTICHE INDUSTRIALE
Istituto Centrale di Statistica

Italian annual c280pp

Yearbook of industrial statistics including data on the production and consumption of principal energy forms.

1028 ANNUARIO STATISTICO DELLA NAVIGAZIONE MARITTIMA
Istituto Centrale di Statistica

Italian annual c380pp

Annual statistics of shipping, number of vessels and tonnage at individual Italian ports. Traffic analysed by commodity, country of origin/destination and flag.

1029 ANNUARIO STATISTICO ITALIANO
Istituto Centrale di Statistica

Italian annual c450pp

Statistical yearbook of Italy. Includes data on: production of coal, oil and gas; electricity production capacity and output; consumption by sector and industry; imports/exports of energy products. Some data analysed by province.

1030 L'ATTIVITA DELL' ENEL NEL 19—
Ente Nazionale per l'Energia Elettrica

Italian annual c120pp

Review of the operations in the previous year of the state electricity supply undertaking. Sections deal with: production and consumption; developments during the year; new plant; the construction programme; research and development.

1031 AZIENDA ELETTRICA MUNICIPALE DI MILANO—CONTO CONSUNTIVO
Azienda Elettrica Municipale di Milano

Italian annual c100pp

Annual report of the supervisory board of the Milan electricity supply authority. Includes a brief review of the Italian economy and general energy situation and analysis of electricity output and sales by the authority.

1032 BOLLETTINO MENSILE DI STATISTICA
Istituto Centrale di Statistica

Italian monthly c270pp

Monthly bulletin of official statistics including series for industrial production and activities of the energy industries.

1033 BOLLETTINO STATISTICO: SULLE FONTI DI ENERGIA E SULLA PRODUZIONE INDUSTRIALE
Ministero dell' Industria del Commercio e dell' Artigianato

Italian half-yearly c90pp

Statistics on a monthly basis for energy production and supply and industrial production in general. Some figures for individual provinces.

1034 CHEMFACTS ITALY
IPC Industrial Press Ltd

English 1979 138pp £40.00

Analysis of market trends, plant capacity and investment; trade in individual chemicals and profiles of the leading companies.

1035 IL CHILOWATTORA
Azienda Elettrica Municipale di Milano

Italian monthly c50pp

Monthly journal dealing with topical news and issues and analyses of electricity supply and distribution in Italy.

1036 ENEL—RELAZIONI DEL CONSIGLIO DI AMMINISTRAZIONE
Ente Nazionale per l'Energia Elettrica

Italian annual c120pp

Report of the supervisory board of the state electricity supply undertaking. Review of the principal activities of ENEL, the general situation of the electricity industry and analysis of revenues and costs.

1037 ENERGIA ED IDROCARBURI
Ente Nazionale Idrocarburi

English/Italian annual

Commentary with substantial statistical element, dealing with energy supply and demand. Produced in English and Italian editions.

1038 ENI—RELAZIONE
Ente Nazionale Idrocarburi

Italian annual

Annual report of the state-owned hydrocarbons undertaking. Includes a detailed survey of the Italian energy situation and its international context and statistics on many aspects of energy in Italy.

1039 GAS
Editrice Palombi

Italian monthly 45pp L17,500 p.a.

Technically orientated journal for the gas industry, but includes statistics and general information about gas in Italy.

1040 INPUT-OUTPUT TABLES—ITALIA 1970
Eurostat

Italian/French 1978 119pp $10.10

Standardised tables showing the expenditure on fuels in individual sectors of the economy and their relative cost significance.

1041 KOMPASS ITALIA
Etas Kompass Periodici Tecnici SpA

Multi-language annual 2 vols

Directory of Italian firms and their principal fields of activity. Includes leading suppliers of energy and related goods and services. Vol 1 gives information on goods and services. Vol 2 gives basic company information.

1042 NOTIZIE STATISTICHE
Unione Petrolifera

Italian monthly c8pp

Statistical bulletin of the oil industry association, containing up-to-date figures for production and deliveries of oil products and comment on the main product markets.

1043 PETROLIO
Publicazione Petrolifera SpA

Italian (English/French summaries) L10,000 p.a.

Periodical containing news and articles about the oil and gas industries of a technical and economic nature.

1044 PIPE LAYING IN DEEP WATER
International Gas Union

French 1979 10pp

Summarises the historical stages and technical aspects of the project to lay a natural gas pipeline across the Mediterranean and Straits of Messina to the Italian mainland. Paper given at the 1979 congress.

1045 LE PRINCIPALE SOCIETA ITALIANE
Mediobanca

Italian annual c270pp

Information on key enterprises in the Italian economy. Includes sections on petroleum, minerals, chemicals and public utility services. Data on turnover, employment and assets.

1046 PROGRAMMI DELL' ENEL
Ente Nazionale per l'Energia Elettrica

Italian 1979 96pp

Details of the forward programme of the state electricity authority. Detailed review of the demand for electricity up to 1990; plant construction programme; the distribution system and rural electrification; electricity, energy and the economy; final consumption of electricity.

1047 RASSEGNA PETROLIFERA
ESPETROL

Italian weekly c40pp L120,000 p.a.

Regular journal of events in the Italian oil industry including details of legislative proposals and enactments, reports on the oil sector and basic statistics.

1048 RELAZIONE SULL' ATTIVITA DEL 19—
Unione Petrolifera

Italian annual 28pp

Survey and basic statistics of the Italian energy situation: energy consumption pattern by region; sources of oil imports; pattern of consumption; domestic price and tax information; refinery capacities; official policies and measures.

1049 STATISTICA ANNUALE DEL COMMERCIO CON L'ESTERO
Istituto Centrale di Statistica

Italian annual 2 vols

Annual statistics of foreign trade: Vol 1 (c450pp): Summary data on imports and exports by countries of origin and destination subdivided by commodity groups; transit trade. Vol 2 (c1360pp): Detailed tables of imports and exports arranged by commodity classifications (BTN) and subdivided by countries of origin and destination; tables of re-imports; re-exports.

1050 STATISTICA MENSILE DEL COMMERCIO CON L'ESTERO
Istituto Centrale di Statistica

Italian monthly

Monthly statistics of foreign trade: tables showing exports and imports arranged by commodity classification (BTN) subdivided by countries of origin and destination. Other tables show imports and exports within the EEC.

**1051 STATISTICHE PETROLIFERE**
Unione Petrolifera

Italian annual 30pp

Oil statistics for Italy for the previous year with comparative data for earlier years, also including data on the international oil supply situation and the Italian energy balance. Statistics include: Italian port facilities; imports/exports of crude oil and products by source/destination; refinery operations; crude oil costs; deliveries; prices and taxes.

# Luxembourg

**1075 L'ANNEE ECONOMIQUE 19— ET PERSPECTIVE POUR 19—**
STATEC

French annual 168pp F120

Annual review of the Luxembourg economy. Contains comment on developments in the energy sector and statistics on production, trade and consumption of individual energy products.

**1076 ANNUAIRE DES SOCIETES ANONYMES**
Banque Internationale à Luxembourg SA

French annual c900pp

Annual handbook of financial and other information for companies registered in Luxembourg. Includes notes on objectives and activities and balance sheet information for most recent years.

**1077 ANNUAIRE STATISTIQUE**
STATEC

French annual c390pp

Statistical yearbook of Luxembourg. Contains a section on energy with data on: electricity production by various groups; sources of energy; consumption of fuels by sector; sales of electricity by type of distributor; imports/exports of energy; some price data.

**1078 LE COMMERCE EXTERIEUR DE L'UNION BELGO-LUXEMBOURGEOISE**
Office Belge du Commerce Extérieur

French annual

Annual statistics in detail of trade between the BLEU and other principal countries and regions.

**1079 COMMERCE EXTERIEUR DU LUXEMBOURG**
STATEC

French annual

Detailed statistics of imports/exports of Luxembourg by commodity and by country of origin/destination, identifying trade in principal energy products.

**1080 L'ECONOMIE LUXEMBOURGEOISE EN 1976 ET 1977**
STATEC

French 1978 282pp

General review with statistics and analysis of the Luxembourg economy. Includes a review of energy developments. Published as No 57 in the series 'Cahiers Economiques'.

**1081 KOMPASS BELGIUM LUXEMBOURG**
Kompass Belgium SA

Multi-language annual 2 vols

Directory of firms in Belgium and Luxembourg including concerns engaged in the production or supply of energy and related goods and services. Vol 1 gives information on goods and services. Vol 2 gives basic company information.

**1082 LA SITUATION ECONOMIQUE AU GRAND-DUCHE**
STATEC

French quarterly 90pp F300 p.a.

Regular official survey of the Luxembourg economy containing data on energy production, trade and consumption. Figures given for individual products and sectors of consumption. Subscription includes the annual review 'L'Année Economique'.

# Netherlands

**1100 CHEMFACTS NETHERLANDS**
IPC Industrial Press Ltd

English 1978 150pp £40.00

Analysis of market trends, plant capacity and investment; trade in individual chemicals and profiles of the leading companies.

**1101 DE CONTINUITEIT VAN DE GASVOORZIENING**
VEG-Gasinstituut NV

Dutch 1978 88pp

Report by VEG-Gasinstituut on the outlook for the Dutch gas industry with reference to technical aspects of maintaining public supply under changing patterns of gas types. Includes annexes dealing with: world energy resources; the Dutch energy situation; possible patterns of energy supply; coal gasification technology.

## 1102 ECN—JAARSVERSLAG
Energieonderzoek Centrum Nederland

Dutch annual 80pp

Annual report of the Netherlands energy research centre. Gives details of progress on research and experimental work on exploitation, processing and use of all main energy forms in the ECN programme.

## 1103 GAS
Drukkerij en Uitgeversbureau Van Lonkhuyzen BV

Dutch monthly 70pp Fl 65.00 p.a.

Journal of the gas industry associations with general news of industry developments and economic and technical articles on aspects of gas distribution in the Netherlands and other countries.

## 1104 GAS MARKETING PLAN
NV Nederlandse Gasunie

English annual 16pp

Annual review of the natural gas supply situation in the Netherlands and general policies on exploitation, conservation, the pattern of disposals on the domestic market and export contracts.

## 1105 GASUNIE—ANNUAL REPORT
NV Nederlandse Gasunie

English annual 40pp

Review of the natural gas supply situation in the Netherlands, the state of individual fields, liquefied natural gas developments. Includes sales and revenue statistics and operational details for the previous ten-year period.

## 1106 INPUT-OUTPUT TABLES—NEDERLAND 1970
Eurostat

Dutch/French 1978 119pp $10.10

Standardised tables showing the expenditure on fuels in individual sectors of the economy and their relative cost significance.

## 1107 JAARBOEK VAN DE OPENBARE GASVOOR-ZIENING
VEG-Gasinstituut NV

Dutch annual 238pp Fl 31.20

Yearbook of the public gas supply industry. Details of: organisations and companies; distribution areas; activities of the industry associations.

## 1108 JAARCIJFERS VOOR NEDERLAND
Centraal Bureau voor de Statistiek

Dutch (English headings)

Statistical yearbook of the Netherlands. Includes statistics on all aspects of the Dutch economy: data on the availability of oil, coal, gas and electricity and their use.

## 1109 KOMPASS HOLLAND
Kompass Nederland NV

Multi-language annual 2 vols

Directory of Dutch firms and their principal fields of activity. Includes firms engaged in the supply of energy and related goods and services. Vol 1 gives information on goods and services. Vol 2 gives basic company information.

## 1110 MAANDSTATISTIEK VAN DE BUITENLANDSE HANDEL PER GOEDERENSOORT
Centraal Bureau voor de Statistiek

Dutch (English headings) monthly c200pp Fl 122.25 p.a.

Monthly statistical bulletin of foreign trade by commodities; data on imports and exports by commodities (BTN classification) and subdivided by countries of origin and destination.

## 1111 MAANDSTATISTIEK VAN DE BUITENLANDSE HANDEL PER LAND
Centraal Bureau voor de Statistiek

Dutch (English headings) monthly c150pp Fl 71.00 p.a.

Monthly statistical bulletin of foreign trade by countries; detailed data on imports and exports subdivided by commodities, identifying energy products according to the SITC commodity classification. Also totals of storage in, and removal from, bonded warehouses by countries.

## 1112 MAANDSTATISTIEK VAN DE INDUSTRIE
Centraal Bureau voor de Statistiek

Dutch (English headings) monthly 88pp Fl 79.75 p.a.

Monthly bulletin of industrial statistics. Includes production series for crude oil, natural gas, coal, and individual fuel products, electricity production and gas supply.

## 1113 MAANDSTATISTIEK VAN HET INTER-NATIONAAL ZEEHAVENVERVOER
Centraal Bureau voor de Statistiek

Dutch (English headings) monthly

Monthly statistical bulletin of international port traffic; details of foreign trade by principal commodity groups, means of transport and port of arrival or departure.

## 1114 MAANDSTATISTIEK VAN VERKEER EN VERVOER
Centraal Bureau voor de Statistiek

Dutch (English headings) monthly Fl 74.00 p.a.

Monthly bulletin of transport statistics; data on: international goods traffic; inland shipping; international inland shipping; sea-going shipping; rail traffic; road traffic; tourist traffic.

## 1115 NATURAL GAS IN HOLLAND
NV Nederlandse Gasunie

English 1977 38pp

Information booklet on the development of natural gas as a major energy form in the Netherlands. Deals with the role of Gasunie, gas resources, natural gas in the energy supply pattern and pricing.

## 1116 NATURAL GAS IN THE NETHERLANDS—PAST, PRESENT AND FUTURE
Institution of Gas Engineers

English 1975 12pp £1.00

Paper by the commercial manager of Nederlandse Gasunie summarising the development of natural gas production and distribution in the Netherlands, the individual markets for gas and changing policies on future sales.

## 1117 DE NEDERLANDSE ENERGIEHUISHOUDING
Centraal Bureau voor de Statistiek

Dutch (English contents) quarterly

Basic energy statistics, including results of monthly and quarterly surveys on the supply and use of energy.

## 1118 NORTH SEA PROGRESS
Shell International Petroleum Co Ltd

English 1979 10pp free

Brief survey of North Sea development activity. Notes on the situation in the Dutch sector. Published in the series 'Shell Briefing Service'.

## 1119 PEB—JAARSVERSLAG
Provinciaal Electriciteitsbedrijf in Friesland

Dutch annual c70pp

Report of the electricity supply authority for Friesland. Includes details of the distribution network, generating plant, plant utilisation, fuel costs and pattern of consumer sales.

## 1120 PLEM—JAARSVERSLAG
Provinciale Limburgse Electriciteits-Mij

Dutch annual c50pp

Report of the provincial electricity supply undertaking in Limburg province. Contains detailed statistics of production and consumption and information on exchanges with other producers in Netherlands and West Germany and electricity prices.

## 1121 PZEM—JAARSVERSLAG
Provinciale Zeeuwse Energie-Mij

Dutch annual 95pp

Annual report of the electricity supply undertaking for the south-west of the Netherlands, including the main nuclear plant at Borssele. Details of electricity production and distribution in the region and of exchanges with other power suppliers in the Netherlands and in Belgium.

## 1122 RECENT AND FUTURE GAS MARKETING ASPECTS IN THE NETHERLANDS
VEG-Gasinstituut NV

Dutch 1979 21pp

Presentation by G Spee of VEG-Gasinstituut dealing with the historical development of the Dutch gas industry, its present day organisation, marketing aspects of natural gas up to the present and the impact of the changed outlook for energy and gas supply.

## 1123 ROTTERDAM
Der Hafenkurier Rotterdam

English/German annual c200pp

Yearbook and directory of the port of Rotterdam. Review of the development and activities of the port. Directory of firms involved in port activities. Index of traders, agents and brokers. Also information on: Rhine transport; road transport; Rotterdam Airport; banking and insurance facilities.

## 1124 THE ROTTERDAM OIL MARKET
Petroleum Press Bureau Ltd

English 1979 20pp

Analysis by J Roeber of the Rotterdam market, including an assessment of the trade and the relationship of bulk market prices to domestic price levels in Netherlands and other neighbouring countries.

## 1125 SHELL IN THE NETHERLANDS
Shell Nederland BV

English 1978 20pp

Information about Royal Dutch/Shell group activities in the oil, petrochemicals and natural gas industries of the Netherlands. Includes data on operations, plant and subsidiary companies.

1126 SHELL NEDERLAND RAFFINADERIJ EN SHELL
NEDERLAND CHEMIE
Shell Nederland BV

Dutch 1976 14pp

Information booklet giving background information
and details of operations and facilities at the major
refining and petrochemicals plants of the Royal
Dutch/Shell group in the Netherlands.


1127 STATISTICAL YEARBOOK OF THE
NETHERLANDS
Centraal Bureau voor de Statistiek

English annual c400pp

English version of 'Jaarcijfers voor Nederland'. Contains long-run data on the availability and disposal
of energy products and details of the pattern of
energy consumption.


1128 STATISTICS OF TRADE, INDUSTRY AND
TRAFFIC
Rotterdam Chamber of Commerce & Industry

English/Dutch/French/German annual c125pp

Contains statistical information about the industries,
trade and services connected with Europe's largest
oil port.


1129 STATISTIEK VAN DE ELEKTRICITEITS-
VOORZIENING IN NEDERLAND
Centraal Bureau voor de Statistiek

Dutch annual 36pp

Detailed statistics for electricity supply, covering:
supply undertakings, production, distribution, consumption, revenues, costs. Data analysed by province.


1130 STATISTIEK VAN DE GASVOORZIENING IN
NEDERLAND
Centraal Bureau voor de Statistiek

Dutch annual 28pp

Statistics of gas supply: total supply by type/source
of gas; structure of gas supply industry; supplies by
region and type of undertaking; main groups of
consumers; average prices; employment and earnings
in the supply industry; financial situation of the
public gas industry.


1131 STATISTIEK VAN DE KOOPVAARDIJVLOOT
Centraal Bureau voor de Statistiek

Dutch (English contents) annual c30pp

Statistics of the merchant marine; annual data on the
merchant marine of the Netherlands, its overseas
territories and the world merchant marine fleet.


1132 STATISTIEK VAN HET INTERNATIONAAL
GOEDERENVERVOER
Centraal Bureau voor de Statistiek

Dutch annual c250pp Fl 29.25

Statistics of international goods traffic; giving data on:
total transport; sea-going shipping; inland shipping;
road, rail and air transport; transit trade with transhipment. Figures for imports/exports/transit trade,
analysed by commodity, mode of transport and
country of origin/destination.


1133 STATISTIEK VAN HET INTERNATIONAAL
ZEEHAVENVERVOER
Centraal Bureau voor de Statistiek

Dutch (English contents) quarterly

Statistics of international port traffic; data on:
imports, exports, transit trade and goods loaded and
unloaded, for seaborne shipping, inland shipping,
railways, road transport, civil aviation. International
trade analysed by commodity, by port, and by
country of origin/destination.


1134 VAN OSS' EFFECTENBOEK
Uitgeverij J H de Bussy NV

Dutch annual

Handbook of stock, share and other financial information on Dutch companies. Includes company and
financial data and information on activities. Produced
as an up-dated loose-leaf file.


# Portugal


1150 ANUARIO ESTATISTICO
Instituto Nacional de Estatistica

Portuguese/French annual c440pp Esc500.00

Statistical yearbook for Portugal, Madeira and the
Azores. Contains sections dealing with energy. Data
on: production of coal and gas; output of electricity;
fuels used in power generation; value of energy produced; energy balances; employment.


1151 BOLETIM MENSAL DA ESTATISTICA
Instituto Nacional de Estatistica

Portuguese/French monthly 70pp Esc800.00 p.a.

Monthly bulletin of statistics, including coal production, output of refined products, electricity production by region.

**1152 BOLETIM MENSAL DAS ESTATISTICAS DO COMERCIO EXTERNO**
Instituto Nacional de Estatistica

Portuguese/French monthly c40pp Esc400.00 p.a.

Monthly bulletin of statistics, including data on primary energy and electricity, coal production, output of refined products, electricity production by region.

**1153 BOLETIM MENSAL DAS ESTATISTICAS INDUSTRIAIS**
Instituto Nacional de Estatistica

Portuguese/French monthly 100pp Esc800.00 p.a.

Monthly bulletin of industrial statistics, including indicators for output, employment and prices. Includes section on energy, covering: production of coal, petroleum products, gas and electricity; consumption of electricity by industrial sector; consumption of gas by sector.

**1154 ESTATISTICA DAS INSTALAÇÕES ELECTRICAS EM PORTUGAL**
Direcção-Geral dos Serviços Electricos

Portuguese annual

Annual statistics of electrical plant in Portugal. Details of location, capacity and fuel type.

**1155 ESTATISTICAS DA ENERGIA**
Instituto Nacional de Estatistica

Portuguese/French annual c100pp Esc140.00

Commentary on the energy sector. Statistics on: production, consumption and labour in the power industries; revenue and investment; production of primary and secondary power; consumption of fuels by sector.

**1156 ESTATISTICAS DO COMERCIO EXTERNO**
Instituto Nacional de Estatistica

Portuguese/French annual 640pp Esc500.00

Statistics of foreign trade including imports and exports of solid and liquid fuels. Tables of imports and exports arranged by commodities, subdivided by countries of origin and destination. Tables of imports and exports and transit trade arranged by countries of origin and destination, subdivided by commodities.

**1157 ESTATISTICAS INDUSTRIAIS**
Instituto Nacional de Estatistica

Portuguese/French annual 2 vols

Results of the annual survey of industry. Statistics on: establishments; output volume and value; cost of materials; fuels used; employment, wages and hours of work; value added; fixed capital; stocks; some analysis by region. Vol 1 covers extractive industries, electricity, gas and water: Vol 2 manufacturing industries, including data on energy consumption by industry.

**1158 PETROGAL**
Petroleos de Portugal

English 1979 20pp

Information brochure on the state oil company. Background to the setting up of the company. Details of organisation, operations and facilities.

**1159 PETROGAL—ANNUAL REPORT**
Petroleos de Portugal

English annual 46pp

English edition of the annual report of the state oil company. Contains a brief review of the economy and the oil sector and details of the company's operations.

# Spain

**1175 ANUARIO DE ENERGIA**
Ingeniera Quimica SA

Spanish annual 520pp

Energy yearbook of Spain including statistics, analysis and commentary. Detailed figures for consumption of primary fuels, reserves and production. Long-run data on individual provinces and locations.

**1176 ANUARIO DEL MERCADO ESPAÑOL**
Banco Español de Credito

Spanish 1979 720pp

Statistics on all aspects of the Spanish economy with numerous socio-economic series for individual provinces. Includes data on consumption of individual fuels and consumption per head.

**1177 ANUARIO ESTADISTICO DE ESPAÑA (EDICION MANUAL)**
Instituto Nacional de Estadistica

Spanish annual c300pp

Pocket edition of the statistical yearbook for Spain. Coverage is similar but with less detail.

**1178 ANUARIO ESTADISTICO DE ESPAÑA (EDICION NORMAL)**
Instituto Nacional de Estadistica

Spanish annual c800pp

Statistical yearbook of Spain. Data relating to the energy sector include: production of coal and individual oil products; consumption of electricity and energy by sector; foreign trade in fuels; employment in the energy sector.

**1179 BOLETIN INFORMATIVO**
Hidroelectrica de Cataluña SA

Spanish half-yearly c10pp

Regular review of the electricity situation and activities of the Catalonian electricity company.

**1180 CHEMFACTS SPAIN**
IPC Industrial Press Ltd

English 1978 £40.00

Analysis of market trends, plant capacity and investment, trade in individual chemicals and profiles of leading companies.

**1181 COMERCIO POR ADUANAS Y TRAFICO DE PERFECCIONAMIENTO EN NDB**
Direccion General de Aduanas

Spanish annual Ptas500

Statistics of foreign trade, including commodities for further processing or re-export, classified according to Brussels tariff nomenclature.

**1182 COMERCIO POR PRODUCTOS Y POR PAISES EN CUCI**
Direccion General de Aduanas

Spanish annual c100pp Ptas500

Statistics of the foreign trade of Spain; trade by commodities under the SITC classification, subdivided by countries of origin/destination.

**1183 COMERCIO POR PRODUCTOS Y POR PAISES EN NDB**
Direccion General de Aduanas

Spanish quarterly c1,000pp

Statistics of foreign trade, identifying energy products, according to Brussels tariff headings, subdivided by countries of origin/destination. Figures for the quarter and cumulatively for the year. Issues for first three quarters Ptas 500 per issue. Fourth quarter issue Ptas 1,000.

**1184 EFECTOS DIRECTOS DE UNA MORATORIA NUCLEAR EN ESPAÑA**
Forum Atomico Español

Spanish 1979 146pp

Detailed study of the implications of proposals of the national energy programme and alternative patterns of energy supply with various levels of use of nuclear power. Evaluation of the requirements for equipment, investment and other resources in the event of a cessation of nuclear construction work.

**1185 EL CICLO DEL COMBUSTIBLE NUCLEAR**
Forum Atomico Español

Spanish 1979 521pp

Detailed survey and analysis of the use of nuclear power both in Spain and abroad. Considers the Spanish energy situation and gives information on activities in Spain of industries involved in nuclear power developments.

**1186 ENCICLOPEDIA NACIONAL DEL PETROLEO PETROLQUIMICA Y GAS**
Club Español del Petroleo

Spanish annual

Handbook of information and statistics about the Spanish oil, gas and petrochemicals industries. Published as an annual in conjunction with the CEP's monthly journal 'Oilgas'.

**1187 ESTADISTICA INDUSTRIAL DE ESPAÑA**
Instituto Nacional de Estadistica

Spanish annual c700pp

Annual statistical review of Spanish industries. Details of: output; turnover; value added; employment; energy consumption; production costs; wages; hours of work; numbers of establishments; size-structure.

**1188 ESTADISTICAS DE PRODUCCION INDUSTRIAL**
Instituto Nacional de Estadistica

Spanish annual c900pp

Annual review of industry, containing statistics on: establishments; employment; material costs; output; turnover; value added. Analysis by individual sector, by region and by size of establishment.

**1189 ESTADISTICAS DE PRODUCCION INDUSTRIAL: INFORMACION MENSUAL**
Instituto Nacional de Estadistica

Spanish monthly c50pp

Monthly bulletin of statistics on output, employment, wages and hours of work in the principal industrial sectors. Includes basic series for energy production and supply.

## 1190 GAS 79
Sedigas SA

Spanish 1979 222pp

Annual review of the Spanish gas industry association. Contains information on gas undertakings, the development of gas in Spain and notes of Sedigas activities. Articles include numerous statistics on energy in Spain and on the gas sector.

## 1191 HISPANOIL—ANNUAL REPORT
Hispanoil

English annual 60pp

Annual report of the state-owned oil exploration and production company. Contains information about the activities of Hispanoil in securing supplies of crude oil for Spanish refiners and details of overseas exploration and development activity.

## 1192 INFORME ANUAL
Banco de Bilbao

Spanish annual 380pp

Detailed review of the Spanish economy for the past year. Includes statistics and comment on energy production, consumption and trade and figures for the balance of payments relating to energy.

## 1193 KOMPASS ESPAÑA
Kompass España SA

Multi-language annual 2 vols

Directory of Spanish firms and their principal fields of activity. Includes many concerns engaged in the supply of energy or related goods and services. Vol 1 gives information on goods and services. Vol 2 gives basic company information.

## 1194 LAS 1500 MAYORES EMPRESAS ESPAÑOLAS
Fomento de la Produccion

Spanish 1978 304pp

Comparative financial and economic data on the 1,500 largest Spanish companies. Includes many key energy enterprises. Data cover: turnover, profits, value added and employment.

## 1195 MEMORIA ASAMBLEA TECNICA DE GAS 1978
Sedigas SA

Spanish 1979

Proceedings of the 1978 annual gas conference, including papers dealing with: energy conservation in industry; natural gas in the national energy balance; marketing gas in the commercial sector; the future of towns gas.

## 1196 MEMORIA ESTADISTICA ELECTRICA
Unidad Electrica SA

Spanish/English annual 56pp

Annual statistics of the electricity supply industry prepared by the producers' association. Review of the energy situation in Spain and statistics of: production and consumption by region; plant capacity, new plant and types of plant; long-run series for electricity output; investment by the industry; average electricity prices.

## 1197 OILGAS
Club Español del Petroleo

Spanish monthly Ptas1,200 p.a.

Journal of the oil industry association in Spain. Contains news of developments affecting the industry of an economic, legislative or technical nature and longer articles on technico-economic subjects.

## 1198 PETROLIBER—MEMORIA
Compania Iberica Refinadora de Petroleos SA

Spanish annual 16pp

Annual report of the operating company of the Corunna refinery. Includes a brief general review with statistics, of the oil sector in Spain in the previous year and details of crude oils used and products manufactured at the refinery.

## 1199 TRAFICO MARITIMO COMERCIO POR VIAS DE TRANSPORTE
Direccion General de Aduanas

Spanish annual c950pp Ptas500

Annual presentation of foreign trade statistics according to point of entry/departure and by mode of transport, sub-divided by country of origin/destination.

# Switzerland

## 1200 ANNUAIRE STATISTIQUE DE LA SUISSE
Bureau Fédéral de Statistique

French/German annual c700pp

Statistical yearbook of Switzerland. Includes long-run data on electricity consumption by main sectors and production by energy source. Statistics of refinery output. Energy consumption pattern. Oil and gas pipeline movements. Price indices for fuels.

1201 ATEL—GESCHÄFTSBERICHT
Aare-Tessin AG für Elektrizität

German annual 32pp

Annual report by a leading Swiss electricity producing company, containing information about demand and supply situation for electricity and data on several major plants including nuclear power stations in which ATEL has interests.

1202 BULLETIN SEV/VSE
Schweizerischer Elektrotechnischer Verein

German/French fortnightly c50pp SwF60.00 p.a.

Information bulletin of the Swiss electro-technical association and the association of power station operators. Includes articles of a technical and technico-economic nature. Alternate issues include 'Elektrizitätswirtschaft', containing statistical section covering energy supply and consumption in Switzerland.

1203 DIE ELEKTRIZITÄT
Verband Schweizerischer Elektrizitätswerke

German/French/Italian quarterly 36pp

Journal of the electricity supply companies, covering a wide range of matters of general interest in the field of electricity: use of electricity in households; rational use of electricity; general and special applications of electricity.

1204 ELEKTRIZITÄTSVERWERTUNG
Verband Schweizerischer Elektrizitätswerke

German/English/French 10 issues p.a.
SwF57.00 p.a.

Periodical concerned with applications of electricity, containing articles and news of a technico-economic nature.

1205 ENERGIE—KERNENERGIE
Verband Schweizerischer Elektrizitätswerke

German/French 1976 48pp SwF3.00

General information booklet on the Swiss energy situation and the prospective need to develop nuclear power in order to meet electricity demand.

1206 ERDÖL-VEREINIGUNG—GESCHÄFTSBERICHT
Erdöl-Vereinigung

German/French annual 50pp

Annual review of the oil industry in Switzerland, development of the general oil situation; balance of supply and disposal; product markets; prices; import/export movements; refining; transportation; taxation; exploration; marketing.

1207 GAS WASSER ABWASSER
Schweizerischer Verein von Gas- und Wasserfachmännern

German/French monthly 50pp SwF70.00 p.a.

Reports on activities of the Verein and other official bodies, policies and measures affecting the gas industry, recent statistics on gas supply and consumption, and developments in the industry.

1208 INFORMATIONSBLÄTTER
Verband Schweizerischer Elektrizitätswerke

German/French irregular SwF0.20 each

Series of information sheets issued irregularly. Subjects covered include: heat pumps, electric space heating, insulation, tariffs, heat recovery, economies in lighting, refrigeration.

1209 KOMPASS SCHWEIZ/SUISSE
Editions Kompass Suisse SA

Multi-language annual 2 vols

Directory of Swiss firms and their principal fields of activity. Includes many firms involved in the supply of energy and related goods and services. Vol 1 gives information on products and services. Vol 2 gives basic company information.

1210 NUCLEAR NEWSLETTER FROM SWITZERLAND
Schweizerische Vereinigung für Atomenergie

English quarterly 10pp free

Short articles of current interest concerning nuclear power in Switzerland: power station operations; new developments; political initiatives. Also information on equipment and contracts of Swiss nuclear engineering firms.

1211 DIE SCHWEIZERISCHE ELEKTRIZITÄTS-WIRTSCHAFT UND DER AUSTAUSCH ELEKTRISCHER ENERGIE
Vereinigung Exportierender Elektrizitätsunternehmungen

German/French/Italian 1978 27pp SwF3.00

Analysis and comment on the practice and importance of power exchanges between Switzerland and neighbouring countries.

1212 LES SERVICES INDUSTRIELS DE GENEVE
Services Industriels de Genève

French 1975 48pp

Booklet of information about the supply of oil, gas and water to Geneva. Historical development of the municipal utility, with data on plant and facilities, customer markets and sales.

**1213 STATISTIQUE ANNUELLE DU COMMERCE EXTERIEUR DE LA SUISSE**
Direction Générale des Douanes

French/German annual 3 vols

Annual statistics of foreign trade. Vol 1: imports/exports of commodities under the Swiss tariff headings sub-divided by country of origin/destination; aggregate figures for value of trade for each country or commodity. Vol 2: imports/exports listed by country, sub-divided by commodity under BTN headings; Vol 3: data on transit/trade, customs revenue, rates of duty.

**1214 STATISTIQUE DU COMMERCE EXTERIEUR DE LA SUISSE: COMMENTAIRES ANNUELS**
Direction Générale des Douanes

French/German annual 2 vols

Annual commentary on foreign trade statistics. Vol 1 groups products according to country of origin/destination. Vol 2 is classified by product.

**1215 STATISTIQUE SUISSE DE L'ELECTRICITE**
Verband Schweizerischer Elektrizitätswerke

French/German annual 45pp SwF7.00

Official statistics of electricity for the past hydrological year: production capacity, output and consumption data.

**1216 STROM-TATSACHEN**
Verband Schweizerischer Elektrizitätswerke

German/French/Italian annual 20pp SwF0.20

Booklet containing basic data on energy supply and demand in Switzerland with details of the electricity supply industry and main sectors of consumption. Breakdown of electricity supply by types of plant.

**1217 SVA—JAHRESBERICHT**
Schweizerische Vereinigung für Atomenergie

German/French annual 40pp

Annual review of the activities of the Swiss atomic energy association. Includes notes on developments in the energy economy relating to nuclear power, information about other organisations and agencies concerned with nuclear power and official measures and policies.

**1218 SWISS ATOMIC YEARBOOK**
Schweizerische Vereinigung für Atomenergie

English/French/German annual 120pp SwF15.00

Directory and handbook of organisations and firms involved in the nuclear power industry. Details of Swiss nuclear installations. Notes on official agencies, legal framework of nuclear power. Directory of suppliers of equipment.

**1219 VEREINIGUNG EXPORTIERENDER ELEKTRIZITÄTSUNTERNEHMUNGEN— JAHRESBERICHT**
Vereinigung Exportierender Elektrizitätsunternehmungen

German annual 30pp

Annual report of the association of electricity exporters. Includes a review of electricity production and details of cross-border movements. Much data on exchanges is presented in graphic form.

**1220 LA VIE ECONOMIQUE**
Département Fédéral de l'Economie Publique

French monthly 90pp

Regular bulletin and review of the Swiss economy. Includes statistical series for quantity and value of foreign trade in coal and oil and prices or price indices for coal, coke and main oil products.

**1221 VSE—GESCHAFTSBERICHT**
Verband Schweizerischer Elektrizitätswerke

German annual 28pp free

Review of the Swiss electricity industry. Analysis of the energy balance and developments in supply and consumption. Detailed statistics of electricity production, new plant projects, cross-border exchanges and the transmission network.

# West Germany

**1250 ARBEITSBERICHT**
Vereinigung Deutscher Elektrizitätswerke eV

German annual 80pp

Annual report of the association of electricity supply undertakings. Includes a survey of all aspects of electricity supply: energy supply and demand pattern; political measures and initiatives; power station projects; investment, costs and prices.

**1251 ATOM UND STROM**
Verlags- und Wirtschaftsgesellschaft der Elektrizitätswerke mbH

German bi-monthly DM70.00 p.a.

Periodical of the association of electricity producers dealing with nuclear power and its role in overall electricity supply systems.

**1252 AUSFUHR DER BRD AN KOHLEN UND KOKS**
Statistisches Bundesamt

German monthly 2pp

Basic statistics of coal and coke exports. Data given in terms of tonnage and value for individual grades of coal and coke.

**1253 AUSSENHANDEL**
Statistisches Bundesamt

German 7 series

Regular official statistics of foreign trade; comprising the following series: 1 General summary (monthly and annual). 2 Imports and exports classified by commodities and subdivided by countries (monthly). 3 Imports and exports by countries subdivided by commodity groups (quarterly). 4 Imports and exports of selected commodities. 5 Imports and exports for selected countries. 6 Transit trade. 7 Imports and exports classified by industry sector.

**1254 BERGBAU-ELEKTRIZITÄTS-VERBUNDGEMEINSCHAFT—JAHRESBERICHT**
Bergbau-Elektrizitäts-Verbundgemeinschaft

German annual 10pp

Annual statistical publication of the association of coal producing electricity companies. Includes data on capacity and production.

**1255 BGW—JAHRESBERICHT**
Bundesverband der Deutschen Gas- und Wasserwirtschaft eV

German annual c80pp

Report of the gas and water supply industries' association. Includes statistical section covering: supply of manufactured gas by type and source; consumption of gas; investment by gas undertakings.

**1256 BGW SCHRIFTENREIHE**
Verlag R Oldenbourg

German

Series of occasional publications by the Bundesverband der Deutschen Gas- und Wasserwirtschaft (BGW), including an annual review of the German gas industry, dealing with topical subjects such as the use of energy, coal gasification and other economic, technical and regulatory questions.

**1257 BLICKPUNKT BRAUNKOHLE**
Rheinische Braunkohlenwerke AG

German 41pp

Information booklet on brown coal production activities in the Rhineland, dealing with production, disposal and related economic and environmental issues.

**1258 BRAUNKOHLE**
Verlag Die Braunkohle

German monthly c40pp DM168.00 p.a.

Journal carrying articles of an economic and technical nature concerning the development of West German coal resources and including some statistics of the industry.

**1259 BRENNSTOFFSPIEGEL**
Ceto-Verlag GmbH

German monthly DM42.00 p.a.

Periodical for fuel distributors carrying news of oil and solid fuel markets and current consumption statistics.

**1260 CHEMFACTS FEDERAL REPUBLIC OF GERMANY**
IPC Industrial Press Ltd

English 1976 £35.00

Analysis of market trends, plant capacity and investment; trade in individual chemicals and profiles of the leading companies.

**1261 DEMINEX—ACTIVITY REPORT**
DEMINEX

English annual 24pp

Annual review of the activities of the German exploration consortium, including developments in the North Sea and background information on the DEMINEX group.

**1262 DEUTSCHE VERBUNDGESELLSCHAFT—BERICHT**
Deutsche Verbundgesellschaft

German annual 26pp

Annual report of the organisation of major electricity supply undertakings. Survey of electricity supply in the previous year. Basic data on generation capacity and the transmission network.

**1263 DEUTSCHES SCHIFFAHRT UND HAFEN JAHRBUCH**
Schiffahrts-Verlag 'Hansa'

German annual 550pp

Directory of organisations and institutions in shipping. Index of shipowners. Details of ports (including main Dutch ports). Foreign section with international maritime information.

**1264 EINFUHR DER BRD AN KOHLEN UND KOKS**
Statistisches Bundesamt

German monthly 2pp

Basic statistics of coal and coke imports into West Germany. Figures for tonnage and value of imports by grade of fuel.

### 1265 EIN- UND AUSFUHR VON MINERALÖL
Statistisches Bundesamt

German monthly 44pp DM6.00 per issue

Import and export statistics for oil products. Figures for volume and value for the latest month and cumulatively for the year. Reihe 4.1 of the Fachserie 7 (Aussenhandel).

### 1266 ELEKTRIZITÄT 19—
Vereinigung Deutscher Elektrizitätswerke eV

German annual 8pp

Brief commentary and basic statistics of electricity supply in the past year, including fuels used, plant capacity by type, electricity and energy consumption.

### 1267 ELEKTRIZITÄTSWIRTSCHAFT
Verlags- und Wirtschaftsgesellschaft der Elektrizitätswerke mbH

German fortnightly DM275.00 p.a.

Journal of the electricity producers' association carrying general, economic and technical news of the industry. Subscription includes the bi-monthly publication 'Atom und Strom', concerned with nuclear power development.

### 1268 DIE ELEKTRIZITÄTSWIRTSCHAFT IN DER BUNDESREPUBLIK DEUTSCHLAND
Bundes Ministerium für Wirtschaft

German annual 40pp

Statistical yearbook of the electricity industry. Details of the use of electricity in individual sectors of the economy; fuels used; investment in electricity production and distribution; statistics on combined heat and power systems. Data given on a monthly basis and for individual Lander.

### 1269 ELEKTRIZITÄTSWIRTSCHAFT ZUM ENERGIEPROGRAMM
Vereinigung Deutscher Elektrizitätswerke eV

German 1978 15pp

Statement of the VDEW's position with regard to the second continuation of the government's energy programme for the period 1977-80, including comment on the nuclear power programme, the role of coal, energy conservation, district heating and pricing.

### 1270 ENERGIEPROGRAMM DER BUNDESREGIERUNG
Bundesministerium für Wirtschaft

German 1977 64pp

Review of the existing energy programme 1973-77 and presentation of the new programme for 1977-80. Survey of the energy supply and demand position and projected forward energy requirements. Contains many statistics including long-run data in graphic form.

### 1271 ENERGY RESEARCH AND ENERGY TECHNOLOGIES PROGRAM 1977-80
Bundesministerium für Forschung und Technologie

English 1977 172pp

Details of the government's research and development programme in the energy field. Chapters on: basic principles and objectives; initial situation in energy policy, research programmes, technology and organisational structure; efficient uses of energy; coal and other fossil sources; new sources of energy; nuclear energy; systems analyses; programme implementation; international co-operation; legislative basis.

### 1272 DIE ENTWICKLUNG DER ELEKTRIZITÄTSWIRTSCHAFT IN DER BRD IM JAHRE—
Deutsche Verbundgesellschaft

German annual 235pp

Comprehensive review of the electricity sector in the past year, with detailed statistics of production, transmission and consumption.

### 1273 DIE ENTWICKLUNG DER GASWIRTSCHAFT IN DER BUNDESREPUBLIK DEUTSCHLAND
Verlag R Oldenbourg

German annual

General review of the gas industry. Details of: gas supply and consumption by type of gas; exploration; investment; employment; prices, analysed by region. Published in the series 'BGW Schriftenreihe'.

### 1274 ERDOEL ERDGAS ZEITSCHRIFT
Urban-Verlag GmbH

German (English summary) monthly c40pp DM130.00 p.a.

Journal of the Deutsche Vereinigung der Erdölgeologen und Erdölingenieure, the Fachverband der Erdölindustrie and the Österreichische Gesellschaft fur Erdölwissenschaften. Contains news and articles of a technico-economic nature on the oil and gas industries and information about general developments, including statistics.

### 1275 ERDOEL INFORMATIONS DIENST
A H Stahmer

German weekly c8pp

News and information service reporting on developments in the West German oil and gas market. Includes basic statistics of reserves, production, refining, consumption, stocks and some price information. Also summaries of company annual reports.

**1276 ERDOEL UND KOHLE ERDGAS PETROCHEMIE**
DGMK

German (English summaries) monthly c50pp
DM158.40 p.a.

Journal carrying technico-economic news and articles
on the oil and gas industries, including basic energy
statistics. Deals with energy in West Germany and its
international context.

**1277 EUROP OIL-TELEGRAM**
Oil-Telegram GmbH

German twice weekly c10pp DM380.00 p.a.

News information service on developments in the
West German oil market. Reports on West German
companies, statistics of production and consumption
and regular market prices series.

**1278 GAS ERDGAS**
Verlag R Oldenbourg

German monthly 110pp DM186.00 p.a.

Journal of the Deutscher Verein des Gas- und Wasser-
faches (DVGW), the Bundesverband der Deutschen
Gas- und Wasserwirtschaft (BGE) and the Technische
Vereinigung der Firmen im Gas- und Wasserfach
(FIGAWA). Carries news of the gas industry and
articles on economic, general and technical topics.

**1279 GAS VERWENDUNG**
ZfGW-Verlag GmbH

German monthly c70pp DM53.00 p.a.

Journal dealing with aspects of distribution and
markets for gas, and including information about
environmental factors in marketing/consumption.

**1280 GERMAN OIL INFORMATION SERVICE**
A H Stahmer

English fortnightly c10pp

English edition of selected items of news and
statistics which have appeared in 'Erdoel Informations
Dienst'.

**1281 GESAMTVERBAND DES DEUTSCHEN
STEINKOHLEN- BERGBAUS—JAHRESBERICHT**
Gesamtverband des Deutschen Steinkohlenbergbaus

German annual c85pp

Annual report of the association of German hard coal
producers. Contains a review of the West German
energy situation and statistics for the coal industry,
including some long-run series. Data covers employment, investment and productivity.

**1282 GLÜCKAUF**
Verlag Glückauf GmbH

German/English DM162.00 p.a.

Journal carrying economic and technical articles on
mining, current statistics and news. An additional
English translation is available at a total cost of
DM 396.00 p.a.

**1283 DIE GROSSE 500**
Hermann Luchterhand Verlag

German loose-leaf

Continuously up-dated survey and analysis of leading
German enterprises. Includes numerous key concerns
in the supply and distribution of coal, oil, gas and
electricity. Data cover: turnover, employment,
output and balance sheet figures for recent years.

**1284 HANDBUCH DER DEUTSCHEN
AKTIENGESELLSCHAFTEN**
Verlag Hoppenstedt & Co

German annual loose-leaf

Up-dated file on German companies with analysis
of recent results. Details of companies include:
directors; historical development; activities; products;
shareholdings; contractual arrangements; capital
structure; dividends; financial performance; salient
points of the latest year's activity.

**1285 INPUT-OUTPUT TABLES—BR DEUTSCHLAND
1970**
Eurostat

German/French 1978 124pp $10.10

Standardised tables showing the expenditure on fuels
in individual sectors of the economy and their relative
cost significance.

**1286 JAHRBUCH FUR BERGBAU, ENERGIE
MINERALÖL UND CHEMIE**
Verlag Glückauf GmbH

German annual c1,100pp

Guide to firms, agencies and associations in the
mining, energy, oil and chemicals sectors. Includes
organisational, administrative and operations information.

**1287 KOHLE UND HEIZOEL**
Verlag Dr Hoffmann KG

German monthly 28pp DM4.00 per issue

Commentary on the West German energy situation
and its international context. Includes articles and
statistical analysis.

**1288 KOMPASS DEUTSCHLAND**
Kompass Deutschland Verlags- und
Vertriebsgesellschaft mbH

Multi-language annual 2 vols

Directory of German firms and their principal fields
of activity. Includes many firms engaged in the
supply of energy and related goods and services.
Vol 1 gives information on goods and services. Vol 2
gives basic company information.

**1289 LANGFRISTIGE VORSCHAU ÜBER
LEISTUNGSBEDARF UND DECKUNG 1977-90**
Deutsche Verbundgesellschaft

German 1978

Estimates the demands for electricity from the public
supply system in the period to 1990 and the implications in terms of plant and investment.

**1290 MINERALOELRUNDSCHAU**
UNITI

German monthly DM26.00 p.a.

Bulletin of the association of independent oil companies, reporting on developments in bulk supply
markets, oil product markets and official regulations
and standards.

**1291 MINERALÖL—ZAHLEN**
MWV-AEV

German annual 68pp

Detailed statistics of the oil industry, produced by
the main industry associations. Statistics cover:
refining capacity, imports/exports, production, consumption by sector. Many series analysed by province.

**1292 OEL**
Oel Verlag GmbH

German (English/French summaries) monthly
c50pp DM101.00 p.a.

Journal carrying articles of an economic and technical nature about the West German oil industry.
Also includes basic current statistics and general
energy news items.

**1293 DIE OFFENTLICHE ELEKTRIZITÄTS-
VERSORGUNG**
Verlags- und Wirtschaftsgesellschaft der
Elektrizitätswerke mbH

German annual c50pp

Comprehensive annual review of the West German
electricity supply industry. Commentary and statistics in detail on: primary energy, electricity supply;
financial performance of electricity producers; power
plant; district heating; output and utilisation; the
high-tension grid; fuels used in generation; electricity
consumption; energy conservation.

**1294 PREISE**
Statistisches Bundesamt

German 10 series

Regular official statistics on prices. Series are: 1 Prices
and price indices for agriculture and forestry. 2 Prices
and price indices for industrial products. 3 Index of
raw material prices. 4 Price indicators for building
and construction. 5 Prices for building land. 6 Index
of wholesale prices. 7 Prices and price indices for
the cost of living. 8 Prices and price indices for
imports and exports. 9 Transport prices. 10 International comparisons of the cost-of-living. Several
series include data on energy prices.

**1295 PRODUZIERENDES GEWERBE**
Statistisches Bundesamt

German 8 series

Regular official statistics on industry in the following
series: 1 Summary data. 2 Indices for production
industries. 3 Output. 4 Mining and processing industries. 5 Construction. 6 Energy and water supply.
7 Handicrafts. 8 Iron, steel, chemicals and timber
industries. Several series include data on energy
industries and consumers.

**1296 RHEINISCHE BRAUNKOHLENWERKE—
GESCHÄFTSBERICHT**
Rheinische Braunkohlenwerke AG

German annual

Annual report of the principal West German producer
of brown coal. Includes details of production,
collieries and employment. Review of the coal sector
and coal as a fuel for electricity generation.

**1297 RUHRKOHLE—GESCHÄFTSBERICHT**
Ruhrkohle AG

German annual

Annual report of the leading West German hard coal
producing company. Review of the coal market and
general economic situation in West Germany. Details
of mining operations in the Ruhr area, including
output in individual mines, employment, coke production, disposals of coal and coke.

**1298 RWE—ANNUAL REPORT**
Rheinisch-Westfälisches Elektrizitätswerk AG

English/German annual 68pp

Annual report of West Germany's major electricity
supplier. Includes a general review of the West
German energy situation and aspects of electricity
production and supply. Statistics of production,
transmission and consumption.

**1299 SALING AKTIENFÜHRER**
Verlag Hoppenstedt & Co

German (English index) annual 1,100pp

Guide to companies quoted on German stock exchanges. Includes leading energy companies. Information on financial structure, operations, holdings and balance sheet analysis.


**1300 SICHERHEIT DER STROMVERSORGUNG HAT VORRANG**
Verlags- und Wirtschaftsgesellschaft der Elektrizitätswerke mbH

German 1979 24pp DM1.20

Statement by the chairman of VDEW, giving an analysis of the energy supply position facing West Germany and affirming the need for continued development of nuclear power and coal-fired plant. Addresses the issues of the environment and costs.


**1301 STATISTISCHES JAHRBUCH FÜR DIE BUNDESREPUBLIK DEUTSCHLAND**
Statistisches Bundesamt

German annual c750pp

Contains ections on mining and energy supply industries. Statistics cover: turnover, employment, investment, cost-structure and output value of energy undertakings: supply and demand for individual products: price indices.


**1302 STROM FÜR BAYERN**
Bayernwerk AG

German 1979 32pp

Information book about the operations of Bayernwerk. Describes electricity and heat generation plant, the transmission network and principal consuming sectors.


**1303 STROM UND WÄRME FUR BERLIN**
Berliner Kraft- und Licht AG

German 1979 60pp

Historical development of Berliner Kraft- und Licht AG (BEWAG) with details of all major electricity and heating plant in West Berlin. Information and data on consumption of electricity and other aspects of BEWAG's operations.


**1304 STROMERZEUGUNGSANLAGEN**
Statistisches Bundesamt

German annual 28pp DM3.50

Statistical data on electricity plant in the mining and processing industries: capacity and production of electricity supply undertakings, mining companies, oil refining, petrochemical and other processing industries; federal railways. Data analysed by consuming sector, by fuel type and by province. Reihe 6.4 of the main Fachserie 4.


**1305 STROMPRAXIS**
Hauptberatungsstelle für Elektrizitätsanwendung eV

German bi-monthly 30pp DM25.00 p.a.

Periodical of the advice centre for electricity utilisation, dealing with the range of uses of electricity and its efficient utilisation.


**1306 USEFUL ENERGY BALANCE SHEETS**
Eurostat

English/French/German 1978 38pp

Explains the structure and composition of balance sheets of useful energy and gives a statistical analysis of the West German and French energy economies in 1975.


**1307 VEBA OEL AG—ANNUAL REPORT**
Veba Oel AG

English annual 70pp

English edition of the annual report of the principal West German oil company. Includes general information about the oil and petrochemicals markets in West Germany, availability of crude oil to the group and data on activities of group companies in exploration/production, transport and storage, processing and distribution.


**1308 VEREIN DEUTSCHER KOHLENIMPORTEURE— JAHRESBERICHT**
Verein Deutscher Kohlenimporteure

German annual 140pp

Annual report of the association of German coalimporters. Contains detailed review of the West German hard coal trade: production, consumption, imports and exports by principal company and by region. Details of electricity generating plant and electricity supply.


**1309 VERKEHR**
Statistisches Bundesamt

German 6 series

Regular official statistics on transport. Monthly and annual publications of statistics in the following series: 1 Goods traffic by mode. 2 Railway traffic. 3 Road traffic. 4 Inland shipping. 5 Seaborne shipping. 6 Air transport.

**1310 WEG—JAHRESBERICHT**
Wirtschaftsverband Erdöl- und Erdgasgewinnung eV

German annual c80pp

Annual report of the industry association for oil and gas producers. Brief commentary. Statistics on: oil and gas production and reserves by field by province and by producing company; drilling and exploration activity; operations of German companies abroad.

**1311 ZAHLEN DER KOHLENWIRTSCHAFT**
Verlag Glückauf GmbH

German annual 104pp

Compendium of statistics of the West German coal industry covering production, consumption and foreign trade. Includes data on individual mines and companies, long-run statistical series and analyses by province.

# Indexes to Publications

# Index 1: Publications A-Z

# C

# D

# E

# Index 2: Publications by Subject and Country

## 2.2 GENERAL ENERGY STATISTICS

## 2.3 ENERGY TRADE

### INTERNATIONAL

### AUSTRIA

### BELGIUM

## 2.4 ENERGY MARKET ANALYSES

### INTERNATIONAL

## 2.5 ENERGY POLICIES

### INTERNATIONAL

### FRANCE

### IRELAND

### NETHERLANDS

## 2.6 ENERGY INDUSTRIES

### 2.6.1. OIL *(See Also 2.7)*

## 2.6.2. COAL

### INTERNATIONAL

### AUSTRIA

### BELGIUM

### FRANCE

### GREECE

### SWEDEN

### UNITED KINGDOM

### WEST GERMANY

## 2.6.3. GAS *(See Also 2.7)*

### INTERNATIONAL

## 2.6.4. ELECTRICITY SUPPLY

### INTERNATIONAL

### AUSTRIA

### BELGIUM

### DENMARK

### FINLAND

### FRANCE

### GREECE

### IRELAND

### ITALY

### NETHERLANDS

### NORWAY

### PORTUGAL

## 2.6.5. NUCLEAR POWER

## 2.6.6. ENERGY-RELATED INDUSTRIES

### INTERNATIONAL

### BELGIUM

### FRANCE

### ITALY

### NETHERLANDS

### SPAIN

### SWITZERLAND

### UNITED KINGDOM

### WEST GERMANY

## 2.7 OFFSHORE EXPLORATION AND DEVELOPMENT

### INTERNATIONAL

# 2.8 CONSERVATION/UTILISATION

## INTERNATIONAL

## 2.9 NEW ENERGY TECHNOLOGIES

### INTERNATIONAL

## 2.10 ENERGY AND ENVIRONMENT

### INTERNATIONAL

### IRELAND

### SWEDEN

### UNITED KINGDOM

# Index 3: Publishing Bodies and Addresses

## A

**AARE-TESSIN AG FÜR ELETRIZITÄT**
Bahnhofquai 12
CH-4600 Olten
Switzerland
Tel: (062) 21 61 51

Entry: 1201

**ADMINISTRATION DE L'ENERGIE**
30 Rue de Mot
B-1040 Bruxelles
Belgium
Tel: (02) 233 61 11

Entries: 854  858  876  884  885

**ADMINISTRATION DES MINES**
30 Rue de Mot
B-1040 Bruxelles
Belgium
Tel: (02) 233 61 11

Entries: 857  882

**AGENCE POUR LES ECONOMIES D'ENERGIE**
30 Rue Cambronne
F-75737 Paris Cedex 15
France
Tel: (1) 578 61 94

Entries: 913  937

**AGIP SPA**
San Donato Milanese
20097 Milano
Italy
Tel: (02) 53 53 60 74

Entries: 001  1026

**AMCOAL**
44 Main Street
Johannesburg
South Africa

Entry: 003

**AMERICAN ENTERPRISE INSTITUTE FOR PUBLIC POLICY**
1150 17th Street NW
Washington DC
USA
Tel: (202) 862 5800

Entry: 068

**APPLIED SCIENCE PUBLISHERS**
22 Rippleside Commercial Estate
Barking IG11 0SA
England
Tel: (01) 595 2121

Entries: 072  178

**THE ARAB PETROLEUM RESEARCH CENTER**
7 Avenue Ingrès
F-75781 Paris
France
Tel: (1) 524 33 10

Entries: 013  014

**ASSOCIATED OCTEL LTD**
20 Berkeley Square
London W1
England
Tel: (01) 499 6030

Entry: 286

**ASSOCIATION ROYALE DES GAZIERS BELGES**
4 Avenue Palmerston
B-1040 Bruxelles
Belgium
Tel: (02) 230 43 85

Entry: 879

**AZIENDA ELETTRICA MUNICIPALE DI MILANO**
Corso di Porta Vittoria 4
Milano
Italy
Tel: (02) 77 20

Entries: 1025  1031  1035

# B

**BANCO DE BILBAO**
Administracion Central—Servicio de Estudios
Alcala 16
Madrid
Spain
Tel: (1) 232 86 01

Entry: 1192


**BANCO ESPAÑOL DE CREDITO**
Servicio Estudios Economicos
Alcala 1
Madrid
Spain
Tel: (1) 232 58 91

Entry: 1176


**BANQUE INTERNATIONALE A LUXEMBOURG SA**
2 Boulevard Royal
BP 2205
Luxembourg
Tel: 47 91-1

Entry: 1076


**BAYERNWERK AG**
Blutenburgstrasse 6, Postfach 200340
D-8000 München 2
West Germany
Tel: (089) 12 54-1

Entry: 1302


**BENN PUBLICATIONS LTD**
25 New Street Square
London EC4A 3JA
England
Tel: (01) 353 3212

Entries: 114 465


**BENN PUBLICATIONS LTD (TUNBRIDGE WELLS)**
Directories Division
Union House
Eridge Road
Tunbridge Wells TN4
England

Entries: 210 437


**BERGBAU-ELEKTRIZITÄTS-VERBUNDGEMEINSCHAFT**
Bismarckstrasse 54
D-4300 Essen 1
West Germany
Tel: (0201) 79 94-1

Entry: 1254


**BERLINER KRAFT- UND LICHT AG**
Stauffenbergstrasse 26
D-1000 Berlin
West Germany
Tel: (030) 267 24 13

Entry: 1303


**BONNIERS FÖRETAGSINFORMATION AB**
Sveavägen 56, Fack 3303
S-10366 Stockholm
Sweden
Tel: (08) 22 91 20

Entry: 740


**BRITISH GAS CORPORATION**
59 Bryanston Street
London W1A 2AZ
England
Tel: (01) 723 7030

Entries: 362 429 446 657


**BRITISH GAS CORPORATION/HMSO**
Available from HMSO—See below

Entry: 360


**THE BRITISH NATIONAL OIL CORPORATION**
150 St Vincent Street
Glasgow G2 5LJ
Scotland
Tel: (041) 204 2525

Entries: 357 516


**THE BRITISH NATIONAL OIL CORPORATION/HMSO**
Available from HMSO—See below

Entry: 363


**BRITISH PETROLEUM CO LTD**
Britannic House, Moor Lane
London EC2Y 9BU
England
Tel: (01) 920 8000

Entries: 021 176 195 243 427


**BUILDING RESEARCH ESTABLISHMENT**
Building Research Station
Garston
Watford WD2 7JR
England
Tel: (092 73) 74040

Entry: 061


**BUNDESMINISTERIUM FÜR FORSCHUNG UND TECHNOLOGIE**
Stresemannstrasse 2
D-5300 Bonn-Bad Godesberg
West Germany
Tel: (02221) 59-1

Entry: 1271


**BUNDESMINISTERIUM FÜR HANDEL GEWERBE UND INDUSTRIE**
Schwarzenbergplatz 1
A-1010 Wien
Austria
Tel: (0222) 73 35 11

Entries: 804 805 820 823

**BUNDESMINISTERIUM FÜR WIRTSCHAFT**
Villemombler Strasse 76
D-5300 Bonn-Duisdorf
West Germany
Tel: (02221) 76-1

Entries: 1268 1270

**BUNDESVERBAND DER DEUTSCHEN GAS- UND
WASSERWIRTSCHAFT EV**
Postfach 140152
D-5300 Bonn 1
West Germany
Tel: (0228) 61 10 01

Entry: 1255

**BUREAU DE DOCUMENTATION MINIERE**
4 Ruc Las-Cases
F-75700 Paris
France
Tel: (1) 555 93 00

Entry: 901

**BUREAU FEDERAL DE STATISTIQUE**
Hallwylstrasse 15
CH-3003 Bern
Switzerland
Tel: (031) 61 88 36

Entry: 1200

**BUSINESS STATISTICS OFFICE/HMSO**
Available from HMSO—See below

Entries: 365 377 395 435 457 490

# C

**CAMBRIDGE INFORMATION AND RESEARCH
SERVICES LTD**
Sussex House, Hobson Street
Cambridge CB1 1NJ
England
Tel: (076 383) 615

Entries: 069 070 361 407 408 412 430 431 446
466

**CENTRAAL BUREAU VOOR DE STATISTIEK**
Prinses Beatrixlaan 428, PB 959
2270 AZ Voorburg
Netherlands
Tel: (070) 69 43 41

Entries: 1108 1110 1111 1112 1113 1114 1117
1127 1129 1130 1131 1132 1133

**CENTRAL BANK OF IRELAND**
Fitzwilton House, Wilton Place
Dublin 2
Republic of Ireland
Tel: (01) 76 05 41

Entry: 553

**CENTRAL ELECTRICITY GENERATING BOARD**
Sudbury House, 15 Newgate Street
London EC1A 7AU
England
Tel: (01) 248 1202

Entries: 350 366 367 368 398 492 495 499

**CENTRAL FORENINGEN AF BENZINFORHANDLERE**
Nordkrog 24
D-2900 Hellerup
Denmark
Tel: (01) 62 77 70

Entry: 600

**CENTRAL STATISTICAL OFFICE/HMSO**
Available from HMSO—See below

Entry: 459

**CENTRAL STATISTICS OFFICE**
St Stephen's Green House, Earlsfort Terrace
Dublin 2
Republic of Ireland
Tel: (01) 76 75 31

Entries: 557 560 563

**CENTRALA DRIFTLEDNINGEN**
Brahégatan 47, Fack
S-10240 Stockholm
Sweden
Tel: (08) 63 54 60

Entry: 738

**CEPCEO**
Hobart House, Grosvenor Place
London SW1X 7AE
England
Tel: (01) 235 2020

Entries: 077 096

**CETO-VERLAG GMBH**
Goethestrasse 34, Postfach 104029
D-3500 Kassel
West Germany
Tel: (0561) 7 45 17

Entry: 1259

**CHARBONNAGES DE FRANCE**
9 Avenue Percier, BP 39608
F-75360 Paris 8
France
Tel: (1) 563 11 20

Entries: 906 943 945

**CHASE MANHATTAN BANK**
1 Chase Manhattan Plaza
New York
USA
Tel: (212) 552 2222

Entry: 023

CHICHESTER DESIGN ASSOCIATES LTD
26a East Street
Chichester, Sussex
England
Tel: (0243) 88344

Entry: 359


CLUB ESPAÑOL DEL PETROLEO
Serrano 57
Madrid 6/E
Spain

Entries: 1186  1197


COMITE DE CONTROLE DE L'ELECTRICITE ET DU
GAZ
8 Boulevard du Régent
B-1000 Bruxelles
Belgium
Tel: (02) 511 81 63

Entry: 861


COMITE PROFESSIONNEL DU PETROLE
51 Boulevard de Courcelles
F-75008 Paris
France
Tel: (1) 227 48 12

Entries: 911  926  927  932  933  934  935  940


COMMISSARIAT A L'ENERGIE SOLAIRE
208 Rue Raymond-Losserand
F-75014 Paris
France
Tel: (1) 545 67 60

Entry: 918


COMMISSION OF THE EUROPEAN COMMUNITIES
Available from:
Office des Publications Officielles des Communautés
Européennes
BP 1003, 5 Rue du Commerce
Luxembourg
Tel: 49 00 81

Entries: 039  040  047  083  088  097  098  099  124
          138  196  227  254  255


COMPAGNIE FRANCAISE DES PETROLES
5 Rue Michel-Ange
F-75781 Paris Cedex 16
France
Tel: (1) 524 46 46

Entries: 041  909


COMPAGNIE NATIONAL DU RHONE
2 Rue André Bonin
F-69316 Lyon Cedex 1
France
Tel: (78) 29 04 31

Entry: 910


COMPANIA IBERICA REFINADORA DE PETROLEOS
SA
Avenida Jose Antonio 20
Madrid
Spain
Tel: (1) 448 00 39

Entry: 1198


COMPASS-VERLAGSGESELLSCHAFT MBH
Wipplingerstrasse 32
A-1013 Wien
Austria
Tel: (0222) 63 66 16

Entry: 815


COMPTOIR BELGE DES CHARBONS
99-101 Rue de la Loi, Boîte 8
B-1040 Bruxelles
Belgium
Tel: (02) 513 28 10

Entry: 883


CONCAWE
Van Hogenhoucklaan 60
2596 TE Den Haag
Netherlands
Tel: (070) 24 50 35

Entries: 052  102  127  220  225


CONFEDERATION OF BRITISH INDUSTRY
21 Tothill Street
London SW1
England
Tel: (01) 930 6711

Entry: 508


COTE DESFOSSES/DAFSA
Cote Desfossés
42 Rue Notre-Dame-des-Victoires
Paris 2
France
Tel: (1) 233 21 30

DAFSA
125 Rue Montmartre
F-75081 Paris
France
Tel: (1) 233 21 23

Entry: 902


CROOM HELM LTD
2-10 St John's Road
London SW11
England
Tel: (01) 228 5088

Entries: 390  476  651

# D

## DANATOM
Allégade 2
DK-3000 Helsingør
Denmark
Tel: (03) 36 00 22

Entry: 614

## DANMARKS STATISTIK
Sejrøgade 11
DK-2100 København
Denmark
Tel: (01) 29 82 22

Entries: 601 602 612 615 616 617 620

## DANSK ELVAERKERS FORENING
Rosenørns Allé 9
DK-1970 København
Denmark
Tel: (01) 39 01 11

Entry: 603

## DANSK ESSO A/S
Sankt Annae Plads 13
DK-1298 København
Denmark
Tel: (01) 14 28 90

Entry: 604

## DANSK GASTEKNISK FORENING
Strandvejen 72
DK-2900 Hellerup
Denmark
Tel: (01) 48 12 00

Entry: 610

## DANSK KEDELFORENING
Gladsaxe Mollevej 15
København
Denmark
Tel: (01) 69 65 11

Entry: 609

## DANSK OLIE & NATURGAS A/S
Kristianiagade 8
DK-2100 København
Denmark
Tel: (01) 14 28 96

Entry: 605

## DAVID & CHARLES LTD
Brunel House, Forde Road
Newton Abbot TQ12 4PU
England
Tel: (0626) 61121

Entry: 474

## DELEGATIONEN FÖR ENERGIFORSKNING
Sveavägen 9-11
S-11157 Stockholm
Sweden
Tel: (08) 763 10 00

Entries: 706 707 708 711 714 715 743

## DEMINEX
Dorotheenstrasse 1, Postfach 100944
D-4300 Essen
West Germany
Tel: (0201) 72 61

Entries: 515 1261

## DEPARTEMENT FEDERAL DE L'ECONOMIE PUBLIQUE
Bundesgasse 8
CH-3003 Bern
Switzerland
Tel: (031) 61 21 11

Entry: 1220

## DEPARTMENT OF ENERGY
Thames House South, Millbank
London SW1P 4QJ
England
Tel: (01) 211 3000

Entries: 372 373 375 376 411 424 438 440 483
486 512 529

## DEPARTMENT OF ENERGY/CIRIA
Available from:
CIRIA
6 Storey's Gate
London SW1 3AU
England
Tel: (01) 839 6881

Entry: 484

## DEPARTMENT OF ENERGY/COI
Available from:
Central Office of Information, Circulation Section (H)
Hercules Road
London SE1 7DU
England
Tel: (01) 928 2345

Entry: 420

## DEPARTMENT OF ENERGY/HMSO
Available from HMSO—See below

Entries: 351 352 353 354 371 379 383 384 386
403 404 409 414 416 417 419 428 432
439 442 445 456 461 462 463 471 481
489 496 500 501 506 517 526

## DEPARTMENT OF INDUSTRY (LEEDS)
Priestley House, Park Row
Leeds LS1 5LF
England
Tel: (0532) 443171

Entry: 485

**DEPARTMENT OF TRADE/HMSO**
Available from HMSO—See below

Entries: 488 519

**DEPARTMENT OF TRADE AND INDUSTRY/HMSO**
Available from HMSO—See below

Entry: 513

**DEUTSCHE BANK AG**
Grosse Gallusstrasse 10-14
D-6000 Frankfurt/Main 1
West Germany
Tel: (0611) 21 41

Entry: 186

**DEUTSCHE VERBUNDGESELLSCHAFT**
Ziegelhäuser Landstrasse 5
D-6900 Heidelberg 1
West Germany
Tel: (06221) 4 50 17

Entries: 1262 1272 1289

**DGMK**
Deutsche Gesellschaft für Mineraloelwirtschaft und
Kohlechemie
Ernst-Mey-Strasse 8, Postfach 1380
D-7022 Leinfelden
West Germany
Tel: (040) 2 80 22 77

Entry: 1276

**DIRECCAO-GERAL DOS SERVIÇOS ELECTRICOS**
Direcção-Geral de Energia
241 Benef
Lisboa
Portugal
Tel: 77 10 13

Entry: 1154

**DIRECCION GENERAL DE ADUANAS**
Guzman el Bueno 125
Madrid
Spain
Tel: (1) 254 32 00

Entries: 1181 1182 1183 1199

**DIRECTION DES HYDROCARBURES**
3-5 Rue Barbet-de-Jouy
F-75700 Paris
France
Tel: (1) 555 93 00

Entry: 900

**DIRECTION DU GAZ, DE L'ELECTRICITE
ET DU CHARBON**
3-5 Rue Barbet-de-Jouy
F-75700 Paris
France
Tel: (1) 555 93 00

Entries: 938 948

**DIRECTION GENERALE DE L'INDUSTRIE**
68 Rue de Bellechasse
F-75700 Paris 7
France
Tel: (1) 555 93 00

Entry: 946

**DIRECTION GENERALE DES DOUANES**
Monbijoustrasse 40
CH-3003 Bern
Switzerland
Tel: (031) 61 61 11

Entries: 1213 1214

**DIRECTION GENERALE DES DOUANES ET DROITS
INDIRECTS**
192 Rue St Honoré
Paris 1
France
Tel: (1) 233 66 33

Entries: 949 950 951

**DISTRIGAZ SA**
Avenue des Arts 31
B-1040 Bruxelles
Belgium
Tel: (02) 230 50 20

Entry: 864

**H P DREWRY**
34 Brook Street, Mayfair
London W1Y 2LL
England
Tel: (01) 629 5362

Entries: 234 237 252 256

**DRUKKERIJ EN UITGEVERSBUREAU VAN
LONKHUYZEN BV**
Montaubanstraat 13
3701 HM Zeist
Netherlands
Tel: (03404) 12441

Entry: 1103

# E

**ECONOMIST INTELLIGENCE UNIT**
27 St James's Place
London SW1A 1NT
England
Tel: (01) 493 6711

Entries: 182 183 248

**EDF—DIRECTION DE LA PRODUCTION ET DU
TRANSPORT**
2 Rue Louis Murat
F-75384 Paris 8
France
Tel: (1) 764 22 22

Entries: 947 953

**ENTE NAZIONALE IDROCARBURI**
Piazzale Enrico Mattei 1
00144 Roma
Italy
Tel: (06) 59 00 1

Entries: 055  093  1037  1038


**ENTE NAZIONALE PER L'ENERGIE ELETTRICA**
Via GB Martini 3
00198 Roma
Italy
Tel: (06) 85 09

Entries: 1030  1036  1046


**ERDÖL-VEREINIGUNG**
Zentralstrasse 70
CH-8003 Zürich
Switzerland
Tel: (01) 66 14 30

Entry: 1206


**ERNEST BENN LTD**
25 New Street Square
London EC4A 3JA
England
Tel: (01) 353 3212

Entry: 029


**ESPETROL**
Via Pompeo Magno 4
00192 Roma
Italy

Entry: 1047


**ESSO PETROLEUM COMPANY LTD**
Esso House, Victoria Street
London SW1E 5JW
England
Tel: (01) 834 6677

Entry: 423


**ESSO SAF**
6 Avenue André Prothin
F-92080 Courbevoie, Paris
France
Tel: (1) 788 50 00

Entries: 919  920


**ETAS KOMPASS PERIODICI TECNICI SPA**
Via Montegna 6
20154 Milano
Italy
Tel: (02) 34 70 51

Entry: 1041


**EUROECONOMICS**
9 Avenue Hoche
F-75008 Paris
France
Tel: (1) 766 04 00

Entries: 179  218


**EUROP-OIL PRICES**
Star House, 104-8 Grafton Road
London NW5 4BD
England
Tel: (01) 485 8792

Entry: 103


**EUROSTAT**
Office des Publications Officielles des
Communautés Européennes
BP 1003, 5 Rue de Commerce
Luxembourg
Tel: 49 00 81

Entries: 004  005  006  019  036  038  048  049  053
        091  092  109  110  111  117  121  129  131
        149  192  197  198  205  212  222  244  450
        873  930  957  1040  1106  1285  1306


**EXXON CORPORATION**
1251 Avenue of the Americas
New York NY 10020
USA
Tel: (212) 398 3000

Entries: 105  270


# F

**FACHVERBAND DER ERDÖLINDUSTRIE ÖSTERREICHS**
Erdbergstrasse 72
A-1031 Wien
Austria
Tel: (0222) 73 23 48

Entries: 803  809


**FEDERATION DE L'INDUSTRIE DU GAZ**
4 Avenue Palmerston
B-1040 Bruxelles
Belgium
Tel: (02) 230 43 85

Entries: 853  856  870


**FEDERATION PETROLIERE BELGE**
4 Rue de la Science
B-1040 Bruxelles
Belgium
Tel: (02) 512 30 03

Entries: 869  871


**FEDERATION PROFESSIONNELLE DES PRODUCTEURS ET DISTRIBUTEURS D'ELECTRICITE**
34 Avenue de Tervueren, Boîte 38
B-1040 Bruxelles
Belgium
Tel: (02) 733 96 07

Entries: 851  855  863  872  878  886  887


**THE FINANCIAL TIMES LTD**
Bracken House, 10 Cannon Street
London EC4P 4BY
England
Tel: (01) 248 8000

Entries: 101  154  156  169  170  174  265  280  426
        656

FINNISH PETROLEUM FEDERATION
Öljyalan Keskusliitto
Fabianinkatu 8
SF-00130 Helsinki
Finland
Tel: (90) 65 58 31

Entry: 629

FOMENTO DE LA PRODUCCION
Casanova 57
Barcelona 11
Spain
Tel: (3) 253 06 97

Entry: 1194

FORLAGET BØRSEN A/S
Montergade 19
DK-1014 København
Denmark
Tel: (04) 15 72 50

Entry: 611

A/S FORLAGET KOMPAS-DANMARK
Hovedgade 4
DK-2800 Lyngby
Denmark
Tel: 88 60 00

Entry: 613

FORUM ATOMICO ESPAÑOL
Claudio Coello 20
Madrid 1
Spain
Tel: (1) 276 56 71

Entries: 1184 1185

FUEL & METALLURGICAL JOURNALS LTD
Queensway House, 2 Queensway
Redhill RH1 1QS
England
Tel: (0737) 68611

Entries: 136 378 443

# G

GASTECH LTD
2 Station Road
Rickmansworth WD3 1QP
England
Tel: (092 37) 71037

Entry: 113

GAZ DE FRANCE
23 Rue Philibert-Delorme
F-75840 Paris Cedex 17
France
Tel: (1) 766 52 62

Entries: 922 923 924 952

GESAMTVERBAND DES DEUTSCHEN
STEINKOHLENBERGBAUS
Friedrichstrasse 1, Postfach 1708
D-4300 Essen
West Germany
Tel: (0201) 10 51

Entry: 1281

GRAHAM & TROTMAN LTD
Bond Street House, 14 Clifford Street
London W1X 1RD
England
Tel: (01) 493 6351

Entries: 015 016 017 100 152 164

GULF PUBLISHING CO
3301 Allen Parkway
Houston TX 77019
USA
Tel: (713) 529 4301

Entry: 278

# H

DER HAFENKURIER ROTTERDAM
Westblaak 180
Rotterdam
Netherlands
Tel: (010) 14 72 11

Entry: 1123

HAMISH HAMILTON LTD
90 Great Russell Street
London WC1B 3PT
England
Tel: (01) 580 4621

Entry: 358

HARPER AND ROW
10 East 53rd Street
New York NY 10022
USA
Tel: (212) 593 7000

Entry: 031

HAUPTBERATUNGSSTELLE FÜR
ELEKTRIZITÄTSANWENDUNG EV
Am Hauptbahnhof 12
D-6000 Frankfurt/Main 1
West Germany
Tel: (0611) 23 35 57

Entry: 1305

HEDDERWICK, STIRLING GRUMBAR & CO
1 Moorgate
London EC2
England
Tel: (01) 600 4011

Entry: 094

**HELSINGIN KAUPUNGIN ENERGIALAITOS**
Kampinkuja 2, PL 469
SF-00101 Helsinki
Finland
Tel: (90) 61 71

Entries: 626  630

**HERMANN LUCHTERHAND VERLAG**
Heddesdorfer Strasse 31, Postfach 1780
D-5450 Neuwied
West Germany
Tel: (02631) 80 11

Entry: 1283

**HEYDEN & SON LTD**
Spectrum House, Hillview Gardens
London NW4 2JQ
England
Tel: (01) 203 5171

Entries: 213  214  215  216  217

**HIDROELECTRICA DE CATALUÑA SA**
Avenida Jose Antonio 632, 5º
Barcelona 7
Spain
Tel: (3) 317 86 85

Entry: 1179

**HISPANOIL**
Pez Volador 2
Madrid
Spain
Tel: (1) 274 72 00

Entry: 1191

**HMSO**
The Government Bookshop

13A Castle Street,
Edinburgh EH2 3AR
Tel: (031) 225 6333

80 Chichester Street
Belfast BT1 4JY
Tel: (0232) 34488

41 The Hayes
Cardiff CF1 1JW
Tel: (0222) 23654

258 Broad Street
Birmingham B1 2HE
Tel: (021) 643 3740

Southey House
Wine Street
Bristol BS1 2BQ
Tel: (0272) 24306

Brazennose Street
Manchester M60 8AS
Tel: (061) 834 7201

(Counter)
49 High Holborn
London WC1V 6HB

(Mail Order)
PO Box 569
London SE1 9NH
Tel: (01) 928 1321

Entries: 396  401  413  425  433  464  498  520  524

**HOLT-SAUNDERS LTD**
1 St Anne's Road
Eastbourne BN21 3UN
England
Tel: (0323) 638221

Entries: 002  065  122  241  453  660

# I

**ICAP HELLAS SA**
64 Vas Sophias Avenue
Athens 615
Greece
Tel: 72 56 51

Entry: 1002

**IEA COAL RESEARCH**
14/15 Lower Grosvenor Place
London SW1W 0EX
England
Tel: (01) 828 4661

Entry: 219

**IMATRAN VOIMA OY**
Malminkatu 16, PL 138
SF-00101 Helsinki
Finland
Tel: (90) 64 78 11

Entry: 631

**INGENIERA QUIMICA SA**
Triana (Pinares) 51
Madrid
Spain
Tel: (1) 457 64 00

Entry: 1175

**INSEE**
Institut National de la Statistique et des Etudes
Economiques
18 Boulevard Adolphe Pinard
F-75675 Paris
France
Tel: (1) 540 01 12

Entries: 903  917

**INSTITUT NATIONAL DE STATISTIQUE**
44 Rue de Louvain
B-1000 Bruxelles
Belgium
Tel: (02) 513 13 68

Entries: 852  859

**INSTITUT NATIONAL DES INDUSTRIES EXTRACTIVES**
200 Rue du Chéra
B-4000 Liège
Belgium
Tel: (041) 52 71 50

Entry: 850

**INSTITUTE OF ENERGY**
18 Devonshire Street
London W1N 2AU
England
Tel: (01) 580 7124

Entry: 421

**INSTITUTE OF GEOLOGICAL SCIENCES/HMSO**
Available from HMSO—See above

Entries: 276  525

**THE INSTITUTE OF PETROLEUM**
61 New Cavendish Street
London W1M 8AR
England
Tel: (01) 636 1004

Entries: 177  203  279  281  380  469  477  491  521
523  527

**INSTITUTE FOR INDUSTRIAL RESEARCH AND STANDARDS**
Ballymun Road
Dublin 9
Republic of Ireland
Tel: (01) 37 01 01

Entry: 561

**THE INSTITUTION OF GAS ENGINEERS**
17 Grosvenor Crescent
London SW1X 7ES
England
Tel: (01) 245 9811

Entries: 043  078  107  112  120  264  382  387  388
410  415  422  434  436  455  467  510  1116

**INSTITUTO NACIONAL DE ESTADISTICA**
Avenida de Generalissimo 91
Madrid 16
Spain
Tel: (1) 279 93 00

Entries: 1177  1178  1187  1188  1189

**INSTITUTO NACIONAL DE ESTATISTICA**
Avenida Antonio Jose de Almeida
Lisboa 1
Portugal
Tel: 80 20 80

Entries: 1150  1151  1152  1153  1155  1156  1157

**INTERCOM**
7 Place du Trône
B-1000 Bruxelles
Belgium
Tel: (02) 512 67 00

Entry: 874

**INTERNATIONAL ATOMIC ENERGY AGENCY**
Kärntner Ring 11, PO Box 590
A-1011 Wien
Austria
Tel: (0222) 52 45 11

Entries: 132  190  191  211  258  260

**INTERNATIONAL GAS TECHNOLOGY**
3424 South State Street
Chicago, Illinois 60616
USA

Entry: 133

**INTERNATIONAL GAS UNION**
62 Rue de Courcelles
F-75008 Paris
France
Tel: (1) 766 03 51

Entries: 125  155  228  239  262  284  392  447  502
925  1044

**INTERNATIONAL PUBLISHING CORPORATION LTD**
King's Reach Tower, Stamford Street
London SE1 9LF
England
Tel: (01) 261 5000

Entry: 161

**IPC ELECTRICAL-ELECTRONIC PRESS LTD**
40 Bowling Green Lane
London EC1R 0NE
England
Tel: (01) 837 3636

Entries: 393  394

**IPC INDUSTRIAL PRESS LTD**
40 Bowling Green Lane
London EC1R 0NE
England
Tel: (01) 837 3636

Entries: 024  025  044  095  135  370  860  907  1034
1100  1180  1260

**IPC SCIENCE AND TECHNOLOGY PRESS**
Westbury House, Bury Street
Guildford GU1 3AW
England
Tel: (0483) 31261

Entries: 081  272

**IRISH GAS BOARD**
Little Island
Cork
Republic of Ireland
Tel: (021) 50 90 99

Entry: 554

ISTITUTO CENTRALE DI STATISTICA
Via Cesare Balbo 16
00184 Roma
Italy
Tel: (06) 46 73

Entries: 1027 1028 1029 1032 1049 1050

# J

JOHN I JACOBS AND CO LTD
19 Great Winchester Street
London EC2N 2DB
England
Tel: (01) 588 1255

Entry: 282

JUPITER VERLAGSGESELLSCHAFT MBH
Robertgasse 2
A-1020 Wien
Austria
Tel: (0222) 24 22 94

Entry: 814

# K

KELLY'S DIRECTORIES LTD
East Grinstead House
East Grinstead RH19 1XB
England
Tel: (0342) 26972

Entry: 451

KOGAN PAGE LTD
120 Pentonville Road
London N1
England
Tel: (01) 837 7851

Entries: 158 172 173 193 269

KOMPASS BELGIUM SA
256 Avenue Molière
B-1060 Bruxelles
Belgium
Tel: (02) 345 19 83

Entries: 875 1081

KOMPASS DEUTSCHLAND VERLAGS- UND
VERTRIEBSGESELLSCHAFT MBH
Wilhelmstrasse 1, Postfach 964
D-7800 Freiburg
West Germany
Tel: (0761) 13 13 31

Entry: 1288

KOMPASS ESPAÑA SA
Avenida del General Peron 26
Madrid 20
Spain
Tel: (1) 455 97 53

Entry: 1193

KOMPASS NEDERLAND NV
Van Stolkweg 6
2585 JP Den Haag
Netherlands
Tel: (070) 54 53 00

Entry: 1109

KOMPASS NORGE A/S
Nobelsgaten 23
Oslo 2
Norway
Tel: (02) 11 40 55

Entry: 659

KOMPASS PUBLISHERS LTD
East Grinstead House
East Grinstead RH19 1XD
England
Tel: (0342) 26972

Entry: 452

KOMPASS SVERIGE
Sveavägen 36, Fack 3303
S-10366 Stockholm
Sweden
Tel: (08) 22 91 20

Entry: 722

KRÅNGEDE AB
Birger Jarlsgatan 41A, Box 7593
S-10393 Stockholm
Sweden
Tel: (08) 23 30 25

Entry: 724

# L

LÄMPÖLAITOSYHDISTYS RY
Fredr.k. 61
Helsinki
Finland
Tel: (90) 694 25 88

Entry: 632

LIBERFÖRLAG
Available from:
Liber Distribution
Sorterargatan 23
S-16289 Vallingby
Sweden
Tel: (08) 89 02 00

Entries: 705 732

LIBERLÄROMEDEL
Sorterargatan 23
S-16289 Vällingby
Sweden
Tel: (08) 89 02 00

Entry: 741

**LIESS**
Dr Otto R Liess
Universitätsstrasse 11
A-1010 Wien
Austria
Tel: (0222) 42 01 50

Entry: 807


**LLOYD'S**
71 Fenchurch Street
London EC3M 4BS
England
Tel: (01) 709 9166

Entries: 139  140


**LONGMAN**
Longman House, Burnt Mill
Harlow, Essex
England
Tel: (0279) 26721

Entry: 441


# M

**MACLEAN-HUNTER LTD**
30 Old Burlington Street
London W1X 2AE
England
Tel: (01) 434 2233

Entry: 185


**McGRAW-HILL PUBLICATIONS**
457 National Press Building
Washington DC 20045
USA
Tel: (202) 624 7561

Entries: 074  208  209


**MACMILLAN PRESS LTD**
4 Little Essex Street
London EC2R 3LF
England
Tel: (01) 836 6633

Entry: 263


**MARTIN ROBERTSON & CO LTD**
108 Cowley Road
Oxford OX4 1JF
England
Tel: (0865) 49109

Entry: 494


**MECHANICAL ENGINEERING PUBLICATIONS LTD**
Northgate Avenue
Bury St Edmunds
England
Tel: (0284) 63277

Entry: 391


**MEDIOBANCA**
Via Filodrammatici 16
20121 Milano
Italy
Tel: (02) 88 29

Entry: 1045


**MICROINFO**
PO Box 3
Alton GU34 2PG
England
Tel: (0420) 84300

Entry: 086


**MIDDLE EAST PETROLEUM & ECONOMIC PUBLICATIONS**
Box 4940
Nicosia
Cyprus

Entry: 143


**MILLER FREEMAN PUBLICATIONS**
500 Howard Street
San Francisco CA 94105
USA
Tel: (415) 397 1881

Entries: 075  231  267  268  277


**MINING JOURNAL LTD**
PO Box 10
Edenbridge TN8 5NE
England
Tel: (0732) 864333

Entries: 144  145  146


**MINING JOURNAL BOOKS LTD**
PO Box 10
Edenbridge TN8 5NE
England
Tel: (0732) 864333

Entries: 137  257


**MINISTERE DE L'INDUSTRIE**
85 Boulevard du Montparnasse
F-75270 Paris
France
Tel: (1) 555 93 00

Entries: 905  908  912  944


**MINISTERO DELL' INDUSTRIA DEL COMMERCIO E DELL' ARTIGIANATO**
Via Vittorio Veneto 33
00100 Roma
Italy
Tel: (06) 49 85

Entry: 1033


**MINISTRY OF PETROLEUM AND MINERAL RESOURCES**
Economics Department
Riyadh
Saudi Arabia

Entry: 204

DEN NORSKE CREDITBANK
Kirkegaten 21
Oslo 1
Norway
Tel: (02) 48 10 50

Entry: 650

DEN NORSKE STATS OLJESELSKAP A/S
Lagårdsveien 78, PO Box 300
N-4001 Stavanger
Norway
Tel: (045) 33 18 0

Entries: 674  675

NOROIL PUBLISHING HOUSE
Hillevågsveien 17, PO Box 480
N-4001 Stavanger
Norway
Tel: (045) 89 00 0

Entries: 153  275  663

NORTH EAST SCOTLAND DEVELOPMENT AGENCY
57 Queens Road
Aberdeen AB1 6YP
Scotland
Tel: (0224) 321211

Entry: 482

NORTH OF SCOTLAND HYDRO-ELECTRIC BOARD
16 Rothesay Terrace
Edinburgh EH3 7SE
Scotland
Tel: (031) 225 1361

Entry: 470

NORTH SEA OBSERVER
Teknisk Presse A/S
Hovfaret 17
Oslo 2
Norway
Tel: (02) 55 48 80

Entry: 157

NORTHERN IRELAND ELECTRICITY SERVICE
Danesfort, 120 Malone Road
Belfast BT9 5HT
Northern Ireland
Tel: (0232) 66 11 00

Entry: 468

AB NYNAS PETROLEUM
Nybrogatan 11, Box 5842
S-10248 Stockholm
Sweden
Tel: (08) 24 35 80

Entry: 700

# O

OECD
2 Rue André Pascal
F-75775 Paris Cedex 16
France
Tel: (1) 524 82 00

Entries: 020  027  050  051  057  058  059  060  062
063  064  079  080  082  084  085  089  090
119  142  160  166  167  184  199  223  238
245  246  247  249  259  266  271  283

OEL VERLAG GMBH
Alsterkamp 20
D-2000 Hamburg 13
West Germany
Tel: (040) 4 10 46 52

Entry: 1292

OFFICE BELGE DU COMMERCE EXTERIEUR
162 Boulevard E Jacqmain
B-1000 Bruxelles
Belgium
Tel: (02) 219 45 50

Entries: 862  1078

OFFSHORE INTELLIGENCE LTD
Marshalsea House, Merchant's Quay
Dublin 8
Republic of Ireland
Tel: (01) 71 99 66

Entries: 555  556

OFFSHORE SUPPLIES OFFICE
Alhambra House, 45 Waterloo Street
Glasgow G2 6AS
Scotland
Tel: (041) 221 87 77

Entry: 487

OIL-TELEGRAM GMBH
Carl-Petersen-Strasse 70-76, Postfach 260443
D-2000 Hamburg 26
West Germany
Tel: (040) 25 11 13

Entry: 1277

A/S ØKONOMISK LITERATUR
Ebbellsgate 3
Oslo 1
Norway
Tel: (02) 20 90 73

Entry: 676

OLJEDIREKTORATET
Lagårdsveien 80, Box 600
N-4000 Stavanger
Norway
Tel: (045) 33 16 0

Entry: 668

OLJEKONSUMENTERNAS FÖRBUND
Sveavägen 153-5
S-11387 Stockholm
Sweden
Tel: (08) 736 00 00

Entry: 727

ÖMV AG
Otto-Wagnerplatz 5, Postfach 15
A-1090 Wien
Austria
Tel: (0222) 42 36 21

Entry: 817

**ORGANIZATION OF ARAB PETROLEUM EXPORTING COUNTRIES**
PO Box 20501
Kuwait

Entries: 066  165  194

**ORGANIZATION OF PETROLEUM EXPORTING COUNTRIES**
Obere Donaustrasse 93
A-1020 Wien
Austria
Tel: (0222) 26 55 11

Entries: 187  188

**OSLO LYSVERKER**
Sommerrogate 1
Oslo 2
Norway
Tel: (02) 56 41 60

Entries: 661  670

**ÖSTERREICHISCHE DONAUKRAFTWERKE AG**
Hochhaus Gartenbau, Parkring 12
A-1011 Wien
Austria
Tel: (0222) 52 66 71

Entry: 818

**ÖSTERREICHISCHE ELEKTRIZITÄTS- WIRTSCHAFTS- AG**
Am Hof 6A
A-1010 Wien
Austria
Tel: (0222) 66 13-0

Entries: 824  825

**ÖSTERREICHISCHE VEREINIGUNG FÜR DAS GAS- UND WASSERFACH**
Gusshausstrasse 30
A-1041 Wien
Austria
Tel: (0222) 65 17 57

Entry: 811

**ÖSTERREICHISCHES STATISTISCHES ZENTRALAMT**
Neue Burg, Heldenplatz
A-1014 Wien
Austria
Tel: (0222) 52 46 86

Entries: 800  801  802  812  813  816  821  822  826
829

**OTTO VIETH VERLAG**
Alfredstrasse 1
D-2000 Hamburg 76
West Germany
Tel: (040) 25 60 58

Entry: 007

**OVE ARUP & PARTNERS**
13 Fitzroy Street
London W1
England
Tel: (01) 636 1531

Entry: 449

# P

**PERGAMON PRESS**
Headington Hill Hall
Oxford OX3 0BW
England
Tel: (0865) 64881

Entries: 028  035  054  123  126  250  473

**PETROFINA SA**
33 Rue de la Loi
B-1040 Bruxelles
Belgium
Tel: (02) 513 69 00

Entry: 877

**PETROLEOS DE PORTUGAL**
Rua das Flores 7
1200 Lisboa
Portugal
Tel: 32 80 35

Entries: 1158  1159

**PETROLEUM INTELLIGENCE WEEKLY INC**
49 West 45th Street
New York NY 10036
USA
Tel: (212) 575 1242

Entry: 202

**PETROLEUM PRESS BUREAU LTD**
5 Pemberton Row, Fleet Street
London EC4A 3DP
England
Tel: (01) 353 4517

Entries: 189  201  233  1124

**PETROLEUM PUBLISHING CO**
1421 South Sheridan Road, Box 1260
Tulsa OK 74101
USA
Tel: (918) 835 3161

Entries: 168  175  200  207  226  285

**PHILLIPS PETROLEUM CO**
Phillips Building
Bartlesville OK 74004
USA

Entries: 206  652

**PROVINCIAAL ELECTRICITEITSBEDRIJF IN FRIESLAND**
Emmakade 59, PB 413
8901 BE Leeuwarden
Netherlands
Tel: (05100) 94 91-1

Entry: 1119

**PROVINCIALE LIMBURGSE ELECTRICITEITS-MIJ**
Prins Bisschopsingel 22
Maastricht
Netherlands
Tel: (043) 84 88 88

Entry: 1120

**PROVINCIALE ZEEUWSE ENERGIE-MIJ**
Poelendaelesingel 10, PB 48
4330 AA Middelburg
Netherlands
Tel: (01180) 25 35-1

Entry: 1121

**PUBLIC POWER CORPORATION**
30 Chalcocondylis Street
Athens 102
Greece
Tel: 64 41 11

Entry: 1004

**PUBLICAZIONE PETROLIFERA SPA**
Piazza della Lega 24
Alessandria
Italy

Entry: 1043

# R

**RESOURCES FOR THE FUTURE INC**
1755 Massachusetts Avenue NW
Washington DC 20036
USA

Entry: 076

**RHEINISCH-WESTFÄLISCHES ELEKTRIZITÄTSWERK AG**
Kruppstrasse 5, Postfach 27
D-4300 Essen
West Germany
Tel: (0201) 18 51

Entry: 1298

**RHEINISCHE BRAUNKOHLENWERKE AG**
Stüttgenweg 2
D-5000 Köln 41
West Germany
Tel: (0221) 4 80-1

Entries: 1257  1296

**RIBA PUBLICATIONS LTD**
66 Portland Place
London W1
England
Tel: (01) 637 8811

Entry: 528

**ROTTERDAM CHAMBER OF COMMERCE AND INDUSTRY**
Coolsingel 58
Rotterdam
Netherlands
Tel: (010) 14 50 22

Entry: 1128

**ROYAL DUTCH/SHELL GROUP**
Available from:
Shell International Petroleum Co Ltd
Shell Centre
London SE1 7NA
England
Tel: (01) 934 1234

Shell International Petroleum Mij BV
30 Carel van Bylandtlaan
Den Haag
Netherlands
Tel: (070) 77 66 55

Entry: 106

**ROYAL SOCIETY OF ARTS**
6 Carlton House Terrace
London SW1Y 5AG
England
Tel: (01) 839 5561

Entry: 230

**RUHRKOHLE AG**
Rellinghause Strasse 1, Postfach 5
D-4300 Essen 1
West Germany
Tel: (0201) 1 77-1

Entry: 1297

# S

**SÄHKÖNTUOTTAJIEN YHTEISTYÖVALTUUSKUNTA**
Lönnrotinkatu 4
Helsinki
Finland
Tel: (90) 64 84 35

Entry: 638

**SCHIFFAHRTS-VERLAG HANSA**
Stubbenhuk 10
D-2000 Hamburg
West Germany
Tel: (040) 36 49 81

Entry: 1263

SCHWEIZERISCHE VEREINIGUNG FÜR
ATOMENERGIE
Bärenplatz 2, Postfach 2613
CH-3001 Bern
Switzerland
Tel: (031) 22 58 82

Entries: 1210  1217  1218


SCHWEIZERISCHER ELEKTROTECHNISCHER
VEREIN
Seefeldstrasse 301
CH-8008 Zürich
Switzerland
Tel: (01) 53 20 20

Entry: 1202


SCHWEIZERISCHER VEREIN VON GAS- UND
WASSERFACHMÄNNERN
Grütlistrasse 44, Postfach 658
CH-8027 Zürich
Switzerland
Tel: (01) 36 56 37

Entry: 1207


SCIENCE REVIEWS LTD
International Institute for Environment and
Development
27 Mortimer Street
London W1
England
Tel: (01) 580 7656

Entry: 454


SCIENTIFIC PRESS LTD
PO Box 21
Beaconsfield HP9 1NS
England
Tel: (04946) 5139

Entries: 150  180


SCOTTISH COUNCIL
1 Castle Street
Edinburgh EH2 3AJ
Scotland
Tel: (031) 225 7911

Entry: 522


SCOTTISH ECONOMIC PLANNING DEPARTMENT
New St  Andrew's House, St James Centre
Edinburgh EH1 3SX
Scotland
Tel: (031) 556 8400

Entry: 478


SCOTTISH ECONOMIC PLANNING DEPT/HMSO
Available from HMSO—See above

Entries: 389  504


SCOTTISH OFFICE/HMSO
Available from HMSO—See above

Entry: 503


SECRETARIAT FOR FUTURE STUDIES
Regeringsgatan 65
Stockholm
Sweden
Tel: (08) 763 10 00

Entry: 733


SEDIGAS SA
Balmas 357
Barcelona 6
Spain
Tel: (3) 247 28 04

Entries: 1190  1195


SERVICE DE CONSERVATION DES GISEMENTS
D'HYDROCARBURES
366 Avenue Napoléon Bonaparte
F-92501 Rueil-Malmaison
France
Tel: (1) 749 27 75

Entry: 939


SERVICES INDUSTRIELS DE GENEVE
Pont de la Machine, CP 272
CH-1211 Genève
Switzerland
Tel: (022) 20 88 11

Entry: 1212


OY SHELL AB
Ulappasaarentie 4, PL33
SF-00980 Helsinki
Finland
Tel: (90) 31 90 1

Entry: 636


SHELL UK LTD
Shell-Mex House, Strand
London WC2R 0DX
England
Tel: (01) 438 3701

Entry: 505


SHELL INTERNATIONAL CHEMICAL CO LTD
Shell Centre
London SE1 7NA
England
Tel: (01) 934 1234

Entry: 026


SHELL INTERNATIONAL PETROLEUM CO LTD
Shell Centre
London SE1 7NA
England
Tel: (01) 924 1234

Entries: 032  056  067  070  128  130  171  235  236
240  480  619  667  1118


SHELL NEDERLAND BV
Shellgebouw, Hofplein 20, PB 1222
3000 BE Rotterdam
Netherlands
Tel: (010) 69 69 11

Entries: 1125  1126

STATISTISKA CENTRALBYRÅN
Karlavägen 100
S-10250 Stockholm
Sweden
Tel: (08) 61 67 12

Entries: 701 702 703 704 716 718 719 720 723
725 729 730 734 744 745 746 747

STERLING PROFESSIONAL PUBLICATIONS LTD
86-8 Edgware Road, PO Box 839
London W2 2YW
England
Tel: (01) 402 7368

Entry: 475

STORA KOPPARBERG
Åsgatan 22
S-79180 Falun
Sweden
Tel: (023) 80 00 0

Entry: 735

STRATHCLYDE REGIONAL COUNCIL
Industrial Development Unit
21 Bothwell Street
Glasgow G2 6NJ
Scotland
Tel: (041) 221 4296

Entry: 511

SUOMEN ATOMITEKNILLINEN SEURA
Valtion Teknillinen Tutkimuskeskus
Lönnrotinkatu 37
SF-00180 Helsinki
Finland

Entry: 646

SUOMEN BENSIINIKAUPPIAITTEN LIITTO RY
Mannerheimintie 40
SF-00100 Helsinki
Finland
Tel: (90) 49 93 48

Entry: 625

SUOMEN SÄHKÖLAITOSYHDISTYS RY
Mannerheimintie 76, PL 100
SF-00260 Helsinki
Finland
Tel: (90) 40 81 88

Entries: 635 639 640

SVENSKA ELVERKSFÖRENINGEN
Norrtullsgatan 6, Box 6405
S-11382 Stockholm
Sweden
Tel: (08) 22 58 90

Entries: 713 742

SVENSKA GASFÖRENINGEN
Norrtullsgatan 6, Box 6405
S-11382 Stockholm
Sweden
Tel: (08) 34 09 85

Entry: 717

SVENSKA PETROLEUM INSTITUTET
Sveavägen 21
S-1134 Stockholm
Sweden
Tel: (08) 23 58 00

Entry: 737

SVERIGES INDUSTRIFÖRBUND
Storgatan 19, Fack 5501
S-11485 Stockholm
Sweden
Tel: (08) 63 50 20

Entry: 736

THE SWEDISH INSTITUTE
Hamngatan 27, Fack 7434
S-10391 Stockholm
Sweden
Tel: (08) 22 32 80

Entry: 710

SWEDISH STATE POWER BOARD
Statens Vattenfallsverk
Jämtlandsgatan 99
S-16287 Vällingby
Sweden
Tel: (08) 87 00 00

Entry: 748

# T

TAUERNKRAFTWERKE AG
Rainerstrasse 29, Postfach 161
A-5021 Salzburg
Austria
Tel: (06222) 72 50 10

Entry: 806

TEKNISK FORLAG A/S
Skelbaekgade 4
DK-1717 København
Denmark
Tel: (01) 21 68 01

Entry: 606

TEXACO INC
200 Westchester Avenue
White Plains, New York NY 10650
USA
Tel: (914) 253 4000

Entry: 253

TEXACO LTD
1 Knightsbridge Green
London SW1X 7QJ
England
Tel: (01) 584 5000

Entry: 514

**THOM'S DIRECTORIES LTD**
38 Merrion Square
Dublin 2
Republic of Ireland
Tel: (01) 76 74 81

Entry: 562

**TILASTOKESKUS**
(Mail Order)
PL 516
SF-00101 Helsinki
Finland
Tel: (90) 53 90 11

(Counter)
Annankatu 44
SF-00101 Helsinki
Finland
Tel: (90) 17 34 1

Entries: 627 641 642 643

**TRADE POLICY RESEARCH CENTRE**
1 Gough Square
London EC4A 3DE
England
Tel: (01) 353 6371

Entries: 163 479 666

**TULLIHALLITUS**
Erottajankatu 2
Helsinki
Finland
Tel: (90) 66 14 11

Entries: 644 645

# U

**UCSIP**
16 Avenue Kléber
F-75116 Paris
France
Tel: (1) 502 11 20

Entry: 929

**UITGEVERIJ J H DE BUSSY NV**
Keizersgracht 810
Amsterdam
Netherlands
Tel: (020) 24 24 49

Entry: 1134

**UN ECONOMIC COMMISSION FOR EUROPE**
Palais des Nations
CH-1211 Genève 10
Switzerland
Tel: (022) 34 60 11

Entries: 008 009 010 011 012 037 045 046 108
118 151 221 287

**UNERG SA**
Chaussée d'Ixelles
B-1050 Bruxelles
Belgium
Tel: (02) 512 58 40

Entry: 890

**UNIDAD ELECTRICA SA**
Francisco Gervas 3
Madrid 20
Spain
Tel: (1) 270 44 00

Entry: 1196

**UNION DES EXPLOITATIONS ELECTRIQUES EN BELGIQUE**
4 Galerie Ravenstein, Boîte 6
B-1000 Bruxelles
Belgium
Tel: (02) 511 19 70

Entries: 867 881

**UNION DES INDUSTRIES CHIMIQUES**
64 Avenue Marceau
Paris 8
France
Tel: (1) 720 56 03

Entry: 956

**UNIONE PETROLIFERA**
Viale della Civilta del Lavoro 38
00144 Roma
Italy
Tel: (06) 591 58 69

Entries: 1042 1048 1051

**UNITED KINGDOM ATOMIC ENERGY AUTHORITY**
11 Charles II Street
London SW1Y 4QP
England
Tel: (01) 930 5454

Entry: 355

**UNITED NATIONS (GENEVA)**
Palais des Nations
CH-1211 Genève
Switzerland
Tel: (022) 34 60 11

Entry: 148

**UNITED NATIONS (NEW YORK)**
United Nations Publications
A-3315
New York NY 10017
USA

Entries: 229 273 274

**UNITI**
Buchstrasse 10
D-2000 Hamburg 76
West Germany

Entry: 1290

**URANIUM INSTITUTE**
New Zealand House, Haymarket
London SW1Y 4TE
England
Tel: (01) 930 5726

Entry: 162

**THE URANIUM INSTITUTE/MINING JOURNAL BOOKS LTD**
Available from Mining Journal Books Ltd—See above

Entry: 018

**URBAN-VERLAG**
Alfredstrasse 1
D-2000 Hamburg 76
West Germany
Tel: (040) 25 60 58

Entries: 181  808  1274

**US DEPARTMENT OF ENERGY**
20 Massachusetts Avenue NW
Washington DC 20545
USA
Tel: (202) 376 4358

Entry: 042

# V

**VALTION YHTIÖIDEN TOIMISTO**
Aleksanterinkatu 10
Helsinki 17
Finland

Entry: 637

**VEBA OEL AG**
Pawikerstrasse 30, Postfach 45
D-4660 Gelsenkirchen-Buer
West Germany
Tel: (0209) 3 66-1

Entry: 1307

**VEG-GASINSTITUUT NV**
Wilmersdorf 50, PB 137
7300 AC Apeldoorn
Netherlands
Tel: (055) 23 08 08

Entries: 1101  1107  1122

**VERBAND DER ELEKTRIZITÄTSWERKE ÖSTERREICHS**
Brahmsplatz 3
A-1040 Wien
Austria
Tel: (0222) 65 17 27-0

Entry: 819

**VERBAND SCHWEIZERISCHER ELEKTRIZITÄTS-WERKE**
Bahnhofplatz 3, Postfach 3295
CH-8023 Zürich
Switzerland
Tel: (01) 211 51 91

Entries: 1203  1204  1205  1208  1215  1216  1221

**VEREIN DEUTSCHER KOHLENIMPORTEURE**
Bergstrasse 7
D-2000 Hamburg 1
West Germany
Tel: (040) 32 74 84

Entries: 261  1308

**VEREINIGUNG DEUTSCHER ELEKTRIZITÄTSWERKE EV**
Stresemannallée 23
D-6000 Frankfurt/Main
West Germany
Tel: (0611) 63 04-1

Entries: 1250  1266  1269

**VEREINIGUNG EXPORTIERENDER ELEKTRIZITÄTS-UNTERNEHMUNGEN**
Parkstrasse 23, Postfach NOK
CH-5401 Baden
Switzerland
Tel: (056) 20 31 11

Entries: 1211  1219

**VERLAG DIE BRAUNKOHLE**
Martin Luther Platz, Postfach 1122
D-4000 Düsseldorf 1
West Germany
Tel: (0211) 88 56 35

Entry: 1258

**VERLAG GLÜCKAUF GMBH**
Franz-Fischer-Weg 61, Postfach 103945
D-4300 Essen 1
West Germany
Tel: (0201) 10 51

Entries: 116  1282  1286  1311

**VERLAG DR HOFFMANN KG**
Tullastrasse 18, Postfach 2545
D-6800 Mannheim 1
West Germany
Tel: (0621) 40 81 65

Entry: 1287

**VERLAG HOPPENSTEDT & CO**
Havelstrasse 9, Postfach 4006
D-6100 Darmstadt
West Germany
Tel: (06151) 8 80-1

Entries: 1284  1299

**VERLAG R OLDENBOURG**
Rosenheimer Strasse 145, Postfach 801360
D-8000 München
West Germany
Tel: (089) 41121

Entries: 1256  1273  1278

**VERLAGS- UND WIRTSCHAFTSGESELLSCHAFT DER ELEKTRIZITÄTSWERKE MBH**
Stresemannallée 23
D-6000 Frankfurt/Main 70
West Germany
Tel: (0611) 63 04-1

Entries: 1251  1267  1293  1300

**VORARLBERGER ILLWERKE**
Josef Huter-Strasse 35
A-6901 Bregenz
Austria
Tel: (055 74) 24 59 10

Entry: 827

# W

**THE WATT COMMITTEE ON ENERGY LTD**
75 Knightsbridge
London SW1X 7RB
England
Tel: (01) 245 9238

Entries: 073  104  224  381  405  518

**WELSH OFFICE/HMSO**
Available from HMSO—See above

Entry: 385

**WIENER STADTWERKE**
Schottenring 30
Wien 1
Austria
Tel: (0222) 63 66 06

Entry: 828

**WIRTSCHAFTSVERBAND ERDÖL- UND
ERDGASGEWINNUNG EV**
Brühlstrasse 9
D-3000 Hannover 1
West Germany
Tel: (0511) 32 60 16

Entry: 1310

**WOOD, MACKENZIE AND CO**
68-73 Queen Street
Edinburgh EH2 4NS
Scotland
Tel: (031) 226 4141

Entries: 159  472  665

**WOODHEAD-FAULKNER**
8 Market Passage
Cambridge CB2 3PF
England
Tel: (0223) 66733

Entry: 418

**WORLD ENERGY CONFERENCE**
34 St James's Street
London SW1
England
Tel: (01) 930 3966

Entry: 251

# Y

**AB YRITYSTIETO OY**
Kalevankatu 45A
Helsinki
Finland
Tel: (90) 64 82 92

Entry: 628

# Z

**ZfGW- VERLAG GMBH**
Theodor-Heuss-Allée 90-98, Postfach 901080
D-6000 Frankfurt/Main 90
West Germany
Tel: (0611) 77 08 77

Entries: 810  1279

**ZINDER-NERIS INC**
1828 L Street NW
Washington DC 20036
USA
Tel: (202) 862 3400

Entry: 034

# Appendix:
# Energy Units and Terms

## ABBREVIATIONS

| | | | |
|---|---|---|---|
| KW | kilowatt | KWh | kilowatt hour |
| MW | megawatt | MWh | megawatt hour |
| GW | gigawatt | GWh | gigawatt hour |
| TW | terawatt | TWh | terawatt hour |
| Kcal | kilocalorie | Kj | kilojoule |
| Mcal | megacalorie | Mj | megajoule |
| Gcal | gigacalorie | Gj | gigajoule |
| Tcal | teracalorie | Tj | terajoule |
| $cf$ | cubic foot/feet | cfd | cubic feet per day |
| $M^3$ | cubic metre | bbl | barrel |
| b/d | barrels per day | Btu | British thermal unit |

## MULTIPLE UNITS

kilo- = x 1,000 ($10^3$)
mega- = x 1,000,000 ($10^6$)
giga- = x 1,000,000,000 ($10^9$)
tera- = x 1,000,000,000,000 ($10^{12}$)

## CONVERSION FACTORS

Heat and Power

1 calorie = 4.187 joules
1 Btu = 252 calories or 1055.06 joules
1 therm = 100,000 Btus or 25,200 Kcals
1 Kwh = 859.6 Kcals or 3411 Btus

Gas

1 $M^3$ = 35.2 cubic feet
1 bbl = 5.61 cubic feet
$10^9 M^3$ p.a.= 96.7 x $10^6$ cfd

*(Conversion Factors contd)*

Oil

| | | |
|---|---|---|
| 1 bbl | = | 35 Imperial gallons or 42 US gallons |
| 1 tonne of crude oil | = | 7.3 bbls (average) |
| 1 $M^3$ motor gasoline | = | 0.75 tonne |
| 1 $M^3$ gas oil | = | 0.84 tonne |
| 1 $M^3$ fuel oil | = | 0.94 tonne |
| 1 million b/d | = | 50 million tonnes per annum (average) |

## APPROXIMATE CALORIFIC VALUES

|  | Mcals per tonne |
|---|---|
| crude oil | 10,000-11,000 |
| hard coal | 5,700-7,700 |
| lignite | 1,700-4,500 |
| coke | 6,300-7,600 |

|  | Kcals per $M^3$ |
|---|---|
| Natural Gas | |
| —Groningen | 8,400 |
| —Ekofisk | 9,800 |
| —Algeria | 10,000 |
| —Soviet Union | 10,000 |
| —Italy | 8,200 |
| Manufactured Gas | 3,800-4,500 |

## DEFINITIONS

'billion' means thousand million ($10^9$)
'tonne' means 1,000 kilogrammes